The Facts On File
DICTIONARY OF AMERICAN POLITICS

The Facts On File
DICTIONARY OF AMERICAN POLITICS

Kathleen Thompson Hill
and
Gerald N. Hill

Checkmark Books®

An imprint of Facts On File, Inc.

The Facts On File Dictionary of American Politics

First published in 1994 as *Real Life Dictionary of American Politics: What They're Saying and What It Really Means.*

Checkmark Books
An imprint of Facts On File, Inc.
132 West 31st Street
New York NY 10001

Library of Congress Cataloging-in-Publication Data
Hill, Kathleen, 1941–
The Facts on File dictionary of American politics/
   by Kathleen Thompson Hill and Gerald N. Hill.
       p. cm.
   Includes index.
   ISBN 0-8016-4519-4 (hardcover)—ISBN 0-8016-4520-8 (pbk.)
    1. United States—Politics and government—Dictionaries. 2. Political science—Dictionaries. I. Hill, Gerald N. II. Title.
JK9.H54 2001
320.973'03—dc 21   2001018770

Cover design by Cathy Rincon

Printed in the United States of America

MP FOF 10 9 8 7 6 5 4 3 2 1
  (pbk) 10 9 8 7 6 5 4 3 2 1

This book is printed on acid-free paper.

CONTENTS

ACKNOWLEDGMENTS

The first edition of this book was a lonely project, as is most writing. This edition was far less lonely, thanks to the world becoming more aware of political language.

Dear friends Mary Evelyn Arnold, Susan Weeks, and Sue Holman all served as sounding boards and word patrol experts. Eternal gratitude goes to Professor Art Warmoth for encouraging Kathleen's passion for political psychology and political language.

Encouragement comes from all sorts of places: our children Erin, Mack, Megan, and David; friends at the University of California at Berkeley's Institute of Governmental Studies; and friends and colleagues in the University of British Columbia Political Science Department in Vancouver.

We especially thank our agent, Mike Hamilburg, for his faith and trust.

—Kathleen Thompson Hill
—Gerald N. Hill

FOREWORD

People of all ages in North America and throughout the world suddenly became greatly interested in politics at the dawn of the new millennium due to nearly constant media coverage of the prolonged exercise of counting presidential ballots in Florida.

In the process, we all learned new political and legal words, including the various stages of pregnancy of "chads," before the presidential election was resolved over a month after election day. Attempts to identify and define words like chads, whether they were dimpled, hanging, pregnant, or swinging, were made by linguists and translators everywhere. Figuring out what politicians, elected officials, and government workers meant by the words they used developed into a spectator sport, as well as serious research.

People have always wondered what in the world politicians are talking about and why they keep changing what they say. In truth, some candidates and officeholders do make skillful use of words to change their minds and their positions. Others use different language for each audience to communicate in the local language to enable as many people as possible to understand them. They recognize that we speak slightly different forms of the same language and use varied meanings of the same words. And conservatives and liberals may use the same words and phrases with substantially different understandings of their meetings.

The *Facts On File Dictionary of American Politics* translates and demystifies American and Canadian "politbabble", tells what everyone is talking about, and provides readers with accepted, historical context where appropriate. It tells you what a buzzword is and defines its meaning. We have included some Canadian political terms because we believe it is important for Americans and Canadians to understand each other's political language.

Politics impacts a far greater part of our lives than most of us realize or are willing to admit, from issues concerning income taxes and health care to building permits, wars, flag raisings, and prayer in schools.

Television, the medium through which most North Americans receive information, employs the lowest common denominator of words to both communicate with the most people at once and to achieve the greatest understanding of its message. In the process, it reduces the public's vocabulary and the number of words with which people think and make choices about many things, including politics.

Since many politicians communicate with the public almost solely through television, candidates and officeholders have become removed from direct contact with the people, resulting in the depersonalization of politics. This depersonalization creates distance, lack of connection, and reduces involvement between those who govern and the governed. Millions of Americans respond by not responding: They don't care, they don't trust, and they don't vote.

We must re-personalize the political process and take it back from the speech writers and spin doctors. We must rebuild our common language and our understanding of each other and our leaders. We must communicate with each other in a way we can all understand. We must participate. We must vote.

The *Facts On File Dictionary of American Politics* is a step toward better personal and public communication and understanding.

—Kathleen Thompson Hill
—Gerald N. Hill

AA   administrative assistant or top staff person, usually to a legislator.

AARP (American Association of Retired Persons)   the largest membership organization (33 million) in the United States comprised of Americans over 55 and their spouses. AARP sells health and other insurance, prescription drugs at discount rates, and financial services to its members, and it lobbies state and federal governments. It publishes *Modern Maturity,* the largest circulation magazine in the country. AARP works for health care reform (some form of national health care and prescription drug benefits), retirement income security, and preservation of social security benefits. AARP frightens elected officials due to its sheer numbers and the commitment of elderly Americans to vote. Address: 601 E Street, N.W., Washington, D.C. 20049. Tel.: (800) 424-3410; e-mail: member@arp.org; website: www.aarp.org

ABC Warfare   atomic, bacteriological, and chemical weapons used in 20th-century wars.

abolition   (1) annulment or making a rule, custom, or decree void. (2) destruction. (3) the movement to end slavery in the United States, which grew as a political force in the 1840s and 1850s, culminating in the Civil War.

Aboriginals   (1) original inhabitants of a place, region, or country. (2) Canada: a politically correct name for Indians (see FIRST PEOPLE).

abortion   (1) the act of inducing miscarriage or "birth" before the fetus is perfectly formed. (2) extraction and termination of life and formation of a fetus from a woman's womb. Conservative political and religious beliefs blend curiously on this issue. Some conservatives, born-again Christians, and Catholics argue that abortion is murder because a person's life begins at conception. Abortion opponents call themselves "pro-life," and those favoring the right to choose abortion call themselves "pro-choice." Pro-lifers generally consider pro-choicers to be killers, sinners, radicals, and dangerous to their way of life. Pro-choicers think of pro-lifers as conservative, racist, reactionary, and living contradictions in their often simultaneous support for death by capital punishment. Historically, abortion was not considered a sin by the Roman Catholic Church until the ninth century.

The U.S. Supreme Court ruled abortion legal if done within the first trimester of pregnancy in *Roe v. Wade* (January 22, 1973), although state laws may vary slightly. As a result, more abortions occur in medically safe environments, such as hospitals, instead of in back alley abortion "mills" where coat hangers were used as medical tools. To repay political support they received from pro-life constituencies, presidents Ronald Reagan and George H. W. Bush appointed pro-life judges to the U.S. Supreme Court, culminating with Clarence Thomas. Efforts to outlaw abortion by constitutional amendment have failed. Surprisingly, in the spring of 1993, the Court, with a majority of Reagan and Bush appointees, upheld the principle of *Roe v. Wade*, while allowing some state limitations. Justice Sandra Day O'Connor worked out a compromise, resulting in the 5-4 decision. President Bill Clinton appointed pro-choice justices Ruth Bader Ginzberg (1993) and Stephen Breyer (1994) to the Supreme Court.

Abortion became a major issue in the 2000 presidential election, because the next president would have the chance to appoint Supreme Court justices who might or might not reverse the *Roe v. Wade* ruling. See also LATE TERM ABORTION and PARTIAL BIRTH ABORTION.

absentee ballot   a voting ballot that a voter can obtain by mail or personal appearance, allowing that person to vote without going to the polls. Absentee ballots may be mailed in or deposited at city halls, designated county buildings, or with designated county officials.

In the 1980s and 1990s, absentee ballots became a sophisticated means of getting out the vote. For many years primarily conservative or Republican voters took advantage of absentee ballots because they had the money to travel and be away at election time. Now both major political parties take advantage of the device to obtain and deliver absentee ballots to their voters, occasionally to mark them, and even to return them to designated collectors. Less scrupulous campaigns provide postage and phony absentee ballots and "lose" ballots cast for opposition candidates.

absolutism   a system of government in which there are no limitations on what the legitimate government may do legally. Authority of the government and its leader is unchecked by any balance of powers.

While absolutism is usually associated with dictatorships and oligarchies, some American presidents have engaged in short-term absolutism by using war powers. Initially President George H. W. Bush engaged in a form of absolutism when he undertook a war with Iraq without consulting Congress or asking that body for a declaration of war.

accord (1) agreement, usually between opposing parties such as labor and management or between countries. (2) a negotiated new agreement replacing a prior, now unworkable one.

accountability (1) responsibility of elected officials and governments to show they have executed and exercised their powers according to the public's wishes. The public may use its ultimate check on that accountability by reelection, recall, or elective replacement. (2) a process of power and responsibility delegation through which those receiving power must report on their accomplishments and justify their work and worth to a superior authority. Liberals and conservatives appear to share interest in accountability of public officials. Both partisan interests judge the other's public servants more harshly than their own. Because of their different perspectives they almost inherently view their opponent's representatives as not representing their interests, and therefore not acting completely or accountably.

activist a person with the motivation and energy to work at and organize goal-specific and sometimes intense activities. Political activists, many of whom are unpaid volunteers, form the mainstay of American politics, although conservatives often regard liberal activists as extremists, whereas liberal activists sometimes see conservative activists as reactionaries.

adjournment the closing or ending of a meeting, often putting off action on proposals or issues until another day. For legislative bodies adjournment usually means the end of a session, as distinguished from a recess or temporary postponement of activity.

administration (1) the elected and appointed executives of a government, such as the department secretaries in the United States. It may also include appointed high-level assistants to the president, such as the "Bush administration." (2) a lumped together reference to everyone who is employed by or who advises a particular president, usually used by critics to target blame or by the president to enlarge the target from just him/herself to a group.

advance man a person charged with preceding a high official, particularly the president, vice president, cabinet members, or governors or candidates to a place they are going to away from their office. An advance man or woman is often involved in planning the trip, and goes to the city or town, checks all the surroundings where the individual will appear—including sound systems, visual impact, size of the expected crowd, availability of favorite foods or drinks—and brings everything involved up to the expected standards of the person for whom he/she is "advancing" by getting local people to do the things felt to be deemed necessary. An advance person might discover that the microphone does not work at a rally and demand one that does. He/she might discover the brand of gin in the hotel room is the wrong one and get the brand favored by the candidate or officeholder, or find a need to get more people to attend an event than were expected. Advance people also verify press interviews and protocol matters.

Advice and Consent Article II, Section 2 of the U.S. Constitution details the Senate's responsibility to provide "advice and consent" to the president to "make treaties" and appointments. In essence, the Senate can block appointments if they find substantial deficiencies in the nominees, and they can veto treaties.

Advise and Consent (1960) America's most popular political novel, written by Allen Drury and made into a successful movie. A long-time best-seller, the book deals with the Senate confirmation process and blackmail with unprecedented realism in exposing behind-the-scenes political maneuvering. Part of the book's allure was that it seemed to confirm the public's suspicions about politicians.

AFDC (Aid to Families with Dependent Children) originating with the Social Security Act of 1935, AFDC provides federal, state, and local government help to needy families with children and is part of the package generally known as welfare. The actual aid may include monetary grants, food stamps, nutrition programs, housing subsidies, Department of Housing and Urban Development funds for housing homeless families, and project Head Start specifically to assist children under five years of age in low-income families. For specific information contact your county government.

affirmative action the policy of giving preferential treatment in hiring or educational opportunities to racial minorities or women on the basis that they have been disadvantaged because of discrimination, neglect, and/or government policies. Liberals favor affirmative action generally but white liberals sometimes have second thoughts when their children fail to gain acceptance to prestigious universities because minority students receive special consideration and admission by "lower" standards. Conservatives often contend that affirmative action translates to "quotas" of minority or female hiring, promotions, and admissions and they believe that minorities and women deserve no special treatment. They prefer "merit" promotions and admissions on the basis of accomplishment, which generally benefits white, middle- and upper-income men. In the 1990s the concept also came to include elderly and handicapped people and women who have not received equal treatment in promotions, opportunities, or pay.

affluent society a concept used by economist John Kenneth Galbraith in the book *The Affluent Society*, to describe a society, such as the United States from the 1950s through the 1980s, that enjoys economic riches and is insensitive to poverty at home or abroad.

AFL-CIO See AMERICAN FEDERATION OF LABOR-CONGRESS OF INDUSTRIAL ORGANIZATIONS.

African American citizen of the United States whose ancestors came from Africa. The term arose in the 1980s and 1990s to replace "Negro" and "black" as the expression of choice by those to whom it applies.

Afro-centrism   the focus of teaching history from the African perspective, beginning with identifying Africa as the beginning of civilization. Several private schools feature this approach to history and are popular among African Americans.

Agricultural Adjustment Act (AAA) of 1933   a law passed by the U.S. Congress (May 12, 1933) on the recommendation of President Franklin D. Roosevelt's Secretary of Agriculture Henry A. Wallace, to increase farmers' income by reducing agricultural production and thereby increasing demand for existing foods. By this scheme, farm prices would rise due to demand in proportion to supply, a sort of reverse of President Ronald Reagan's supply-side economics. Farmers who reduced their production would receive cash for their lack of effort, the money for payments to be raised from a tax on food processors (people, not Cuisinarts), who of course would pass the tax on to consumers. The program aimed to achieve "parity prices" and established the Commodity Credit Corporation with crop loan and storage programs. By 1936 benefit payments to farmers totaled $1,500,000,000, the same year the U.S. Supreme Court declared the AAA unconstitutional. While commodity prices rose, the increases were attributed to the severe drought of 1933–1936. Under later agricultural legislation, some American farmers are paid not to grow crops to this day, occasionally buying additional land so that they can be paid even more not to grow anything.

aide   assistant to a government official who performs professional, and sometimes personal, services for that official.

AIDS   (acquired immune deficiency syndrome)   a disease that reached worldwide epidemic status in the 1980s. It is caused by viruses that destroy some of the body's white blood cells (lymphocytes), resulting in impairment of the body's natural defense system. The victim becomes vulnerable to a variety of other diseases, including pneumonia, tuberculin infections, and some forms of lymphoma. Some people may carry the disease with no symptoms while many others may die. AIDS is transmitted by sexual contact, exchange of bodily fluids, or sharing of contaminated intravenous needles, either in unsanitary medical facilities or through illegal drug injection.

Since many homosexuals and other minorities have contracted AIDS and subsequently died, the disease's treatment, research, and prevention have become highly volatile, politicized issues. For a time, conservative Republicans, including presidents Ronald Reagan and George H. W. Bush, tried to ignore the disease as something not experienced by "normal" people (conservative, Christian Republicans), and therefore not worth bothering to acknowledge or solve. In the meantime, estimated deaths due to AIDS reached 136,000 in the United States and 500,000 worldwide in five years ending in 1991. Only after movie star Rock Hudson's death in 1985 did fellow actor President Reagan begin to take the disease seriously. Basketball hero Magic Johnson's announcement that he carries the HIV virus (a precursor to "full blown" AIDS) prompted President Bush to appoint Johnson to the National AIDS Commission, but Johnson resigned from the commission in protest at the lack of adequate research funding. Millions of African children will never reach their teens due to ignorance of preventative means, the resulting increased spread of AIDS to heterosexuals, and neglect by the developed nations. AIDS is the worst worldwide epidemic since the Black Death in the 14th century and no medical cure has been found to date, although some expensive medicinal "cocktails" have been found to hold the disease in remission.

aisle   a passageway between the two sides of the Senate and House chambers. Traditionally (from British parliamentary practice) the Republicans sit on the right side of the aisle and the Democrats sit on the left side of the aisle.

alderman   name in some parts of the United States for members of a city council or city board. Aldermen (alderpeople) usually represent districts or wards and are important power links in big city political machines. They work with the mayor and staff to run the city, represent constituents' interests, and deliver favors and communication back to voters who, hopefully, will thank him/her by reelecting him/her to office. Chicago is the largest American city with this form of government.

alien   (1) a person who is a citizen of another country. (2) immigrant resident of a country who has not yet become a citizen of that country. (3) someone from another planet. The word bears a negative, distancing connotation of someone desiring to reside in a country whose government or people might deem him/her to be undesirable.

Alien and Sedition Acts (1798) a series of four laws passed by Congress to restrict civil liberties of aliens, silence criticism of the Federalist Party's move toward war with France, and stifle possible electoral success of its opponents, the Jeffersonian Republicans. Aimed at French and Irish immigrants, many of whom were Jeffersonians, the laws raised the waiting period for naturalization from five to 14 years. They also allowed detention of subjects of an enemy nation (to be determined at will), and allowed the president to expel any alien he considered dangerous (read opposition). Many French immigrants had fled to the United States in fear of the "reign of terror" in the 1790s. The Sedition Act prohibited publication of "false or malicious writings" against the government and inciting opposition either to any act of Congress or to the president. Anti-Federalists vociferously affirmed that such restrictions were unconstitutional. Government officials made 25 arrests and obtained 10 convictions. Censorship was rampant. Unexpectedly, the government's victims became martyrs and heroes, resulting in cessation of the practice. Misuse of the acts actually helped Democratic-Republican Thomas Jefferson defeat Federalist John Adams for president (1800). All four acts either expired or were repealed between 1800–1807.

alienation   a feeling of separation from sources of satisfaction or security, which may include one's government, church, sexual group, or family unit. Particularly in a society such as the United States, in which the family as a cohesive unit has become rarer and weaker, faith in the government, church, cult, or sexual group or community becomes more important. Presidents Reagan and George H. W. Bush, while decentralizing government and reducing "people programs," may have increased a feeling of alienation from the government as an instrument of public service and driven the public to churches and other entities in search of community. A long-range side effect may be a distancing and increased distrust of government and incumbent elected officials.

Alliance for Progress　an idealistic 10-year, $20 billion program proposed by President John F. Kennedy on March 27, 1961, to develop agricultural, economic, and social reform in Latin America, and funded with an initial $600 million on May 27, 1961. The United States and 22 Latin American nations developed the Charter of Punta del Este (Uruguay), where they met (August 17, 1961) to work toward creating and maintaining democratic governments through economic and social development. Other aims included sustained growth in per capita income, more equitable distribution of income and wealth, agrarian reform and industrial development, improved health care and welfare, and stabilization of both export and domestic prices. While it lasted, funding came half from the United States and half from international lending and private sources. The program was a partial success with only a few new schools and hospitals actually built. Tensions rose between the United States and the Latin American countries, possibly due to resentment of the United States' somewhat patronizing management of the program and local skimming of funds that never got to designated projects.

All Quiet on the Western Front (1929)　a pacifist novel, later made into a movie, by Erich Maria Remarque about young German soldiers in World War I. Both had substantial antiwar impact on the American public. The movie starred Lew Ayres, who became a conscientious objector in World War II. It won Academy Awards for Best Director (Lewis Milestone) and Best Picture (1930).

America First　(1) originally a nationwide committee of isolationists and German sympathizers who opposed American aid to the Allies and any steps to prepare for war from 1940 to 1941. Air flight pioneer Charles A. Lindbergh served as the committee's spokesperson. The committee collapsed when the Japanese attacked Pearl Harbor and America entered the war. (2) During the 1991–92 presidential campaign conservative Republican candidates David Duke and Patrick Buchanan resurrected the term to express what they believed to be prevailing public sentiment that American taxpayers' dollars ought to be spent at home rather than in foreign aid to help rebuild eastern European countries following the Soviet Union's breakup. They generally favored drastic foreign aid reductions and aimed their criticism at incumbent president George H. W. Bush's globe-trotting policy to solve other countries' problems while ignoring America's economic problems.

American (1) a native of North America, South America, or Central America. (2) a native or person residing in America. (3) the citizens of the United States of America. (4) English language spoken in the United States. (5) anything pertaining to or of the United States. (6) to conservatives, people living in the United States who agree with them.

American Civil Liberties Union (ACLU) a membership organization founded in New York City by Roger Baldwin and others (1920) to watch out for, defend, and protect "the rights of man set forth in the Declaration of Independence and the Constitution." The ACLU researches the legalities of public policies and actions, issues statements on issues and positions, and defends clients in court when civil liberties are in question. The group has active committees on academic freedom, state issues, media rights, free speech and association, due process, equal rights, labor unions/business, and privacy. It also supports its Voting Rights Project, Reproductive Freedom Project, Women's Rights Project, and Lesbian and Gay Rights Project.

The ACLU's first big case was in support of John T. Scopes, who was accused of violating Tennessee statutes by teaching evolution. Scopes was tried in the "Monkey Trial" (July 1925) at which Clarence Darrow defended him and lost. On occasion the organization has angered some of its liberal supporters by defending American Nazis' rights to free speech and 1992 presidential candidate David Duke's right to appear on election ballots. The ACLU's position remains that it exists to defend the civil liberties of all people in the United States.

In the 1988 election presidential candidate George H. W. Bush used opponent Massachusetts governor Michael Dukakis's membership in the ACLU as a political weapon to label Dukakis as a "liberal," playing on public misunderstanding of the ACLU's role as guardian of the fights of people of all persuasions. Although Dukakis lost, the ACLU gained membership after Bush's attack. Address: 125 Broad Street, New York, N.Y. 10004-2400. Tel.: (212) 549-2500; e-mail: aclu@aclu.org; website: www.aclu.org

American Conservative Union (ACU) a political organization founded in 1964 to communicate "the goals and principles of conservatism," it works to advance the agenda of traditional conservatives. ACU's clout has diminished due to internal scandal and the rise of more combative conservative organizations. It provides a safe haven for proponents of the MX missile, the B-1 bomber, and supporters of Senator Jesse Helms (R–N.C.), and the Nicaraguan *contras*. It supported the Supreme Court nomination of Clarence Thomas and reveres Oliver North and former vice president J. Danforth Quayle. Board members include Helms, Richard Viguerie, noted effective conservative fundraiser, and Angela "Bay" Buchanan, sister and campaign manager of Patrick Buchanan. ACU co-sponsors the annual Conservative Political Action Conference (CPAC). Address: 1007 Cameron Street, Alexandria, Va.

22314. Tel.: (703) 836-8602; FAX: (703) 836-8606; e-mail: acu@conservative.org; website: www.conservative.org

American dream a term whose definition varies for everyone, because everyone has different dreams. Generally it refers to American opportunity and goals of making more money and living a better lifestyle than one's parents, owning a home and an automobile or two, and being able to raise and educate one's children comfortably. Variations range from little houses with picket fences to inventing a new gadget or computer program and earning a fortune. The American dream suffered some adjustments in the early 1990s recession, with simply retaining one's job and home and affording health care becoming worthy goals.

American Federation of Labor-Congress of Industrial Organizations (AFL-CIO) a federation of most American labor unions resulting from the merger (1955) of the AFL and CIO. Originally the AFL, founded in 1886, consisted of craft unions such as carpentry and plumbing. Samuel Gompers was the first president of the AFL (1866–1924). In 1935 the CIO was organized on the basis of industry, instead of by craft or skill, so that all workers in an industrial plant belonged to the same union. The United Mine Workers' John L. Lewis was the CIO's first president (1935–1941). AFL-CIO political endorsements through political action committees (PACs) and the Committee on Political Education (COPE) wielded clout and made contributions, particularly for Democratic Party candidates, whom they generally supported. Their political influence diminished during the 1970s and 1980s because of declining membership and inability to deliver their members' votes in blocs. In the late 1980s and 1990s AFL-CIO members voted more conservatively for Ronald Reagan and George H. W. Bush, but they began to return to the Democratic fold in 1992, partly due to economic recession during the Reagan and George H. W. Bush administrations. Address: 815-16th Street, N.W., Washington, D.C. 20006. Tel.: (202) 637-5000; FAX: (202) 637-5058; e-mail: feedback@aflcio.org; website: aflcio.org

American Freedom Coalition a right-wing conservative organization allegedly funded by Korean Reverend Sun Myung Moon and his Unification Church. With access to millions of dollars, the AFC mailed 35,000,000 slick brochures to voters (1988) favoring then-vice president George H. W. Bush's presidential candidacy. Such political activity and influence by a foreign national came under closer scrutiny in the early 1990s, although it has been ignored by Republican administrations that have benefited from the group's activities and largesse. Address: 800 K Street, N.W., Suite 830, Washington, D.C. 20001. Tel.: (202) 371-0303.

American Independent Party (AIP) a political party formed in anticipation of avowed segregationist Alabama governor George Wallace's dissatisfaction with Republican and Democratic nominees (not himself) and need to have a vehicle to run for president in 1968. AIP nominated

Wallace in Dallas, Texas (September 17, 1968), and announced its platform on October 13, including its demand for an end to federal enforcement of public school desegregation, increased police powers, and larger social security and Medicare benefits. In the interim, Wallace finally settled on a running mate, General Curtis LeMay, who had advocated bombing North Vietnam "back into the Stone Age" by "use of anything we could dream up—including nuclear weapons." Wallace and LeMay won 45 electoral votes and 9,906,141 popular votes (13%). AIP surfaces periodically and has no known headquarters address.

American Labor Party (ALP) an American political "third" party from 1936 to 1956 that backed strong social legislation in New York City and New York State elections. The movement was organized by a coalition of liberal Democrats, Socialists, and some labor union leadership. It rarely ran its own candidates but supported existing candidates who shared its positions and goals. Left-liberal congressman Vito Marcantonio of New York was ALP's one elected official. The party backed the Progressive Party's candidates in 1948 and disappeared by 1956 as its members drifted back to the Democratic Party or the Liberal Party of New York.

American Legion the largest veterans' organization in the United States with 3,000,000 members, the American Legion was founded in 1919 in France after the armistice ending World War I. "Posts" (local chapters) emerged in most American cities and towns immediately after

World Wars I and II. It has concentrated its main efforts on lobbying for veterans' benefits, patriotism, strong national defense, and against communism. Politically powerful and conservative through the 1950s, its power waned as World War I veterans aged and died. Veterans of World War II and the Korean War were originally less interested in veterans' organizations than were their predecessors, but many joined the American Legion and Veterans of Foreign Wars. Neither organization was very supportive of or interested in Vietnam veterans, which unfortunately reflected the public's sentiments. *Legion* magazine still boasts a circulation of 2,800,000. Address: P. O. Box 1055, Indianapolis, Ind. 46204. Tel.: (317) 630-1200; FAX: (317) 630-1223; e-mail: tal@legion.org; website: www.legion.org

The American Presidency (1956) a popular book by Professor Clinton Rossiter, which emphasized the powers a dynamic president could exercise. Reportedly John F. Kennedy read the book carefully and often, and he adopted some of its strategies both in his 1960 campaign and in his brief presidency. Rossiter's praise of Harry Truman as an activist president instigated a favorable public reappraisal of Truman, who had rated low in opinion polls when he left office.

American Veterans' Committee (AVC) a liberal veterans' lobby group established in 1944. AVC's slogan was "Citizens first, America Second." Its policies included favoring the United Nations, civil rights, and electoral reapportionment, in contrast to the conservative American Legion. The group participated in organization of the World Veterans Federation, headquartered in Paris, France, which opposed legislation overly favorable to veterans, censorship, and racism. Representing left of center veterans, AVC flourished briefly and achieved many of its goals. It was red-baited as welcoming communist influence and, by 1950, was no longer a major political force. It still claims 20,000 members. Conservative Republican president Ronald Reagan was active in AVC during his liberal days and was defeated in an election for president of the Hollywood chapter. Address: 1717 Massachusetts Avenue, N.W., Suite 203, Washington, D.C. 20036. Tel.: (202) 667-0090.

Americans for Democratic Action (ADA) a liberal, mostly Democratic membership organization formed in 1947 to insure that communists would not dominate the liberal movement or image in the United States and to promote an economically just, liberal, and progressive agenda. ADA was founded by publisher James Loeb Jr. and lawyer Joseph Rauh with the guidance of Eleanor Roosevelt, who served as Honorary Chairman. Others on the organizing committee included labor leaders David Dubinsky and Walter Reuther, Franklin D. Roosevelt Jr. and Charles Bolte, chairman of the American Veterans Committee. Even Ronald Reagan once belonged to the ADA during his liberal period, although eventually he attacked the group as "soft" on the communist threat. ADA advocated national health insurance, wage and price controls, increased federal funding of education, a national housing program, repeal of the Taft-Hartley Act's right-to-work laws, abolition of the House Un-American Activities Committee, rights of free speech for communist or any other student organization on university campuses, and peaceful coexistence with the Soviet Union. It opposed the use of wiretaps, and currently favors campaign reform, the Family and Medical Leave Act (passed), the Freedom of Choice Act, reduction of the defense budget, and international human rights.

At its inception, ADA included an influential group of New Dealers, including Leon Henderson and Hubert Humphrey. Today it continues as a smaller, somewhat elitist liberal force with a few remaining local chapters and 35,000 household members. Address: 1625 K Street, N.W., Washington, D.C. 20005. Tel.: (202) 785-5980; FAX: (202) 785-5969; e-mail: adaction@ixnetcom.com; website: www.adaction.org

amnesty (1) a general pardon given to a group following a shared offense. (2) a general pardon given for offenses against a government. (3) a proclamation of pardons such as those described above. (4) a deliberate overlooking of an offense or an act. Amnesty may be given to a group of war veterans forced to commit heinous acts against their will, and a public library may declare amnesty for everyone who returns overdue books and not charge fines just to get the books back.

Amnesty Act (1) an act passed by Congress (1872) to end Reconstruction problems by restoring political privileges to most Confederate officers. The act resulted in removal of the carpetbagger leadership in southern states at that time. (2) President Jimmy Carter granted a blanket pardon to draft resisters following the Vietnam War, signing the pardon January 25, 1977, four days after taking office.

Amnesty International a worldwide organization founded in 1966 and dedicated to discovering and revealing human rights violations and illegal political imprisonments and seeking amnesty for political prisoners throughout the world. It is the primary investigative source of information on human rights violations in the world and received the Nobel Prize for Peace in 1977. Address: 322 Eighth Avenue, New York, N.Y. 10001. Tel.: (212) 807-8400; e-mail USA: admin-us@aiusa.org; e-mail Canada in English: info@amnesty.ca; e-mail Canada in French: info@ amnistie.qc.ca; website: www.amnesty.org

anarchism a political theory based on somewhat negative principles that: (1) authority is evil and unnecessary. (2) freedom is absolute. (3) government is not legitimate unless it is totally consented to by all those governed. Anarchism was originally based on the positive concept of the natural goodness of man, although some supporters saw violence and terrorism as worthy and valid means to destroy government. It enjoyed a vogue among radicals in czarist Russia in the 19th century, led by Mikhail Bakunin, as well as in France and Italy. Anarchism attracted some prominent philosophical advocates in the United States, such as Mollie Steimer, Emma Goldman, Alexander Berkman, and the Jewish anarchist group Pioneers of Liberty. President William McKinley's assassin, Leon Czolgosz, claimed to be an anarchist. The 1920s and 1930s were the high point of the anarchist movement in the United States. Radical student groups in the 1960s, such as the Weathermen, believed that society or "the system" had to be destroyed before there could be a new beginning. A strong mutual antagonism has existed between liberals, who claim to be working within the system to change society, and anarchists, who believe in destroying the system to bring about social change.

anarchy a condition in which there is no government running a country, society, organization, or even family. Anarchy can be created consciously from the inception of an organization or it can occur when a government is destabilized or overthrown. It includes the absence of government, laws, courts, law enforcement agencies. The chaotic period between destabilization or destruction and reconstruction of a system may be seen as anarchy.

Anti-Defamation League (of B'nai B'rith) (ADL) a membership and educational organization originally formed in 1913 to discover and fight discrimination against Jews, and now against Jews and other minorities. It sponsors studies and reports, investigates discriminatory activities, and promotes interreligious understanding and tolerance. Address: 823 United Nations Plaza, New York, N.Y. 10017. Tel.: (212) 490-2525; e-mail: webmaster@adl.org; website: www.adl.org

Anti-Masonic Party (1827–1836) a political party founded by non-Masons who deeply suspected and distrusted the secret fraternal order's activities. Suspicion and fear were ignited by the unsolved disappearance of William Morgan, a Freemason who was on the verge of publishing many secrets of the Order of the Masons. He was criminally charged with stealing and owing money, imprisoned, released, and supposedly kidnapped. Masonic leaders refused to cooperate with the investigation of malfeasance. Churches, the press, antislavery, and temperance groups condemned Morgan's probable "murder." The Anti-Masonic Party emerged after 15 Anti-Masonic candidates gained election to the New York State Assembly (1827). The party held the first national political conventions in America at Philadelphia (1830) and Baltimore (1831), nominating former U.S. attorney general William Wirt of Virginia for president. They required an unusual three-fourths majority vote to nominate, which the Democrats modified to require a two-thirds majority, and set the precedent for national party conventions. By 1836 most members had joined the Whig Party.

anti-politics a general feeling among some people that they do not want to participate in politics, due to politicians' unkept promises, hot air speeches, discussion of issues of little interest, long campaigns, insults, and the power of money, among other complaints.

anti-Semitism discrimination against Jews for being Jewish, which many people believe is both a religious and racial quality. Anti-Semitism, based upon belief that the Jews killed Jesus Christ, another Jew, existed centuries before Nazi aggressions and attempted eradications of Jewish populations. Much anti-Semitism results from jealousy of perceived Jewish intellectualism and business acumen. The resulting prejudice exists in the United States and throughout the world. Subtle demonstrations of anti-Semitism include exclusion of Jews from organizations, such as country clubs, fraternities and sororities, secret societies, and certain housing neighborhoods. Blatant violence against Jewish institutions and other discriminatory activities are popular among some conservatives, including born-again Christians, fundamentalists of all sects, the John Birch Society, the Ku Klux Klan, and 1992 Republican primary presidential candidate David Duke.

Some observers saw Al Gore's selection and the Democratic Party's nomination of Senator Joseph Lieberman (D.–Conn.) as the vice presidential nominee as a test of whether the American people harbored anti-Semitism.

antitrust legislation laws written to restrict business practices considered to be monopolistic, such as preventing cartels or other large businesses from buying out smaller competitors in their field to control the business from top to bottom, its supplies, its prices, and its markets. The Sherman Anti-Trust Act of 1890 declared illegal "every contract, combination . . . or conspiracy in restraint of trade or commerce" between states or with foreign countries. The Clayton Anti-Trust Act of 1914, amended by the Robinson-Patman Act (1936), prohibits discrimination among customers through price adjustments and disallows mergers, acquisitions, or takeovers of one firm by another if the effect will "substantially lessen competition." Enforcement of these acts has resulted from activities of the Anti-Trust Division of the United States Department of Justice and by private lawsuits filed to stop suspected anti-trust activities. In the early 1900s the federal courts ordered the breakup of such monopolies as Standard Oil in petroleum and Du Pont in the chemical industry. In 1982 American Telephone and Telegraph was forced to divest itself of regional telephone companies. Yet the public wonders how it is that most banks raise or lower their interest rates the same day and how it is that most airlines raise or lower their ticket prices the same day.

Anti–Vietnam War movement (1965–1973) a political-social movement which began primarily among liberal Democratic activists and campus groups in mid-1965 to oppose the United States's increased military involvement with and support of South Vietnam's government. The movement gained energy and momentum in early 1966 when the war and drafts of American young men escalated rapidly, ostensibly to curtail communist influence in South Vietnam. In 1966 the California Democratic Council and a few Democratic U.S. senators called for peaceful resolution of the conflict. Other organizations advocating peace and withdrawal of American forces from Vietnam included Women's Strike for Peace, MassPax, and various student organizations across the country. Massive peace marches and rallies first took place on April 15, 1967, in New York, San Francisco, Washington, D.C., and in locations around the country as long as the war continued. Some demonstrations resulted in violent confrontations with authorities.

By 1968 many businessmen and labor leaders had joined middle-class activists in protest against the war. During the 1968 Democratic Party's presidential primaries, mainstream partisans were surprised by Minnesota senator Eugene McCarthy's upset of President Lyndon Johnson in the New Hampshire primary. McCarthy's antiwar victory resulted in Johnson's decision not to run. After New York senator Robert Kennedy entered the race, President Johnson announced his withdrawal. Following Kennedy's assassination by Sirhan Sirhan and McCarthy's loss to Vice President Hubert Humphrey at the Democratic National Convention in Chicago, the Anti-Vietnam War movement persevered with renewed aggressiveness and increasing support from the American people.

By changing the public's mood and attitude, it was the first successful people's movement against American foreign policy, military action, and a president. See also PEACE MOVEMENT.

antiwar movements social coalition efforts in opposition to war. See also ANTI–VIETNAM WAR MOVEMENT; PEACE MOVEMENT.

apartheid a South African racist policy formally enacted into law (1946) denying the black majority civic, social, housing, educational, and economic rights equal to those of the white minority. Apartheid kept blacks and other non-whites separated physically from whites, barred from economic opportunities, and in a constant state of repression. During the 1970s and 1980s there was a major effort in the United States to isolate South Africa's government by boycotting products produced there (even by American companies) and promoting divestment of stocks in companies doing business in and cooperating with South Africa. In response to citizens' demands, some American state universities and state governments sold off stocks and investments in South African companies. Through the African National Congress, Nelson Mandela led South Africa's anti-apartheid movement although he was incarcerated as a political prisoner for more than 20 years. Mr. Mandela was released from prison in 1990, and in 1991 the government of South Africa repealed some apartheid laws but did not grant voting rights to blacks. By mid-1993, much of apartheid had been officially dismantled, a black woman was selected as "Miss South Africa," democratic elections appeared to be on the horizon, and Mandela and Frederick W. de Klerk won the Nobel Peace Prize jointly. Mandela won the presidency in the first post-apartheid democratic elections in 1994, and during his term led efforts for equality and reconciliation between blacks and whites. However, racially motivated violence, riots, and murders still occurred on occasion.

appeasement A policy of giving in to the demands of another, often hostile or warlike, power in order to avoid violence or strife. The Munich Pact of 1938 in which British prime minister Neville Chamberlain and French premier Edouard Daladier agreed to allow Nazi leader Adolph Hitler to annex part of Czechoslovakia to Germany just before the outbreak of World War II is a good (or bad) example of appeasement.

apportionment the drawing of congressional or legislative districts according to population. See also REAPPORTIONMENT.

appropriation a legislative body's act of granting money to run the government, usually called an authorization bill. The budget states the amount that may be spent, authorization gives consent to the allocation of funds, and appropriation legislation actually makes the funds available.

aristocracy (1) a segment of society that is a privileged minority thought to be the "upper class," often possessing inherited wealth and controlling societal and governmental systems. (2) one of the factors contributing to the lack of social mobility that accounts for the historic and, to a lesser degree, current flight of emigrants from Europe.

arms control an effort to reduce or limit production of arms or military weapons. Arms control may include international restriction on testing and use or deployment of weapons while acknowledging the continued existence of each country's weapons. This does not prohibit or stop weapon research, production, or sales, but it may deter a leader's ability or inclination to pull the trigger. Arms control implies (1) that it is a principle agreed upon by usually antagonistic states, and (2) that it can be an effort by a single state to influence world peace and security by reducing destruction capabilities. The two basic goals of arms control are: (1) to reduce the risk of war by reducing arms, and (2) to increase the possibility that peace and restraint will triumph when conflict arises. Arms control usually includes periodic inspection by both or all sides. These are mostly post–World War II efforts inspired by the existence of modern weapons and nuclear bombs.

Arms Control Agreements include: The United States, U.S.S.R., and Great Britain agreed to halt nuclear tests in the atmosphere, sea, and space on July 25, 1963, signed by President John F. Kennedy and ratified by the U.S. Senate. The **Nuclear Nonproliferation Treaty** (1968), eventually signed by 60 nations, stated that nuclear nations would not provide nuclear weapons to non-nuclear nations. The U.S. Senate delayed ratification until March 13, 1969, because Soviet troops were marching into Czechoslovakia. President Richard Nixon and Soviet president Nikolai V. Podgorny signed the agreement on November 26, 1969, in Moscow, Russia. The **Strategic Arms Limitation Treaty** (SALT) resulted from meetings in Helsinki, Finland (November–December 1969), and in Vienna, Austria (April 1970), and signed in Moscow. There were two parts to the agreement: (1) the Anti-Ballistic Missiles Treaty Limitation, which permitted missiles only to protect national capitals and existing fields of intercontinental missiles, and (2) an executive agreement to limit offensive ballistic weapons to those

under construction. The **Nuclear Test Pact** was signed on May 28, 1976, by the United States and the Soviet Union and limited nuclear testing to 150-kiloton yield weapons with mutual examination of test sites by the United States and the U.S.S.R. **SALT II** limited nuclear missiles further. Signed on June 18, 1977, by President Jimmy Carter and Soviet leader Leonid Brezhnev, the agreement was never ratified by the Senate, but both nations behaved as if it were in effect. President Ronald Reagan announced on May 27, 1986, that the United States was not bound by Salt Two, but it has informally observed its limitations.

Despite these agreements, nuclear research and development continues throughout the world.

arms limitation the reduction and limitation of a nation's weaponry by international agreement. The first such official talks took place at The Hague (1899, 1907) but the resulting conventions produced little concrete results. Strategic Arms Limitations Talks between the United States and the Soviet Union began in 1970. See also ARMS CONTROL.

arms race the actual as well as imagined buildup of ground and airborne tactical and nuclear weapons by the United States and the Soviet Union to prove strength and therefore superiority. The arms race was based partly on the fear that the United States could again be caught unprepared, as it was by Germany and Japan in World War II. Another American motivation was the possibility that an attack by the Soviet Union could have brought on World

War III and the end of civilization. Of course, an attack by the United States would have produced the same result.

Negative effects of the arms race include federal monies spent on nonproductive military weapons, the danger inherent in the use of those weapons, the lack of investment in more economically beneficial industries, and the constant contrived tension among citizens of competing nations during the cold war.

arm twisting lobbying, trying forcefully to persuade.

Army-McCarthy Hearings nationally televised hearings (April 23–June 17, 1954) of the Senate Permanent Subcommittee on Investigations examining charges by Senator Joseph McCarthy (R–Wisc.) that the United States Department of Defense shielded communists in the army. For five years McCarthy had made unsupported charges that spies and communists were widespread in the government, creating suspicion, firings, and blacklisting of those whom he opposed or "exposed." During the hearings, McCarthy's irresponsible charges, threats, and constant badgering of the committee chairman, combined with whispered asides from his young counsel, Roy Cohn, made an unintentional negative impression on the unprecedented national audience. Staid Boston attorney Joseph Welch, representing the U.S. Army, proved McCarthy's attacks to be politically motivated revenge for the army's refusal to give special treatment to a soldier friend of Cohn. Ironically, the hearings led to the Senate's censure of McCarthy, ending an

era of fear. He died in 1956, partly due to alcoholism.

Arsenal of Democracy President Franklin D. Roosevelt's view expressed in a fireside chat on December 29, 1940, of the role the United States should play in the war in Europe. His statement helped swing public support for American aid to Great Britain's defense against Nazism.

Articles of Confederation an agreement among the first 13 states (1781) affiliating them loosely in a government until the Articles were abandoned in favor of the Constitution (1789). Each state had one vote in the law-making Congress. There was no president or executive branch to enforce laws, no powers to tax, regulate commerce, or make the new states conform to congressional decisions, and no national court system. See Appendix, p. 359.

articles of impeachment charges against the president of the United States brought by a majority vote of the House of Representatives on each charge. Only three times have articles of impeachment been brought by the House: against Andrew Johnson in 1868, Richard Nixon in 1974, and Bill Clinton in 1999. Those articles that are adopted are then sent to the Senate, where a trial is held if the Senate concurs. No president has been convicted by the Senate. Richard Nixon resigned when informed that he would be convicted on one or more articles.

assault weapons rifles, pistols and submachine guns made with large clips of ammunition to fire extremely rapidly to kill human beings. Some assault weapons are created by converting hunting rifles and adding large bullet clips. Increasingly, assault weapons have been used in crimes in the United States. A partial ban on importation, manufacture, and sale of such weapons was enacted by Congress and signed by President Bill Clinton in 1994. Some gun manufacturers have produced weapons similar to those banned. The National Rifle Association opposes such bans.

Assault Weapons Ban a statute championed by Senator Dianne Feinstein (D–Calif.) that bans the manufacture, importation, or sale of certain rapid fire weapons with large clips of ammunition designed to kill human beings. President Bill Clinton signed the bill in 1994. New assault weapons ban legislation has been drafted to close loopholes that allow new designs and conversion of other guns to assault weapons.

assembly (1) a gathering of people or crowd brought together by a common interest to listen or express ideas or positions on issues. (2) a gathering of citizens for any purpose as protected by the First Amendment to the U.S. Constitution. (3) in many states the name of the lower house of the state legislature.

association a group of people united to pursue a common cause and advance mutual interests, demonstrating the U.S. constitutional right to associate and gather publicly and politically.

Atlanta Constitution morning newspaper published in Atlanta, Georgia, considered to be the voice of the more liberal "New South," and featuring a strong editorial page and policy. The paper's political influence is far greater than its circulation (316,000) or its national ranking (30) might indicate. The *Atlanta Journal* is its evening edition.

at large a delegate, representative, or public official elected by an entire elective unit such as a town, county, or state rather than by a district or other subdivision of that town or voting body. Some small states' populations warrant only one "at large" member of Congress.

Atomic Energy Commission (AEC) a U.S. agency (1946–74) composed of five commissioners appointed by the president, with the Senate's consent, to oversee control of atomic energy, building, and stockpiling of nuclear weapons, and development of peacetime uses of atomic energy. The AEC was an extremely powerful commission that also controlled the disarmament of atomic weapons, who should and should not develop nuclear power resources, and how and when. The AEC's functions were subsumed into the Nuclear Regulatory Commission (NRC) by the Energy Reorganization Act of 1974.

attaché (1) French for attached. (2) the person working closely with a diplomatic officer or top public official who may represent his/her country's special business, cultural, or military interests. An attaché is often the closest an inquirer gets to the real authority and, therefore, is the best link between a country's government and its citizenry.

at that point in time a phrase used by Richard Nixon and spokespersons for his administration, particularly those friends who were involved in Nixon's Committee to Re-elect the President (CREEP) and the Watergate cover-up, to mean "then." The phrase implied that what might have been true at an earlier time might not be true later.

Attorney General's List of Subversive Organizations By the Internal Security Act of 1950 (McCarran Act), the attorney general received the power to name organizations he considered to be "subversive," meaning communist or communist connected, without proof. Left-wing organizations complained vehemently that the list and the whim of the attorney general and F.B.I. director were misused for political purposes to weaken or destroy them. On November 15, 1965, the U.S. Supreme Court ruled that the registration and listing were unconstitutional.

atrocities acts of extreme cruelty or massive killings inflicted against political or moral rivals, ethnic groups, prisoners, or civilians, or simply against human beings, by armies or governments.

attack ads political advertisements featuring negative attacks on one's opponent instead of positive ads advocating one's positions or good qualities.

Australian ballot a secret voting ballot that originated in Australia in the early 1880s. It was first introduced to the U.S. electoral system in 1888, and the ballot was generally opposed by party machines, which had often provided the ballots to voters. The Australian ballot supposedly insures that all ballots look alike and are not coded or colored by party affiliation. Voters mark them in secret and place the ballots in a closed ballot box.

authoritarianism a state of government in which forceful, strong control is exercised over the people with no concern for or interest in the people's opinions. The rejection or replacement of civil rights and freedoms accompany the government's right to rule or govern by command, requiring obedience and a lack of opposition (even loyal), argument, or free speech. This kind of power or rule can be exercised by an individual, junta, or council. A recent example of assumption of authoritarian rule was Philippine president Ferdinand Marcos's declaration of martial law (1972), which included elimination of all other constitutional officers and the democratically elected congress and senate.

authority (1) the right to give an order and to follow up to see that it is carried out. (2) the right to make decisions within certain limitations. Authority differs from power in that it is given by those whom it affects and is therefore seen as legitimate. Authority can be granted by a constitution, as in the United States, a law, a delegation, or an organization. Occasionally it is taken and then exercised by force of personality.

autocracy absolute power of one person over others as exists in a dictatorship or despotism, such as the Soviet Union through 1990.

autonomy (1) self-rule or self-government as in self-governing states, groups, or entities within states that enjoy independence and freedom from scrutiny. (2) ultimate freedom. Immanuel Kant, the 19th-century philosopher, defined autonomy as the right of the individual to govern himself according to his own reason, which raises the question: how many American individuals or entities actually enjoy autonomy?

availability the known willingness to be "tapped" or discovered to run for office without overtly pushing oneself forward but hoping it happens. When other potential candidates decide not to run, or their flaws and vulnerabilities become public, availability enhances one's position to become the preferred candidate.

B

baby boomers people conceived following the end of World War II and born between 1946 and 1964. They comprise one of the largest segments of the American population, and their children crowded public schools in the 1990s.

backbenchers (1) in Britain and Canada, the newest members of parliament who are assigned the lowest prestige seats on the back benches or who are not members of the dominant political party or the government's cabinet. Former Canadian prime minister Joe Clark says he avoided ever being a backbencher due to alphabetical luck: there were so many freshmen in his incoming parliamentary class that, because his name was early in the alphabet, he got to sit in the second to last bench. (2) newcomers or members who rank lowest in seniority in a legislative body.

backer a person who supports a candidate by endorsement, financial contribution, or other campaign help ranging from ringing doorbells to legal research.

background conference a non-public informational meeting usually between presidential representatives, government officers, or foreign diplomats and the press at which limited details of statements, positions, or agreements are represented for use by the reporters, often without attribution and sometimes without conveying the whole truth.

backlash unexpected negative response and reaction from the public to a statement, series of statements, position on an issue, or movement.

backscratching a political or business term suggesting "I will help you, and you help me." It implies that favors will be returned for favors done. Legislators sometimes trade votes in this fashion.

bafflegab often meaningless fast talk to avoid making a real commitment or taking a stand, particularly when one does not know an answer to a question.

bagman a person who picks up and carries money or communicates favors from one person to another in a campaign. The term implies corruption or money from illegal sources and, in some cases, is seen as libelous. Bagmen or bagwomen usually have much less influence than they want people to believe and are often just go-betweens.

balance of power from the 1830s until 1992, the theory that peace is more likely when the countries concerned hold equal military and, therefore, political power. In reality, each nation is afraid to have truly equal power and constantly struggles to surpass the other, leading to and fueling a budget-draining arms race. A theoretical economic power balance works the same way. The general theory lost credence in the 1990s with the onset of the age of global economic and military power units and the dissolution of the Soviet Union. Theoretically, a balance of power could be achieved if all nations maintained minimal military strength, since military power is less important in a global equation.

balance of trade the difference between the monetary value of a nation's imports and exports of goods and services over a specific time period, usually a year. Most countries prefer to have an excess of export revenue because it means that new money comes into the country. Occasionally an excess of imports is deemed not to be bad if it is offset by income from foreign investments. The public can become confused when government reporting agencies state unclearly what is included in the balance of trade, and government agencies can deliberately make their reports fuzzy by excluding important data to gloss over bad news.

Balanced Budget Amendment proposed constitutional amendment requiring each annual federal budget to be balanced, with some exceptions for national emergencies. Championed by Senator Paul Simon (D.–Ill.) and backed by a coalition of Democrats and Republicans, it was opposed by the Clinton administration and the congressional leadership and was narrowly defeated in 1994. Opponents argued that (1) it would tie the hands of the administration and Congress, and (2) such an amendment would result in an abrupt disruption of government programs rather than gradual cuts in those programs to reduce the annual deficit. Arguments for the amendment were that: (1) Congress and the executive branch had to be forced to be fiscally responsible, and (2) even the best efforts had only reduced the deficit's rate of increase and had not halted its growth. Almost all state and local government budgets are legally required to be balanced.

balanced ticket a pairing of presidential and vice presidential candidates or others on a slate who attract support for different reasons, including the location of their political bases, religions, and issues for which they are known, thereby tapping the broadest possible appeal to voters. The Democratic ticket of Catholic

John F. Kennedy (D.–Mass.) and Protestant Lyndon Johnson (D.–Tex.) is an example. The election of southerners Bill Clinton (Arkansas) and Albert Gore (Tennessee) over President George Bush (Connecticut/Maine/Texas) and Vice President Dan Quayle (Indiana) discredits the supposed need for geographic balance.

ballot a piece of paper upon which Americans vote anonymously and place in a ballot box to be counted confidentially. See also AUSTRALIAN BALLOT.

ballot, long an election form that usually includes local and state measures, as well as the names of candidates, often utilized when several local, state, and national elections occur jointly. See also BALLOT, SHORT.

ballot rigging any fraudulent and purposeful miscounting or losing of votes or ballots, especially to achieve a particular end or electoral result. Ballot rigging includes cheating on the count, voting on behalf of people who did not vote or who are dead, voting multiple times, putting ballots in the ballot box before voting begins or after it ends, jamming voting machines, and disqualifying legitimate ballots. See also BALLOT STUFFING.

ballot, short a ballot that includes only a few names or propositions in an off-year election without national or state office candidates. See also BALLOT, LONG.

ballot stuffing (1) cheating in an election by filling the ballot box with premarked ballots before the polls open or before the count. (2) altering the counter on a voting machine. (3) voting more than once or casting ballots for absent or dead registrants. See also BALLOT RIGGING.

bandwagon a term used mainly as "to jump on the bandwagon" or "to get on the bandwagon," meaning to join the crowd headed toward assumed success for either a cause or a candidate. Campaign strategists and managers sometimes try to create a premature feeling of success so that crowds will jump on their candidate's bandwagon instead of supporting a suggested loser (the other guy).

bank holiday (1) any weekday on which banks are closed. (2) in the United Kingdom and Canada, six specific weekdays on which banks are closed and which are considered holidays. (3) a day on which all banks throughout a country are closed for a specific purpose, such as when President Franklin D. Roosevelt closed American banks from March 4 to 14, 1933, to prevent withdrawals while there were preliminary audits and to let public emotions cool down and public confidence in the government and economy warm up.

banner district a district in which a candidate or party does so well that those involved see it as the ideal outcome. Often candidates or campaigners work to duplicate elsewhere the methods and results of those in a banner district.

bar (1) all lawyers. (2) a statewide organization of lawyers. (3) a place to purchase and drink alcoholic beverages.

Barnburners members of a liberal faction (1844) of the New York State Democratic Party who opposed the extension of slavery into the territories that had not been admitted as states. The name was pinned on the group by its opposition, the Hunkers, in an effort to associate the liberals psychologically with the apocryphal Dutch farmer who burned down his barn to get rid of the rats. The Barnburners considered former president Martin Van Buren to be their leader. They followed him out of the Democratic Party when it denied him the presidential nomination (1844), into the Free Soil Party (1848), and then back to the Democratic Party (1852).

barnstorming to conduct a thunderously obvious and quick campaign, usually with lots of trips and stops.

base closure closing of military bases in the United States due to military budget cutbacks. Base closures in the 1990s affected surrounding communities whose businesses depended upon traffic from servicemen and women. Base closures increased as needs for ground troops and scattered domestic military establishments seemed to diminish.

battleground state a state where pre-election polls show the race is close and the state's number of Electoral College votes is great enough to cause the candidates to spend much time there fighting for that state's votes.

beauty contest (1) a term used by those who think they will lose a non-substantive election campaign based on popularity instead of issues. (2) an election that is only advisory, such as a nonbinding presidential primary.

bedfellow a legislator or supporter sharing a view and agreeing on a vote. See also STRANGE BEDFELLOW.

Bee papers a powerful group of newspapers in California's agricultural valleys with the McClatchy family owning a controlling interest, including the *Sacramento Bee* (300,000 circulation), the *Fresno Bee* (145,000) and the *Modesto Bee* (85,000). Generally of Democratic persuasion, the Bees receive particular acclaim for their political, economic, and business reporting.

bellwether a word often used in reference to a county or district that exemplifies typical voter characteristics and from which politicians and pundits think they can forecast results in other districts or regions.

beltway (1) an expressway that passes around an urban area. (2) In Washington, D.C., the term refers to all the people in the capital area whose lives revolve around and therefore focus on the capital and so are labeled as being somewhat out of touch with the rest of the world. (3) a lifestyle of pleasant comfort free from financial, employment, health, education, or housing problems, including no contact with people who have these problems, especially minorities. (4) hundreds of thousands of people who work for the U.S. government and make up the bureaucracy. The term "beltway" is used most often by people who do not live inside its boundaries.

beltway bandits companies with lucrative (often defense-related) contracts with the federal government.

bench an inclusive term meaning all court judges in the United States.

bicameral legislature a legislature with two houses or chambers, such as the U.S. Senate and House of Representatives, Britain's House of Lords and House of Commons, and Canada's Senate and House of Commons. All American state legislatures are bicameral except for Nebraska's, which has only one house.

big government a term for invasive, overpowering, taxing, and meddling government that, some people believe, takes over their lives, their money, and their decisions. Conservatives usually dislike "big government," with the implication that it takes money from those making it and gives it to the poor or spends it inefficiently. Liberals traditionally have rarely used the term. The Clinton administration reflected a sensitivity to the concept and worked to reduce the number of government employees.

bigot a narrow minded, intolerant, immovable, racist, prejudicial person.

big stick a term first used by President Theodore Roosevelt to connote a strong military to back up his policies. America should "speak softly and carry a big stick." The term now means quiet, but potentially threatening, power.

big tent a term used to suggest that a political party is so big, inclusive,

and expansive that it is open to many ideas, some of which conflict. All perspectives may be considered and debated, and all ethnicities and backgrounds are supposedly welcomed and included.

bilateralism diplomatic, trade, or military activities between two countries, usually on reasonably equal terms and footing.

bilingualism the principle that two languages share equal status within a country, state, or province. In Canada, they are English and French.

bill a written proposal to amend or create a new law in a legislature. The proposal remains a bill until it is passed and signed; then it is called an act, statute, or law.

Bill of Rights the first 10 amendments to the U.S. Constitution. They were adopted on December 15, 1791, to guarantee certain basic freedoms and individual rights. Those favorable to the new Constitution had promised that the omission of the 10 amendments in the original draft of the Constitution would be rectified by the addition of a Bill of Rights in order to persuade states, particularly New York, Virginia, and Massachusetts, to ratify the Constitution. See Appendices.

bimetallism the legalized use of a two-metal standard, such as silver and gold, as the official coinage or currency of a country.

As a compromise between silverites who wanted cheaper inflationary money and hard-money gold standard backers, President Franklin D. Roosevelt announced its adoption in 1933, ending reliance on gold alone to back paper currency.

bipartisan a term suggesting that there has been participation by two political parties in creating or supporting a policy, position, resolution, or legislation.

bipolar (1) having to do with polar or opposite views or interests. (2) something pertaining to or occurring at both poles. (3) new term for what used to be called "manic depressive."

Bircher member of the John Birch Society. See also JOHN BIRCH SOCIETY.

birth control regulation of child conception, especially by contraceptives. In some states birth control was as controversial up through the 1950s and 1960s as "choice" and abortion have been from the 1970s to the present day. Birth control controversy stemmed partly from Roman Catholic convictions that birth control artificially altered God's will. The issues developed into ones of free speech and privacy and whether government or private entities had the right to disseminate information on birth control. Connecticut disallowed sale or advertisement of birth control devices until the Supreme Court ruled on June 7, 1965, that the ban was unconstitutional.

Some groups claimed that it should be a matter of a woman's right of choice. Others saw it as an issue of social reform—of reducing child producing and raising by the poor (read minorities), and creating or reducing financial burdens on the state. Some minority leaders regarded birth control and sterilization as racist efforts to curb the political power of darker skinned races by holding down their numbers.

Birth control pills arrived in the 1960s for "family planning," a polite euphemism for avoiding unwanted pregnancies. Intrauterine devices (IUDs) and diaphragms inserted in the woman's vagina were other birth control methods that have proved sometimes unsuccessful and even harmful. Other methods of birth control that have met with varied success and popularity include condoms, the rhythm method, vasectomies and tube tying, and sponges. Female condoms and the RU-486 morning-after pill are two new devices.

bite the bullet take responsibility and make a decision, often in a difficult situation.

blackball to reject a person who has applied for a job or membership in a club, organization, or profession because of his/her race, religion, or political beliefs. The term comes from an ancient Greek means of casting secret or anonymous votes with marbles dropped into a box in which white meant yes (acceptance) and black meant no (rejection). Traditionally some collegiate fraternities and sororities required only one vote (blackball) to reject a prospective member.

black hats evil plotters or bad guys who usually wore black hats in western movies. See also WHITE HATS.

blackleg (1) in England a person who works for an employer while the unionized employees are on strike. (2) strikebreaker. (3) scab.

blacklist   a listing of persons as an order or strong suggestion that they should not be hired or taken into an organization because of their alleged political views or affiliations. Blacklisting occurred in the 1930s to keep names and personal data of prominent liberals, Jews, and union organizers, leaders, and members from working. In the 1950s, movie writers who refused to implicate themselves or others as communists before the House Un-American Activities Committee were blacklisted from the entertainment industry.

Black Panthers (Black Panther Party)   a militant and occasionally violent black movement founded in Berkeley and Oakland, California, by Bobby Seale and Huey Newton (October 1966), who were influenced by Malcolm X to demand help for poor blacks. Eldridge Cleaver, who later wrote *Soul on Ice,* joined the Black Panther Party in 1967 and soon took over its leadership. The group entered the California state capitol building in Sacramento with guns, uniforms, and black berets, but they did not hurt anyone. Cleaver became the 1968 presidential nominee of a coalition formed by the Black Panther Party and the Peace and Freedom Party. Black Panthers served hot meals in church basements in black ghettos and brought attention to their cause. By the early 1970s the Black Panthers had faded from prominence for many reasons, including arrests, violent deaths, police and F.B.I. intervention, and defection of some members to less violent civil rights organizations.

Black Power   (1) a term first used publicly by Representative Adam Clayton Powell (D.–N.Y.) in a May 29, 1966, baccalaureate speech at Howard University. He saw "black power" as "the power to build black institutions of splendid achievement." (2) a 1960s–1970s slogan popularized by Stokely Carmichael, leader of the Student Non-Violent Coordinating Committee (SNCC), and the stated goal of the younger and left-wing black or African-American civil rights movement toward political, social, and cultural equality and pride for black people.

bleeding   heart (liberal)   term used usually by conservatives for a person who is overly sensitive to other people's plight and problems and throws himself/herself into trying to solve those ills without the ability to actually do so and who, it is claimed by opponents, fails to put those problems into perspective.

bloc   a coalition of parties, partisans, or nations formed for a common cause, purpose, or goal. In the U.S. Congress this can mean a farm bloc, southern bloc, or oil bloc, the members of which vote together. The republics of Eastern Europe formed the Eastern Bloc of nations to negotiate, trade, and purchase arms together, a unity dismantled by the dissolution of the Soviet Union and the breakup of Yugoslavia.

block grant   federal government grants of financial aid (money) to state and local governments for specific purposes, such as welfare, community development, and some health services. Conceived by Republican administrations in the 1970s and 1980s, block grants were intended to give money to local agencies to manage services and projects, thereby relieving federal government of the burden, responsibility, and expense of employment, and creating the impression of less federal government involvement and interference.

blue-collar worker originally workers whose bosses demanded that they wear uniforms, often blue shirts, which over time came to indicate the wearer was a semi-skilled worker. They include workers who engage in physical labor, such as carpenters, plumbers, and auto workers. In the United States many blue-collar workers were organized into unions and usually voted Democratic on most issues. Many blue-collar workers followed presidents Reagan and George H. W. Bush toward conservatism and increased racism, encouraged by 1992 presidential primary candidates David Duke and Patrick Buchanan. Blue-collar workers began to return to the Democratic Party during the recession of 1991–1993.

blue dog Democrat a conservative Democrat who often votes with Republicans.

blue laws certain state and county laws prohibiting sales of alcoholic beverages or staging entertainments or sports events on Sundays, particularly during the late 1800s and early 1900s. They were employed in the New England colonies controlled by Puritans who kept the Sabbath sacred. "Blue" was slang for puritanical. Realistically, people who enjoy drinking alcoholic beverages in states with

blue laws stock up during the week or on Saturday.

blue ribbon panel a group of top experts set up to investigate or study a problem or matter.

boat people People who leave their homeland's oppressive governments and economic conditions for other countries by boat, usually risking their lives in the process and arriving in the new nation with little or no possessions. Originally the term was used to describe Vietnamese who fled their country after the fall of Saigon (1975), but the term now includes emigrés primarily from Vietnam, Haiti, Cuba, and China. In most cases, the United States has granted them political asylum.

In 1992 the U.S. government forced hundreds of Haitians to "repatriate," that is, return to their country by boat. Most arriving boat people work and study hard, resulting in local workers' resentment of their intrusion and competition. They became a political issue in the rising dispute over immigrants in the early 1990s. Racism and envy are more likely to be at the root of this demand to keep boat people away.

In 1993, boat people from China, who allegedly had paid smugglers up to $30,000 for safe passage, were intercepted off the California and Mexican coasts, arrested, and returned to China.

body politic any group of people governed by others.

boll weevil (1) a conservative southern Democrat who makes himself/herself a pest by gnawing at the

Democratic mainstream's foundation, named for a bug that destroys cotton balls by eating from the inside. (2) a southern Democratic member of Congress who votes Republican.

Bolshevik (1) originally one segment of the revolutionary movement in pre-1917 Russia. Bolshevik comes from the Russian word for "majority," as distinguished from Menshevik, Russian for "minority." (2) left-wing creators of the Communist Party who were hard-line Marxists. (3) a generic term used (1917–90) as a Western term for communists or those suspected of being communist. (4) a common description of anyone who held left-wing or radical beliefs. (5) term once used for anyone who did not accept authority or value institutions.

bolt to resign or withdraw from one's majority traditional party or group position over an issue with which one does not agree. A legislator who bolts usually does it in such a way, and it is so obviously out of his/her expected behavior, that publicity results. See also BREAK RANKS.

bonds, public a means of funding public projects, education costs, and other municipal, county, and state proposals by selling government-guaranteed bonds to private individuals and banks to be paid off over a long period. Bond issues usually require a public vote, often with two-thirds approval. To many purchasers, bonds offer investment safety, and tax-free profit to offset low-interest returns.

bookburners people who decide it is their responsibility to censor books and destroy them. The term comes from the public burning of books by the Nazis in Germany in the 1930s.

boondoggle (1) a valueless, sometimes contrived work or useless occupation. The term originated during the Great Depression when the government created jobs to give citizens income to relieve unemployment and lack of spending. (2) braiding leather or plastic strips into a watch fob or bracelet by a series of alternate overlays.

border state (1) originally five states that wavered between the Union and the Confederacy during the Civil War (1861–65): Delaware, Kentucky, Maryland, and Missouri remained loyal to the North, and West Virginia split from confederate Virginia (1863) to create a new state for the Union. (2) a state bordering the Mason-Dixon line, which divides northern and southern states, specifically Pennsylvania and Maryland. Border states usually include Delaware, West Virginia, Kentucky, Maryland, Missouri, Oklahoma, and Tennessee. Political attitudes and consensus are less predictable among the border states than in the northern or southern states, because the population generally exhibits characteristics and reflects attitudes of both regions. (3) U.S. states that border on Canada or Mexico.

born again (1) a Christian (usually Protestant) who believes he or she has experienced a rebirth in the Christian faith in Jesus through a spiritual experience. (2) a nonreligious "born again" gains a new enthusiasm for and commitment to a crusade or cause.

In the 1980s and 1990s many born-again Christians voted conservatively, actively evangelized their Christianity, and rationalized prejudice against Jews and other minorities. Many have switched from the Democratic Party to conservatism and the Republican Party, with parties' or candidates' positions against abortion or "choice" crucial for their endorsement or support. Ironically, many born-again Christians also favor the death penalty. Billy Graham was the first born-again Christian minister to deliver a bloc of votes to the candidate of his choice, Ronald Reagan. Born-again televangelists played important roles of delivering votes to elections of conservative Republicans in the 1980s, and thereafter.

Many born-again Christians have not joined the religious right and do not equate their commitment to Christ with conservative political or racial concepts. Former president Jimmy Carter is a prime example of this kind of born-again Christian.

boss   a dominating, controlling leader of a political machine or office. They included William M. "Boss" Tweed of New York City (1870s), Ed Kelly of Chicago (1940s), Frank Hague of Atlantic City (1940s), Edward Crump of Memphis (1930s–1950s), and Richard Daley Sr., of Chicago (1950s–1970s).

Boston-Austin Axis   a term symbolizing (1) need to balance a presidential ticket with regional origins and support such as John F. Kennedy (D.–Mass.) with Lyndon B. Johnson (D–Tex.); and (2) need to balance a ticket with philosophically complementary candidates.

both sides of the aisle   a term that refers to bipartisan agreement. Both the Republicans on the right side and the Democrats on the left side agree on something. See also AISLE.

bounce   a candidate's jump upward in the polls, usually after a positive event, such as a nationally publicized party convention.

bourgeois   (1) French word meaning one who lives in a town or city, particularly the upper middle and upper classes, as distinct from both the lower classes in cities or anyone with a rural background. (2) wealthy yuppie aristocrats gave the word a pejorative connotation referring to those on whom they look down, meaning their rivals. (3) Marxist view: the class who rises and creates capitalism but lacks aristocratic connections. (4) middle class and professionals who dominate and run a political government or economy and set standards of behavior. (5) from the liberal perspective, a pejorative comment meaning insatiable, conformist, somewhat conservative, and nonintellectual. (6) radicals use "bourgeois" to epitomize middle-class narrow values. (7) particularly in the United States, dull and culturally stunted.

boycott   a refusal to purchase products or associate with an individual or organization to attract attention and bring about a change of social or political policy. Labor union members and sympathizers have boycotted lettuce and grapes not picked by union farm workers, and some people avoided purchasing products from companies whose owners supported South African apartheid. The term originally came from Irish captain Charles C. Boycott's neighbors' ostracizing him as a land agent during Ireland's 1880 Land League problems.

"bozos" a term (based on a popular TV clown named Bozo) used by Republican president George H. W. Bush toward the end of the 1992 presidential campaign to refer to his Democratic opponents, Governor Bill Clinton and Senator Albert Gore. Bush's apparent goal was to demean his opponents as the lowest (even lower than liberal) possible being, also stating that his dog knew more about foreign policy than did Clinton.

bracket creep a method of increasing taxes on people with certain incomes by lowering the reaches of tax brackets to include them. This technique is often used by governments pretending to lower taxes.

Brady Bill (Brady Handgun Prevention Act) a bill and now law named for James S. Brady, President Ronald Reagan's White House press secretary who was shot in the head and permanently disabled in John Hinckley Jr.'s attempted assassination of President Reagan on March 30, 1981. The Brady Bill, passed by Congress and signed by President Bill Clinton in 1993, took effect in February 1994 and creates a national waiting period between one's application for a permit to purchase a gun and the actual purchase. Ostensibly the waiting period gives authorities time to investigate the applicant's criminal history and gives enraged purchasers

time to cool down. President Reagan opposed the bill and President George H. W. Bush, a member of the National Rifle Association (NRA), threatened to veto it unless it came to him as part of his own crime bill, which did not happen.

Gun dealers claimed record sales of guns between passage of the Brady Bill and the day it took effect. See also GUN CONTROL; HANDGUN CONTROL, INC.; NATIONAL RIFLE ASSOCIATION.

Brahmin (1) originally the highest Indian Hindu caste. (2) aloof, snobbish, self-designated social or political aristocracy that plays power games to their own benefit. Boston Brahmins were despised particularly by the politically active Irish.

brain drain the enticement of one country's best educated and most intelligent citizens to leave their native country and go to another, usually for higher-paying jobs and more pleasant living conditions. The brain drain from a country can leave that country with a loss in collective brain power, and it can result in reduced possibilities to compete in scientific and high-tech fields.

Brain Trust (1) the term Franklin D. Roosevelt applied during his 1932 presidential campaign and early years of his administration to his first group of advisers as part of his "New Deal." Three prominent political economists, Raymond Moley, Adolf A. Berle, Jr., and Rexford G. Tugwell, led the Brain Trust, which also included several college and university professors and scholastic experts. (2) a group of advisers to the public official who calls upon their services. (3) any group of advisers, predominantly academics with special knowledge. (4) a term often used derogatively by opposition to mean "eggheads" or unelected insiders. Andrew Jackson's group was called the "kitchen cabinet."

branches of government   the three parts of the American government designed to create a balance of influence and a system of checks and balances: executive, judicial, and legislative.

bread and butter issues   issues based on basic economic concerns, such as jobs, inflation, and housing costs, that affect average households and individuals' take-home pay and purchasing ability.

break ranks   to vote or speak out contrary to one's party's or leadership's prevailing position. See also BOLT.

bribery   the act of giving, offering, or taking rewards (usually money) for corrupt acts such as changing votes as a result of being paid, giving false testimony, or doing something known to be illegal.

briefing   (1) meeting to explain or inform. (2) giving background and/or detailed information.

briefing book   usually a binder containing carefully prepared summaries of issues to be dealt with by a candidate, politician, or diplomat.

brinkmanship   a president or political leader's act to push a dangerous crisis to the brink of war or disaster before pulling back or watching the opponent pull back. There seems to be a sexual parallel here. The term came to prominence to describe the diplomatic methodology of Secretary of State John Foster Dulles during the Eisenhower administration in the 1950s.

broad construction   a constitutional law theory that broad (unilateral) interpretation of the U.S. Constitution is legitimate and appropriate according to the social and political mores of the times and the justices of the Supreme Court. Liberals tend to favor broad construction, as do presidents who do not wish to be constrained by decisions based on a literal reading of the Constitution. See also LIBERAL CONSTRUCTION.

brokered convention   a political party convention at which commitments have been or are made to deliver favorite sons' or daughters' delegates and those of other leading candidates to the eventually triumphant candidate. Often favors or future appointments result from such deals. With an increased number of primaries designed to select committed delegates, brokered conventions have become rare.

brownfield   a contaminated former industrial site.

Brown Act   A California statute that requires that all meetings of governmental decision-making bodies such as city councils and commissions, be public and prohibits meetings of a majority of that decision-making body, including "serial" phone calls among members.

Brown v. Board of Education of Topeka (1954) a case in which the U.S. Supreme Court ruled that separate educational facilities for whites and blacks are inherently unequal "and that equal conditions for all races must be provided with all deliberate speed." Basically, the Supreme Court ruled that racial segregation in public schools is unconstitutional, reversing the 1896 ruling of "separate but equal" in *Plessy v. Ferguson.* The plaintiffs' case was supported by an *amicus curiae* brief from President Harry Truman's Justice Department when it was filed in 1952. The decision was written by Chief Justice Earl Warren for a unanimous court and is considered to be the single most influential case in civil rights history. At the time conservatives criticized the ruling as social engineering rather than constitutional interpretation.

bug (1) to eavesdrop without the other person's knowledge or permission. (2) to spy by electronic device. (3) the electronic device used to secretly listen in on a conversation when one is not in the same room with the speaker(s).

Bull Moose Party See PROGRESSIVE PARTY.

bullet ballot voting for only one candidate when several are to be elected, thereby increasing your preferred candidate's chances while decreasing those of the other candidates, such as when many candidates are running for two or more city council seats.

bump (1) to dump or kick off (a committee). (2) a candidate's sudden rise in poll ratings caused by an event, such as a party convention and the media attention it brings.

bundling soliciting and gathering together campaign contributions, which the bundler then passes on to the campaign and usually gets credit for raising those funds.

buppies Acronym for *black urban professionals*, with the connotation that they tend toward white yuppiedom and away from their roots. Also inherent in the word is the implication that blacks cannot be ordinary (white) yuppies and need their own designation. See also YUPPIES.

bureaucracy (1) an institution's functions combined with the people who make up its organization and perform its functions with a certain degree of efficiency, inefficiency, and impersonality. (2) the institution's hierarchy and chain of command. Rewards come from salary and theoretically not from power or influence sensations. Appointments and promotions are supposed to be by skill and accomplishment and not by influence or patronage and are protected by both civil service and hierarchical pyramid systems. (3) pejorative word for petty time-servers who appear to be indifferent to the public and incapable of personal or collective initiative or innovative work. In many counties and states the bureaucracy is protected and institutionalized by civil service. Bureaucracies retain power because functionaries understand, control, and manipulate the system and the routine functions of government, whereas elected officials come and go.

bureaucrat a person who works for the government who may enter the bureaucracy with idealism and ideas for reform, but who may adopt to its system and its inefficiencies, stiflings, and securities while performing expected functions perfunctorily. Bureaucrats always seem to leave a little something unfinished and enjoy the power they feel over the public.

bureaucratic state A governmental and societal condition in which bureaucrats unite, intimidate, and control elected officials who theoretically make decisions.

business as usual the public's view of the way government and politicians continue to operate in the same old way and ignore public protestations favoring reform, responsiveness to the voters, fiscal responsibility, and resistance to lobbyists' influence.

busing an effort to move students from their residential neighborhood to a school in another geographic area in order to mix races and end de facto segregation in schools as required by *Brown v. Board of Education of Topeka*. Busing often becomes a political issue but is usually required by courts to achieve integration. Conservatives saw busing as a fearful policy, which would force mixing of their children with blacks, waste students' time and public funds, and compel students to attend schools too far from home in hostile and unsafe neighborhoods. Liberals, particularly outside the South, favored busing to equalize educational opportunities.

button-hole to keep a person in conversation longer than they want to be held, as if clutching a man's button-hole collar and pulling his face to yours, connoting a form of force. The implication is that the speaker is forcing him/herself upon the listener. Button-holing is a technique often used in legislatures or at political conventions to urge one's position or candidate.

buzzword a word selected and used to trigger an additional reaction beyond that of the word's normal meaning.

by-election (1) an election held in a constituency or district to fill a legislative seat rendered vacant between general elections. (2) special election.

cabal (1) a small group of people who unite on a specific issue or plan. (2) a plot by a group of insiders to oust a superior, take over an organization, or change the conduct or direction of an organization or agency, such as a political party or White House staff members.

cabinet (1) United States: group of major federal government department heads, gathered originally during George Washington's first presidential term. Some presidents have included the U.S. representative to the United Nations and the vice president in their cabinet discussions. The cabinet traditionally advises the president. Individual members or secretaries are removable by the president without consent of the Senate. Members include (in order of succession after the vice president, secretary of state, secretaries of treasury, defense, attorney general, secretaries of the interior, agriculture, commerce, labor, health and human services, housing and urban development, transportation, energy, education, and veteran's affairs. President Bill Clinton added several positions to "cabinet level" without actually making them part of the cabinet, partly to satisfy his self-imposed need to bring ethnic and gender diversity to the cabinet. President George W. Bush elevated the office of National Security Advisor to cabinet level. (2) parliamentary systems: in Great Britain, Canada, Japan, and other countries cabinets are constituted from members of parliament's ruling party.

cabinet solidarity an unwritten rule that members of a government cabinet stick together to support their president or prime minister, as well as each other's programs. This is particularly characteristic of parliamentary governments in which cabinet members come from the parliament.

cadre-style party   a term coined by Dr. R. Kenneth Carty, chair of the Department of Political Science at the University of British Columbia, to describe a strong political party that controls its operation, possesses an active permanent staff, recruits a force of local volunteers and follows an established set of principles.

California Democratic Council (CDC)   a Democratic volunteer organization of clubs founded in 1953, following Democratic presidential candidate Adlai Stevenson's loss to Gen. Dwight D. Eisenhower. It reached a membership of over 50,000 in 500 clubs by 1966. The CDC coalesced Democratic Party support around primary candidates by early endorsements. It provided precinct organization and issues materials, leading to victories for California Democrats in the 1950s and 1960s, including the governorship and majorities in the California state legislature and congressional delegation after long dominance by the Republicans. The largest volunteer political organization in the United States, the CDC was the first party group to question (1966) and oppose (1967) President Lyndon Johnson's Vietnam War policy. The CDC first questioned Johnson's renomination and then instigated the candidacy of Senator Eugene McCarthy. The CDC's power and influence waned during the 1970s as campaign media advertising replaced volunteerism, but it still represents 100 clubs of liberal volunteers as grass-roots activity regains importance. Address: 8124 West 3rd Street, #207, Los Angeles, Calif. 90048. Tel.: (323) 653-1091 or (800) 353-4335.

California Republican Assembly   a club-like organization founded in 1934 by moderate Republicans, such as Earl Warren, as a volunteer arm of the California Republican Party. The CRA actively sought, developed, and supported candidates. It remained an important force in California politics through the 1950s, and it was then taken over by extreme conservatives in the early 1960s. Since then it represents primarily the conservative wing of the party and, subsequently, is only one of several Republican volunteer organizations in California. Address: P. O. Box 276101, Sacramento, Calif. 95827. Tel.: (916) 858-1469; FAX: (916) 858-8274; e-mail: editor@ca-ra.org; website: www.ca-ra.org/

campaign   (1) originally a series of military operations with specific goals. (2) organized, planned activities aimed at convincing the electorate to vote for a particular candidate for public office or to support one side of an issue, and at making sure those favorable to a candidate or a position vote.

campaign consultant   a person who offers himself or herself to advise or manage a campaign for money. Campaign consultants abound, and no standards exist to inform candidates or campaigns about the level of experience or competency they can expect. Anyone who has ever worked professionally—and some people who have never been paid—in campaigns can print business cards and call himself/herself a campaign consultant.

campaign contributions   money, gifts in kind, or services donated to a political campaign ostensibly to fund campaign expenses such as mailings, staff, advertising, get out the vote efforts, and a candidate's and staff's travel expenses.

While currently necessary to finance American political campaigns, candidates usually spend more time raising money than they do listening to the opinions of the citizens they hope to represent. Contributors to campaigns too often get the ear of the officeholder they supported and have undue influence on that person because of the officeholder's supposed indebtedness to the donor. Influence and presidential appointments are often in direct proportion to the size of the contribution. In 1993 the Democratic National Committee actively solicited $15,000 per couple contributions from lobbyists and corporate presidents in return for promises of private meetings with President Clinton, his top economic advisers, and his Chiefs of Staff or overnight stays in the White House. Subsequently both Democrats and Republicans have raised hundreds of millions of dollars from dedicated, large givers.

campaign finance reform   political issue brought to awareness by Senator John McCain (R–Ariz.) in the 2000 presidential primary campaign and as the McCain-Feingold Bill in the U.S. Senate. Those favoring campaign finance reform want to limit contributions and spending, increase disclosure of contributors and their affiliations, and eliminate "soft money" contributions to political parties. (See SOFT MONEY.)

campaign manager   the person who organizes and runs a campaign to persuade the voters to elect his/her candidate to public office or to vote in favor of his/her side of an issue or ballot measure. Usually this individual is paid and is responsible for hiring and overseeing staff, coordinating strategic planning, fund raising, advertising, publicity, scheduling the candidate's appearances and appointments, and getting out the vote.

campaign reform   proposals to reorder, monitor, and control campaign contributions and expenditures, most recently via the McCain-Feingold Bill.

Traditionally legislators have avoided implementing campaign reform, primarily because the current system benefits incumbents (themselves), and campaign reform might benefit challengers and the people. The 1992 presidential candidate and former California governor Edmund G. "Jerry" Brown Jr. campaigned nationally for political reform, advocating limitations on campaign contributions. Congress offered a "reform package" in 1993 limiting expenditures for congressional races to $600,000. Few challengers have any hope of legitimately raising $600,000. Republican presidential candidate Senator John McCain (R–Ariz.) campaigned in the 2000 primaries advocating campaign finance reform.

True campaign reform would include limitations on both campaign contributions and campaign expenditures. By contrast, the British system limits monies raised and spent, guarantees equal electronic media time for candidates, and forces the candidates to truly mingle with and listen to potential constituents and voters. Voter turnout is consistently high in Britain due to personal and direct identification with candidates and issues. Canada limits parliamentary candidates' expenditures with the same result.

Canadian Alliance nickname of the Canadian Reform Conservative Alliance Party, Canada's most conservative party, which morphed in 2000 from the Reform Party, briefly into the Canadian Conservative Reform Alliance Party (CCRAP), and the Conservative Alliance Reform Party (CARP). In 2000 the Canadian Alliance elected Stockwell Day as leader over its founder, Preston Manning. While its positions shift frequently, the Canadian Alliance is against gun control and abortion, and for the death penalty and a flat tax, and enjoys its greatest popularity in the Canadian plains and western provinces. Address: #600-833 4th Avenue, S.W., Calgary, Alberta T2P 3T5. Tel.: 1-888-733-6761 or (403) 269-1990; FAX: (403) 269-4077; website: www.canadianalliance.ca

candidate a person who offers himself or herself to run for elective office.

cannibalism (1) to eat one's own. (2) attempts by opposition party senators, members of Congress, and the press to denigrate the program and/or person of a president.

canon law rules of the Roman Catholic Church originating from c.1100–c.1500 that deal with personal morality, church and personal discipline, administration of the sacraments, and the status and powers of the clergy. It is still used in church courts. Canon law sets precedents and influences concepts that move from the religious to the political, such as constitutional law, the development of secular politics, and elections. Formulators of Canon law drew from natural law, Roman and civil law, and secular experience.

canvass (1) to examine carefully, or discuss in detail, a subject, policy, or measure. (2) to walk through a geographic area soliciting votes or opinions for a candidate or on an issue. Campaign workers often go door to door asking people's views in a candidate's district. In this sense canvass is a form of poll. (3) the post-election count of votes by a designated official to determine the winner. States' secretaries of state tabulate statewide election counts, and county registrars of voters record county and city election results.

capitalism an economic system that combines the principles of private property and free and competitive enterprise—or business with workers employed primarily by private business—with that of production for profit. Capitalism was first delineated by Scottish economist Adam Smith in his monumental work *Inquiry into the Nature and Causes of the Wealth of Nations* (1776), and it constitutes the economic basis of most industrialized nations. Some capitalist economies utilize socialist elements such as state ownership or control of some functions and industries. Liberals usually favor capitalism but want it to be humane and in the public interest, preferring regulation and some welfare funded by taxes on profits. Conservatives sometimes view liberals' positions, such as favoring nationalization of the health care system, as communistic or socialistic and thereby threatening to capitalism. Some conservatives favor deregulation of industries and favor capitalism as a form of economic Darwinism (survival of the financially most capable) on the basis that anyone in America can succeed financially if he or she will just try, "pull him/herself up by his/her bootstraps or bra straps," and get a job. Liberals complain that such remarks are made by people who grew up in comfortable circumstances or who are insensitive to the needs of others and do not face economic stress. They contend that such job searches are particularly demoralizing and humbling experiences in times of recession and depression, often created and ignored by conservative national administrations.

capital punishment (1) death penalty for a crime. (2) executing a person for committing a crime. See also DEATH PENALTY.

Capitol Hill (1) the low hill in Washington, D.C., on which the Capitol building, the House and Senate chambers and office buildings are located. Geographically, and sometimes politically, it is at the opposite end of Pennsylvania Avenue from the White House.

capture the candidate a phrase used to describe some people's need to get a candidate or person of perceived power into their own control at all costs. Capturing the candidate may mean simply insisting on driving him/her in one's own car and thereby controlling his/her next actions or conversation for a short period of time. Often the candidate capture is not in the best interest of the candidate. People who play capture the candidate often annoy other campaign workers or contributors and, sometimes, even the candidate.

carpetbagger (1) originally a northern office seeker who moved to the South during post–Civil War reconstruction to take advantage of white and newly freed black southerners in unsettled political and economic conditions. (2) roving bankers in the Old West who carried their money in bags made of old carpets. (3) a person from outside a particular political district who moves into it for the purpose of running for political or public office. In the United States a person does not have to live in a congressional district to represent it, although candidates from outside or those who move into a district so that they can run for office in that district are often referred to as carpetbaggers.

caucus (1) from an Algonquin Indian word (*Kaw-kaw-asu*) meaning to speak or to counsel. (2) a meeting of residents of an electoral district belonging to the same party to nominate and select convention delegates, recommend party policy and platform, plan campaigns, or, in a legislature, select their own party leaders. (3) a grouping of voters with interests or ethnicity in common who meet to discuss their commonalties and try to educate and influence others. (4) a closed-door meeting to plan or deflect problems and/or blame. (5) between 1796 and 1828, the groups of congressional leaders who chose presidential and vice presidential candidates, nicknamed "King Caucus."

(6) a meeting of party activists used to nominate and/or elect convention delegates as in the Iowa caucuses or the California Democratic caucuses in which candidates run to be elected delegates to the Democratic National Convention.

CCRAP Canadian Conservative Reform Alliance Party, the momentary 2000 "new" name of Canada's Reform Party abandoned within 24 hours when the press pointed out the acronym. Now the Canadian Alliance or Canadian Reform Conservative Alliance Party. See also CANADIAN ALLIANCE.

censorship the act of censoring, overseeing of public morals, or imposing one's morals on others by forbidding certain words, phrases, musical lyrics, video games, Internet web sites, and movies to keep the public from being exposed to them.

Censorship is accomplished directly and indirectly in the United States by rating of movies; v-chips blocking reception of some television programs, and stamping warnings of vulgarity on records, cassettes, and CD albums to alert parents to language deemed offensive by self-appointed censors or moral arbiters. Other means of censorship include investigations of citizens whose acts, comments, writing, or art are offensive to a particular presidential administration by the FBI, IRS, or other regulatory agency or congressional committee. Most presidents have used indirect censorship by withholding news tidbits from reporters whose stories have offended them. President George H. W. Bush's personal news censorship became well known, partly because reporters talked about it more openly than ever before.

During the Iraqi/Gulf War, the Defense Department actually forbade print or televised photos of Iraqi or American bombing victims and destruction.

In totalitarian countries all news is subject to censorship to keep bad news, mistakes, and opposition views from the public. See also DEMOCRATIC WIMP FACTOR, POLITICAL CORRECTNESS.

censure a judgment or resolution condemning a member of a body for misconduct without expulsion. The U.S. Senate's censure of Senator Joseph McCarthy for his irresponsible charges of treason in the U.S. Army in 1954 ended his campaign of wild claims of communist influence on Democrats and liberals and destroyed his effectiveness. After the House of Representatives impeached President Bill Clinton in 1999, the Senate discussed censuring Clinton but decided not to punish him.

Center for the Study of Democratic Institutions an American think tank established in Santa Barbara, California in 1959 by the Fund for the Republic to identify and study particular public issues. Under the presidency and chairmanship of former University of Chicago president Robert M. Hutchins (1954–69) the center changed its emphasis from supporting groups working for civil rights and civil liberties to clarification of social reform's basic issues of freedom and justice in the second half of the 20th century. Prize-winning editor Harry S. Ashmore became president in 1969, and the center attracted scholars from all over the world, held

national and international conferences, and created *The Center Magazine* (1967) and *The Center Report*
(1970). The cost of these publications
contributed to the Center's financial
ruin and reduction in size. Address:
10951 West Pico Blvd., 3rd Floor, Los
Angeles, Calif. 90064. Tel.: (310)
474-0011.

Central Intelligence Agency (CIA)
America's official spy and intelligence
organization created in 1947 by Congress under the National Security Act
to coordinate various intelligence
operations that existed throughout
the U.S. government and to advise the
president and National Security
Council on security matters, foreign
governments, and espionage.

The CIA has been criticized for the
ill-fated "Bay of Pigs" invasion of
Cuba and attacked in recent years for
its involvement in politics, rumored
death plots against Fidel Castro,
favorable treatment of drug dealers
who agree to act as agents, the Iran-
Contra Affair, failure to kill Khadafi
when bombing Libya, and misreading
Iraq's intentions toward Kuwait.

Since its budget and activities are
officially secret, and its analyses (good
or bad) are often not made public, the
CIA has raised suspicion and doubts
as to its mission, effectiveness, and
usefulness. Address: Washington,
D.C. 20505. Tel.: (703) 482-0623;
FAX: (703) 482-1739; (does not
accept e-mail); website: www.cia.gov/

centralization the concentration of
a national government in a large city
as opposed to distribution of powers
and responsibilities among national,
state, and local authorities. Extreme
examples included the former USSR
and China. President Ronald Reagan
attempted to decentralize government
by shifting duties and financial
responsibilities to the states, making
the action appear positive when actually he was trying to shed responsibilities and financial blame.

Conservatives usually claim to
favor decentralization and local control, while liberals usually prefer a
mix of centralization and local control. See also DECENTRALIZATION.

centrist a person whose political
position is firmly in the center of the
political thinking spectrum, being neither totally leftist nor rightist, and neither liberal nor conservative. Centrist
refers to people who genuinely believe
in positions fitting this description,
and not those lacking the will to make
a choice. President Bill Clinton and
the Democratic Leadership Council
were centrists who tried to combine
liberal social policy with conservative
fiscal principles. See also MIDDLE OF
THE ROAD.

chad the small piece of paper voters
punch out with a stylus to cast a vote
on some ballots, such as those used in
Florida in the 2000 election. Machines that count the kind of paper
ballot used by this system count holes,
do not count chads that are partly
punched out, and reject ballots with
partial holes they cannot read. The
degree to which a chad is or is not
punched out led to controversy in the
close 2000 presidential election and
produced new names for pieces of
paper: **dimpled chad** is a small piece
of paper that is dented but has minute
paper attachments from the ballot
card that are not broken; **hanging
chad** is one that is partially punched

out and has one or more of its minute paper connections broken through; **pregnant chad** is a small piece of paper that significantly bulges away from the ballot card but is not detached at more than one point; **swinging chad** is a small piece of paper that hangs from only one of its attachment points on the ballot.

challenged a late-20th-century politically correct term for "handicapped" or somehow lacking perfection. A person may be mobility challenged if he/she needs a wheelchair or educationally challenged if he/she has a learning disability.

chamber (1) the room in which a legislative body meets. (2) an abbreviation for a chamber of commerce.

chamber of commerce an organization of business owners or high-level employees. Most towns and cities in the United States have chambers of commerce which promote business development in their area and advocate business' interests before local, state, and national legislative bodies.

Chambers of commerce are usually fairly conservative and thought to favor all kinds of development, sometimes without regard for overall environmental and economic consequences. Republicans often see chambers of commerce as their grass roots, sensible organizational foundation, whereas some Democrats may see chambers as Republican, conservative, selfish, self-promoting organizations. Nationally they are represented by the U.S. Chamber of Commerce. Address: 1615 H Street, NW, Washington, D.C. 20062. Tel.:

(202) 659-6000 or look in local phone books.

Chambers v. Florida a U.S. Supreme Court case in which Justice Hugo Black wrote the decision (1940) ruling that the use of coerced confessions in state law cases is a violation of "due process," thereby extending the due process protection to local police practices. This case was an important step in applying the Fourteenth Amendment equal protection clause to states as well as to the federal government.

Chappaquiddick (1) an island in Nantucket Sound off the coast of Martha's Vineyard, Massachusetts. (2) a "problem" for Senator Edward M. Kennedy (D.–Massa.). (3) a generic term for the 1969 incident in which Senator Kennedy drove off a narrow bridge into the water with fellow party-goer Mary Jo Kopechne in his car. Senator Kennedy escaped through the driver's side door window and Kopechne drowned. Senator Kennedy, his cousins, friends, and their dates delayed reporting the accident to authorities while they considered what action to take, and prepare alibis. The incident crippled Ted Kennedy as potential presidential material. Republicans use the event to disparage Kennedy and all Democrats by association, with comments such as "Fewer people died at Three Mile Island than at Chappaquiddick."

character issue under the guise of general moral standards, "character issue" most often means playing around with members of the opposite sex to whom a candidate or office holder is not married. Republicans campaigned on the character issue in 2000, attacking President Bill Clinton's (and therefore Vice President Al Gore's) character based on Clinton's reputation as a womanizer due to Paula Jones's accusations, his White House affair with Monica Lewinsky, charges that he lied under oath, and his 1999 impeachment trial.

charisma (1) originally a Catholic concept of "a gift of grace" attributed to saints. (2) a quality of attractive charm that allows the possessor to exercise psychological power and inspire devotion and political loyalty over large numbers of people. (3) personal magnetism. Well-known examples of people possessing charisma include Mahatma Gandhi, Adolf Hitler, Gloria Steinem, and John F. Kennedy. The word became popular in reference to Kennedy's charm in the 1960s.

charismatic authority extraordinary authority unofficially granted to a leader based on a public's or following's admiration of the individual's personal qualities, such as good looks, intellect, or spiritual comforts.

chauvinism (1) belligerent, demonstrative, absurd, fanatical patriotism. (2) unreasoned commitment to one's sex or race while bearing contempt for another sex or race. (3) term used to describe out-of-date attitudes that men dominate or are superior to women.

Checkers the name of a cocker spaniel which had been given to Richard Nixon's daughters while he was running for vice president in 1952. Following revelation by the *New York Post* in September 1952, that Nixon's friends had set up a secret fund to receive gifts to cover political, and perhaps personal, expenses, Nixon first claimed that the exposure of this legal but embarrassing fund was a communist plot to smear him.

Pressure built for him to resign from the Eisenhower-Nixon Republican ticket to protect Gen. Dwight Eisenhower's pristine image. Former New York governor Thomas E. Dewey urged him privately and former Minnesota governor Harold Stassen begged him publicly to drop out of the race. Nixon boldly appeared on national television live with his own emotional half-hour defense, talking little about the secret fund and lots about his humble assets, referring to his wife Pat's cloth coat, and about his beliefs that the secret fund reports were part of a smear campaign.

Ironically, the most remembered part of his speech came when, with a tear in his eye and a cracking voice, he vowed that he was going to keep Checkers because his children loved the dog. Hence, his monologue became known as the Checkers speech, and undoubtedly saved Nixon's career for the moment. A few days later Eisenhower embraced Nixon and announced that he was his man and would remain on the Republican ticket.

checks and balances the principle of separation of powers in government, giving powers to legislative, executive and judicial branches in order for "the efforts in human nature toward tyranny can alone be checked and restrained, and any degree of freedom served in the constitution" (John Adams). The principle derives from the writings of French philosopher Montesquieu, and James Madison built it into the U.S. Constitution by giving each branch a check on the other two.

Chernobyl location in Ukraine where a nuclear power plant's generator melted down in April 1986. Radioactive gases floated throughout Ukraine and to other European countries. Authorities evacuated 40,000 people from the immediate area. Deaths, illnesses, animals born with grotesque deformities (multiple heads and appendages), anemia, eye problems, oversized fish in waters downstream and contamination of rivers, produce, and cattle feed, have resulted. Total damage may never be recorded, known, or revealed.

Chicago Seven Rennie Davis, David Delinger, John Froines, Tom Hayden, Abbie Hoffman, Jerry Rubin, and Lee Weiner, radical antiwar activists who were charged with conspiring to incite a riot (against the establishment and against the Vietnam War) outside the Democratic National Convention in Chicago, Illinois, in 1968. An eighth participant, Bobby Seale of the Black Panthers, insisted that he be tried separately, which reduced the group to the Chicago Seven. They were cleared of conspiracy charges, but five were convicted of crossing a state line to incite a riot. The Appeals Court overturned the conviction in 1972 on the basis that remarks by the judge in the original trial had prejudiced the jury, and the defendants were not re-tried.

Chicago Sun Times the most liberal daily newspaper in the Midwest, ranking 11th in the country in circulation with 400,000 readers. It survives in a highly competitive and shrinking market, providing a political balance to the *Chicago Tribune,* and its editorial efforts include syndication of its opinion columns. Address: 401 North Wabash Avenue, Chicago, Ill. 60611 Tel.: (312) 321-3000; FAX: (312) 321-3084; website: www.suntimes.com

Chicago Tribune the most influential newspaper in the Midwest, ranking seventh in circulation in the United States with 750,000 subscribers. Historically a citadel of isolationism and conservatism, the *Tribune* has become more balanced editorially in recent years with nationally syndicated features. It is also famous for its embarrassingly untrue headline in 1948 proclaiming "Dewey Defeats Truman." Address: 435 North Michigan Avenue, Chicago, Ill. 60611. Tel.: (312) 222-3232; website: www. chicagotribune.com

chief executive president of the United States.

chief of staff the top manager of any office, if so designated, particularly in congressional and White House staffs. The most powerful chief of staff in Washington is that of the president, a job created in 1939 by President Franklin Delano Roosevelt to direct White House business. The chief of staff's power and status derive from his/her assumed daily contact and communication with the president, apparent power to direct the operation of the president's staff and business, and oversight of the president's appointments calendar.

Some chiefs of staff have abused their influence, including President Dwight D. Eisenhower's Sherman Adams, who took gifts from influence peddlers, and H. R. Haldemann, who helped President Nixon conduct the Watergate cover-up and who subsequently went to jail. Others have proved ineffective, too easy going or subservient to the president, vain, or petty. The best chiefs of staff are those who submerge their personal egos and agendas in service to the president of member of Congress for whom they work, such as President Lyndon Johnson's Bill Moyers and President George H. W. Bush's James Baker.

child labor   a major American and international reform issue during the 19th and 20th centuries. Since before World War I efforts were made to outlaw or regulate child labor. The National Child Labor committee worked for legislation, the Department of Labor's Children's Bureau began investigations in 1912, and the Keating-Owen Act (1916) forbade trading in interstate commerce of products made by children 14 years of age or under, later to be wiped out by *Hammer v. Dagenhart* (1918). Congress created a 10 percent tax of net profits on child employers, which was overruled in 1922 in *Bailey v. Drexel Furniture Co.* The Cotton Textile codes outlawed child labor in the cotton industry (1933), and the Walsh-Healey Act (1936) prohibited government contracts with firms hiring workers under the age of 18. The Fair Labor Standards Act (1938) set a minimum age of 14 for employment outside school hours, 16 for employment during school hours in interstate commerce, and 18 for occupations deemed hazardous by the secretary of labor. Today, many employers require work permits from high school counselors while many young children are still exploited in agriculture and "piece" industries, in which the family gets paid by the "piece" picked or produced, regardless of the worker's age.

choice   a buzzword for a woman's right to choose whether she wants to have an abortion or give birth to a child she is carrying.

Division lines between Americans who are pro-choice (favoring a woman's right to choose whether she has an abortion over legislation against same) and those who are anti-choice or "pro-life," (which are synonymous with anti-abortion) generally parallel political lines between liberals and conservatives, and religious lines between liberal religions and Roman Catholics and born-again Christians. Some Catholics favor "choice" but may face excommunication from the church for voicing their views.

Christian   (1) a believer in the teachings of Christ. (2) in the born-again Christian sense of the word used politically in the 1980s, 1990s, and 2000s, "Christian" has become a buzzword for those who call themselves that to signal that they believe in Jesus Christ and the "right to life," and that they are righteous people. Many try to distinguish themselves from everyone else by the implication that they belong to a correct group and will be saved for eternity.

Christian Coalition   the newest name preferred by the religious right to label their organizational umbrella of conservative political positions and religious views on issues such as reproductive rights, (Christian) prayer in schools, and school vouchers. See also MORAL MAJORITY, RELIGIOUS RIGHT.

Christian Conservative   See MORAL MAJORITY, RELIGIOUS RIGHT.

Christian Right   See NEW RIGHT.

church and state   separation of church and state is required in the First Amendment of the U.S. Constitution. The specific language reads: "Congress shall make no law respecting an establishment of religion, or prohibiting the free exercise thereof." Challenges continue regarding Christian prayer in public schools, posting of the Ten Commandments in classrooms, displaying Christian scenes or creches on public property, and even the added "under God" phrase of the Pledge of Allegiance.

citizen   a member of a state or nation by birth or naturalization who is entitled to full civil rights.

citizenship   the duties, rights, and privileges of membership in a nation, especially in a republican form of government with full civil rights.

city commissioners   (1) name for city council members or aldermen in some cities. They are persons elected to make city policy and budgetary decisions. The mayor usually presides over meetings. (2) appointed city officials who serve on specific purpose boards or commissions to hold hearings, make decisions, and make recommendations to the city council. These commissioners are usually appointed to the body for their expertise or political influence.

city council   the governing body of a city, made up of commissioners, city council members, or aldermen.

city manager   (1) an individual appointed by a city council to professionally administer a city government and enforce city ordinances who also manages city finances, public works, recreation, police, water, and other services. (2) one of three prevailing forms of city government. The city manager system was first introduced as a reform in Staunton, Virginia in 1908.

city planning   an effort to plan growth and development with zoning systems designating certain areas for residential homes, apartments, multiuse, business, manufacturing, recreation, open space, and transportation. Planning began with William Penn's design for a new Philadelphia (1692), and later Major Pierre L'Enfant came to the United States from Paris to design the new national capital on the Potomac River (Washington, D.C.). Upper New York City was originally planned by a special commission (1807). Today most cities, towns, counties, and some states have official general plans and planning commissions using zoning laws as the legal basis for planning and regulating development.

civil defense   (1) a national system to protect civilians and property during war or threat of war. (2) a preparedness weapon whose existence supposedly deters attack from the outside.

Fear of bombing by Japan and of German and Japanese espionage in World War II led to a national civil defense system, including volunteer air raid wardens (1941–45).

President John F. Kennedy's administration advocated a civil defense program including bomb shelters (1961–62) in response to Soviet and Cuban crises. Active liberals considered such moves as ridiculous hysteria, while conservatives believed enemy communists might bomb the United States. Little actual organizing occurred besides the establishment of a hierarchy of a civil defense officialdom with regional offices. As the foreign threat of attack dissolved, the system was converted for use in earthquake and other natural disaster preparedness, although earthquakes and storms in the 1980s and 1990s raised questions about the bureaucracy's effectiveness.

civil disobedience   a form of nonviolent protest developed and popularized by Mahatma Gandhi in his campaign from the 1920s to the 1940s to liberate India from the British Empire. Civil disobedience occurs when a group of people publicly defy a law or rule to which they object or would like to have changed. Theoretically, the protesters' intermediate goal is to provoke appropriate authorities to react by drawing broad attention to the regulation or law they want changed. If the responsive action by the governmental body is not worth the effort or embarrassment, protesters may cave in or compromise.

Essayist Henry Thoreau (1817–1862) was America's most articulate advocate of civil disobedience. In the United States it has included suffragettes chaining themselves to public buildings, "sit-ins" at segregated business establishments by civil rights advocates, and blockades at university campuses and military buildings by antiwar students.

Liberals generally are tolerant toward nonviolent civil disobedience as the right and obligation of citizens. Conservatives usually have viewed civil disobedience as radical and almost treasonous. Ironically, some conservatives view civil protests begun by anti-abortion Operation Rescue advocates as justified even when they become violent or result in murder. Liberals consider civil disobedience as their right and obligation.

civil liberties   rights or freedoms given to the people by the First Amendment to the U.S. Constitution, by common law, legislation, or basic fairness, allowing the individual to be free to speak, think, assemble, organize, and worship without government interference or restraints. Civil liberties usually are lacking in dictatorships, totalitarian states, or under martial law. They also can be threatened in democracies by conservative legislators or executives who think it is their job to decide when other people's civil liberties infringe on the public welfare. For example, Senator Jesse Helms (R–N.C.) believes that he should control funding of the National Endowment for the Arts based on his personal views of art, obscenity, and propriety.

civil rights   those rights guaranteed by the Bill of Rights, the 13th and

14th Amendments to the U.S. Constitution, and acts of Congress: exemption from slavery, equal treatment of all people regarding enjoyment of life, liberty, and property, and protection under the law. Positive civil rights include the right to vote, rights to enjoy the benefits of a democratic society, including the use of and equal access to public schools, recreation, transportation, and public facilities, equal and fair treatment by police and judges, right to vote, and housing. See also CIVIL LIBERTIES.

civil rights acts a series of laws enacted regarding civil rights in the United States. They are: (1) 1866: vetoed by President Andrew Johnson, but over ridden on April 9, this was a federal law to protect the rights of newly freed (black) people by defining citizenship and protecting civil rights with enforcement by the federal courts. (2) 1875: passed March 1, to protect all citizens' legal rights regardless of "nativity, race, color, or persuasion, religious or political," this law was intended to give equal rights and access to accommodations, "advantages," facilities, public transportation, theaters, and "other public amusements." Enforcement was to be in district and circuit courts. (3) 1957: passed August 29, this act basically gave weak voting rights to blacks and created a six-member Civil Rights Commission. (4) 1960: weakly provided for enforcement of the 1957 act. (5) 1964: the strongest legislation since the Civil War providing equal rights to voting, education, public accommodations, and federal programs. It is supposed to be enforced through the Department of Justice and other federal agencies regardless of a person's race, color, religion, or national origin. (6) 1968: adopted six days after Rev. Martin Luther King Jr.'s assassination on April 4 at Memphis, Tennessee, this law prohibited discrimination in housing because of race, color, religion, or national origin by giving the applicant the right to file complaints of discrimination with the Department of Housing and Urban Development. (7) the Civil Rights Act for Indians (1969) introduced the Bill of Rights into Indian Tribal Law. (8) 1991: a broader civil rights act was vetoed by President George H. W. Bush on his claim that it set up a quota system, and the veto was upheld by Congress.

civil rights movement Although there had been concern for Negroes' civil rights dating back to post–Civil War reconstruction days, the civil rights movement dates from the 1950s. It gained momentum with the school desegregation ruling in *Brown v. Board of Education* (1954), which led to sit-ins and demonstrations in southern states to bring about desegregation of buses, whites-only colleges, restaurants, and other public accommodations and facilities. In 1956 Rosa Parks refused to sit in the "colored only" section at the back of a public bus and triggered a bus boycott by blacks in Montgomery, Alabama. Fannie Lou Hamer instigated a crusade to register black voters in Mississippi and Alabama (1961) in response to existing intimidation, poll taxes, impossible literacy tests, and closed primaries. The Rev. Martin Luther King Jr. and other nonviolence advocates led the movement, which rallied supporters to employ marches, sit-ins, persuasion, legal actions, and publicity in the face of beatings, jailings, murder, arson, and resistance by state and local governments. Thousands of "freedom riders" from the North and West joined southern civil rights activists in marching at Selma, Alabama, and working to register voters.

Two hundred thousand civil rights supporters walked in the "March on Washington" and heard Martin Luther King's "I Have a Dream" speech on August 28, 1963. The 24th Amendment to the Constitution abolished poll taxes (January 23, 1964). The Voting Rights Act of 1965 guaranteed voting rights. With help from "modern" southern leaders such as by Georgia governor and future president Jimmy Carter and the federal government, many of the movement's goals were achieved by the 1970s. Economic and social equality still elude African Americans.

Coretta Scott King, Medgar and Myrlie Evers, James Farmer, Jesse Jackson, the NAACP, Andrew Young, Julian Bond (the first modern black legislator in Georgia), and many other individuals and organizations are among the movement's leaders. Medgar Evers (June 1963), freedom riders Andrew Goodman, Michael Schwerner, and James Chaney (August 1964), Rev. James Reeb and Viola Liuzzo (March 1965), and Rev. Martin Luther King Jr. (April 1968) are among those who gave their lives for the civil rights movement.

civil service   (1) originally all nonmilitary government employees of the British Crown. (2) government employees who are supposed to implement policies of a government, advise elected officials, and implement decisions of political leaders of a government and its agencies. Such employees are supposed to be nonpartisan, although higher level employees are often political appointees who change with each administration. Civil Service employees (civil servants) are protected from firing as long as they do their work, although they can be manipulated and made subject to politics within government or agency departments.

The civil service concept in the United States developed in response to ineffectiveness and corruption within government systems. The first American civil service act (Pendleton Act, passed January 16, 1883) followed the assassination of President James A. Garfield by a deranged office seeker. The Pendleton Act placed 14,000 jobs on a merit promotion system. By 1900, civil service encompassed another 100,000 jobs free from political control and influence.

During the 20th century more than 90 percent of federal government jobs have been brought into the civil service system with established levels of pay for each job, tests for promotion, and job protection.

Liberals traditionally favored civil service despite its weaknesses, including the inability to dismiss inadequate workers, lack of inspiration and creativity among workers, inefficiency, and promotion of power games within the system. Conservatives usually emphasize these weaknesses.

Civilian Conservation Corps (CCC) (1933–42)   an early New Deal program to relieve the Great Depression's effects. It employed single men in conservation work, including planting trees, building flood dikes, fighting forest fires, and maintaining forest roads and trails. CCC men lived in quasi-military camps where they followed a strict regimen, received medical care, $30 cash per month, and food. Employing 500,000 men at its peak, the CCC provided work for three million men. President John F. Kennedy considered revitalizing the CCC for ghetto youths (1961) but did not follow through with his plan. California governor Jerry Brown implemented a CCC-type workforce during his tenure in the 1970s.

Clarity Bill   a Canadian parliamentary bill enabling the Canadian government to review language of any ballot measures proposed in Quebec to separate Quebec from Canada.

class   a group of people who share similar economic or social status. While "class" is downplayed as theoretically nonexistent in the United States, it does exist. Class designations are usually claimed by those seeing themselves as better or "higher" than others. Karl Marx saw society as divided into two classes: the bourgeoisie elite who control commerce and business, and the proletariat or rest of the people who work for the owners. Social science theory usually ascribes social status as determined by wealth or income, with education and family genealogy contributing to class distinctions.

In the United States there are upper, middle, and lower classes. Theoretically, there is class mobility in a capitalistic democracy, enabling citizens to rise from class to class. Politically, upper and middle classes tend to vote conservatively or Republican, and the working classes traditionally

vote more liberally or Democratic. However, in the 1980s traditional identifications became scrambled with workers joining management and voting conservatively, leaving white liberals and minorities voting Democratic.

class warfare   contention that working and poor people are at odds with wealthy people.

clean sweep   a win by one party or philosophy of every office in a political race, often replacing incumbents with all new people.

clear and present danger   a somewhat *unclear* standard, set by the U.S. Supreme Court to decide when freedom of speech may and should be limited to "protect" society or when information on public affairs should be kept secret in the name of national security. The uncertainty of what constitutes a "clear and present danger" is also a potentially dangerous political weapon to silence opposition or to judge when a president has the right to withhold information from the public.

Generally those being silenced or not receiving information feel the standard is unclear and unjust, while those deciding when information presents a "clear and present danger" interpret the vagueness as specificity, and assume their standard is the correct one. Justice Oliver Wendell Holmes pointed out that freedom of speech did not include the right "to yell 'fire' in a crowded theater," but he did not provide limits on the restriction.

Conservatives usually interpret the president's right to make the decision broadly and trust the president's (particularly one of their own party) judgment, while liberals often see withholding of information as treasonous and rarely trust a president to make that decision for them. Conservatives vehemently supported President George H. W. Bush's decision not to allow photos of dead Iraqis in the 1991 War to appear in the American press, while liberals accused him of distorting the truth to sway public opinion.

clickocrasy political discussion groups on the Internet.

Clinton Fatigue a notion that the American public and voters were tired of hearing about and from President Bill Clinton, partly due to hyperattention to his extramarital affairs.

Clinton Nostalgia an emotional public response following President Bill Clinton's House of Representatives impeachment, during which the public was willing to overlook his shortcomings and focus instead on his accomplishments.

cloakroom backrooms off congressional floors where members "rest" and deals are made.

closed primary a primary election in which only members of a party can vote for its candidates for nomination.

closed shop a factory or business that hires only union members, although the Labor-Management Relations Act of 1947 prohibits existence of closed shop practices. Manufacturers, contractors, restaurant owners, and other unionized businesses now theoretically give prospective employees the choice of union membership, although usually incoming workers join the union if the majority of workers belong to a union certified as the bargaining agent for employees. Conservatives who dislike unions blame increased costs, prices, and exportation of jobs on unionization of plants and industries, whereas liberals criticize employers who break or oppose unions as being greedy and inhumane. See also OPEN SHOP.

cloture the process to limit debate in the Senate, which takes a three-fifths vote to enforce and results in limitation of one hour speaking per senator and prevents filibusters.

clout the influence a person may have on other voters or on officeholders to get things done. Clout is seen by the beholder as positive and good, and by the person lacking it as corrupt, unfair, and oppressive.

CNN the leading worldwide television news station, based in Atlanta, Georgia, and owned by AOL Time Warner. Website: www.cnn.com

coalition a grouping of political interest entities to attain a common goal or face a common enemy on a single issue or a long-term alliance. A coalition may be made up of disparate groups that agree on essential principles. Its leadership is often volatile and seemingly unstable because of challenges by groups making up the coalition, partly because their leaders do not want to relinquish power to someone else.

Conservative Republicans and Democrats might form a coalition against abortion, while liberal Republicans and Democrats might form a coalition against a war. Coalitions formed by factions within a party are often viewed by members of the opposing party as dangerous and suspicious. In Great Britain, France, Italy, Israel, and other multiparty countries, coalitions are needed to form a government (administration) when no one party wins an electoral majority.

coalition government a government, administration, or cabinet made up of representatives of leading political parties that ran candidates in the previous election, as opposed to a government made up only of members of the winner's party.

coattail effect the result when an extremely popular ticket leader for president or governor wins by a large majority and carries candidates for lower offices into power with him/her. Riding into office on someone else's coattails is considered fortunate although slightly embarrassing for those who do it and dishonorable and unfair by those who do not.

coffee klatch (kaffee klatch) an informal get together between a candidate and a few constituents, usually women, who meet in one person's home, to create a personal familiarity between voters and candidates. Often the attendees remember much more of the encounter than do the candidates, who may attend several such meetings in a day.

coffer a campaign bank account.

cold war a condition in which extreme hostility between countries exists, although military action is avoided. Administrations discredit the "opponent" (read competitor), which does not really exist since no war has been declared. A cold war existed between the United States, allied with other NATO countries, and the Soviet Union, together with its East European "satellites" between 1948 and 1990. Each side believed it had to keep ahead of the other in the ability to eliminate the other, constantly increasing arms production and the threat of disaster.

Conservatives claim victory in the cold war due to the dissolution of the Soviet Union and the apparent rise of democracy in formerly communist countries. Liberals contend that conservatives need an enemy and will develop a cold war with another country or with a faction of Americans. They also believe that if the demand for military and nuclear weapons is reduced, a "peace dividend" should emanate from reduced military spending. Conservatives retort that liberals want to weaken the U.S. defense system.

collective bargaining a process of determining and negotiating terms and relationships between workers' and employers' representatives such as wages, hours, hiring and firing practices, layoffs, benefits, pension plans, and discipline. Collective bargaining began in 1790s England and in New York and Philadelphia on behalf of a printers' union. Some employers see collective bargaining as a necessary evil that can result in their having to compromise, and sometimes results in their breaking or busting unions. Some employers consider collective bargaining as a confrontational battle, and others think of it as an opportunity to bring stability and certainty to their relations with their work-forces. Workers usually view collective bargaining optimistically as a means by which they will get as much as possible.

collective (group) rights rights or privileges due to a public or constituency by the state or government.

collectivism a system by which a group of people who choose to own, share, and produce goods together, operating on consensus and lacking coercion or force. In concept it has been utilized by China (since 1948), Cuba (since 1960), and the Soviet Union (1918–90). While theoretically voluntary, collectivism was compulsory in those authoritarian regimes, in which even those who objected were forced to participate.

Liberals often favor moderate collectivism and some have experimented with it in establishing co-housing, communes, and alternative communities. Conservatives often view collectivism as communistic and therefore suspicious, although some corporations and agricultural industries engage in a form of collectivism when joining trade associations and cooperative distribution networks.

Comeback Kid what Bill Clinton called himself after coming in second (25%) to Paul Tsongas (33%) in the 1992 New Hampshire Democratic presidential primary. Clinton saw a second place finish as a "comeback" after Gennifer Flowers announced her alleged long-term affair with Clin-

ton while he was governor of Arkansas.

Commander in Chief president of the United States in his/her constitutional role as top commander of all American military forces.

commissioner (1) an appointed or elected member of a public commission, such as a local member of a local planning commission. (2) a person who has charge of a specific government department. (3) an elected official who holds functions similar to a member of a city council.

Common Cause a liberal public and political watchdog organization founded in 1970 by John Gardner, after serving as President Lyndon Johnson's secretary of health, education, and welfare (1965–68). It issues reports, investigates accusations, and brings legal actions to restrict the political power of special interest groups whose positions it does not share. It also works to limit campaign contributions and reform the electoral process. Common Cause has had great influence on legislation and cabinet appointments during Democratic administrations. Both Gardner and legal scholar and federal special prosecutor Archibald Cox have chaired Common Cause. Many view it as an irritant and a trouble-making organization, but it also has a positive reputation as a watchdog of electoral practices. Address: 1250 Connecticut Ave., 6th Floor, NW, Washington, D.C. 20036. Tel.: (202) 736-5723; web: www.commoncause. org

common good a goal or objective deemed by those making a decision to be in the best interest of its public. The decision makers tend to see their position as the correct one for the entire citizenry. The more sensitive to others' experience and views the decision makers are, the more they realize how difficult it is to decide what goals and objectives are desirable or beneficial to the most people.

commune (1) historically the European or Israeli basic unit of government parallel to an American township. (2) in America communes are patterned after the Israeli *kibbutz* in which people live together sharing responsibilities and pleasures, including food, land, housing, and supplies, without individual ownership. Often these are founded on religious or philosophical beliefs, occasionally leading to cult development. Some evolved through the "back to the land" movement in the 1960s. (3) in the Soviet Union Premier Joseph Stalin endorsed communes to share scarce heavy agricultural equipment and, in the 1930s, the Soviet government starved to death thousands of kulaks who refused to join communes. (4) since 1948, the People's Republic of China has used communes as a basic political-economic-social unit in rural areas.

communism (1) a form of governance and commerce in which resources and individual ownership are limited, and communal sharing and participation are necessary for survival. (2) Marxist view: a purist theory first laid out in *Das Capital* (1867) by German philosopher Karl Marx and completed by Friedrich Engels in which equality theoretically reigns, everyone lives harmoniously

sharing resources, work, and benefits, and no private property or social class divisions exist. (3) modern political communism, as defined by Soviet Union founder V. I. Lenin, included little or no private ownership of property, the state owned and ran business and agriculture, and the Communist Party served as a nondemocratic government. The pre–1991 Communist Party in the Soviet Union broke Marx's rules by allowing the party elite to gain privileges and ownership, such as the party leadership occupying the biggest apartments, owning the best automobiles, and enjoying such privileges as sending their children to "Young Pioneer camps." Although scorned by Marx, religion was on the rise even before the Soviet dissolution. The 1990–91 upheaval and breakup of the Soviet Union, regarded by conservative Westerners as the triumph of capitalism over communism, has resulted in increased crime, shortages of goods and food, and general upheaval as the country attempts to adopt a market economy with little preparation and no recent experience. (4) a name used for most stringent forms of socialism. Other communist governments include China (1948–), North Korea (1946–), Vietnam (1954–), Cuba (1959–), and Eastern European Soviet "satellite" nations until 1990.

American liberals have felt antagonistic toward modern communist leaders' elitism, excesses, and promotion of empire building, but many have adopted a "wait and see" attitude in giving it a chance to succeed or fail. American conservatives consider communism to be the United States's enemy to be opposed and stopped from spreading at all costs, including war and possible use of nuclear weapons. Ironically, Soviet liberals favor a move toward democracy, while Soviet conservatives demand a return to strict, stern Marxist-style communism.

communitarianism a philosophical movement created by Washington University sociologist Amitai Etzioni (né Werner Falk of Germany and Israel) as a "third way" approach that merges the stereotypes of liberalism and conservatism to solve America's problems. Etzioni summarizes communitarianism as "a group of people who want to restore the moral, social and political foundations of our country. We want to act together to restore civility to our society." Supporters or interested parties in communitarianism include former president Bill Clinton, Republican presidential aspirant Jack Kemp, and Senator Bill Bradley (D–N.J.). Etzioni's principles of communitarianism stress responsibilities over rights, community over individual, new priorities for spiritual values, and a 10-year moratorium on "manufacturing of new rights." Communitarians strive to encourage schools to return to teaching moral values, promote two-parent families, and compel community groups to take on fighting crime and aggressive panhandling. Many favor putting parents' social security numbers on their children's birth certificates to discourage desertion, placing mandatory program blockers on television sets, banning private gun ownership, instituting welfare reform, making divorce more difficult to allow time to consider effects on children, and establishing sobriety driving checkpoints. The Communitarian Network produces a quarterly journal, *The Responsive Community,* and Etzioni's latest book, which sat on President Clinton's desk, is *The Spirit of Community: Rights, Responsibilities and the Communitarian Agenda.*

While community qualities have diminished in the United States and it is generally agreed that community bonds are necessary in a civilized society, communitarianism raises serious questions. Whose spiritual values are the correct ones? Whose moral values should the schools teach? And how are these decisions reached? How many constitutional civil rights might be violated in such selection processes?

Libertarians oppose communitarianism in the belief that it imposes views and values of the majority over the minority. American Civil Liberties Union members suggest that the movement actually advocates increased government intervention in citizens' lives, and they deride its suggestions that individuals should sublimate individual and human rights violation complaints to the greater good of the whole community.

comprehensive benefits a term used in President Bill Clinton's health care plan (rejected by Congress) and defined in the "Glossary of Terms" of his *Health Care Update* (August 1993) as "the health care services that will be guaranteed to every American citizen and legal resident. . . . The Clinton plan will guarantee a comprehensive benefits package for every American" (p. 43). It will include preventative care and "your health care will be guaranteed, so your boss or insurance company can't take away your benefits or tell you to go read the fine print in your policy when you get sick" (p. 21). "you will get the security that you will never lose your insurance—whether you switch jobs, lose your job, get sick or start a small business. The Clinton plan will guarantee you health care that's always there" (p. 22). The term appears to have meant guaranteed health insurance coverage for all Americans but remained unclear.

concession speech a speech a losing candidate makes admitting that the person who beat him/her won. A winner usually waits until after his/her opponent's concession speech to make his/her victory speech. In a famous case, President Jimmy Carter conceded defeat in 1980 before the polls closed on the West Coast, greatly reducing voter (particularly Democrats) turnout after 5:00 P.M. Pacific Time.

concurrent power jurisdiction shared between federal and state governments in the United States, and power shared by parliament and provincial legislatures in Canada.

confederation uniting of states, provinces, or nations in a permanent league or organization, often for the purpose of governing. Canada was originally a confederation and retains many such aspects. U.S. president Andrew Jackson said: "The Constitution of the United States forms a government and not a league."

conference committee a committee formed from members of House and Senate committees to resolve differences between similar bills passed by each house and reach agreement on a bill that will be submitted to and hopefully passed by both houses.

confirmation hearings U.S. Senate hearings held to investigate backgrounds and appropriateness of presidential nominations to the cabinet, sub-cabinet, federal judgeships and other appointments designated as requiring the advice and consent of the Senate. After the hearings at which evidence is presented, the Senate then votes on whether or not to confirm the president's appointments.

Attitudes toward confirmation hearings vary depending on which major party holds the presidency and the Congress. During Ronald Reagan's and George H. W. Bush's administrations (1981–93), the White House was Republican and the Congress was Democratic, resulting in many major appointment hearings becoming partisan duels, irritating Republicans, who wanted to place their people in judgeships and high offices, and delighting Democrats who saw the hearing process as their only chance to have any influence on the courts and high offices while putting the screws to an opposition president.

After President Bill Clinton took office in 1993, Republican senators decided to confirm most of his appointments without challenges to let him live with his choices, an attitude conservatives believed would do him in. After taking control of Congress in the 1994 election, the Republicans rejected or delayed confirmation of many Clinton appointments, particularly federal judgeships. In 2001, a 50-50 Senate confirmed President George W. Bush's cabinet nominees, but only after extensive questioning of some.

conflict of interest (1) a situation in which a public official or public employee makes a decision where her/his personal interests may be in conflict with the public's best interest. (2) a situation in which a person gains privileged information by her/his position and uses it to her/his own benefit. Examples: A city planner or city council member (alderman) quickly buys land around a parcel he expects to be approved for development or recommends approval of development on a parcel in which s/he is a silent partner.

In 1992 the *New York Post* suggested that Democratic presidential primary candidate Bill Clinton had a conflict of interest because of part ownership in an investment bank that he regulated as governor of Arkansas. (See WHITEWATER.) Democrats and liberals often claim side business dealings by Republican cabinet members and White House officials are conflicts of interest, whereas Republicans seem to believe their own dealings are not. In fact, the party not holding the White House often claims conflict of interest on the part of that in the White House. Rarely do members of one's own party make such claims against each other. Each party tries to interpret conflict of interest more stringently toward the other party than it does toward itself.

congress (1) general: a meeting of representatives of constituencies to discuss and debate issues. (2) the legislative branch of the U.S. government consisting of a 435-member House of Representatives elected by district every two years and a 100-member Senate elected (two per state) with rotating six-year terms. Congressional powers are set forth in Article 1 of the U.S. Constitution. (3) the House of Representatives, con-

sisting of 435 members, each representing approximately 572,466 constituents (1990).

In the 1980s and early 1990s Republican presidents Ronald Reagan and George H. W. Bush regarded the Democratic-controlled Congress as an opponent and an obstacle to implementing a conservative agenda, including deregulation of industries and increased military spending. During the same period, Democrats saw their control of Congress as the only hope for reinstating social programs and controlling military spending.

President George H. W. Bush campaigned against Congress in his reelection bid in portraying it as the enemy and as a scapegoat for "gridlock" between the executive and Congress. While President Harry Truman won a come-from-behind reelection campaign in 1948 by attacking what he called the "do-nothing" Republican-controlled Congress, Bush's attack on the Democratic-controlled Congress did not work. In 1994, a Republican campaign against a Democratic-run Congress led to Republican control of both houses. In 2000 the Senate elections resulted in 50 members of each party with the Republican vice president empowered to vote in case of a tie.

Congressional Black Caucus a group formalized in February 1970 to unify position and enhance clout among black members of Congress after President Richard Nixon refused to meet personally with them. In 1993 the Congressional Black Caucus was believed to represent blacks throughout the United States.

congressional campaign committees political committees organized by members of Congress of each party to raise money, select targeted districts, and find winning candidates for their parties. The chairs of these committees are usually vigorous, ambitious members of Congress, who have the chance to travel around the United States meeting influential people, thus enlarging their personal contact lists.

Congressional Caucus on Women's Issues a U.S. congressional caucus to study and further women's issues, whose ability to earmark individual congressional staff members to caucus work was ended by then speaker Newt Gingrich. Gingrich also ended the caucus's right to have an office on Congressional Hill.

Congressional Hispanic Caucus members of U.S. Congress of Hispanic backgrounds who lobby on behalf of Hispanic/Latino causes and issues, including health care, immigration, welfare, education, and voter registration.

congressional liaison a person or persons who represent the president's views to Congress and, ostensibly, communicate members' interests and needs back to the president or his staff.

Congress of Racial Equality (CORE) an organization founded by James Farmer and George Houser in Chicago in 1942 whose members led some of the first efforts to desegregate restaurants, theaters, and swimming pools in large cities around the country. James Farmer led the "Journey of Reconciliation" integrated bus trip (1947) and later challenged segregation of transportation facilities throughout the South (1961). CORE became one of the leading and most respected civil rights groups in the 1960s. Address: 817 Broadway, New York, N.Y. 10003. Tel.: (212) 598-4000; FAX: (212) 598-4141; e-mail: coreny@msn.com; website: www.core-online.org/

conscience one's knowledge or feeling of what is right or wrong, correct or incorrect, or moral judgment that may prevent violation of an ethical principle. Members of different parties often accuse the other of having no conscience. Each party holds different values of right and wrong, which results in both lacking comprehension of the others' views and language, leading to the judgment that the other has no conscience because it does not match theirs.

conservation preserving and protecting from loss, decay, damage, and violation, pertaining to principles, old objects, or resources. Conservatives, whose own name derives from the same root and principle, ironically tend to think conservation of natural resources is unnecessary, un-American, job and profit threatening, and as an approach in opposition to their own supply-side views, which hold that one should sell it and use it if you think you need or want to. Liberals see conservation as a necessity for survival so that the planet does not run out of natural resources. They do not think conservatives understand the urgency and they encourage recycling, reuse of products, and higher mileage-per-gallon automobiles. The cold war view had been to make the best use of national resources for whatever national needs might surface without regard for conservation.

conservatism (1) historically: political thought based on belief in tradition, existing institutions, the status quo, private ownership of property and business, and preservation of established authority with the spirit of "conserve the best" of principles. (2) United States in the 1990s: beliefs in these principles have led many conservatives to support increasing nationalism, subtle and overt racism, prejudice, censorship of news (information) and the arts, social conformity, supply side economics, environmental protection opposition, and international conflict resolution by means of threats or force of arms instead of negotiation to preserve democracy and fight communism. Conservatism includes the belief that those who fail economically or educationally lack initiative to pull themselves up by their own efforts. It favors deregulation, and resists taxes for social programs on the basis that individual initiative and hard work can cure problems of the poor and undereducated. Generally it favors a "slow but sure" approach to problem solving. (3) Soviet successor states after 1990: the right end of the political spectrum favoring the hardest line, strictest Marxist communism possible.

conservatives those who believe in conservatism. In *The Devil's Dictionary,* Ambrose Bierce defines conservative as: "A statesman who is enamored of existing evils, as distinguished from the Liberal, who wishes to replace them with others." In Canada, "Conservatives" usually refers to members of the Progressive Conservative Party (Tories), but Progressive Conservatives are not the most conservative party in Canada. See also CANADIAN ALLIANCE CONSERVATISM.

constituency (1) a group of voters. (2) an electoral district or riding (Canada). (3) any group of people with common interests who expect representation.

constituency association an electoral district party organization in Canada.

constituent (1) a person who can and or does vote for a local, state, or federal representative. (2) an individual who believes he/she is represented by another on a philosophic or some other basis. For example, many African Americans see themselves as constituents of Jesse Jackson, although he has never held elective office.

constitution a set of laws and principles upon which a government is based. See also U.S. CONSTITUTION.

constitutional monarchy a government run under a constitution with a prime minister, premier, or president with a legislature, and a king, queen, or emperor as head of state. Examples include Great Britain, Canada, Denmark, Norway, Sweden, Spain, and Japan.

consumerism (1) the function of informing consumers of defective and unsafe products, misleading business practices, labeling, and advertising. (2) the conscientious search and purchase of good, ethical products by the consumer. Republican and conservative administrations and members of Congress have long hesitated to require provision of consumer-beneficial information on products, partly due to their position against government intervention, and partly due to lobbying on behalf of friends and campaign contributors who represent corporate manufacturers who believe it is not in their best interest to inform the public. Democrats have suffered the same inclination, but liberals have long advocated dissemination of such information and favor consumerism.

Contract with America a 10-point Republican 1994 campaign document developed by then House minority leader Newt Gingrich and Representative Dick Armey (R–Tex.) that promised the following: (1) a balanced budget amendment and a line item veto; (2) "effective" death penalty laws and increased funding for law enforcement and prisons; (3) "welfare reform" that would cut off aid to dependent children of women who became pregnant while on welfare, ending welfare for those on AFDC for five years and for noncitizens, "workfare" and general cuts in spending on welfare; (4) "child help" by credits for adoption, tougher child support enforcement, rights of parents in children's education, and stronger child pornography laws; (5) tax cuts, including end to so-called marriage bias; (6) more spending on the military, prohibiting U.S. troops to be under United Nations command, and a new missile defense system; (7) help for seniors by raising earnings limits when receiving social security; (8) cut capital gains taxes, greater regulatory flexibility, and other changes in calculating taxable business profits; (9) so-called Tort Reform such as limits on

punitive damages, loser pays costs, excluding "junk science" evidence; (10) term limits for members of Congress.

Democrats referred to the document as the "Contract on America."

contributions See CAMPAIGN CONTRIBUTIONS.

convention a large meeting at which delegates representing members of political parties get together and officially discuss and decide issues, positions, and platforms and select nominees for president and vice president or governor and lieutenant governor.

convention bounce new popularity a presidential nominee often gets and feels immediately after a party convention in which there is much celebration and good publicity. Sometimes the "bounce" refers to momentary jumps in the candidate's standing in public opinion polls. See BOUNCE.

conversion an early 1990s term for the need for industries and military bases geared to wartime or cold war economies to change to peacetime production of useful goods and retrain displaced and laid-off employees whose skills were no longer required. While the need for a conversion plan and a suggested conversion coordinator continues, little coordination exists. In 1945–46, following World War II, a national debate over conversion took place, but no official plan resulted.

copperhead (1) a name for a poisonous snake indigenous to the Southeast. (2) originally a term for northern

Democrats during the Civil War (1861–1865) who either supported the Confederacy or urged an early peace allowing the South to secede. (3) traitor.

corporate welfare   substantial subsidization or tax breaks for groups of businesses or industries, such as agriculture, arms manufacturers, and pharmaceuticals in the United States.

corruption   a change for the worse toward deterioration of moral principles and loss of integrity. The term is usually used in politics by the public (nonpoliticians) in reference to elected officials who gain power claiming to be solid, honest citizens, give way to temptation, lose their purity, and become corrupt, wicked, or evil. Corruption's purpose is usually to gain control or financial and/or political power. The implication is that corrupt politicians cheat and take money to which they are not legitimately entitled, pad expense accounts, give contracts to unqualified cronies, and vote in response to the donors of that money rather than in response to their constituents and the general public.

coup d'état   a sudden, brilliant, skillful stroke or move in politics, resulting in a forcible overthrow of a government.

Coups d'état often result from a small group of trusted insiders in a leader's administration or military departing from that loyalty and scheming to overthrow the leader to install themselves as leaders.

court packing   (1) proposals to change the number of justices or force retirements to gain a majority who shares the president's or governor's beliefs. The most famous example of court packing was President Franklin D. Roosevelt's unsuccessful attempt in 1937 to "pack" the Supreme Court, whose older, conservative members regularly declared Roosevelt's New Deal legislation as unconstitutional. Roosevelt proposed that for every justice who did not retire at age 75, a new justice could be added to the Court. The public's reaction was unfavorable, accusing Roosevelt of executive tinkering with the independence and sanctity of the judicial branch. After Roosevelt withdrew the plan, justices's deaths, retirements, and changes of view gave FDR a more accommodating Court.

More subtle forms of court packing include making court appointments based on a conservative or liberal outlook and candidates' potential positions on sensitive issues, such as abortion; and campaigns to remove state justices, such as the recall of three California Supreme Court justices who opposed the death penalty.

cover-up   an ultimately unsuccessful attempt to hide evidence of wrongdoing to deceive the public and protect the alleged wrongdoers. President Richard Nixon, his staff, and associates tried to put in place a cover-up of the break-in at the Democratic Party headquarters in the Watergate complex. Members of Ronald Reagan's administration allegedly attempted a cover-up of their involvement in the Iran-Contra affair; President Bill Clinton attempted a cover-up of his affair with a young female intern.

CREEP (Committee to Re-elect the President)   the Republican committee set up to raise funds and manage the expected reelection campaign of President Richard M. Nixon in 1972. Then Republican National Chairman senator Robert Dole (R–Kans.) first turned Committee to Re-elect the President to CREEP in resentment of what he saw as snubbing of the National Committee by White House staffers. After it was revealed that the CREEP financed the break-in at Democratic Party headquarters in the Watergate complex, the term came into broader use.

Crime Strike a crime-fighting unit of the National Rifle Association of America (NRA). Address: 1800 Rhode Island Avenue, NW, Washington, D.C. 20036. Tel.: (202) 828-6000.

crony (1) an intimate friend or companion. (2) a friend from whom one expects trust, loyalty, and protection due to personal or political expediency. An officeholder might appoint his/her cronies to important jobs because he/she feels safe surrounded by them, owes them payoffs for their loyalty, or fears the consequences of not keeping them around.

crossover primary similar to an open primary, in which one can vote in a primary election for a candidate of a party to which one does not belong. See also OPEN PRIMARY.

crossover vote voters who are likely to vote for candidates of a party other than their own.

Crown (Canada) a symbolic name for governmental and state institu-

tions, deriving from the British usage for the power of the monarch or officials representing that authority; ultimately, the people. Used for Crown counsel, Crown corporation.

Crown agencies (Canada) governmental organizations or agencies outside established departments.

cult a group of followers, particularly of a fad, based on devotion, admiration, worship of the leader, or a set of principles. Some cult members follow their leader in quest of answers to personal or public questions and problems, salvation, protection from the rest of the world, or commitment to a way of life. Some cult devotion is seen as irrational by the outside world, and those involved often deny that their group is a cult. The best known American cults are those whose disasters and demise have revealed the extremes of leaders' control and members' devotion, such as James Jones's People's Temple and David Koresh's Branch Davidians in Waco, Texas. Studies of cults may reveal deep problems in a society from which those in political office could learn about unpublicized and misunderstood public needs.

cultural elite a term used by Republican vice president J. Danforth Quayle (1989–1993) to refer to a group concept he deemed to be the enemy. Apparently he referred to movie and television moguls, producers, directors, and stars as America's "cultural elite" and, more specifically, to sitcom fictional character Murphy Brown. Murphy Brown, played by Candice Bergen, was an independent, fairly liberal television news reporter who became pregnant and chose to deliver her baby as a single mother.

Quayle's implication, which he never really explained, was that character Murphy Brown's actions and decisions were contrary to moral America's, which he apparently equated with born-again Christian "values."

culture (1) improvement, refinement, development of the mind, thought, emotion, manners, and way of being. (2) the collective concepts, habits, skills, philosophy, arts, instruments, and institutions of a people or civilization.

Because of the American population's diverse countries of origin, backgrounds, and geographic distribution, there is little identifiable national culture. Regional cultures exist, as in New England or the deep South, and cultural clusters preserved from countries of national origin still exist, such as among Norwegians and Finns in Minnesota and Germans in Wisconsin.

The lack of a single, unifying, and unified culture, which gives reassurance, grounding, and identity to a people, seems to lead to an apparent disunity or shallowness among Americans. An identifiable culture is most possible in a homogeneous society, which the United States is not.

As economic conditions motivate the world's people to move from their native country to another in quest of earning power and security, societies become less homogeneous. Perhaps after the initial clashes common between and among peoples in mobile societies, prejudices and fears will dissipate, peoples will learn to live with others, and unifying and unified cultures will emerge.

damage control (1) manipulation of the media to minimize, twist, and combat the fallout from an apparently damaging occurrence, statement, or just plain mistake. (2) an intentional attempt to turn a negative into a positive.

Then Democratic presidential candidate Bill Clinton's 1992 campaign statement that he "didn't inhale" when his sampling of marijuana was revealed is a most blatant and humorously obvious attempt at damage control.

dance card a legislator's or lobbyist's busy calendar schedule.

Darby v. United States 1941 Supreme Court case that sustained that portion of the Fair Labor Standards Act of 1938 that prohibited child labor and regulated wages and maximum work hours. Justice Harlan Stone's decision stated that the federal government's power to regulate interstate commerce included the authority to promote commerce as well as to prohibit it, a position Oliver Wendell Holmes had argued in a 1916 dissent. The case demonstrated that the older Supreme Court members would no longer vote to declare all New Deal legislation unconstitutional.

dark horse a candidate considered to have only the slimmest chance to win a nomination or election. Political pundits usually admit in advance that they will be surprised if the "dark horse" candidate wins, but at the same time suggest that the door is open to the possibility. Often candidates prefer to describe themselves as the "dark horse" to evoke curiosity and interest in their campaigns and to appeal to Americans' penchant for the long shot or underdog. The last dark horses who actually became presidential nominees were Republican Wendell Willkie (1940) and Democrat Adlai Stevenson (1952).

dead-beat dads divorced or single fathers who fail to make court-ordered child support, alimony, or spousal support payments.

dead broke dads divorced or single fathers who make too little money to make court-ordered child support, alimony, or spousal support payments.

death penalty capital punishment, execution, or killing of a person found guilty of committing a crime by hanging, electrocution, gas, lethal injection, or military firing squad.

England once had more than 200 offenses qualifying for the death penalty but now has abandoned it entirely. The death penalty exists in most American states but is exercised only after lengthy appeals and is infrequently applied in many states.

Basic arguments in favor are that: (1) the death penalty is justified as retribution ("eye for an eye"); (2) it deters crime; and (3) criminals executed will never commit another crime. Opposition arguments include: (1) it is wrong for the state to kill; (2) it is wrong for anyone to kill; (3) it is not a deterrent; (4) the poor and uneducated (particularly minorities and those who cannot afford expensive lawyers) are those executed; (5) the danger exists of executing persons later found to be innocent; (6) some forms of the death penalty itself are cruel and unusual punishment.

Ironically, many born-again Christians and conservatives favor the death penalty and oppose abortion or "choice" because it is killing. Many liberals oppose executions on the basis that the state should not be in the killing business, although most favor a woman's right to choose to have an abortion.

However, particularly heinous crimes, such as the 1993 kidnap and murder of Polly Klaas, often stir pro-death penalty feelings among people intellectually opposed to capital punishment.

The U.S. Supreme Court vacillates on the issue according to the conservative/liberal leanings of the justices. In the *Furman* decision (1972) it held that capital punishment was a violation of the U.S. Constitution's Eighth Amendment prohibiting "cruel and unusual punishment" in certain cases, leading to a temporary halt in executions. Polls show that a majority of Americans favor the death penalty with restrictions and limitations varying by region or state. In recent years executions have resumed primarily in southern states, with one in California (1993).

As a result of several cases in which DNA evidence proved persons convicted of murder to be innocent, there have been increased calls for a moratorium on executions. Such a moratorium was ordered by the governor of Illinois in 2000. The largest number of executions in recent years have occurred in Texas, which made the death penalty a sensitive issue for Republican presidential nominee Governor George W. Bush in 2000. Bush declared he was certain that all persons executed "on my watch" were properly represented and convicted.

debates public discussion of opposing opinions or views by candidates from different parties before a general election and from opposing views of the same party in a primary election.

Usually the debate is "demanded" by the underdog or candidate most needing exposure, who seeks a public forum from which to challenge the leader's views. Organizations ranging from the League of Women Voters to Irish-American and Filipino-American societies and Chambers of Commerce hold debates to help voters comprehend candidates' positions, personalities, and commitment. Debates can—but rarely do—show unrehearsed or spontaneous reactions to questions.

In 1960 John F. Kennedy's good looks and charm helped him win over some voters in contrast to Richard Nixon's lack of same. In 1992 President George H. W. Bush refused to meet Democratic presidential candidate Bill Clinton in televised debates until nationwide public ridicule forced Bush to reverse his position. With independent candidate Ross Perot in the race, the debate dynamics resulted in Perot attacking President Bush and allowing then-governor Clinton to sail through relatively unbruised.

The granddaddy of all debates was the series between Abraham Lincoln and Stephen Douglas for the U.S. Senate seat in Illinois (1858). Douglas won the election, but the debates gave Lincoln national prominence. Two years later Lincoln defeated Senator Douglas and two other candidates for the presidency on the eve of the Civil War. See also KENNEDY-NIXON DEBATES.

decentralization a sharing of responsibilities, decisions, and funding by the federal government with state governments and local agencies.

Conservatives favor decentralization to get "big brother" government off their backs and out of their lives, supposedly giving more control to local agencies and, realistically, placing the burdens (with few benefits) on local government. Liberals see decentralization as a cop-out by conservative administrations to bypass a Congress they see as liberal and to create the appearance of local control while actually shifting moral and fiscal responsibility and hard decision making to others.

Declaration of Independence the document by which the 13 American colonies declared independence from Britain. Primarily written by Thomas Jefferson for a committee appointed by the Continental Congress of 1776, it was passed on July 2, 1776, and announced July 4, 1776. It stated that the colonies "are, and of right ought to be free and independent states." Fifty-six delegates signed the Declaration of Independence.

Thought, then and now, to be a revolutionary document, and without actually being law, the Declaration of Independence boldly affirmed so-called natural rights of man yet without reference to women or racial minorities: "All men are created equal," it proclaimed. Jefferson drew upon his own ideas and those of 18th-century English philosophers John Locke and David Hume. Jefferson's draft condemned slavery, but that part of the text was removed by the delegates.

The Declaration of Independence is on display at the National Archives, 8th Street at Pennsylvania Avenue, Washington, D.C. 20408. Tel.: (202) 501-5202. See Appendices.

declaration of war a power granted exclusively to Congress by Article I of the U.S. Constitution.

U.S. presidents Madison, Polk, McKinley, Wilson, and Franklin D. Roosevelt all asked Congress to declare war. President Truman employed U.S. forces in Korea as part of a United Nations "police action" without a declaration of war. Moderately liberal president Lyndon Johnson (in Vietnam) and conservative president George H. W. Bush (in Iraq) both interpreted the Constitution broadly, reading into it their own permission to wage war without obtaining a formal declaration of war from Congress.

As commander in chief, President Bush challenged accepted interpretations of Article I and started a war with Iraq (1990) to "liberate" Kuwait from Iraq's invasion without asking Congress to declare war. Instead, Bush asked the United Nations to sanction a world punishment of Iraqi president Saddam Hussein for his Kuwaiti border crossing. After some members of Congress expressed outrage at his action, Bush then went to Congress to ask for approval of military action without an official Declaration of War. Congress narrowly approved American military backing of the United Nations resolution. In the last week of his presidency, Bush launched new air strikes with the help of French and British pilots in military action approved by the United Nations but without sanction by the U.S. Congress.

In 1993, President Bill Clinton approved American Tomahawk missile attacks on Iraq's intelligence headquarters in retaliation for an attack on America—an alleged plot to assassinate former president Bush on a visit to Kuwait City in April 1993. President Clinton informed Congressman Ron Dellums, chair of the House Armed Services Committee, after the attack and asked the U.N. Security Council to support his actions after the fact. In 1999, President Bill Clinton directed a U.S. air war, including bombing of cities, against Yugoslavia to end atrocities in Kosovo province.

Most liberals believe the president should consult Congress for a declaration of war before engaging in hostilities, although President Lyndon Johnson moved from dove to hawk in liberals' eyes when he used the Tonkin Gulf Resolution (1964) to justify fighting an undeclared war in Vietnam. Conservatives have supported military operations without a formal declaration of war, but by mid-1993, under a Democratic president, they had become more cautious about sending troops into unsettled foreign countries without congressional approval.

decline to state a person who wants to vote and registers to vote but chooses not to affiliate with any known political party or simply prefers not to state his/her party preference. Instead, that person can register "decline to state."

Professional politicians of both major parties are perplexed by those who decline to state since they are unpredictable.

In fact, people of varied political views, and some with no positions, register this way, often to avoid junk mail from established parties or from fear of having others know their political views. A disadvantage is that in most states those who so register cannot vote in party primaries and presidential caucuses. Under so-called open primary laws, they can vote in party primaries. See also OPEN PRIMARIES.

deep ecology a belief system in which environmentalism and nature are valued more highly than individual human needs, practices or desires. All questions are considered in relation to the environment.

deep-six to hide, bury, or get rid of evidence, papers, or unpopular ideas, nominations, proposals, or programs.

Deep Throat (1) a popular 1970s pornographic movie. (2) confidential source who talks lots, usually on a potentially scandalous matter. (3) a code name for an anonymous source to *Washington Post* reporters during the Watergate scandal.

de facto translates from Latin to mean "reality" or "truth." De facto has come to imply the true power or the actual ruling class that is in a position to control a political entity while it appears that another is running the system.

Whereas some Democrats and Republicans have been elected as populist, grass-roots, or average people, they have, in fact, come from wealthy, well-educated families who have groomed them to serve in high public office. This can be seen as de facto rule by elites in a democratic society.

De facto segregation applies when segregation is outlawed but exists in truth or reality. A de facto government is one that controls a country without following an official system such as an election.

defense cuts a hot political issue in U.S. politics, particularly since the end of the cold war. Democrats generally favor some specific defense cuts, while Republicans criticize Democrats for jeopardizing national security. Republicans generally favor a stronger defense, while Democrats criticize Republicans for spending on bombs and missiles and sacrificing health care and education needs.

deficit (1) a government's budgetary situation in which more money is spent than is taken in by taxes, fees, and tariffs. (2) a 1990s denial buzzword for deficit is "shortfall."

Republicans accuse Democrats of overspending on social programs and creating an unhealthy deficit while claiming to balance budgets themselves. In 1993, after 12 years of Republican presidents, the United States had the largest deficit in history, jumping from one trillion dollars to four trillion in 12 years due to tax cuts, unparalleled peace-time military spending, and expansion of government. A large deficit requires heavy borrowing through treasury notes and bonds and multiplies the deficit through interest payments on itself.

Deficits lead to age-old arguments of whether to cut programs to save money, cut taxes when deficits are turned to surpluses, or find a workable combination. Republicans favor cutting social (read liberal, minority) programs such as Aid to Families with Dependent Children, Social Security, aid to the blind, abortion clinics, and subsidies to the arts, particularly those endeavors or artists whose work they deem to be of moral question. Democrats generally favor cuts in military spending to save billions of dollars while maintaining social, educational, and health benefits.

Beginning in 1992, Republican and Democratic leaders, as well as former independent presidential candidate Ross Perot, claimed that budget deficits were the most important issue facing the nation and that the public was clamoring to have it reduced.

As a result of the mid-1990s economic boon, there was an expected government revenue surplus over mandated expenditures, resulting in a presidential candidate argument over what part of the monies should be used to reduce the national debt and annual deficit. Republicans generally favored tax cuts and partial privatization of services with minimal program expansion, while Democrats generally favored national debt reduction with expansion of services.

deficit-neutral spending former Secretary of Health and Human Services Donna E. Shalala's term for new programs that will not increase or reduce national debt because they are covered by new taxes or use of other funds.

de jure from Latin meaning "by right" or by law. De jure rule or power means a particular official or group is legitimately entitled to control or give orders because of legal authority from local laws or structure, such as elections.

De jure rule contrasts with de facto rule.

delegate a person elected or selected to represent a constituency, group, candidate, or ideology at a gathering or meeting where issues will be discussed and decisions will be made by the group.

In politics, "delegate" is most commonly used as a delegate to a conven-

tion, such as those held quadrennially by Republicans and Democrats. Theoretically delegates present the views of the people who sent them to represent their ideas, although many simply attain delegate status and then vote their own views, if they get to vote at all.

Delegate nomination and election methods vary by political party. Republican delegates are often chosen because of their loyalty to the appointer, while Democrats often participate in self-consciously democratic processes to elect delegates at community or congressional district caucuses in addition to office holders, party officials and major contributors ("Super Delegates"). Official Democratic Party rules require an equal number of men and women delegates while the Republican have no such strictures.

Delegates to national party conventions are supposed to attend seminars, special interest caucus meetings, and listen to endless speeches. They are also expected to spend money to transport themselves to the convention site, for hotel rooms and meals, and for party or candidate fundraisers held during the convention. Delegates are generally expected to "go along with the program" of the dominant party faction and often find themselves frustrated if they attempt to represent minority views.

delegation (1) giving authority or power to others to carry out responsibilities (also called "delegation of power" in constitutional law). (2) a group selected to represent the views of a constituency, group, candidate, or ideology at a state or national party convention.

deliver   to do what one promised to do in return for another favor.

demagogue   a person who stirs up a people's emotions by appealing to mass prejudices in order to become or maintain himself or herself as a leader for personal or selfish gain. Demagogues sometimes use believable lies, incite fear, and distort the truth, consistently appealing to the listeners' self-interests and baser instincts. Examples include Adolf Hitler, Benito Mussolini, one-time Louisiana governor and senator Huey Long, Philippine president Ferdinand Marcos, and former Ku Klux Klan leader turned politician David Duke.

demobilization   dismantling military systems and weapons stockpiles, and redirecting popular attitudes from wartime to peacetime pursuits while dismissing military troops who had been called up. It usually occurs at the end of a war or threat of war.

democracy   (1) a political theory of government based on the Greek words *demos,* meaning "people" or "mob," and *kratos,* meaning "authority." (2) any government in which the ultimate power of control lies with the people. Key elements of modern democracy include voting rights for all adults, the right of all political parties to have access to the ballot, the right to campaign without unreasonable restrictions, and the civil rights of speech and assembly.

Often democracy is theoretical and idealistic since men, the wealthy, owners of the media, majority ethnic groups and other controllers of the power levers dominate the process while women, the poor, the unedu-cated, and minorities have their votes as their sole power. And often they have to fight for those.

democracy, direct   a democratic government in which all citizens participate directly and at an equal level in voting, making decisions, and passing laws. No representatives or delegates may perform these functions in place of the collection of individuals.

Arguments in favor: (1) its laws are truly in the whole public's interest since only the entire citizenry can pass a law; (2) Jean-Jacques Rousseau believed "direct democracy is necessary for true freedom, because a man is only free when he is obeying a law he himself has willed." Direct democracy occasionally evolves by public demand in reaction to fear of governance by a few. Arguments against: (1) it is nearly impossible to assemble all those governed to make decisions on how they are to be governed; (2) it is nearly impossible for all citizens to participate in every decision. The town meeting, which still takes place in some New England communities, is the best American example of direct democracy, but it is fading as a procedure and forum.

democracy, representative   a form of democratic government in which the people choose representatives to act and make decisions for them, such as in legislatures, parliaments, congresses, city councils, and boards of supervisors or commissioners.

Strengths: (1) it is the only practical democratic system since it is impossible for the whole public to decide all issues; (2) political power ultimately rests in the hands of the adult population, theoretically on a one-adult/one-vote system; (3) it gives individual citizens maximum freedoms along with responsibility. Weaknesses: (1) inability to consult the people in times of crises; (2) requires high level of public education and understanding; (3) can improperly control the public's decisions by controlling information citizens receive on which to base their decisions and votes in elections.

Representative democracy constantly grapples with the question of whether elected representatives should base their vote on how they believe their constituents would want them to vote or on what they personally believe is proper policy.

Democrat (1) a member of the Democratic Party. (2) a person registered to vote who states that he/she prefers the Democratic Party and can vote in Democratic primaries. (3) with a small "d," a person who favors and believes in democracy.

Democratic Leadership Council (DLC) an informal organization of Democratic officeholders organized by somewhat conservative southern Democrats, including former senator Charles Robb (D–Va.), who urged the Democratic Party to take more pragmatic positions on issues. President Bill Clinton belonged to the group when he was governor of Arkansas and drew on the members' ideas and support to formulate his presidential candidacy. Vice presidential nominee Senator Joseph Lieberman (D–Conn.) served as chair from 1995 to 2000. The DLC has also been known as the (National) New Democratic Coalition and the New Democrats. Address: 600 Pennsylvania Avenue, S.E., Washington, D.C.

20003. Tel.: (202) 546-0007; FAX: (202) 544-5002; e-mail: press@dlcppi.org or membership@dlcppi.org; website: www.dleppi.org

Democratic Party one of two major American political parties, founded by Thomas Jefferson and James Madison of Virginia with New York anti-Federalists in 1793, and originally called the Democratic-Republican Party to emphasize the founders' antimonarchical sentiments.

The first Democratic-Republican president was Thomas Jefferson (1801–09), who saw his party as the popular people's party of yeoman-workers and farmers, although he, Madison, and James Monroe were all aristocrats. It officially became the Democratic Party in 1828 and elected President Andrew Jackson that year. It held its first convention in 1831. The party supported slavery on a states rights or protection of property basis (1850s) and lost members favoring abolition of slavery to the new Republican Party.

The Democratic Party declined during and immediately after the Civil War except where new immigrants bolstered it in urban areas and in the South, which was resentful of Republican reconstruction. Except for Grover Cleveland's two nonconsecutive presidential terms, it remained out of power until Woodrow Wilson's election in 1912.

Until the 1940s Democrats embodied two conflicting wings, liberal (intellectual, pro-blue collar, and small farmer) and conservative (big business and southern all-white segregationists). Moderate liberals took control of the party with Franklin Delano Roosevelt's election (1932) and they have prevailed in party control since, with redefinition of "moderate" and "liberal" nearly annually. F.D.R.'s New Deal programs stressed reform, welfare policies such as social security and consumer protection, measures favoring organized labor, environmental protection, publicly owned power and utilities, and active stimulation of the economy.

The Democratic Party declared itself in favor of civil rights for blacks at its national convention in 1948 and began to lose its conservative "Solid South" support while building support among racial minorities. A second major schism occurred when President Lyndon Johnson pressed the increasingly unpopular Vietnam War (mid-1960s). In 2001, Democrats' took the formerly conservative position of paying down the deficit before tax-cuts.

Since 1932, Democrats have controlled Congress for all but 18 years and led in state and local elections in most years, but they had difficulty winning presidential elections between 1968 and 1992.

Pre–Civil War Democratic presidents include Andrew Jackson, Martin Van Buren, James K. Polk, Franklin Pierce, and James Buchanan. Other Democratic presidents are: Grover Cleveland (1885–89 and 1893–97), Woodrow Wilson (1913–21), Franklin D. Roosevelt (1933–45), Harry S. Truman (1945–53), John F. Kennedy (1961–63), Lyndon Johnson (1963–69), Jimmy Carter (1977– 81), and Bill Clinton (1993–2001).

Well-known losing Democratic presidential candidates include Samuel J. Tilden (1876), William Jennings Bryan (1896, 1900, and 1908), Al Smith (1928), Adlai Stevenson (1952 and 1956), Hubert Humphrey (1968), Walter Mondale (1984), Michael Dukakis (1988), and Albert Gore Jr., 2000.

Democratic-Republican Party a political party founded by Thomas Jefferson and James Madison in 1793 when Jefferson left George Washington's cabinet after continuing disputes with Federalist Alexander Hamilton. Once known as the Anti-Federalist Party and as "Republicans," its leaders added "democratic" to the Republican name to disassociate themselves from the radical French Revolution "republicans." In 1828 it became the Democratic Party.

Democratic Study Group an organization of liberal reform Democratic members of the House of Representatives, founded in January 1957 by Representative (later Senator) Eugene J. McCarthy and formally structured (1959) with Representative Lee Metcalf as chairman. Membership grew to 100 members of Congress and developed a "whip" system, legislation, staff, and enough clout to break archaic seniority rules, block legislation, and curb the power of conservative southern Democratic congressmen. While the organization still exists, it achieved most of its original goals for congressional reform. The founding group was called "McCarthy's Marauders" or "McCarthy's Mavericks." Address: 1422 Longworth House Office Building, Washington, D.C. 20515. (202) 225-5858.

Democratic Wimp Factor submission of Democratic members of Congress to Republican proposals, pressure, and intimidation during the Ronald Reagan and George H. W. Bush administrations out of fear of reprisal by conservative Democratic and Republican voters. As a result, few Democrats had the courage to speak in favor of traditional Democratic programs and values.

demonstration   a gathering of people who express themselves with their voices, signs, and/or bodies to make their views known. Demonstrations were often used to communicate the public's opposition to the wars in Vietnam and Iraq, in favor of civil rights or for or against legality of abortions.

demonstrators   people who gather to express their views on a subject. Often demonstrators are willing (an even anxious) to get arrested to draw attention to their causes.

dependency theory   a liberal view of conservative countries' subjugation of Third World countries based upon a form of capitalistic imperialism. So-called economic and financial aid are given to these countries, sometimes called "client countries," for agricultural and industrial development with contingencies that render the recipient country dependent upon the donor country for product markets. There is also an implied commitment to purchase necessary goods from the donor country, completing the circle of economic imperialism.

Conservatives generally see this activity as the free enterprise system helping others, while, in fact, enjoying economic and political control over recipient countries. Such has been the practice with some countries in Latin America, Africa, Asia, and the former Soviet Union. Liberals favor aid and encourage development toward economic independence through various means such as the Peace Corps.

deportation   forced departure of an immigrant from a country because of illegal or political acts deemed dangerous by or to a government. Deportation may occur for not having proper entry documents and includes loss of civil rights in the country deporting.

Deportation has become a point of argument over principle between conservatives and liberals. Conservative Republican president George H. W. Bush and California governor Pete Wilson advocated aggressive deportation on the basis that "immigrants" are taking citizens' jobs and bleeding the welfare system, since they are willing to take entry-level jobs otherwise filled (or rejected as unsuitable) by unskilled Americans. Liberals and Democrats see this form of deportation as discriminatory against minorities from countries whose people have dark skin and in favor of European and certain Asian immigrants. Often Irish immigrants who work without green cards are overlooked, whereas Mexican immigrants are rounded up in vineyards and deported, only to return again and again.

Deportation is also employed to rid the United States of known criminals (read Mafia), anti-government terrorists, suspected spies, and former Nazis. If the potential deportees are naturalized American citizens, deportation requires hearings and, occasionally, court trials to determine the basis for deportation, including falsifying data and immigration papers when entering the country.

depression   an extreme and prolonged down turn in the economy, including lasting declines in employment, productivity, prices, wages, stock market prices, and confidence. It is more severe than a recession. See also GREAT DEPRESSION.

deregulation   the removal of regulations governing prices, controls, standards of manufacture, and other forms of governmental regulation of industry.

President Jimmy Carter's deregulation of America's airlines was hailed as pro-consumer on the basis that competition would result in lower prices and improved service (Industrial Darwinism). Actually it resulted in higher ticket prices and airline bankruptcies and job losses in many of the largest airlines such as Eastern and Pan American. President Ronald Reagan's deregulation of the savings and loan industries resulted in corporate pilfering by executives, risky loans, bankruptcies, depositors' losses, and the need to spend billions of tax dollars to bail out deposit insurance funds.

Despite these disasters, debate continues with conservatives, Libertarians, and some Independents arguing that deregulation gets government out of people's lives and allows free competition, while liberals defend regulation as necessary to protect consumers and workers and as a brake against recession.

desegregation   abolition of segregation by races, with the incumbent inclusion of equal use of education, transportation, housing, recreation, and public facilities. In the United States, desegregation was achieved primarily by federal government legal action in the 1960s and 1970s, following *Brown v. Board of Education of Topeka* (1954), and civil rights demonstrations in the 1960s. Various means have been implemented to desegregate communities, such as busing students from their segregated neighborhood to school in another neighborhood. Usually the students continue to cluster at lunchtime or recess according to race or ethnicity in a self-imposed, comfort zone segregation.

Some conservatives see desegregation as government interference in natural law, unnatural, and unnecessarily provoking problems. Liberals see desegregation as correct and necessary.

despotism   ruling by one person who controls and governs others through fear and who is not accountable to the people or a legal system.

destabilization (of government) a theory that a government can be so disrupted that it can become unstable and collapse. Destabilization can be achieved by terrorism, sabotage, rumor, military takeover, or divide and conquer techniques. In theory, and occasionally in reality, collapse is followed by chaos and upheaval, leaving an opening for new ideas and reconstruction.

Destabilization is often a feature of revolution or the overthrow of a particular government by those who want another form of government and want to achieve it by means other than elections or military revolution. People who aim at destabilization are usually seen as radicals or anarchists.

detente   a lessening of tensions or hostilities, usually between nations, by agreement, whether implied or explicit and written. Detente resembles peaceful coexistence and was referred to frequently in the 1960s and 1970s to denote the unofficial and delicate process aimed at easing tension between the United States and the then U.S.S.R. In this case detente included supposed economic cooperation, often benefiting American businesses whose officers were good friends of or large contributors to the campaigns of presidents. Detente was also believed to include steps toward reducing conventional and nuclear armaments on both sides and efforts to promote a theoretical halt to the cold war.

deterrence   a theory or plan used by military planners and defense "experts" based upon the notion that the best way to protect oneself or one's country is to develop, hold, and threaten to use greater, more powerful, and more frightening weapons than one's potential enemies.

Deterrence gained credence when the United States held a monopoly on atomic weapons in the late 1940s and the 1950s. It is often used as an excuse to build a country's supply of weapons, leading to an arms race. Such mutual stockpiling raises fears that large arsenals intensify pressure to use the weapons (partly to require more production by the weapons industry), which can ultimately lead to war.

developing nation   a euphemism for a country whose people are poor and whose economy lags behind those of industrialized nations. "Developing" puts a supposedly positive spin on disastrous circumstances by suggesting that conditions are in the process of improving.

devolution   the return of power from a central source to a more local one, such as granting semi-independence to a protectorate or colony. Irish Republican officials refer to the United Kingdom's potential relinquishment of the six counties of Northern Ireland as devolution. Proponents of independence in Quebec occasionally refer to their plans to secede from Canada and take control of their own "country" as devolution.

devolve   to pass authority or power on to another.

dialectical materialism   a philosophy developed by Karl Marx's successors in Germany and the Soviet Union. Basic premises include: (1) all mental processes derive from material processes; (2) dialectical character of all natural or human processes are expressed in three laws: transformation of quantity into quality, unity of opposites, and negation of the negation. Based on the theories of Georg Hegel (1770–1831) applied to economics, it translates to thesis that produces antithesis and results in synthesis. Some say this equates to positivism.

dictator   (1) in ancient Rome, a magistrate appointed by the Senate and given absolute power and authority in emergencies. (2) a ruler, sometimes self-appointed, who has absolute, unlimited, uncurbed, and unchecked political power and prescribes rules for his public to follow.

Under a dictator's rule, the people lack civil rights and liberties. Most dictators suppress or outlaw their political opposition. Examples of dictators include "Papa Doc" Duvalier of Haiti, Ferdinand Marcos of the Philippines, Adolf Hitler of Germany, Benito Mussolini of Italy, Idi Amin of Uganda, Saddam Hussein of Iraq, communist leaders of the former Soviet Union such as Joseph Stalin, and various Latin American military "presidents."

American administrations of both parties have tended to support foreign dictators for political and business expediency, ostensibly because of fear of communism rising or drug markets expanding should the dictator depart. Democrats claim to eschew all dictators, but they have hesitated to advocate the use of military force to depose them.

dictatorship a form of government in which one person controls all political, economic, and social elements of a political entity. A dictatorship lacks civil rights and civil liberties for the people and is characterized by the complete suppression of apolitical opposition.

Dictators are occasionally appointed by a military or legislative body to govern in an emergency. More often they are self-appointed as a result of a coup d'état that they may have led or for which they serve as a front or "puppet." A dictatorship may be a small group, such as "The Colonels" in Greece during the 1970s.

diehard (1) an immovable, committed partisan or person loyal to a cause, party, or person even in the face of limited prospects. (2) loyalist.

digital divide the gap between the United States's affluent population in which most homes have computers, and its poorer people who have no personal computer or computer training and rarely have access to either, creating an abyss in the information accessible to the two groups.

dimpled chad See CHAD.

diplomatic immunity a general international standard by which ambassadors are not subject to the laws of the land in which they are serving. Basically, this means for example, that cars with "diplomatic" license plates can speed or park illegally. For more serious offenses, the host country's recourse is to expel the diplomat from the country.

direct action a form of civil disobedience in which participants attempt to physically obstruct functions of government policy they find objectionable instead of engaging in direct political lobbying or protest.

Democrats and liberals tolerate direct action, but most object to direct action that damages property or injures people. Conservatives generally see direct action as indicative of the subversive nature of those participating, although conservative anti-abortionist members of Operation Rescue employ direct action by blocking entrances to abortion clinics and even go to extreme of burning down some clinics.

direct democracy See DEMOCRACY, DIRECT.

direct mail a way to communicate with voters by sending them brochures or letters for or against a candidate or soliciting campaign funds.

direct primary a nomination system by which the people vote directly to select party nominees. Devised to break the bosses' power to control hand-picked candidates and convention nominations, the direct primary was a principal goal of progressives of both major parties in the early 1900s. The direct primary had a resurgence in popularity in the 1970s and is used in most states today. In some states, such as Louisiana, both parties' candidates for state office run in the same direct primary, and the top two vote-getters—regardless of party—compete in the final election. See also BLANKET PRIMARY, CLOSED PRIMARY, OPEN PRIMARY.

direct taxation collection of taxes from the people by government agencies, such as income taxes.

dirty laundry a person's previously unmentioned indiscretions that may be exposed in campaigns or congressional hearings.

dirty tricks vicious or humorous efforts to spy on, misrepresent, or foul up the opposition's campaign. Efforts by the 1972 Committee to Re-elect the President (Nixon) to vandalize and bug the Democratic National Committee's offices and phones in the Watergate Complex is a perfect example of a vicious dirty trick. Democrat Dick Tuck's donning a railroad conductor's outfit and waving 1960 Republican presidential candidate Richard Nixon's train out of the station while Nixon was still talking on the ground has been treated as a humorous dirty trick. Tuck's classic dirty tricks also included one during a Nixon visit to San Francisco's Chinatown after public accusations that Nixon's brother had borrowed big money from industrialist Howard Hughes. Nixon was pleased at the number of Chinese-Americans who turned out to see him but did not know that nearly all the signs they held said "What about the Hughes loan?" in Chinese. Of course, determination of which dirty tricks are vicious and which are humorous may vary with the trickster or the trickee.

disadvantaged a euphemism for poor.

disarmament (1) destruction or reduction of arms of a defeated country. (2) abolition of all armaments. (3) a bilateral or multilateral agreement applying to a specific geographic area, such as the Rush-Bagot Agreement, which prohibited military buildup on the Great Lakes.

Some conservatives think the United States may lose its world power advantage if it retains fewer arms than the total possessed by its enemies. Some may have friends in the weapons industry whose interests they want to protect since they donate liberally to conservatives' campaigns. Liberals are more likely to see disarmament as a noble effort necessary for global survival. See also ARMS CONTROL.

disconnect a lack of comprehension or understanding between peoples or ideas.

discretionary spending spending not earmarked for any particular purpose.

discrimination unequal treatment or mistreatment of groups singled out because of race, religion, sex, impairments, ethnic or national origin, or language.

Discrimination takes many forms including refusal of employment or promotion, disallowing use to public facilities or transportation, creation of ghettos and prohibition (overt or covert) of living in certain neighborhoods, restrictions on interracial marriage, unequal education opportunities, limitation of voting rights, deportation of dark-skinned immigrants, and restrictions on participation in political systems.

Extreme examples of discrimination were Nazi treatment and killing of millions of Jews, and American southern whites' oppression of blacks. Other current flagrant examples include the late Ayatollah Khomeini regime's execution of people simply for believing in a faith other than the Shi'ite form of Islam and South Africa's apartheid laws denying blacks and "coloreds" civil and economic rights.

Some conservatives are believed to tolerate and engage in discrimination more than liberals. Some liberals actively and self-consciously work against discrimination.

disenfranchise taking away a person's right to vote, usually for commitment of certain crimes or through aggressive government action such as apartheid in South Africa. It can also include denial of voting privileges by roadblocks to voting such as "constitutional" tests, poll taxes, or threats.

disinformation politbabble for wrong or misleading statements purported to be serious information and meant to mislead the recipients.

disinvestment politbabble for cutting back on or reducing federal spending for whatever program is affected. Conservatives usually favor disinvestment, and liberals often favor investment in programs and new business categories.

dissident a person who dissents from the religious or political views of those in the majority or in power.

During certain administrations, particularly those of Lyndon Johnson and Richard Nixon, dissidents were discouraged and intimidated by various means, such as Internal Revenue Service audits, so-called security investigations, FBI infiltration of organizations, massive police actions against peaceful demonstrations, and use of private means such as denial of credit.

In his unsuccessful 1992 reelection campaign, President George H. W. Bush attempted to discredit Democratic candidate governor Bill Clinton by suggesting Clinton's youthful dissent against the Vietnam War had been unpatriotic and treasonous, thereby disqualifying Clinton as a candidate for president. Bush did not understand that dissent against the Vietnam War became the majority position, which was partly the reason the Vietnam War ended. Occasionally today's dissidenter is tomorrow's member of the majority if there is a shift in public sentiment.

Dissidents also can bring about changes in public opinion by bringing their opposition views before the public, increasing public awareness of their positions, and convincing others that theirs are correct.

dissolution (of government— Canada) the end of a government or parliament when a prime minister's party has lost a parliamentary majority, loses a parliamentary vote of confidence, or when the prime minister calls an election for a new parliament.

district a geographic area with boundaries within which voters living in that area vote for a person to represent them.

diversity a new, politically correct term for carefully balanced integration of races and nationalities in the job market, government, and higher education. Those whom "diversity" annoys often see it as subtle quota requirements.

divestment to strip one's investment from an entity. Divestment often occurs with negative overtones and effects. Some American state governments and universities pulled their money or investments out of American and other businesses in South Africa to protest apartheid. Some Americans boycotted businesses that refused to divest themselves of their South African branches or manufacturing plants. The goal of this divestment was to have a negative effect on the South African economy in order to force fair political, personal, and economic treatment of blacks. In this case divestment had the desired impact, and it, along with many other group and personal efforts, eventually brought about the abandonment of apartheid.

divided government a government in which the president or premier is of one party and its legislature is of another party. A divided government may lead to argument and stagnation. Recent examples include Democratic president Bill Clinton and a Republican Congress from 1995 to 2001.

division of labor a system of running economic and industrial production and administrative policymaking in which the parts of a task or job are split up among several people who usually perform and repeat their function over and over. An example is assembly line workers who all place door handles on left side doors of automobiles.

While this method had been thought to be a key to modern industrial productivity, its inherent lack of independent and creative thought and feeling may account for high stress levels and lack of self-confidence among industrial workers.

Modern attitudes may usher in collaborative, creative contributions by everyone involved in the labor process, encouraging and utilizing creativity shared by and with all participants. Japanese auto firms manufacturing both in Japan and the United States already implement the latter premise, which is thought to increase productivity.

Dixiecrats States' Rights Democrats organized on July 17, 1948, to include 6,000 rightwing southern Democrats who objected to the Democratic Party's civil rights program, but who would not join the Republican Party and preferred to start a third political party.

The Dixiecrats first met at Birmingham, Alabama, and nominated

Governor (now U.S. Senator) Strom Thurmond of South Carolina for president and Governor Fielding L. Wright of Mississippi for vice president. Their platform supported states' rights to make decisions, opposed federal regulations that they believed interfered with states' rights, and opposed Fair Employment Practices proposals.

In the 1948 presidential election the Dixiecrats carried South Carolina, Mississippi, Louisiana, and Alabama, gaining 1,169,021 popular votes and 39 electoral votes, many more than any 20th-century third party or, for example, wealthy Independent candidate Ross Perot, who won no electoral votes in 1992.

Alabama governor George Wallace restructured the Dixiecrats as the American Independent Party in 1968, but by the mid-1970s membership had dwindled to an insignificant number.

doist a person who is capable of observing and relating what he/she learns from practical experience and whose knowledge comes from real world activity, as opposed to a theorist, whose knowledge comes from reading and talking about other people's activity and thoughts. Both develop political thought.

dole, the (1) the distribution of money, food, and medicine to the poor by a government. (2) welfare. The term is used more commonly in Great Britain and Ireland than in the United States.

"He (She) is on the dole" is a pejorative expression used primarily to denigrate the recipients. Conservatives object strongly to and disparage those on the dole as people not willing to work, and their attitudes sometimes display racist undertones. Liberals generally believe a dole of some form is necessary for many people who are unemployable and unable to help themselves.

domino theory a political and international relations concept that appeared during the rise of communism which held that if a country "fell to communism," others nearby would also fall "like a line of dominoes."

The term was first used by President Dwight D. Eisenhower in the 1950s, and then by presidents John F. Kennedy and Lyndon Johnson in the 1960s to rationalize American involvement in the Vietnam War. The theory was that if South Vietnam went communist (as North Vietnam was), so would all of Southeast Asia. President Ronald Reagan also used the domino theory to justify his invasion of the British Commonwealth Republic of Grenada in October 1983.

donkey the graphic symbol of the Democratic Party introduced in political cartoons as early as 1837.

By the 1992 elections, traditional symbols of political parties were rarely used, perhaps indicating (1) abandonment of traditional party identities and definitions; (2) abandonment of traditional party symbols and affiliations; and (3) attempted redefinition of parties.

don't ask, don't tell Senate Armed Services Committee chairman Senator Sam Nunn's (D–Ga.) proposed solution to the gays in the military debate raised by candidate and then-

President Bill Clinton, who had proposed removing the ban on gays in the military forces. Senator Nunn's suggestion, which became official policy of the American military in 1992, means that homosexuals cannot be discharged from the armed services provided they do not reveal their sexual orientation publicly or to other service people, and that the military cannot ask questions about sexual orientation. Discharges continue for those who state they are gay.

double dipper   a person who takes at least two pensions or paychecks from a government. Former California governors George Deukmejian and Jerry Brown both receive two state pensions: Deukmejian as former attorney general and governor, and Brown as former secretary of state and governor.

dove   (1) a pejorative term usually used by "hawks" or conservative Republicans in time of war to refer to pacifists who prefer a gentle, peaceful, negotiated, nonviolent approach to the settlement of differences or controversy.

The term originated in American debates of the Vietnam War in the 1960s, and it was generally used to describe those who wanted the war to stop. (2) a white bird that has become the symbol of peace.

downsizing   a word contrived to make more acceptable or cast a positive spin on firing or laying off employees to economize or increase profits. During the recession in the early 1990s many companies laid people off to reduce expenses and show higher profits for themselves or for

stockholders. Downsizing rarely includes reduction in salaries of those employed, particularly of those doing the cutting.

draft   (1) compulsory enrollment in military service used first in the United States by the Union in the Civil War, revived in World War I and World War II, and then kept in force. While registration was required of all males over 18, actual call-ups were renewed during the Vietnam War through 1971.

When the draft was in force, the order of call-up was determined by a national drawing of numbers that local draft boards had assigned to each young man. Officially it was called the Selective Service System and applied to males only. The Vietnam era draft fell heavily on the less educated and minorities, since college students were exempt. The draft law expired in 1973, but 1980 legislation required all males to register at 18. Registration is currently required of all male university students to be eligible for federal student loans and grants. (2) to choose a presidential or other candidate at a partisan convention who had not declared his/her candidacy or campaigned for the nomination. Presidential nominees drafted as candidates were Democratic winner James K. Polk (1844), Republican winner James Garfield (1880), and Democratic loser Adlai Stevenson (1952). (3) to write new legislation.

draft dodger   a person who goes to extremes to avoid the draft into military service without filing as a conscientious objector (who may get a legal exemption from military service.)

During the Vietnam War draft dodgers hid out in the woods, fled to Canada and other countries, and burned their draft cards as a protest against the war.

Some conservatives and Republicans generally saw draft dodgers as traitors and cowards. Many liberals and anti-war activists viewed them as conscientious, honest, and courageous human beings who dodged participation in a war in which they did not believe.

A draft dodger is distinguished from a person who refuses induction because of moral opposition to military action, such as Mohammed Ali or conscientious objectors.

In the 1992 presidential campaign, President George H. W. Bush implied that challenger Bill Clinton's studies at Oxford University, after signing up for ROTC, constituted a form of draft dodging.

draw a line in the sand take a fixed position beyond which one will not step toward another person's position or views. The term originated when Spanish conquistador Pizarro drew a line in the sand with his sword on the way to Peru and asked those who were "with him" to step across. Everyone did, and a potential mutiny died. During the Iraqi war, President George H. W. Bush said "a line has been drawn in the sand," meaning "we are tough and will not give in." Reporters accused President Bill Clinton of drawing lines in the sand and then erasing them, meaning he changed some positions after making supposedly firm statements.

due process a U.S. constitutional (Fifth and Fourteenth Amendments) right guaranteeing that a person accused of a crime or who is confronted with legal action against him or her will have his/her rights protected and that he/she is entitled to proper legal procedures in both state and federal courts. The Fourteenth Amendment, adopted after the Civil War, became the basis for extending federal guarantees of due process to state actions.

dyed-in-the wool a total, unabashedly, immovably, loyal supporter of a political party or candidate.

earmarking designation of funds, information, staff, or an organization to be used for a specific purpose. Earmarking of funds for government programs sets and usually guarantees the specific amount of money that a program will get.

Eastern establishment a boundless, mythical group of influential and powerful New York money managers, corporate presidents and directors, and lawyers who believe they can and do determine what directions presidents and the government take. Many people believe this group controls government, although the new economy of the 21st century has altered their role. See also ESTBABLISHMENT.

economic globalization the buying, selling, and manufacturing of goods, foods, services, companies, and computer software around the world by companies possibly located in entirely different parts of the world. Some people believe economic globalization is good because it raises the living standards of countries providing inexpensive labor while increasing markets for goods. Other people believe economic globalization transfers jobs held by workers in a company's own country to cheaper labor pools elsewhere and takes undue advantage of poor workers who work in unbearable conditions for poverty wages. Large corporations engage in buying other large corporations in other countries to enlarge their portfolios in an effort to gain power, wealth, and importance. See also GLOBALIZATION.

economic nationalism the belief that a country's people should grow, manufacture, sell, and buy goods made in their own country, thus preserving jobs at home. Buzz phrases include "Buy American" and "Buy Canadian."

economic patriotism   a belief that buying goods made in one's own country is the loyal thing to do.

edifice complex   a play on "oedipus complex" to refer to government managers or elected officials whose desire to have a building erected with their name on it sometimes outweighs good planning decisions, community needs, or available funds.

education   (1) the process of training and developing the knowledge, skill, mind, and character, particularly through formal schooling, teaching, and training. (2) a political football, tossed to the states by President Ronald Reagan, who essentially abdicated responsibility by returning funding and standards setting to the states in the guise of states' rights and advocated abolishment of the U.S. Department of Education.

Vice President George H. W. Bush campaigned to be the "Education President." But as president, Bush actually cut federal funding to schools and announced plans to initiate one experimental school per congressional district, which never happened. Public education is generally administered by elected local school boards, with heavy funding assistance from the state and special program help from the federal government. Basic curricula are set by state legislatures.

The United States ranks among the lowest of all industrial nations in language and mathematics skills by standardized test scores.

Liberals usually advocate more spending on education than do conservatives, on the basis that education is the key to the country's and the world's futures. Conservative voters tend to be older, believe they have paid their school taxes when their children were students, and therefore feel they do not have any further obligation. They often vote against school bonds and for people who promise to cut budgets, regardless of the long-range cost to the country. Most Americans believe in the importance of education but believe the system is imperfect at best.

In the 2000 election vouchers available for students to use in "better" or private schools, more standardized testing, funding teacher training and preschool educational programs became proposals discussed as means to improve American education.

edutainment   word coined by rapper KRS-One to mean educate young people on social issues by communicating through entertainment they enjoy, such as rap music. Entertainers and propagandists convey important political, social, religious, and moral messages through edutainment. "Christian" musicians engage in a form of edutainment.

EEC   See EUROPEAN ECONOMIC COMMUNITY.

effectiveness of government   a term used often by conservatives as a code to question the expenditure of funds and the role of government in education and in solving social and economic problems, particularly those of the poor, unemployed, disabled, aged, and homosexual.

There is a basic belief that the government's use of tax dollars is inefficient due to high management costs, low visible productivity, overregulation, and lack of competitive drive among bureaucrats.

Liberals would respond that effectiveness of government includes expenditure of money on education, vocational training, drug rehabilitation, sex education, and preventative medicine, which, they believe, will cost less in the long run than the administrative costs of imprisonment, hospitalization, and welfare. Conservatives tend to become skeptical and resistant to spending money without advance proof that it would solve the problem, a nearly impossible guarantee.

egalitarianism   a doctrine or belief that all citizens of a state should have exactly equal political and social rights and privileges. The concept usually includes access to equal rights to vote, practice religion, develop abilities, be considered for employment or promotion, and be free of discrimination on the basis of ethnicity or national origin. Ideally egalitarianism requires education and training of disadvantaged persons to bring their opportunities up to a par with those of other citizens.

Pure egalitarianism is realistically impossible to achieve, since all people are not actually created equal. Their talents and interests vary. While Americans have convinced themselves that a college education is necessary for "success," jobs do not exist for all college graduates at a white-collar level. Society requires functions and services that necessitate different levels of specialized education, such as vocational training for cooks, airplane mechanics, homebuilders, child care givers, and university education for physicists, lawyers, doctors, and teachers.

eighteen-year-old vote   the 26th Amendment to the U.S. Constitution guaranteed the right to vote to American citizens 18 years of age or older when it was finally ratified by the states on June 30, 1971. (Georgia had already allowed 18-year-olds to vote.)

The fervor to lower the voting age from 21 to 18 developed as 18-year-olds objected to being regarded as adult enough to be drafted, to fight, and to lose their lives in the Vietnam War but not enough to vote at home. Parents of those in question generally supported their children's right to vote if they were old enough to be drafted or required to register with the draft.

The 18- to 20-year-old age group has the lowest voter turnout of all age groups.

Eisenhower Doctrine (June 5, 1957)   Also known as the Middle East Doctrine, the document affirmed President Dwight D. Eisenhower's policy, following a joint resolution approved in the U.S. Senate and House of Representatives, to use armed forces to assist any nation or group of nations feeling threatened by armed aggression from communist countries. Since it was devised to give military and economic aid to Middle Eastern countries to stave off aggression by the Soviet Union, the doctrine is largely irrelevant today since the Soviet Union no longer exists the threat of communism has abated.

electeds   a noun used in the 1992 presidential campaign of Bill Clinton as a slightly disparaging reference to anyone who had been elected to office, with the attitudinal implication that because of their having been elected, they would or should demand special, differential treatment, and thereby pose a special problem. Electeds may include members of city councils, county commissioners or supervisors, members of state legislatures, Congress, and statewide elected officers.

election a method of choosing among candidates for a political office by voting or marking ballots, raising hands, moving beans, etc. Elections can be real, fraudulent, fake, or ignored in some dictatorships and countries. They are carried out at club, neighborhood, community, city, county, district, state, and national levels.

U.S. elections for president and vice president can produce popular vote results that do not reflect the voters' true will due to the Electoral College, as in the 2000 presidential election. See also ELECTORAL COLLEGE.

electioneering campaigning.

election returns (1) election results. (2) actual numbers of votes counted and reported.

Elections Canada a Canadian government agency, responsible to the House of Commons, that conducts elections and gathers election results. Website: www.elections.ca

elector (1) a person who elects by voting. (2) a qualified voter. (3) a member of the Electoral College.

Electoral College persons selected or elected from each state to meet exclusively to cast their state's votes for president and vice president, as mandated by the U.S. Constitution. The number of electors from each state is equal to the total number of U.S. senators and members of the House of Representatives from that state.

The winning slate of electors are elected or selected based on their pledges to presidential and vice presidential candidates. Electoral College members are technically elected by the voters and are supposed to reflect their state's voters' wishes, but they are not required to vote for the candidate to whom they are pledged. Often the electors are placed on the slate by their governors, sometimes in return for generous campaign contributions or significant community activity. In all states, except Maine and Nebraska, the winning candidates obtain all of the electors on a "winner-take-all" basis.

Even if the popular vote in a state is close, the loser gets no electoral votes. Electoral College members may elect a person who did not gain the majority of the total public vote. Presidents who did not win the popular vote but won in the Electoral College vote include: Rutherford B. Hayes, who beat Samuel J. Tilden by one electoral vote (1876), Benjamin Harrison, who defeated Grover Cleveland (1888); and George W. Bush, who defeated Al Gore (2000).

The Electoral College does not meet as a body, but each state's electors convene at their state capital on the first Monday after the second Wednesday of December and cast their ballots. The ballots are sealed and sent to the president of the U.S. Senate (the vice president of the United States) and are opened on January 6th before a joint session of Congress.

Presidential campaigns target states with large numbers of electoral votes and ignore some states with few electoral votes. Voters in these smaller states are thereby deprived of attention from, exposure to, and communication with national candidates. National candidates often do not bother to campaign in states where polls show they cannot win or where the electoral votes are not numerous enough to make a difference to them. While Democrat Bill Clinton gained only 43 percent of the popular vote in 1992, his campaign scientifically targeted and worked those states that could deliver enough electoral votes for him to become president. Republican senator Robert Dole "wrote off" California in 1996 since he could not win its electoral votes.

Many attempts and proposals have been made, especially by political outsiders whom it did not benefit, to abolish the Electoral College and elect the president and vice president by popular vote. A direct popular vote would, theoretically, encourage candidates to visit all states without snubbing smaller states with fewer electoral votes and prevent a popular vote loser from winning by calculated electoral vote targeting. Proponents of the abolition of the Electoral College also argue that the original concept of civic leaders being chosen from within each state to elect a president and vice president has not been operative since the 1820s, when electors were chosen by popular vote for the first time, instead of by the state legislatures. By 1828 all states but one chose electors by popular election.

electorate   all people who are eligible, qualified, and registered to vote in an election.

electronic media   the worldwide network of computer communication through the Internet.

elephant   the symbol of the Republican Party introduced by political cartoonist Thomas Nast in 1874.

Eleventh Commandment   an adage, "Thou shall speak no evil of a fellow Republican," coined by California Republican Party state chairman Dr. Gaylord Parkinson (1966) and used widely by then Republican gubernatorial candidate Ronald Reagan. Parkinson's goal was to avoid a nasty primary between Reagan and San Francisco Mayor George Christopher. Reagan urged that they save their vitriol for the Democrats. They did and Reagan defeated two-term Democratic governor Edmund G. "Jerry" Brown.

elites   a select group of people perceived to control thinking, power, or business. Democrats used to refer to Republicans as elites, until Dan Quayle turned the tables and referred to Hollywood stars and producers as elites, as if the word had a dirty, liberal connotation.

elitism   the belief that all political entities are run by the elite, i.e., the "best" and wealthiest part of society or the political power structure. The concept also includes the theory that elected representatives are actually selected or elected by the elite, with the party nominees selected from a political elite of primary candidates, resulting in rival elites vying for the top spots and power.

Elitism was originally a concept in conflict with social democracy and with Marxist theory, which contended there could be a classless society featuring total equality (egalitarianism).

Contrasts in approaches to elitism include Republican Party abilities to preselect candidates so that only one Republican runs in a primary, thereby saving money and energy. Democrats are so publicly anti-elite (but work to preserve and be part of their own elite within their system) that they encourage all comers and often refuse to support any Democrat until after the primary election.

Republicans see their elitist selection by high party officials without consulting the public as the right thing to do to preserve the status quo and make sure the right person runs. Democrats abhor the Republicans' system and state that it is unfair to the public and favors elites, while Democrats drain their financial campaign coffers with intraparty fights. The latter may simply be jealous. See also CULTURAL ELITES.

elitist an attitude favoring the upper class, most intellectuals, and/or the wealthiest part of society. See also CULTURAL ELITES.

embargo a restriction or prohibition imposed to stop communication of information, trade, and movement of goods.

emergency powers powers granted to the executive branch of government to perform certain unusual functions without going through normal and formal legislative processes.

According to the U.S. Constitution, war is supposed to be declared by Congress. Presidents Harry Truman (Korea), Lyndon Johnson (Vietnam), Ronald Reagan (Grenada), George H. W. Bush (Iraq) and Bill Clinton (Yugoslavia) all engaged the United States in war without asking Congress to vote a declaration of war.

Other countries use emergency powers for various purposes. The United Kingdom utilizes them only in a "wartime situation." By France's 1958 Constitution (Fifth Republic) the president must consult four top leaders, namely the prime minister, the president of the Senate, the president of the National Assembly, and the president of the Constitutional Council before declaring a state of emergency powers. Nondemocratic countries employ emergency powers called "states of siege" or martial law in which all civil liberties are suspended, as has happened in Latin America, Africa, and some Pacific and Asian countries.

Emily's List a network through which contributors can donate to women candidates who support "choice" and the ERA for gubernatorial and congressional offices. Emily's List stands for "Early Money Is Like Yeast." It makes dough rise. Founded in 1985 by IBM heir Ellen Malcolm of Washington, D.C., Emily's List became the largest fundraiser and contributor to female political candidates in the country in 1992. Members give a minimum contribution of $100 to the organization, pledging to donate at least $200 more directly to two or more candidates at each election. Address: 805 15th Street, N.W., Suite 400, Washington, D.C. 20005. Tel.: (202) 326-1400; e-mail: information@emilyslist.org; website: emilyslist.org

eminent domain   the right of the government to take property for public use, as provided for in the U.S. Constitution. The government must pay the person whose property they are taking the fair market price.

emphatic negative advertisement a positive ad for a candidate sandwiched between two negative ads or points slamming the opponent.

Empower America   a political organization founded in 1993, of which former football star, congressman, secretary of housing and urban development, and 1996 Republican vice presidential nominee Jack Kemp is co-director. Empower America advocates changes in education, particularly for disadvantaged students in urban areas, improving schools with poor test results, and using the methods devised by the organization for setting standards testing for advancement and graduation, vouchers, charter schools, and merit pay for teachers. Address: 1701 Pennsylvania Ave., N.W., Suite 900, Washington, D.C. 20006. Tel.: (202) 452-8200; e-mail: clowe@empower. org; website: www. empower.org

empowerment   the giving or taking of power or a feeling of control to accomplish something thought to be unattainable before. The term gained acceptance in the 1980s in the context of giving electoral, economic, or personal will power to the weaker segments of society, resulting in the "empowerment" of the poor, minorities, senior citizens, women, and single mothers on welfare.

empowerment zones   depressed geographic (usually urban) areas where some Republicans and Democratic president Bill Clinton hoped to "invest" or spend federal funds on business and housing development.

endorsement   (1) approval, support, or sanction of a person or proposition in an election, usually including the endorser's signature giving a political campaign the right to use the endorser's name in support of the candidate or issue position. (2) published support by newspapers, usually through editorials. Many newspapers print lists of their endorsed candidates.

Endorsements are often sought for symbolic use to entice and influence followers' friends to support the same candidate or issue. Often getting the first endorsements is as difficult as getting a first job. Potential endorsers want to know who else you already have lined up to make themselves feel more comfortable in adding their names to your list. They ask: Can you assure me that you will win or that I will not be embarrassed? Is it the right thing to do? How will it help me?

The negative sides of endorsements include: (1) someone will know something negative about every endorser, and (2) occasionally people's names are published without their permission, leading them to publicly deny support, which may be more harmful than the endorsement would be helpful.

enemies list   a list kept by a politician or elected official of people whom he/she feels crossed him/her or whom he/she wants to "get." Some of President Richard Nixon's staff kept lists of people they wanted harassed, including some members of the media, and Philippines president Ferdinand Marcos allegedly kept an enemies list of people he considered had contributed to his downfall and whom he wanted killed when he left office.

enemy   a person, group of people, or a nation hostile to another person or nation, which another person or country might plot to injure, cripple, destroy, violently or through a cold war.

The United States has traditionally needed an enemy around which to coalesce support and unify its people. In times of war, the target is easy to identify: the Kaiser and German "Huns" in World War I, Nazis and Japanese in World War II, and communists in Korea and Vietnam. In times of peace, some Americans tend to transfer this need for an enemy to a timely domestic issue. Conservatives' peacetime enemies have included Democrats, "liberals," communism, the Soviet Union during the cold war, minorities, immigrants, Iraq, immigrants, and Japan. Democrats and liberals prefer to consider poverty, the extremely wealthy and powerful, big business, racism, Republicans, "conservatives," and intolerance as their enemies.

Enlightenment   an 18th-century European philosophical movement that propounded rationalism, a positive attitude toward learning with a new wave of skepticism toward Christianity, and empiricism in political and social thought. The movement saw history as the record of man's progress toward reason and, therefore, perfection. The Enlightenment's empiricism influenced the American Revolution and political writings, including Thomas Paine's *The Age of Reason* (1794, 1796).

enterprise zone   a concept expounded but not defined by former secretary of housing and urban development Jack Kemp (R–N.Y.) in the *New Republic* (October 12, 1992). Apparently Kemp intended to grant businesses and entrepreneurs capital gains and income tax benefits for establishing themselves in ghettos and other low-income neighborhoods and, ostensibly, improving the local economy. A bill creating enterprise zones was vetoed by Republican president George H. W. Bush (November 4, 1992) on the basis that it included some tax increases. Democratic president Bill Clinton later became an advocate of such zones.

entitlements   government programs granting money to people who qualify to receive the funds, such as Social Security, Aid for Dependent Children, aid to the physically challenged, and many others. The word is used both in the sense of what one is entitled to by government or legislative acts, and as an overall word to avoid actually mentioning the words "social security" or aid to the blind, particularly when discussing reduction of funds. Cutting entitlements funding has been suggested as a way to reduce the national deficit (1993). Senate majority leader George Mitchell (D–Maine) suggested that members of Congress who advocate limiting benefits should have the courage to tell the voters outright that they favor cutting down social security payments.

entryism   an effort (often successful) by members of extreme political movements to join (infiltrate) and eventually take control of established political parties or movements. Entryism may happen to liberals from the socialist left and to conservatives from Nazi or religious right interests.

Examples that have occurred in the United States include communist or Mafia infiltration of some labor unions by means of intelligence, persistence, and organizational talents, left-liberal movements invaded by radicals with their own agendas, such as the 1948 Progressive Party, and born-again Christians infiltrating the Republican Party. In the long run, such entryism usually has resulted in either the infiltrated group's destruction or the group's shaking off of the radicals' takeover due to the obsessiveness of the latter's control agenda.

enumerators   (1) people who count votes or voters; (2) party loyalists who go to the polls and count their party members' votes to make sure they are all tabulated and to get voters out to the polls if they have not already.

environmentalism   a concept that holds as its primary concern human beings, their surroundings, and preservation of nature's balance between consumers and organisms. People interested in environmentalism (environmentalists) work to solve problems such as air and water pollution, overuse of natural resources, burning of rain forests and other timberland, and uncontrolled population growth. The concept usually also includes a position against use of nuclear weapons or energy. Environmentalism gained momentum in the 1960s because of works such as Rachel Carson's *The Sea Around Us.*

Some conservatives see environmentalism as a phony, liberal, hippie, new religion of pot-smokers and tree huggers that impedes what they see as the necessary use and sale of natural resources to make money in the free enterprise system. Liberals tend to favor environmentalism and accuse conservatives of insensitively ruining the planet.

In true semantic irony, conservatives, whose name root means to preserve from loss or decay or preserve what is established, disinvest themselves of that part of their definition when it applies to the environment.

Environmental Protection Agency (EPA)   a federal agency created on July 2, 1965, to protect and enhance the environment by controlling and reducing air and water pollution and regulating solid waste disposal and use and disposal of pesticides, radiation, and toxins. Address: Ariel Rios Building, 1200 Pennsylvania Ave., N.W., Washington, D.C. 20460. Tel.: (202) 260-2090; e-mail: public-access @epamail.epa.gov; website: www.epa. gov.

envoy   an ambassador or a person sent by a leader or government for a specific purpose.

equality   the state of being equal, with no one in a position of superiority or inferiority, and in which everyone has the same rights, privileges, opportunity, and dignity. Equality was first dealt with in the United States in the Declaration of Independence.

Some conservatives seem to be unconcerned with equality and, at times, appear to favor inequality, which favors them, their supposed superiority, and elitism. Radical conservative Republican David Duke's candidacies for Louisiana governor and U.S. president (1991–92) emphasized superiority of whites and "Christians" over everyone else.

Liberals tend to fight for, or at least give lip service to, equality of classes, races, and religious followers, but they often consider themselves to be intellectual superiors.

equal opportunity the premise that everyone should have the same chances in educational, employment and promotion, and housing opportunities regardless of race, religion, sex or sexual orientation, and national or ethnic origin. Tests for employment and promotion are supposed to be the same for everyone.

Abridgements of this principle include past recruitment of top British civil servants from Oxford and Cambridge universities and, in the United States, passing down of longshoremen's, railroad workers', and teamsters' jobs to sons without competition.

Conservatives, claim that equal opportunity leads to a "quota system" or reverse (positive) discrimination by which minorities are hired to give their races a specified percentage of employment opportunities, discriminating against whites who are equally or better qualified, simply because they are white. Real-life examples include a city fire department hiring a minority person who scored 75th on a promotion test over a white male who scored 40th.

Liberals generally favor equal opportunity and claim reverse discrimination when they or their children are affected and cannot get into a particular university or job because they are white. Some feel conservatives' claims about quota systems are guises for breaking down integration and equal opportunity and for gradual return of segregation, unequal opportunity, and hate crimes.

equal protection of the laws a clause in the Fourteenth Amendment to the U.S. Constitution requiring states to guarantee equal rights and protections to all citizens. The original (1868) intention was to prevent abridgement or denial of slaves' rights as human beings. From the U.S. Supreme Court leadership of Chief Justice Earl Warren (1953–1969), the interpretation of equal protection has expanded to eliminate racial and sex discrimination and segregation, and guarantee desegregation. Interpretations and enforcement of this amendment can vary according to the makeup of the Supreme Court and the sitting justices' political leanings and inclinations. In this sense, the president's appointive powers can powerfully influence such rulings.

Equal Rights Amendment (ERA) a proposed constitutional amendment declaring: "Equality of rights under the law shall not be denied or abridged by the United States or any state on account of sex."

It was aimed at guaranteeing women equality in employment, pay, promotion, civil rights, choices, and opportunity. Proposed as early as 1923, after rigorous campaigning by women's groups, the ERA was adopted by the House of Representatives in October 1971 and by the Senate in March 1972. After 10 years, including one extension of time and a series of fights in state legislatures, only 35 states ratified the ERA, falling three short when time ran out on June 30, 1982.

Arguments against the ERA usually center on lack of real benefits not already guaranteed, possible loss of special rights such as alimony, worksafe conditions, and avoidance of the draft, and the claim that the equal protection clause of the Fourteenth Amendment gives women equal rights.

Proponents claim lawsuits under the Fourteenth Amendment are impractical, that women suffer unequal treatment in the workplace and by businesses, and that the ERA is symbolic of women's rights to fair play.

Women's organizations made support or opposition a litmus test for their political support in the 1980s. President George H. W. Bush opposed the ERA while his wife, Barbara Bush, backed it in a genuine political/family division. President Bill Clinton supported the amendment, which was reintroduced in 1992.

equal time   a regulation of the Federal Communications Commission (created 1934) requiring radio or television stations that give free air time to a candidate to give the same amount of free time to other candidates in the same race.

The FCC has varied its rules over the years, particularly regarding news conferences and interviews of incumbents and challengers. In August 1987, the FCC unanimously repealed the "Fairness Doctrine," which required equal time for political parties and candidates.

While the FCC requires that minor party and independent candidates be given some access to broadcast media, those candidates are rarely included in debates with major candidates. The rules generally favor incumbents making "news" over challengers, and major candidates over those with little public support. Ross Perot bought hours of television time throughout the country to get his message across as well as to secure his place in the 1992 presidential debates with incumbent President George H. W. Bush and challenger Governor Bill Clinton.

equal time rule   a rule in the media that requires an outlet to give equal free time to candidates or opponents on both sides of a contest or issue, or make available equal paid advertising time to each side if they have the funds or choose to purchase the time.

escalation   (1) the increase of military or nuclear forces, usually in response to an at least imagined buildup by an enemy. (2) the step-by-step expansion of a local conflict into one covering a larger geographic region, or from conventional weapons (guns) to high-tech bombs and nuclear weaponry. Escalation also implies that such a rise in activity may have fearful consequences.

establishment   (1) originally included the hierarchy of the Church of England, but now includes an intertwining of the Royal Family, the Church of England, and the aristocracy. (2) the ruling inner circle of any state or institution. (3) in the United States: an amorphous group of individuals and the institutions they lead that together exert social, economic, and political power over the rest of society. This use of the term originated in an *Esquire* magazine article by Richard Rovere (1961). (4) a pejorative term for those in whose hands power seems to rest, akin to elitism.

In the United States the establishment supposedly consists of white, Protestant males with power and influence, although a person might gain establishment status in America by acquisition of expertise and/or money. The establishment is also occasionally the target of political demagogues, for example, Spiro Agnew believed it was the evil force behind what he contended was unfair media cover age of him. See also EASTERN ESTABLISHMENT.

ethnic group   See ETHNICITY.

ethnicity   a combination of characteristics that leads to classification, grouping, or affiliation by which some societies divide themselves in social and political contexts. Those characteristics may include race or skin color, religion, national origin, and language.

ethnocentrism   an emotional assumption that one's own race, culture, nation, or religion is superior to all others.

Euro-centrism   a philosophy and way of life that emphasizes following European (white) values, culture, language, politics, cuisine and general lifestyle with the understanding that European (white) morals and history are the most important and correct. Outside of Europe, many societies in countries once invaded or colonized by Europeans and in whose leadership

European descendants dominate practice conscious or subconscious Eurocentrism, often in conflict with native, aboriginal, or migrant peoples. Examples outside Europe include the United States, Canada, Argentina, Brazil, and Mexico.

Euro-communism   a new version of communism found primarily in Western European democracies, such as the Italian Communist Party (PCI) or the Spanish Communist Party (PCE). These efforts evolved among World War II pacifists, anti-fascists, and members of resistance movements against German occupation. In fact Euro-communism resembles socialism more than Marxist communism.

European Economic Community (EEC)   one of five agreements among Western European nations to create common policies, eliminate tariffs, monetary standards, taxes, and generally manage the economic well-being of its member nations. Regarded as a first step toward the unification of Europe, it tries to achieve mutual economic advancement and protect member states from war among and between the members.

The EEC evolved from the European Common Market, created by the Treaty of Rome (1957). The original members included France, Belgium, Luxembourg, the Netherlands, Italy, and West Germany. The United Kingdom, Denmark, and Ireland joined in 1973. Other new member nations included Greece (1981), Portugal (1986), and Spain (1986).

The EEC's European Parliament is a legislative body made up of members elected from each country.

executive branch of government one of three branches of government developed from the writings of Montesquieu and included in the U.S. Constitution in James Madison's first draft. The other branches are the legislative and judicial. The executive branch includes the president and vice president, the cabinet, and, in reality, all of their staffs. In some countries (Great Britain), executives are selected from among the elected legislators, while in the United States and France they may not come from the legislature. They are elected or appointed separately to create and protect the separation of powers.

executive (committee) a small group of people elected either by an organization, political party, or legislature to run the group, set policy, and oversee departments or agencies of a government.

executive order an order by the president of the United States that does not require senatorial or congressional approval, usually following a statute that allows him or her to make that order.

executive privilege the claim by the nation's executive, the president, that he/she does not have to respond to subpoenas or reveal to Congress information he/she does not want to reveal on the basis that Congress or the courts do not have the right to ask the executive for the information. President Richard Nixon claimed executive privilege in confronting the Watergate scandal during the congressional hearings prior to his resignation.

existentialism a Western European philosophy that evolved in France and became popular after World War II. Its original theorist was Soren Kierkegaard in Denmark (1813–55), whose ideas were revived by philosophers and writers Jean-Paul Sartre (1905–80) and Albert Camus (1913–60) in France. The theory includes the principle that each individual exists alone in a world without purpose or meaning. Existentialists see the world, modern society, and government as dehumanizing and alienating. Regarded as somewhat pessimistic by others, and realistic by themselves, existentialists generally oppose organizational power in any form, including left- and right-wing political parties and even themselves. They believe the individual must strive against the politicians for his/her own autonomy and to protect his/her personal creativity.

exit poll questioning and tabulation of voters of their votes as they leave their polling places. Media representatives, candidates' staffs, and campaign workers take exit polls to gauge and predict the election's outcome before the polls close and the results are in, tabulated, and revealed. Exit polls used by nationwide television and radio networks have influenced election results. In response to exit polls, Democratic president Jimmy Carter conceded the 1980 presidential election to Republican Ronald Reagan at 8:00 P.M. Eastern Time, which is only 5:00 P.M. Pacific Time, affecting voter turnout and discouraging western Democratic voters from voting. Exit polls were sharply criticized for inaccurate and hasty reports of state results in the 2000 presidential election.

expat   nickname for an expatriate.

expatriate   a person who has chosen to leave his/her country and take up residency in another country. Expatriates often wish to distance themselves from their own country, if only temporarily, and often for political reasons. Expatriatism usually does not include giving up one's original citizenship.

In the 1920s and 1930s many American artists and writers who opposed the Harding-Coolidge era moved to France and lived in Paris as expatriates. Well-known examples include Earnest Hemingway and Man Ray. Most eventually returned to the United States. Many Americans moved abroad in the 1980s for similar political reasons.

expertise   skill or knowledge held by someone thought to be an expert or who has specific experience in a particular field. Expertise may bring a person close to joining the Establishment if one does not belong to it by birth or, in America, by acquisition of money. Expertise may be seen as equally important by the person possessing it and the person perceiving it.

extortion   the use of one's political or other position or power to take money illegally from others by intimidation or threat.

eyeball to eyeball   a potentially volatile face-to-face confrontation forcing a question and potentially resulting in war.

fact-finding trip   a trip taken by an officeholder and rationalized as important for information gathering on public issues. Fact-finding trips are called junkets by people who do not approve of them or who are not invited to go on them.

faction   a group of people within a political party or other organization who share a common viewpoint, interest, or goal, probably in opposition to the official party's positions or goals. Factions usually expend more energy and enthusiasm than the mainstream organization against which they are rebelling.

As of 1993, the radical right, religious right, or Christian conservative faction had pursued its interests and spread its word so effectively that it had grown from a small pressure group to become a major influence within the Republican Party. In California, the religious right faction within the Republican Party is so large

it prevails on platform issues votes, and the moderate, former mainstream Republicans now qualify as a faction.

Fair Deal   a label given to his domestic programs for progress by Democratic president Harry S. Truman in his first postwar message to Congress (1945). As part of his Fair Deal, Truman asked for "liberal" programs such as expanded social security, new wages and work hours laws, public housing legislation, and a permanent Fair Employment Practices Act, which would prevent religious or racial discrimination in hiring. With a Republican congressional majority from 1946–48, Congress seemed obsessed with inflation and conversion to a peacetime economy following World War II and basically ignored Truman's social and economic requests.

After President Truman's unexpected reelection (1948), he again asked for Fair Deal legislation with the same results. Finally Congress did raise the minimum wage, instituted slum clearance, and added old age benefits for an additional 10,000,000 people, in a rerun version of Franklin Delano Roosevelt's New Deal (1933).

Fair Employment Practices Commission (FEPC) commissions established in several states and cities to enforce or at least watch for violations of laws supposed to guarantee freedom from racial, religious, sexual, or other discrimination in the workplace.

Fala President Franklin D. Roosevelt's scotch terrier dog.

During Roosevelt's 1944 reelection campaign, a false rumor floated widely that Fala had been left behind during a naval inspection tour in Alaska and that taxpayers' money was spent to send a naval destroyer back to get the dog. In a nationally broadcast speech to a Teamsters' Union banquet FDR said in mock seriousness that he was used to attacks on himself, his wife, and his sons, but that they had gone too far in maligning his little dog Fala, whose "Scotch soul was furious. He hasn't been the same dog since." The audience and the nation laughed, and Roosevelt's humor contrasted favorably with his uptight opponent, Thomas E. Dewey.

falangism a fascistic movement that began in 1934 with the Falange Española, the Spanish Fascist movement, and brought General Francisco Franco to power in the Spanish Civil War (1936–39). Falange Española was the only political party Franco allowed in Spain during his dictatorship. Falangism is usually characterized by strong national traditions, a supposed vision of destiny, a powerful right wing, and authoritarian management of a political entity. Falangism has some populist characteristics: it runs across class lines (although most participants tend to be middle class), and religious and national identities are much more important than economic status or class differences. The Christian Falange in Lebanon is church-based.

false consciousness a term that refers to a situation in which a people's beliefs, values, and preferences appear to be false or inappropriate according to their "normal" standards or expected best interests. Many American trade union members supported conservative Republican presidential candidate Ronald Reagan because they believed he would do the most for them and would protect them from higher taxes and communism. By 1992 many union members began to think this confidence was falsely placed and switched back to support Democrat Bill Clinton. Some conservatives who backed Clinton may feel the same way.

family breakup a 1990s term that refers to the facts that the family is no longer the basic unit in America, that more than 50 percent of all American marriages end in divorce, and that often one parent is left to raise children alone and without emotional or financial aid from the other parent. Government leaders, particularly those struggling to blame society's woes on others, often blame family breakup or lack of "family values" for the country's crime culture, evangelical movements, and persistent incidences of children having children.

family issues a vague linkage of issues such as child care, health care, education, marriage and divorce, and growth of adolescent crime.

family medical leave a concept embodied in an act passed by Congress in 1993 in which employers with 15 or more employees must allow time off from work with pay or without penalty for health situations ranging from childbirth to caring for immediate family members suffering from illness.

family values a term used in the late 1980s and in the 1992 presidential campaign and made prominent by Republican vice president J. Danforth Quayle's attack on fictional television character Murphy Brown's birth of a child as a single mother. Exactly what the term means is unclear, although it apparently refers to remaining a virgin until marriage, getting married, raising a family, paying taxes, and living according to traditional Christian standards. President Ronald Reagan's secretary of education William Bennett suggested on December 26, 1993, on N.B.C.'s *Meet the Press* that values are "what you're taught at an early age" and "habits from your youth."

However, each family's values must be different, and members within each family can hold different views of what those values are. Cases where there is no family or where communication is lacking within a family sometimes result in members resorting to gangs for a sense of community, structure, and rules.

Farmer-Labor Party (1) first a section and then an offshoot of the National Labor Party formed on June 12, 1920. At its national convention, members nominated Parley P. Christensen of Utah for president and Max S. Hayes of Ohio for vice president. The party was extinct by 1923. (2) a "third" party of Minnesota small farmers and urban workers who supported Robert M. LaFollette in the 1924 presidential election and Franklin Delano Roosevelt in 1932 and 1936. A spinoff of the Nonpartisan League, the Farmer-Labor Party first nominated candidates for office in 1918 for the Minnesota legislature. Farmer-Labor Party candidate Floyd B. Olsen was elected Minnesota governor in 1930, 1932, and 1934. The Minnesota party merged with that state's Democrats, creating the Democratic-Farmer-Labor Party (DFL) in 1944. Early young DFL activists who became nationally prominent Democrats include Senator and Vice President Hubert Humphrey, Senator Eugene McCarthy, Governor and Secretary of Agriculture Orville Freeman, and Senator and Vice President Walter Mondale.

Farmers' Alliance (National Farmers' Alliance) a nonsectarian farmers' organization (1880), the leaders of which formed the Ocala Demands (1890), which itself led to the National People's (Populist) Party founded in Omaha, Nebraska, in 1892.

Branches of the Farmers' Alliance sprang up in the South and West as agrarian reformers and populists coalesced around discontent with crop and price failures due to bad marketing and credit facilities. They demanded more circulating currency through unlimited silver coinage, a graduated income tax, government ownership of railroads, and the direct election of U.S. senators to give farmers equal influence with business and industry.

The National People's Party's or Populists' first presidential candidate, James B. Weaver, gained 22 Electoral College votes with 1,000,000 popular votes in the 1892 election. In some states they merged with Democrats, resulting in a few members elected to Congress.

The Populists joined with Democrats in 1896 in support of the Free Silver Movement and its champion, presidential candidate William Jennings Bryan. Bryan's defeat brought an end to a separate Populist movement, some of whose causes were picked up by progressives among both Democrats and Republicans. Some of its aims were achieved during President Woodrow Wilson's administration.

Farmers Union (National Farmers Union) a union of liberal farmers founded in Texas (1902) and claiming over 300,000 family members (1992) throughout the states of Wisconsin, Minnesota, and Colorado. The FU began as a radical statement of outrage and discontent among farmers. It remains the most liberal of farm organizations and promotes co-ops as well as education of farmers and the public about farmers' concerns. Its organization resembles a labor union more than do other farmers' organizations. Address: 11900 East Cornell Avenue, Denver, Colo. 80014 Tel.: (303) 337-5500; e-mail: webmaster@nfu.org; website: www. nfu.org

fascism (1) the philosophy of the Fascist Party founded in 1919 by Benito Mussolini to oppose, suppress, and eventually eliminate any and all opponents in Italy. Its name came from the Latin word "fasces," meaning a tied bundle of rods used as a symbol of authority in ancient Rome. Its "Black Shirts" (paramilitary toughs) paraded into Rome in 1922, forcing King Victor Emanuel III to name Mussolini premier. Mussolini took the title *Il Duce* (the leader) and established an actively antidemocratic dictatorship (1922–43), which invaded Ethiopia, Albania, and Greece. (2) a generic name for a political philosophy advocating suppression or elimination of any opposition, achievement of a one-party dictatorship, elimination of unions, and activist violence against minorities and liberals. It included Hitler's German Nazis, Franco's Spanish Falange, and most right-wing dictatorships. (3) current usage: a term applied by liberals and Democrats, and some Republicans, when referring to conservatives more conservative than they are. (4) people who hold extreme totalitarian beliefs, especially if the person uses verbal or physical violence to express or enforce his/her views.

fast-track a verb for speeding international trade legislation through Congress, which can be applied to other issues.

fat cat a slang term for a person who demonstratively gives large amounts of money to political candidates or parties supposedly out of devotion to public service, but usually to buy influence or access to the recipient after he/she is elected to office.

Fat cats' appeal to candidates is often their money, rather than their ideas, expertise, or abilities. Bill Clinton's 1992 presidential campaign assigned staffers to communicate with fat cats after they donated, simply to make them feel as if their input derived from qualities other than their money.

Republicans and most Democratic activists refer to donors of large sums ($10,000–$500,000) as fat cats. Party leaders use the term with slight sarcasm for large donors whom they treat publicly as friendly, noble, concerned, and especially generous and patriotic citizens.

fat cat candidate a candidate who refuses federal government campaign matching funds and uses only his or her own fortune, allowing him or her to ignore spending limits.

favorite son a person nominated for president by his/her state's delegation to his/her party's national convention. A favorite son candidate is usually assumed not to be a serious candidate, willing to serve as a holding individual for a delegation that does not want to commit or wishes to use its withholding of support as a bargaining point with a party faction or potential nominee. The state delegation honors the nominee, and, in some cases, the favorite son is more popular in his state than the known candidates. The last favorite son to win the nomination and presidency was Republican Warren G. Harding in 1920.

featherbedding (1) limiting work productivity or output in order to provide more jobs to produce the same amount of goods and to stifle, prevent, or reduce unemployment. (2)

mandatory hiring when tasks are actually, or are thought to be, unnecessary. (3) unnecessary or undemanding jobs created to employ friends and political supporters, often with marginal effect.

Fed, The nickname for the Federal Reserve Bank.

federal pertaining to a national, central government created by a unified group of states. See also FEDERAL-ISM.

Federal Communications Commission (FCC) federal commission that regulates radio, television, cable and interstate telephone lines and service. Established by the Communications Act of 1934, its decisions can be political since it approves and gives licenses to radio stations and television channels, regulates required public service broadcast time, sometimes limits advertising time, and preserves clear frequencies. If public hearings on license issuance or renewal are unfavorable, the FCC can require improvement in service or deny the license. Address: 445 12th Street, S.W., Washington, D.C. 20554. Tel.: (202) 418-0190, 1-888-225-5322; e-mail: fccinfo@fcc.gov; website: www.fcc.gov

Federal Election Commission (FEC) a commission established in 1975 by the Federal Election Campaign Act that monitors contributions to candidates for presidential and congressional offices, to political party committees that spend money on campaigns, and to political action committees that contribute to campaigns.

The FEC receives, tabulates, and publishes candidates' financial reports, and determines candidates' eligibility for and allocation of matching funds derived from Americans' tax return $1 check-offs for the Presidential Election Campaign Fund.

The FEC has six members, with no more than three members of the same political party, serving staggered six-year terms, appointed by the president and confirmed by the Senate. Address: 999 E Street, Washington, D.C. 20463. Tel.: (800) 424-9530; e-mail: webmaster@fec.gov; web site: www.fec.gov.

Federal Housing Administration (FHA)
federal housing agency established under the National Housing Act on June 28, 1934, that insures home loans, making mortgages easier to obtain and stimulating home purchase and repair. The **Public Housing Administration** was created (September 1937) to finance housing projects for low-income families to be built by local communities and states. **Title I of the 1949 Federal Housing Act** commenced assistance for urban renewal (redevelopment).

Federal Reserve System
the central bank of the United States made up of 12 district banks and a Board of Governors. The Federal Reserve Board has seven members appointed by the president for 14-year terms and is headed by a chairman and vice chairman who serve four-year terms in that post. The board is currently chaired by Alan Greenspan, who was appointed originally by President Ronald Reagan. The Federal Reserve Board and Bank act independently of any other government departments and control monetary policy through regulating interest rates (which most money managers and economists believe control inflation), setting reserve requirements for depository institutions, and controlling open market operations (the sale and purchase of government securities). Such decisions are made based on current and future economic and financial conditions as interpreted by the board.

Federal Trade Commission (FTC)
a federal government commission created in 1914 in response to "muckraking" writers' revelations to regulate "unfair methods of competition," deceptive advertising, price discrimination, and prevention of monopolies. The president appoints the FTC's five members, who must be approved by the Senate. The commission has the power to issue "cease and desist orders" against companies that continue unfair trade practices after warnings. Address: 600 Pennsylvania Avenue at Sixth Street, N.W., Washington, D.C. 20580. Tel.: (202) 326-2222; website: www.ftc.gov (phone numbers for special topics and complaints on website).

federalism
(1) originally an arrangement binding a union of states for specific purposes, usually military or commercial. (2) a union of states in which each one subordinates its power to the central (federal) authority in matters and issues they share, leading to a national government. Most have an upper house (Senate) and lower house (House of Representatives or House of Commons). A system employed by the United States,

Switzerland, Germany, Australia, and Canada, among others, it usually includes a balance and sharing of power between federal and local authorities.

Conservatives believe that the more local governments depend on the federal government for financial help, the more the feds can control usage of the money. Liberals usually believe the federal government should use taxes to help the poor, provide reasonable medical care, and maintain the country's infrastructure.

Federalist Papers a series of 85 essays supporting ratification by the states of the U.S. Constitution. Written by Alexander Hamilton, James Madison, and John Jay, the *Federalist Papers* were published in newspapers between October 27, 1787, and April 4, 1788, and in a book in May 1788. They remain one of the best expositions ever written on representative government.

Federalists those who favored a strong national government in the debate over adoption of the Constitution (1787–88). They dominated the administrations of presidents George Washington and John Adams. More conservative Federalists formed the Federalist Party organized by Alexander Hamilton. Democratic-Republican Thomas Jefferson's election as president (1800) signaled the beginning of the end of the Federalists. Prominent Federalists included Hamilton, Adams, John Jay, and John Marshall.

Feds (1) a term for overbearing, intrusive federal government bureaucrats, usually with the implication that one cannot oppose or contradict their methods or power. (2) slang for federal enforcement officers, including the F.B.I. and I.R.S. auditors.

feeding frenzy a relentless pursuit by the media or opponents when an officeholder makes a tragic mistake, like sharks drawn to blood.

feet to the fire intense need to fulfill a commitment or make a decision, usually when one has put off action and a problem reaches crisis proportions.

fellow traveler (1) 1930s: a person sympathetic to the Communist Party without joining it. (2) 1950s: a disparaging term to apply to many people accused of being communists. (3) 1990s: a person who supports the philosophy of any political or social group with commitment but without actually joining that group. Conservatives usually use the term sarcastically to mean liberalism in the extreme, or linkage of liberals with leftists/communists.

feminazi radio personality Rush Limbaugh's term for feminists, women active on women's issues, or women he dislikes.

The Feminine Mystique a landmark book written on feminism by Betty Friedan (W.W. Norton, New York, 1963), which became a bible for the women's rights movement.

feminism a belief and theory that women should have equal rights with men, including political, economic, social, and sexual rights, equal pay for equal work, free day care to allow women to work and support their families, and free choice of whether or not to have an abortion.

Feminism traces its early beginnings to Jacksonian Democracy when President Andrew Jackson demanded the vote for every white man, an action that, at the time, was considered radical since property ownership had been a requirement previously. In the 19th century, Dorothy Dix, Susan B. Anthony, and Amelia Bloomer fought for woman suffrage.

Feminism gained considerable power and prominence by the early 20th century, winning suffrage in 1920, and then became dormant. Interest revived when women entered the workforce during World War II. It waned again, but resurfaced in the early 1960s with Betty Friedan's *The Feminine Mystique*, Gloria Steinem and *Ms.* magazine, the National Organization for Women (NOW), and the National Women's Political Caucus (NWPC).

Some results of the movement include a few more women in political office (far short of women's 51 percent share of the U.S. population) and important activists in anti-war efforts of the 1960s, environmentalism, Equal Rights Amendment (ERA), gay and lesbian rights, and pro-choice campaigns.

Many conservatives see feminists as an uppity group of undesirable, frustrated, and possibly lesbian women with chips on their shoulders. Former president George H. W. Bush opposed passage of the Equal Rights Amendment on the basis that it was not needed since everyone already has equal rights, although Barbara Bush supported it.

Liberals and many Democrats support feminism and the ERA, but they are occasionally dismayed by the movement's militant leadership.

Feminism's definition has changed over the years from broom-wielding suffragists to bra-burning feminists and now to rational, methodical researchers and activists working within systems to bring about change. The message, messengers, and delivery have softened, attracting women and men who were originally put off by abrasive tactics.

fence mending legislators' efforts to repair hurt feelings or damaged egos of constituents, settle feuds, or patch up divisions or problems that may have developed while the legislators were either away or inattentive.

fence, on the (1) apparently incapable of making a decision. (2) not wanting to offend people on various sides of an issue.

fence-sitter a legislator who has not made a decision on an issue or has a reputation for not making decisions. Fence-sitters often cannot make up their minds on how to vote, but some do refrain from voting in holding out for points of principle.

feudalism an economic, political, and social system that existed primarily between A.D. 1000–1500 in Europe. The system is based on the principle that a king or other overlord holds land, the rights to the use of which he may grant to others in return for favors. Those favors might include political and military loyalty as well as sexual service. Feudalism is based on the overlord-serf relationship rather than on a contractual agreement or basic rights and died out as a system when mercantilism and then industrialism became dominant.

Feudalism has existed in the United States with "company towns," plantation slavery, and even in nonunion retail stores, "sweat shops," and manufacturing plants. Systems resembling feudalism still prevail in Latin America and the Philippines on large estates owned by absentee landlords. In Japan business firms provide homes and entire social lives, including leisure activities, that indenture employees.

FGM female genital mutilation, clitoral mutilation. It is estimated that more than 100 million girls around the world have undergone this brutal procedure.

Fifth Amendment an amendment to the U.S. Constitution as part of the Bill of Rights which grants a series of rights to the accused or defendants in actions by the federal government. These include: (1) no one will be held for a capital or infamous crime (felony) unless he or she is indicted by a grand jury; (2) no person shall twice be put in jeopardy (tried) for the same offense; (3) a person cannot be required to testify against him/herself or incriminate him/herself; (4) a person cannot be deprived of life, liberty, or property without due process of the law (in federal cases); and (5) private property cannot be taken for public use by condemnation without just compensation. These protections have been extended to state legal actions by the Fourteenth Amendment and by the Supreme Court's constitutional interpretation.

"Taking the Fifth" is a maneuver used often in courtrooms when the witness chooses not to testify and wants to protect him/herself from incrimination. The term became well known during the first televised Senate hearings on organized crime (1950–51), chaired by Senator Estes Kefauver (D–Tenn.), in which one mobster after another declined to answer questions. More recently it became familiar during the televised congressional hearings on the Watergate and Iran-Contra scandals in which Nixon, Reagan, and George H. W. Bush administration officials "took the fifth," exercising their rights to protect themselves from discussing possible involvement in criminal activity. In 2001, two friends of and contributors to Clinton campaigns and Clinton's presidential library "took the fifth" to avoid testifying before a congressional committee regarding their roles in his presidential pardon of Marc Rich.

filibuster to obstruct or delay passage of a bill in the U.S. Senate by supporting a minority position and making long-winded speeches including irrelevant issues, yawns, songs, fairy tales, and reading from an encyclopedia. Filibustering can result in withdrawal of a bill. It is supported by a basic Senate policy allowing unlimited debate, but can be cut off by a 60 percent vote of all senators for "cloture," which calls for closing debate.

final election an election usually held in November in which candidates who won primary election nominations, either through party primaries or by placing in the top two finishers, run against each other to decide the winner. The candidate with the most votes wins the final election. Some candidates address different issues or take different positions on the same issues in the final election from those they took in the primary. Final election candidates also try to attract the supporters of defeated primary contenders to win over their supporters and add to the vote.

Financial Disclosure Act   A British Columbia (Canada) regulation that requires local election candidates to disclose contributions and expenditures.

fireside chats   a series of radio chats held by President Franklin D. Roosevelt, beginning on March 12, 1933, to explain his policies to the listening public, allay fears concerning the Great Depression, and outline federal governments steps to reopen the banks. Chats suggest informal and familiar conversation without strict format. FDR's chats were friendly but serious, one-directional, and well planned. The entire nation would pause for these broadcasts, which gave ample opportunity to display President Roosevelt's distinctive, confident, and pleasant voice.

firestorm   a nearly overwhelming series of political reverses, scandals, or revelations occurring in a short period of time and requiring damage control, changes in behavior, thinking, or performance and personnel.

First lady   wife of the president of the United States, first applied to Mrs. Ulysses S. Grant.

first peoples   indigenous peoples, aboriginals, people of First Nations, Native Canadians or Americans, Indians.

first strike   in international political vernacular, the use of nuclear or any other weapons to attack an enemy before the enemy attacks you. First strike probably would also mean "last strike" in nuclear war.

The Japanese attack on Pearl Harbor was a preemptive strike in which they attacked the United States first to destroy the American Pacific fleet, to prevent the United States from attacking them.

First World   (1) a term used occasionally in reference to the prosperous industrialized Western European and North American countries, Australia, and New Zealand. (2) the part of the world that experienced the 19th-century Industrial Revolution. See also SECOND WORLD and THIRD WORLD.

fiscal year   any 12-month period between settlement of accounts. The U.S. government fiscal year begins October 1 and ends September 30 every year, providing a new administration and/or new Congress a substantial period of time to prepare, debate, and adopt a budget.

fishing expedition   legislative investigation for partisan or political purposes to embarrass the subject with the remote hope of finding negative evidence.

flak   strong opposition to a proposal, position, or program.

flat tax   a tax system in which everyone is charged the same percentage of income for taxes, regardless of income level. Democrat Jerry Brown advocated a flat tax in his 1992 presidential bid, Republican Steve Forbes recommended a flat tax in his 1996 and 2000 presidential attempts, and Reform/Canadian Alliance leaders Preston Manning and Stockwell Day advocate flat or single taxes in Canada. See also SINGLE TAX.

flexible response   a military/political strategic doctrine based on the premise that a government should be prepared with a full range of possible defensive and offensive strategies to face serious war or confrontations as a means to keep war from escalating quickly in response to attack. Constant one-upmanship in arms kept on hand leads to arms races or cold war. Flexible response is the opposite of threatened massive retaliation, which has been the usual U.S. strategy. Opponents fear there is no limit or cutoff to this gradual escalation of military violence and that it could lead, step by step, to nuclear war.

flip-flop   changes of position, back and forth from one side of an issue to another.

floater   on election day a person who moves around to different precincts and votes in the name of dead people and people who have moved.

floor   "on the floor of the House or Senate" means (1) that a bill is being considered, or (2) that the senator or representative is actually in the chamber where the full Senate or House meets.

floor fight   an argument of principle, credentials, or position among delegates on the floor of a political convention. Usually a floor fight means leaders could not control followers and force them to agree in committee meetings and that delegates hope to persuade leaders and other delegates to accept their position.

F.O.B.'s   friends of Bill (Clinton). F.O.B.'s surfaced during Arkansas governor Bill Clinton's 1992 presidential campaign. Clinton and his wife Hillary Rodham Clinton saved names, addresses, and phone numbers and seemed to have kept in communication with every person they ever met in their lives. Clinton enlisted F.O.B.'s to start up his campaign in many states, even if they had no political experience. F.O.B.'s primary attribute was loyalty, which made them trusted with campaign, transition, and, for some, administration responsibility and influence.

focus groups   groups of people selected as representative of a cross section or specific interest who are asked questions so that the questioners can discover the group's thinking. Focus groups are sometimes used by candidates to figure out what positions they should take on issues.

Foggy Bottom   (1) the nickname for the U.S. Department of State, whose offices originally were built on Washington, D.C., swampland from which a foggy mist still rises. (2) a residential area near the Department of State. (3) Lee Iacocca's adjective to describe diplomacy theorists. It may be assumed that he referred to establishment, beltway government employees whose thinking he and some liberals regard as limited, narrow, and out of touch with the real world.

food stamps federally supplied stamped paper shaped like money (although smaller) in various monetary denominations. Food stamps are given or sold at less than face value to qualifying unemployed or low-income persons for use as cash equivalents to buy essential foods.

Conservatives see the program as wasteful and inciting fraud on the part of many recipients. Conservative Republican president Ronald Reagan tried to lower the poverty level, i.e., reduce the maximum income one could earn and still receive food stamps, in an effort to reduce the number of recipients.

Liberals tend to favor the food stamp program to help those without jobs and those losing jobs because of the declining economy during the Reagan and Bush presidencies. Some also believe purchases with food stamps keep one segment (food industry) of the economy and national agricultural inventory moving. Conservatives counter that social programs supported by liberals, such as food stamps, burden the country's economy by spending money on people who do not produce anything.

foreign policy the policy of a nation in dealing with other countries and international organizations. In the United States, foreign policy is developed by the president with the assistance of the secretary of state and specialists and diplomats in the State Department. In addition, both houses of Congress have input through committees on foreign relations in the Senate and foreign affairs in the House. The Senate must "advise and consent" in approving treaties, the appointment of high level State Department officials and ambassadors. Also influential in developing American foreign policy can be the CIA (by supposedly, but not always, giving impartial intelligence data on other nations), the National Security Council, and the National Security Adviser, the military and even private contacts of the president and his advisers.

In the 20th century, presidents increasingly dominated final decisions on foreign policy. The role of the Senate diminished, while that of the military, security and intelligence advisers has grown, diffusing determination and responsibility and at times making unclear exactly what American foreign policy is.

Fornigate label given by Democratic members of Congress for divorces and affairs among "family values" preaching Republicans, according to former representative Pat Schroeder (D–Colo.) in her *24 Years of House Work and the Place Is Still a Mess*.

Founding Fathers 39 of the original 55 drafters of the U.S. Constitution who completed and signed the final document. The group included George Washington, Benjamin Franklin, James Madison, Alexander Hamilton, and James Wilson. The term also loosely includes the signers of the Declaration of Independence and patriot leaders not present at the Constitutional Convention, including Thomas Jefferson, John Adams, Patrick Henry, and John Hancock.

Four Freedoms President Franklin Delano Roosevelt's specified social and political objectives stated before Congress on January 6, 1941, in his eighth State of the Union Message. The Four Freedoms are (1) freedom of speech and expression, (2) freedom of worship of one's choice, (3) freedom from want by securing a healthy, peaceful life for all, and (4) freedom from fear by worldwide arms reduction so that "no nation will be in a position to commit an act of physical aggression against any neighbor—anywhere in the world."

Fourteen Points the name given to President Woodrow Wilson's declaration on January 8, 1918, during World War I, in which Wilson outlined the aims for a postwar world, asked for "open covenants," freedom of the seas, the right of nationalities' self-determination, a league of nations, and other efforts to assure long-range, amicable peace, as well as some specific changes in borders.

Fourteenth Amendment to the U.S. Constitution (1868) extended most of the Bill of Rights and the rest of the Constitution to the states. While most of it related to post–Civil War issues, such as protection of former slaves, Section One stated that "no state shall deprive any person of life, liberty, or property, without due process of law; nor deny any person within its jurisdiction the equal protection of the laws." This broad language has been applied to all citizens.

franchise (1) the right to vote. (2) to sell a store or business formula for limited use to someone who will use all the accoutrements and products to run his/her business somewhat independently.

franking privilege a right of members of Congress and members of the government's executive branch to send mail free of cost to them but at the public's expense. Franking has long been controversial, because the line between sending mail at the public's expense for the public's benefit or for the officeholder's campaign benefit is a fine one. Members of Congress tend to flood their districts (especially right before elections) with newsletters, notices of meetings and appearances, and other materials extolling or demonstrating their concern for the voters, using their franking privilege. Opponents of incumbent representatives often challenge their use of postage-free mail as constituting campaign promotions instead of constituent information pieces.

Fraternity (Fraternité) (1) part of the French Revolution cry for "Liberté, Egalité, Fraternité." A term that suggests a concept of mutually beneficial brotherhood that might include communal life, mutual support, and respect, based upon a shared experience or goal. Fraternity may be found in clubs, labor unions, cults, philosophical societies, and political parties. (2) a university student social organization usually with "chapters" on many campuses, and often with reputations for community, high jinks, drinking, and snobbery. Bonds and friendships cemented in college fraternities often carry over into students' adult lives in politics and business.

free-market environmentalism (1) a theory that environmental problems are best handled by commerce, property rights, and self-rule. (2) a system in which commercial companies are offered financial incentives to conduct business in an environmentally sound way.

free vote a legislative vote in which members of the legislative body are told by their leadership that they can vote as they wish, rather than according to the party line.

freedom the state or condition of being free and having the right to do exactly what one wants to do. Freedom was part of the French Revolution cry for "Liberté, Egalité, Fraternité." Three levels of freedom include (1) national freedom from domination by other nations, (2) individual human freedoms, and (3) having the possibility to do something. See also FOUR FREEDOMS.

Freedom Now a chanted, shouted slogan used by Civil Rights Movement activists. Often it is used as an echoing rallying cry: "What do we want?" "Freedom." "When do we want it?" "Now!"

Freedom of Assembly the right guaranteed by the First Amendment to the U.S. Constitution to hold public gatherings and meetings, and to form associations without government interference.

Some law enforcement agencies subjectively judge the quality of focal topics of assemblies and break up gatherings, civil disobedience demonstrations, and some parades, particularly if they disagree with the participants' expressed opinions. Such an act violates both the public's right to assemble and to speak.

In the late 1950s and 1960s southern sheriff's deputies regularly violated citizens' rights to assemble by attacking civil rights demonstrators with clubs, guns, high-powered hoses, and attack dogs.

In 1965, Alameda County, California, sheriff's deputies shot tear gas at anti–Vietnam War demonstrators, and that action witnessed the start of arrests, disruptions, and excess force often used against assemblies of peace advocates, culminating in the Chicago police action against anti-war demonstrators and delegates during the 1968 Democratic National Convention and shootings of student demonstrators at Kent State and Jackson State universities (1970) by national guardsmen. In 1990, the American Civil Liberties Union defended the Ku Klux Klan's right to assemble and the right of former Klan official David Duke to have his name placed on presidential primary ballots from which he had been barred.

Conservatives tend to believe they can interpret the Constitution narrowly and restrict others' freedom of assembly if the purpose offends them. Liberals usually favor everyone's rights to assemble, including those holding opinions contrary to their own.

Freedom of Information Act (1966) a law that requires all government agencies to give to any citizen who requests his/her file unless the information includes certain exclusionary categories such as violations of other people's privacy or national security. This act evolved following the revelation that J. Edgar Hoover's

FBI and the Internal Revenue Service had amassed information on certain individuals who had opposed the government's policies, or were personal enemies of Mr. Hoover or other officials. The act, originally resulting from the efforts of Congressman John Moss (D–Calif.), allowed those subjects to demand a copy of the information gathered about them. Anti–Vietnam War activists Daniel Ellsberg and Tom Hayden were among targeted protestors who asked for their files. In recent years it has been used frequently by news and research organizations to obtain inside information on government policies and actions. Currently a government agency has 10 working days to respond to formal requests, a deadline rarely met.

Freedom of Religion

Freedom of Religion a First Amendment provision that bars any law that prohibits the "free exercise" by any person of the right to believe in and belong to a religion, and to worship privately or publicly without fear of reprisal. Some religious practices, such as animal sacrifice by various Caribbean cults, peyote smoking by American Indians, or intimidating ceremonies by the Ku Klux Klan, have been permitted under this freedom. Conscientious religious objections to serving in the military or saluting the American flag have been found by the U.S. Supreme Court to be protected.

Freedom of Press

Freedom of Press a right guaranteed by the First Amendment to the U.S. Constitution providing the right to publish freely without censorship or governmental interference. The principle is supposed to apply to every size and kind of publication.

Freedom of the press is violated when publishers of material in conflict with a president's or FBI director's statements are intimidated by IRS audits, FBI searches, or blacklisting from employment. The Administration of President George H. W. Bush allegedly violated freedom of the press provisions by prohibiting cameras from photographing or televising shots from the Iraqi war theater or shots of wounded and killed Iraqis.

Freedom of Speech

Freedom of Speech a freedom "guaranteed" by the First Amendment to the U.S. Constitution to include the right to express opinions in public through any medium.

The right has been challenged many times, including the Sedition Act, the Gag Rule in court cases or abortion advice, attitudes of some police toward demonstrators and dissenters, and actions by university executives regarding professors' and students' expressions on issues such as racism against whites and Asians (Berkeley, 1990). A Cincinnati, Ohio, gallery owner was arrested (1990) and later acquitted for hanging Robert Mapplethorpe's photographic exhibit on the basis that it was pornographic. Senator Jesse Helms (R–N.C.) and conservative presidential candidate Patrick Buchanan advocated withholding National Endowment for the Arts funds unless all art works proposed for funding were clearly not controversial (pornographic or irreligious). Such an act limits a person's right to free speech, particularly when the judgment is subjective and inconsistent, as are the guidelines.

Conservatives feel they have an obligation to make such judgments to save the country from offensive "controversy," smut, or the anti-Christ. Liberals consider such potential restrictions to constitute censorship and often are politically motivated.

free ride a situation that arises when an officeholder runs for a higher office during an election when his/her term in his/her current office has not expired. If such a candidate loses, he/she may remain in the office he/she already holds.

Freedom Riders anti-segregation Americans who traveled (usually by bus) between 1961 and 1964 to southern states such as Mississippi, Alabama, and Louisiana to assist in voter registration of blacks and desegregation of public facilities. Freedom riders were mostly young, white students, community activists, and lawyers. Threatened, beaten (Birmingham and Montgomery, Alabama), often jailed, and sometimes murdered (Philadelphia, Mississippi), members and associates of the Congress of Racial Equality (CORE) and the Student Non-Violent Coordinating Committee (SNCC) gave moral and practical support to southern blacks striving for political, civil, and economic equality, and their efforts helped to broaden the civil rights movement.

Free Silver Movement a late 19th-century populist campaign based on the belief that producing unlimited silver money would stimulate the economy and equalize economic chances. Led by Democratic-Populist presidential candidate William Jennings Bryan, the movement was joined by Populists, Grangers, Greenbackers, and economically distressed farmers to expand the economy and escape the clutches of eastern financiers who controlled the gold supply.

The battle raged into the 1896 presidential election campaign and led to the Democratic Party's defeat since it had sided with the Free Silver position. The resulting Republican-dominated Congress passed the Gold Standard Act (1900) ending the debate temporarily. Bimetallism (gold and silver support of currency) was resurrected again during the Great Depression and the issue was settled when President Franklin D. Roosevelt took the United States off the gold standard in 1933.

Free Soil Party (1848) a short-lived political party comprised of anti-slavery New York Democrats known as "Barnburners" who believed the western territories had to join the union as free (no slavery) states, those who favored abolition of slavery and felt dominated by southern slaveholders, former Liberty Party members, and some anti-slavery Whigs. They held a convention (1848), nominating former president Martin Van Buren. With the slogan "free soil, free speech, free labor, and free men," they obtained 10 percent of the vote (1848), and 5 percent for John P. Hale (1852). At their peak, they elected 10 Free Soilers to Congress. Most adherents joined the Republican Party, which was formed in 1854.

Free Speech Movement a political and social movement that began at the University of California at Berkeley (1964), triggered by U.C. officials' denial of political groups' rights to pass out printed information against the Vietnam War and other causes (including even students supporting conservative Republican Barry Goldwater for president), and eventual denial of the right to assemble, both of which are supposed to be guaranteed by the First Amendment to the U.S. Constitution. Student Mario Savio became the symbolic leader of the protest, standing on cars to speak, and leading sit-ins at the university's Sproul Hall. U.C. police, Berkeley city police, and Alameda County sheriffs overreacted with brutality, tear gas, and helicopters. Although temporarily defeated, the student effort led to free expression on almost all American campuses.

free trade an international economic system without trade tariffs or import or export controls between among or the member nations. Occasionally associated nations do impose tariffs against imports from nations not belonging to their free trade group. The European Economic Community (EEC) allows free trade between and among its members, but the organization places import taxes on goods from nations not belonging to the EEC.

Debate rages over whether free trade benefits producers/manufacturers or union labor, since import taxes theoretically protect producers/laborers in the importing country. Scottish economist Adam Smith (1723–90) first theorized that free trade would allow for division of labor, production of what each nation makes best, and even encourage specialization and greater efficiency. President George H. W. Bush advocated free trade with Mexico and Canada to counteract the EEC's economic clout and rectify trade imbalances. President Bill Clin-

ton supported free trade with reservations and brought about "side agreements" to cover topics such as minimum wages and the environment. Opponents claimed free trade would encourage more manufacturers to take plants to other countries to take advantage of cheaper labor, further increasing U.S. unemployment and trade imbalances. The North American Free Trade Act (NAFTA) passed both the House and the Senate in November 1993 and took effect in January 1994, and was also approved by Canada. (See NAFTA.) Trends toward free trade recommended by the World Trade Organization have inspired fear and protests in the United States on the basis that jobs would be lost to countries with lower-cost labor and laborers in other countries would be abused and unprotected.

friendly fire a term first used publicly by U.S. Army spokesmen during the Vietnam War to describe Americans killing Americans and allies in action by error. The term later gained currency during the Iraqi War (1991), in which U.S. military spokespeople chose words carefully to refer to Americans bombing and shooting down planes of their own countrymen. More Americans were killed in the Middle East during the Gulf War by American friendly fire than by the "enemy." Most conservatives generally viewed the term with an attitude of sorrow and sacrifice, whereas many liberals could not imagine any "fire" or killing as "friendly."

front loading a practice in U.S. presidential elections in which states compete to host the early primaries in a presidential election, resulting in bunching of primaries early in a presidential election year. States seek to be first to get media attention, commercial benefits, and advertising revenues.

front runner   the candidate deemed to be leading in the public's favor before an election. The front runner is often expected to win, and he/she becomes the primary target of challengers' rhetoric. He/she is the person to catch and beat.

fruits, flakes, and nuts   Republican insiders' reference to the California Democratic Party and its activists.

Fulbright Act of 1946   an act conceived by Senator J. William Fulbright (D–Ark.) to create a scholarship program to improve international understanding through educational and cultural exchanges between students. The act called for use of money from the sale of foreign war surplus property for educational travel grants. The Fulbright Act and other educational bills resulted in the Fulbright-Hayes Act or Cultural Exchange Act of 1961. Most Fulbright grants go to students, teachers, advanced researchers, trainees, and observers in more than 100 countries around the world.

full-court press   a basketball term used by legislators to mean applying all available pressure to get something done.

full disclosure   complete and honest revelation of all information and documents relevant to an investigation, withholding or hiding nothing.

fund-raiser   (1) a person who raises money for a cause or a candidate. (2) an event at which money is paid by those attending to benefit a cause or candidate.

Professional fund-raisers usually are paid by the committee organized to promote a cause or candidate. Others receive a percentage of funds taken in. At typical fund-raiser events, those who pay for tickets often pay much more for their ticket than the value of what the receive. One might pay $100 for a $10 dinner, or $10,000 for a $100 dinner. Many contributors who go to fund-raisers expect nothing in return and consider their donation to be their public duty while others expect favors in return, such as road-building contracts or appointments to positions of power or influence.

Fusionists   a Liberal Party and Republican Party coalition in New York on whose liberal Republican ticket Fiorello La Guardia first ran successfully for mayor in 1934 and served until 1945. The two parties often combined efforts as Fusionists to prevent Democratic Party victories. Of his opponents, La Guardia chided, "I could run on a laundry ticket and beat these political bums. . . ."

gag rule a rule usually used in courts or in confidential hearings that prohibits discussion of the case or issue outside the formal chambers or with anyone outside the sphere of interrogation and consideration. Usually the gag rule is issued to protect those involved, but it can also be used to hide details of a hearing from the public. President George H. W. Bush applied the gag rule to federally funded medical clinics to prevent them from disseminating abortion information. President Bill Clinton lifted this use of the gag rule on his first day in office as president.

Gallup Poll a public opinion poll devised by George H. Gallup to gauge the thinking and emotions of a voting public. Known officially as the American Institute of Public Opinion, the Gallup Poll is the grandfather of a burgeoning group of opinion survey organizations. In a typical poll, the Gallup organization samples 1,000–2,000 persons, extrapolates results (with a two to five percent margin of error), and forwards them to the medium or entity that paid for the polling services. Often the Gallup Poll and some of its imitators obtain accurate results, but they also predicted Dewey over Truman in 1948, when Truman beat Dewey.

Other hazards include (1) the sampling might not be balanced since it relies on so few responses, (2) wording may be inappropriate or contrived to obtain desired results, (3) the poll may exert undue influence on voters and affect voters' opinions in self-fulfilling prophecy.

game plan agreed upon strategy.

gang a group of people, usually young, who come together to share rules, standards, codes of behavior, community, and family feelings in place of other fulfillments of those needs. Gangs often scare outsiders, fight for turf ranging from the right to stand on a street corner to drug deals, sometimes work for neighborhood good, and perform a social function for those involved. Gang wars have resulted in the early death of thousands of young blacks and Hispanics, and they should be looked at seriously for signals of society's needs and trends. Gang symbols include colors of clothes members wear. Outsiders might be harmed if they unknowingly wear one gang's colors while present in a rival gang's territory. On occasion gangs have participated in get-out-the-vote drives.

GAO   See GENERAL ACCOUNTING OFFICE.

Gaullism   a conservative French political philosophy named for the views of France's autocratic last prime minister of the Fourth Republic and first president of the Fifth Republic, Charles De Gaulle (1890–1970). Gaullism strongly emphasizes national (and personal) independence, a centralized state with a powerful executive, constant distrust and suspicion of international movements or cooperation, and reliance on France's own military forces. Originally comprised of De Gaulle devotees who worshiped him as a near savior, modern Gaullism is a conservative party enjoying support from the middle and upper classes, church goers, and senior citizens.

gay   (1) happy or light-hearted. (2) homosexual, usually referring to a male homosexual.

gay rights movement   a movement originating in the late 1960s to reaffirm that homosexuals have equal rights and freedom from discrimination in medical treatment, housing, employment, health benefits from partners' employers, and insurance benefits, as well as respect. In some cities gay rights activists have learned to manage the political process and language to become influential and forceful political blocs. Gay rights activists have elected four members of the San Francisco Board of Supervisors, including Roberta Achtenberg, nominated by President Bill Clinton (1993) to be assistant secretary of housing and urban development. Ms. Achtenberg was the first openly gay person to be nominated to a federal office requiring Senate confirmation. She was confirmed by the Senate in May 1993.

President Bill Clinton proposed terminating the ban on homosexuals in the military during his first week in office. Because the proposal was strongly opposed by military leaders, many conservative lawmakers and, presumably, by their constituents, Senator Sam Nunn (D–Ga.) proposed a "don't ask, don't tell" solution. Mr. Clinton compromised his statement and then supported a revised measure to allow gays in the military if they do not say they are gay. In return the military will not ask questions about sexual orientation.

Conservatives and the religious right dislike, disparage, and treat the gay rights movement with disapproval. They consider gayness a sin, unnatural, and, to some, a personal and sexual threat. They find more comfort with the old status quo, in which gays kept their gayness "in the closet" or out of sight. A New York judge ruled (1992) that gays could not walk in the city's St. Patrick's Day parade, a controversial issue between religious and liberal Irish Catholics.

Liberals generally tolerate gays and often assist in the gay rights movement. The city of San Francisco and some other local jurisdictions acknowledge "domestic partner" relationships, certifying them in city hall ceremonies and extending benefits to partners of gay city employees. Many other nations are much more tolerant of homosexuality than is the United States. In 1999 Vermont approved gay unions, but stopped short of sanctioning gay marriages.

gender gap a label for lack of understanding or shared premises and language between men and women. In politics it may refer to male or female support for a candidate. Recommended reading: *You Just Don't Understand* by Deborah Tannen (New York: Ballantine, 1990).

General Accounting Office (GAO) a federal agency empowered to audit any and all spending by the executive branch and report its findings directly to Congress. It operates independently and is directed by the comptroller general of the United States, who is appointed by the president for a single 15-year term and confirmed by the Senate. The GAO can also be used by Congress to investigate suspected wrongdoing. The GAO has uncovered mishandling of funds and has alerted Congress to problems and trends in expenditures. Address: 441 G Street, N.W., Washington, D.C. 20548. Tel.: (202) 512-3000; e-mail: webmaster@gao.gov; website: www.gao.gov

General Agreement on Tariffs and Trade (GATT) an international agreement implemented after World War II, in which cooperating countries negotiate reductions in tariffs leading toward free trade.

general election a regularly scheduled election at which winners are determined, often following a primary election. Usually the general election candidates are those who won their party's primary election nomination for office, or in a few states, the two candidates with the highest total vote.

general will a concept developed by Jean-Jacques Rousseau (1712–78) that became the motivating idea for direct or participatory democracy. The theory allowed for collective decisions made by all the people after they have considered what is good for all the people, as opposed to what is good for the individual. Rousseau suggested that liberty could only be enjoyed when every man could participate in the creation of laws over himself and, therefore, only had to obey laws he created. Women were never mentioned because they had no role in the decision process. In the United States, New England town hall meetings come closest to governing by general will.

Generation X early 1990s buzzword affixed to young adults between the ages of 18 and 29 whom the media could not identify with any other descriptive catchword. The term implies that Generation Xers have no group identity, which is their identity. They escape other categorization based on who their parents are, opposition to wars or institutions or any other philosophy.

genetic party identification a feeling of commitment to register in a political party because one's parents did.

geopolitics (1) the study of the relationship of political power and geography. (2) the belief that if a nation controls key geographical areas (heartland) it will be able to dominate the surrounding territory.

Geopoliticians who subscribe to the heartland theory sometimes contend that a controlling area is an ocean (such as the central Pacific) but more often it comprises the heartland of a continent, encompassing key trade routes, natural resources, barriers to invasion, large homogeneous populations, and access to neighbors. The science of geopolitics was first developed by British geographer Sir Halford John Mackinder (1861–1947) of the University of London, and in the United States by Captain Alfred Thayer Mahan (1840–1914), president of the Naval War College (1886–89), who wrote extensively on sea power and geopolitics after his retirement in 1896. Mahan believed that it was vital for the defense and strength of the United States to control the Pacific Ocean region. He influenced assistant secretary of the navy and later president Theodore Roosevelt on the importance of naval power. In Germany the chief exponent of geopolitics was Karl Haushofer (1896–1946), army general, geographer and writer, who influenced and advised Adolf Hitler as to the need to invade and control particular areas in order to permanently dominate Europe, and to join in a partnership with Japan to keep the United States from controlling the Pacific basin. Haushofer committed suicide the year after the German surrender.

Geopolitics should be an important study in the development of the foreign policies of major powers, particularly since geographic position can be one of the determining factors in assessing the strength and importance of other such powers. As the prime example, America's position in the Western Hemisphere, straddling both Atlantic and Pacific oceans, and possessing a large population and natural resources ensures the country from almost any threat of invasion and virtually guarantees that the United States will be a superpower under geopolitical theories. The heartland theory leads to the conclusion that China may dominate mainland Asia once it becomes modernized. It also appears that Germany in Central Europe, Russia in Eastern Europe, and Japan in the Pacific basin can be expected to continue as major powers based on these geopolitical concepts.

gerrymander the practice of drawing legislative districts to create a partisan voting balance to favor the beliefs, party, or candidates of those drawing the district boundaries. The custom was named for Massachusetts governor Elbridge Gerry (pronounced with a hard G) who signed into law (1812) a district drawn to favor a Jeffersonian Republican friend. The tailor-made district's shape resembled a salamander. "Gerry" plus "salamander" equals gerrymander (pronounced with a soft G.)

District lines actually can be drawn so that a state's minority party could win most of the legislative seats by including just enough voters of the party in most districts to prevail, while deliberately sacrificing other districts.

When the governor and the state legislature are of the same political party, they can gerrymander to their own party's benefit. When the governor and the legislature are of different parties, the governor can influence a fairer line drawing through threat of veto. Several states employ impartial commissions to draw district lines to avoid gerrymandering.

The party in control usually enjoys its power, while the party out of power sees the other party's line drawing as gerrymandering.

get out the vote (GOTV) a system organized by campaign staff and/or volunteers to make sure those voters sympathetic to their position or candidate actually vote. The process often involves scanning voter lists at polling places to determine who has not voted in a given election, calling those people to remind them to vote for your candidate or position, and even driving voters to the polls. In the late 1980s GOTV expanded to include use of absentee ballots by encouraging early mailing and hospital visits with ballot applications and then absentee ballots.

Gibbons v. Ogden **(1824)** a U.S. Supreme Court case decision written by Chief Justice John Marshall ruling that Congress had the exclusive right to regulate interstate commerce, and struck down state barriers to such commerce. The case involved a steamboat operator who was denied a license by one of the states that he serviced.

G. I. Forum organization of Hispanic veterans founded after World War II to lobby for Hispanics' rights and to provide valuable political action experience for Hispanic activists in the 1950s.

glad-handing shaking hands and generally jollying up constituents or contributors in a somewhat superficial, phony way to ingratiate oneself. Glad-handing is done in the course of campaigning or when one is thinking of running for political office. One of the most accomplished and best-known glad-handers was "Honey Fitz" Fitzgerald, one-time congressman and mayor of Boston and grandfather of President John F. Kennedy. "Honey Fitz" used to shake one person's hand while nodding to another, making each constituent feel personally recognized for an instant.

glass ceiling invisible promotion, position, and salary barriers that prevent women and minorities from breaking into or rising in some corporate, political, and governmental fields.

global economy the concept that nationalistic self-sufficiency is no longer relevant and that production, distribution, trade, and income occur among and for all nations and not just within a single nation's borders.

globalism economic and political theory and practice that sees the entire world as one economic entity in which communication and production and sale of goods have no barriers. Companies based in one country produce goods in other countries for sale in more countries, while food producers in one country contract with farmers in other countries to produce food to be exported from the growing country back to the first country. Globalism advocates believe less expensive labor in the producing country helps raise the economic level of those workers (however, while occasionally enslaving them to contractors and exposing them to hazardous chemicals), while opponents of globalism view it as taking jobs from one country and sending them abroad and taking advantage of poor foreign workers.

gold standard a monetary system in which all paper money and coinage was supported by stored gold. A major political issue from the 1870s until the 1930s, the existing gold standard was favored by those wanting a stable, noninflationary currency and opposed by debtors who would benefit from mild inflation and also by silver-mining interests. President Franklin D. Roosevelt took the country off the strict gold standard in 1933, turning to bimetallism. In real life, none of the world's currencies is fully backed by gold or gold and silver stockpiles.

good neighbor policy President Franklin D. Roosevelt's Latin American policy as suggested in his first inaugural address on March 4, 1933, which constituted a departure from what had been known as interventionism. With the help and diplomacy of Secretary of State Cordell Hull and Under Secretary Sumner Welles, the United States gave up certain privileges and practices detested by Latin Americans. At the Montevideo Conference (December 1933) the United States renounced its supposed "right" to intervene in other nations' internal affairs. The Platt Amendment sanctioning U.S. intervention in Cuba was nullified (1934) and American marines withdrew from Haiti (August 1934).

The policy's success was measured in U.S. terms by the quickness with which Latin American countries rallied to help the Allies in World War II. Latin America's distrust of American policy and war activity rose again with U.S. postwar involvement in Europe and Asia, as well as following intervention in the Dominican Republic and covert activity in Nicaragua, Chile, and other countries.

good offices political vernacular for influence, position, or power. One might be asked to "use your good offices to get me what I want," for example, a waiver on planning department regulations or a contract for my business.

good ole boys men who generally hold some seniority in belonging to "the club" of decision makers and who live politically by unwritten rules and mystique, which, they believe, give them the right to make decisions on who runs for office, who gets the contributions, who gets elected, and who takes what positions on issues important to their community or constituency. "Good ole boys" often represent the most conservative wing of their parties and uphold the status quo. They believe that women have few roles in truly important political matters. Good ole boys support a woman as their candidate only when that woman's election seems inevitable.

G.O.P. (Grand Old Party) nickname for the Republican Party. There is no equivalent for the Democratic Party, except for Republicans' usage of the word "Democrats," as in "Democrat Party," when they mean Democratic.

GOPAC a Republican political action committee created by House Speaker Newt Gingrich (R–Ga.) in the mid-1990s to provide funding for Gingrich to distribute to Republican projects and congressional candidates who supported his claimed "revolution" and "Contract with America" in the 1994–98 elections. Address: 122 C Street, N.W., Suite 505, Washington, D.C. 20001. Tel.: (202) 484-2282; FAX: (202) 783-3306; e-mail: webmaster@gopac.org; website: www.gopac.org

G.O.P.-TV cable television network funded by the Republican Party to communicate with members, potential members, and the general public.

government assistance financial help from the government, including welfare relief and assistance through farm subsidies, loans, guarantees of private institutional loans, college loans, technical research assistance, and grants to states and individuals in business.

Conservatives generally favor limits on welfare assistance to the poor including lower benefits to single mothers with several children, whom they regard as promiscuous, lazy, and a drain on public funds. Liberals and others claim this is a racist position against African-American welfare mothers. At the same time, Republicans and conservatives favor government assistance to businessmen and farmers, who are mainly white and usually vote Republican. During the 1980s–1990s recession, conservative Republican president George H. W. Bush advocated reduction of Aid For Dependent Children and limitations of unemployment benefits to workers laid off during the recession that Bush said did not exist. President Bush only relented when public outrage became so strong that he could see a political benefit to himself by extending assistance.

Liberals and most Democrats view government assistance as necessary to help those who cannot help themselves, which may include multitudes during a recession/depression. During the Clinton administration, welfare programs were reduced with bipartisan support in Congress.

government interference any action by the government that one can see affecting oneself directly against one's will, that one does not like, or that gives no benefit to the person or business regulated. If a government act helps a person, that person rarely regards the act as government interference.

Conservatives see regulating airlines, banks, savings and loans, and other businesses, setting standards of business conduct, and implementing workers' protections as government interference. This view is sometimes shared by moderates and even liberals in specific instances. There is general resistance to governmental mini-managing in the name of regulation.

Liberals usually favor (as a positive influence) some controls and regulations to protect the public's interest.

They do not regard the government's role as negative interference, per se.

governor   chief elected official of a state.

governor general   representative of the king or queen (Canada) appointed by the monarch on recommendation of the prime minister. The governor general theoretically reports to the monarch, makes appointments recommendations, and delivers the "speech from the throne" for the prime minister.

Governor Moonbeam   California governor Edmund G. "Jerry" Brown Jr. (1975–1983), many of whose environmental and social programs and experimentation with new technologies seemed to his opposition to be from outer space but that appear more reasonable currently. The nickname resurfaced when Governor Brown ran for president in 1976 and in 1992 when he again ran for president, coming in a distant second to Bill Clinton in delegates to the Democratic National Convention. In 1998 Jerry Brown was elected mayor of Oakland, California, where he has proved to be a proactive, practical, and pragmatic administrator.

gradualism   an attitude that favors a gradual, slow approach to change of social, economic, and political institutions through democratic processes instead of violent revolution. Gradualism is often the point of demarcation between liberals who define themselves as gradualists and radicals who demand immediate, total change. In European history, Soviet communists advocated revolution, while the Italian Communist Party and Britain's Fabians (moderate socialists) utilized gradualist tactics.

Conservatives and liberals generally accept gradualism as a means of progress in democratic societies but differ sometimes on issues of speed and degree of change.

graft   (1) taking advantage of one's political position or any position of authority to take money or property dishonestly. (2) that which is taken by this means. Well-known American examples of politicians and their friends who developed webs of graft include New York Boss Tweed, several members of President Warren G. Harding's inner circle, President Lyndon Johnson's pal Billy Sol Estes, Illinois governor Otto Kerner, and Vice President Spiro Agnew. Graft exists at all levels of government and comes in the form of bribes, kickbacks, contracts granted in violation of rules, and other special favors.

Gramm-Rudman (Gramm-Rudman-Hollings Act, 1985)   a statute enacted to lower the federal government deficit by increments until a balanced budget was achieved with a target date of 1991. If the government failed to lower the deficit for any year's quota, Gramm-Rudman would enact the automatic reduction of government spending, cutting every department equally, a provision ruled unconstitutional in 1986 by the Supreme Court in *Bowsher v. Synar*. Because the budget deficit actually increased during President George H. W. Bush's tenure following passage of Gramm-Rudman, Congress extended the deadline for a balanced budget to 1997, when it was achieved under President Bill Clinton.

grandstand to make a flashy, sometimes outrageous and irrelevant speech to draw attention to oneself and/or away from someone else.

grapevine rumor network.

grass roots (1) the common people or general body of voters. (2) a political movement that starts with the people in neighborhoods and filters upward, as opposed to the elites or the establishment who dictate downward.

Republican political organizations talk of the grass roots but do not rely on them for activity. Generally they believe that clubs of young businessmen, Republican Women, and fundraising groups satiate the people's need for participation. Most G.O.P. communication with these groups comes from above instead of ideas originating in the clubs and filtering upward. Democrats often talk about grass roots, the people, and people's efforts in campaigns, and they usually do a better job of pretending that grass-roots people's opinions count. Both parties turn out grass-roots volunteers for elections, but these efforts are more crucial to Democrats who usually raise less money than do Republicans. Some conservative Republicans boast that the Christian churches form their grass-roots network.

The importance of grass-roots politics greatly diminished in the early 1970s by campaign emphasis on "the media." Television advertising became so highly valued that all campaign efforts were aimed at raising money to buy commercial television time. Door-to-door campaigning was replaced by candidates meeting principally with people who could give them large amounts of money, thereby buying special, unequal influence.

Beginning with the 1992 presidential campaign, true grass-roots campaigning has shown some renewed popularity.

gravitas a media catchall term for a combination of charm, sophistication, seriousness, dedication, and credibility.

Gray Panthers (1) originally a coalition of activist senior citizen groups that first exercised their clout in the 1970s. (2) generic term for energetic advocates for rights of the elderly. Address: 1424 16th Street, N.W., Washington, D.C. 20036. Tel.: (202) 387-3111.

gray white men a reference to appearances, personalities, and political views of senior, usually conservative men in power. They are stereotyped as having pale complexions, with diminishing gray hair, and wear expressionless gray suits. See also SUITS.

Great Depression an economically disastrous slump in the United States, Canada, and Europe that began with the crash of the American stock market (October 1929) and was characterized by business failures, high unemployment, and personal and social turmoil and upheaval between 1929 and 1939. In essence, capitalism had failed to cope with the sudden economic contraction following the 1920s economic boom and growth. World trade dropped by one-half.

Politically the Great Depression resulted in widespread dissatisfaction with President Herbert Hoover's conservative, limited problem-solving methods, based on his misplaced belief that the system was basically "sound." Extremist groups, both left and right, flourished everywhere in a desperate search for solutions, and Europeans and Asians succumbed to totalitarianism in search of saviors, including Hitler in Germany and the militaristic clique in Japan. American liberals offered alternatives, including reform of the financial system, broad-scale relief, and job creation by government expenditure. Their champion and leader, Franklin D. Roosevelt, became president in 1933.

Some theorists believe the Great Depression and other recessions are simply part of the natural economic cycle. Most analysts feel that the controls and limitations on speculation slow the process of decline and prevent recessions from becoming depressions as deep and as broad as the Great Depression.

Great Society Democratic president Lyndon Johnson's program of economic and social reforms and assistance programs including his "War on Poverty" to try to solve problems of poverty, malnutrition, poor housing, and access to medical care, announced on May 22, 1964. While Johnson did not expect to solve all these problems, he believed an effort should be made.

The Great Society appeared to be headed for success, but its dream failed, largely due to enormous expenditures diverted to conduct the escalating Vietnam War, although the Head Start preschool program continues.

Conservatives criticized it as "throwing money at problems." Liberals supported the Great Society concept and were ridiculed for favoring social programs over funding the war in Vietnam.

Green Card a document that allows a person from another country to work legally, earn income, and pay taxes in the United States. Potential workers who lack green cards may be referred to as illegals, illegal aliens, undocumented workers, and wetbacks. Certain numbers of immigrants from foreign countries receive green cards on quota-per-country or special circumstances bases.

Green Party USA originally a West German political party formed and led by Petra Kelly in 1979 to elect their candidates to Parliament and preserve the earth's fragile ecological balance. The Green Party's purpose and goals include "a society based on ten key values: ecological wisdom, social justice, grass-roots democracy, nonviolence, decentralization, community-based economics, post patriarchal values, respect for diversity, personal and global responsibility, and future focus." Founder Kelly was murdered, allegedly by her boyfriend, in 1992.

Green Party organizations exist in several countries and states, often so idealistically anarchistic that they have no structure by which to nominate candidates. In the United States they have qualified for the ballot in most states, but seldom field a full slate of candidates. By the late 1990s, Greens elected a few local officials and a California state legislator, who promptly changed her party affiliation to Independent. Consumer advocate Ralph Nader ran for President on the Green Party ticket in 2000 and received more than 2,000,000 votes. Address: 1134 Lawrence, Mass. 01842. Tel.: (978) 682-4353; FAX: (978) 682-4318; e-mail: gpusa@igc. org; website: www.greenparty.org

Greenback Party a post–Civil War 19th-century "third party" that favored printing paper money, not always backed up by stored gold, to inflate currency and enable farmers and other debtors to meet their obligations. The party reached its apex between 1876 and 1884, but its presidential candidates ran a poor third to the major party's candidates. Supporters elected 14 Greenback congressmen (1880), won a few local offices, and became a forerunner to Democratic candidate William Jennings Bryan's silverite bimetallism (1896).

Greenpeace an international (primarily American and Canadian) environmental group dedicated to "preserving the Earth and all the life it supports." Greenpeace came to prominence in October 1969, when its supporters blocked the border between Washington State and British Columbia to protest nuclear testing in the Aleutian Islands. Supposedly dedicated to nonviolence, nonpartisanship and positive internationalism, Greenpeace originally used intervention tactics such as sailing boats into nuclear test areas (first in 1971) and physically interfering with whaling and harp seal harvests. It has occasionally blown up ships engaged in such fishing or involved in nuclear testing. More recently Greenpeace has relied primarily on education and demonstrations.

Conservatives consider Greenpeace members to be troublesome radicals interfering with trade who oppose their philosophy that you should use what you need to in order to make the economy and your income work. Liberals often support Greenpeace's principles to preserve the environment, but they do not always agree with the group's tactics. Address: 1436 U Street, N.W., Washington, D.C. 20009. Tel.: (202) 462-1177; websites: www. greenpeace.org or www. greenpeaceusa.org

Grenada (1) a tiny British Commonwealth island nation in the West Indies. (2) the site of an invasion by U.S. marines (1983) ordered by President Ronald Reagan without a declaration of war by Congress, ostensibly to protect and rescue 1,000 American medical students Reagan believed threatened by Cuban communists he thought had taken over the country. The marines did find some Soviet arms but no substantial military force. President Reagan prohibited the press from accompanying the invasion in a restriction on press freedom and an effort to manage news. (3) a general term referring to American military intervention in small countries by American presidents without a congressional declaration of war.

American conservatives and hawks supported the effort to prevent a so-called domino effect engendered by communist invasion. Liberals thought it was a highly unnecessary effort to create a false enemy and rationalize increased military budget allocations and spending.

gridlock (1) traffic jam in which no one can move. (2) a political, legislative, or governmental impasse in which no progress is made because the system is stuck or blocked due to bureaucracy or lack of compromise, collaboration, or cooperation. Gridlock often occurs when the executive is of one political party and the legislature is dominated by another. See also DIVIDED GOVERNMENT.

Grits Canada: nickname for the Liberal Party.

groundswell a real or imagined development of grass-roots excitement and support for a candidate or position.

Group of Seven (G-7) the world's seven leading industrial nations, including the United States, Japan, Great Britain, Canada, France, Germany, and Italy. The G-7 governmental leaders meet annually to discuss trade balances and other issues of mutual concern. Russia now attends meetings, so the Group of Seven (G-7) has become the Group of Eight (G-8).

grow (the economy) a term created and used by 1992 Democratic presidential candidate Bill Clinton and his staff to express the need to create jobs and improve incomes, taxpaying abilities, and general productivity and buying power. What he meant, or how one grows an economy, no one knows. Apparently President Clinton used the word as a substitute for "develop" or "nurture." By mid-1993 candidates, elected officials, and cabinet members used the term "grow the economy" frequently, usually meaning to improve business and increase jobs.

gucci gulch where lobbyists hang out in Washington, D.C., or any other capital.

guerilla a member of a small, militant group who make surprise raids behind acknowledged battle lines. They often create destabilizing harassment of conventional forces, with the goal of provoking the enemy into an unwise response that would cause it loss of public support. Guerillas rarely allow themselves to get involved in a genuine, life-threatening confrontation with the enemy or another larger, superior group that might defeat them. Examples of guerilla warriors include some American "minutemen" in the American Revolution, Confederate irregulars in the Civil War, Allied partisans in World War II, Viet Cong fighters in Vietnam, and *contras* in Central America.

gun control various efforts to enact laws to register all guns, license gun owners, impose "waiting periods" to purchase guns, and/or ban some types of handguns and military-style weapons. The movement initially resulted from the assassination of President John F. Kennedy and gained momentum after the killings of Rev. Martin Luther King Jr., Robert Kennedy, and the attempted assassinations of Republican presidents Gerald R. Ford and Ronald Reagan.

In recent years gun control has centered around the Brady Bill, named for James Brady, President Reagan's press secretary, who was permanently injured during the attempted assassination of Reagan (March 30, 1981.) The bill requires registration of handguns and attempts to halt public sales of military-style automatic weapons.

Congress passed the Brady Bill and President Bill Clinton signed it in 1993. New efforts at gun control evolved following multiple fatal shootings in offices and schools, such as Columbine High School in Colorado, gang warfare, and possession of guns by children as young as five years old.

Conservatives, gun collectors, and some hunters view gun control as a licensing procedure designed to restrict their claimed constitutional right to bear arms. The National Rifle Association (N.R.A.) has made anti-gun control a crusade and recruiting tool. Liberals contend that the constitutional argument is invalid since the right to bear arms refers to a state's right to maintain a state militia, and that gun control is necessary to restrict sales, purchases, and use of "Saturday Night Specials" (small handguns) and assault weapons used in holdups and in crime- and insanity-driven killings, as well as accidental shootings. Ironically, many liberals who favor gun control to prevent killing also favor "choice" of abortion, while many conservatives who oppose gun control oppose abortion or a woman's right to choose abortion. Congress has enacted legislation making the importation of rapid-fire assault weapons illegal, but there are various loopholes such as failure to describe new weapons in the ban.

guns and butter   a reference to military and domestic programs.

In 1936 Hermann Goering, Hitler's air marshall, urged that Nazi Germany should put "guns before butter" to build up its military machine before its domestic needs. In 1966 President Lyndon Johnson altered the phrase to "guns and butter" as part of his argument to both escalate American involvement in the Vietnam War and continue his domestic "War on Poverty" as part of the Great Society. Johnson claimed the country could support both at the same time, which proved to be impossible.

hack longtime campaign worker, either paid or volunteer, who moves from one campaign to another with little conviction and who often does things with little imagination and based on "the way they have always been done."

halo effect a general impression of a person based on one or more favorable characteristics or impressions.

handbag a verb created in England meaning to treat a person (opponent) ruthlessly. The term comes from former prime minister Margaret Thatcher's practice of carrying a handbag on all important occasions, as well as a reference to the fear she and the handbag created.

Handgun Control, Inc. a prominent advocacy group that favors control of sales and ownership of handguns and semiautomatic weapons, thereby making it the leading adversary of the National Rifle Association. Founded in 1974 as the National Council to Control Handguns (NCCH), the group has gained greater public recognition since the involvement of Sarah Brady, wife of James Brady, President Ronald Reagan's press secretary who was shot and permanently disabled in John Hinckley Jr.'s attempt to assassinate the president. Address: 1225 Eye Street, N.W., Room 1100, Washington, D.C. 20005. Tel.: (202) 898-0792; FAX: (202) 371-9615; website: www.handguncontrol.org. See also GUN CONTROL.

handlers people who tell a candidate or officeholder how to act and what to say to achieve a specific result.

hanging chad See CHAD.

hard hats (1) people who work at laboring jobs that require they wear a hard hat to prevent injury from falling equipment or materials. (2) general reference to laborers, with oblique reference to supposed qualities such as stubbornness, low education level, and conservative, racist, and hawkish views.

hard-liner a person who holds to her/his position without willingness to compromise, negotiate, or change views.

hard money money given directly to a candidate or to his or her campaign, as opposed to "soft money" given to political parties. See SOFT MONEY.

(throw your) hat in the ring an expression meaning that you have become a candidate. It was first used in 1912 when someone asked Theodore Roosevelt if he would seek the Republican presidential nomination, and he answered: "My hat is in the ring."

Hatch Act (1939) an act that states that officers of the executive branch of the federal government "shall not take any active part in political management or in political campaigns." The act effectively prohibited most government employees, including state employees whose salaries come partially from federal funds, from participating in the American political process beyond voting. As it stood, even post office mail deliverers could not run as delegates to national party conventions. In September 1993, Congress passed legislation allowing federal employees to participate in political campaigns. Vice President Al Gore was criticized

for making campaign fund-raising telephone calls from his White House office in 1996.

While the Hatch Act was designed to protect government employees from undue influence and exploitation by candidates and officeholders, some of those employees have questioned whether the act violates their civil rights.

Hatched the constriction of federal employees from participating in politics, due to the Hatch Act. See also HATCH ACT.

hatchetman a person who carries demanding messages from public officials to people who want favors, forces wayward constituents into support against their will, or makes public attacks on behalf of an officeholder.

hate crimes crimes committed because of hate of another individual's or group's lifestyle, religious or political beliefs, or ethnicity. Nazi massive killing of Jews, killing of gays, and Ku Klux Klan burning of crosses at homes of blacks all qualify as hate crimes. The recent killings of gays have enkindled hopes of including violence against gays in hate crimes. Where "hate crimes" are defined in legislation, the result is that the sentences are longer than for the same illegal act (such as assault) without the hate factor.

hawk (1) originally referred to the "war hawks" in Congress who favored war against Great Britain in 1812. (2) an American who supported U.S. military action in Vietnam. During the Vietnam War, Democrats who backed liberal domestic policies, including President Lyndon Johnson, Dean Rusk, McGeorge Bundy, Robert McNamara, and Walter Rostow, became leading hawks and were supported in their views by conservatives. (3) an American who favors war over negotiation as a solution to international problems. (4) opposite of dove or pacifist.

Haymarket Riot a violent confrontation between police and labor in Chicago. On May 3, 1886, newspapers reported that in Chicago six people were killed by police at a McCormick Harvesting Machine Co. strike when strikers threw stones at scabs. The next day's protest at Haymarket Square proved peaceful until police tried to break it up. Someone, believed to have been an antiunion provocateur, intending to discredit the labor unions, threw a dynamite bomb that killed seven policemen. Their fellow officers opened fire, and many people were injured on both sides. Police and the newspapers raised public emotions to the point of hysteria.

Eight anarchist labor leaders were charged and convicted for conspiring with or aiding the unknown bomber. Four were hanged, one committed suicide, and the remaining three were pardoned (1893) by Democratic governor John Peter Altgeld, who found lack of due process and lack of evidence against those convicted after careful review of the trial transcript. This pardon cost Altgeld reelection but made him a legend for his political courage.

Public acceptance of the establishment story that labor radicals incited the riot badly damaged the labor union movement. It destroyed the Knights of Labor and made the American Federation of Labor (AFL) cautious and hesitant.

head of government the top-ranking person or executive in management of a government; the president of the United States, the prime minister of Canada, among others.

head of state (1) in U.S. the chief executive position (president) who holds real power. (2) in some countries, a monarch or other person who represents the nation, but primarily performs ceremonial functions, or has nominal power to appoint a prime minister or other head of government. In Canada and Great Britain Queen Elizabeth II is head of state but has no governing powers, while the **head of government** is the prime minister in each case.

headquarters a place where a campaign is managed and where volunteers and staff gather and do their work. Headquarters are often in vacant stores in downtown neighborhoods because the rent is often inexpensive and they are usually handy to the public. While they house the business of campaign management, they also become social centers for the people who like to work on campaigns.

Head Start a "Great Society" agency created in 1966 to help children (to age five) of low-income families so that the children may begin school with chances equal to their more affluent peers. Programs include nutrition, social competence, learning skills, health, language development, medical, dental, and mental health services. At least 90 percent of Head

Start children must come from below the poverty line, which changes. Head Start is one Great Society (Lyndon Johnson) program that is still supported by congressional leadership. In 2000 both candidates Vice President Al Gore and Governor George W. Bush advocated increased spending on Head Start. Use your local or county telephone book for the closest Head Start number.

health alliances groupings of Americans based upon geography, employment, union membership, religion, physician membership, or other common factors to purchase health insurance.

hearings meetings of state or federal legislative committees at which witnesses testify on legislation, question presidential appointments in the Senate or state executive appointees, or provide information on subjects the committee is investigating. Congressional committees have the power of subpoena and can call favored experts and advocates on various issues to testify.

Confirmation hearings in the Senate used to be settings in which candidates for cabinet posts or other high federal appointments were politely interrogated and affirmed their good reputations, but on occasion the hearings became confrontations between senators and the nominees over positions on issues, candidates' sex lives, drug habits, check bouncing, and club memberships.

Televised hearings have had a profound effect on public opinion on such subjects as organized crime (1950), Joseph McCarthy's claims of communist influence in government

(1954), Watergate (1974), and Iran-Contra (1987).

Using the hearing process to threaten and intimidate witnesses and as a sounding board for unsubstantiated attacks became common in the 1940s through 1960s by the once-powerful House Un-American Activities Committee (HUAC) and Senator Joseph McCarthy's committee on internal security. By charging political foes with being communists or "fellow travelers" the hearings were employed to suppress opinions and free speech, and damage reputations.

hegemony the political dominance of one state or government in a group of nations or of one class over another by imposition of its values and beliefs on the rest of the nations or people. Examples include U.S. influence in much of Latin America, the former domination of China over North Korea, and the control exercised by the Soviet Union over Poland, East Germany, and Czechoslovakia during the cold war.

Heritage Foundation an ultraconservative think tank and lobbying organization that is "dedicated to the principles of free competitive enterprise, limited government, individual liberty, and a strong national defense." Founded in 1973 with funds donated by right-wing partisan Joseph Coors of Coors Brewing Company, the Heritage Foundation often advocates "bombs and bucks" as solutions to international problems. Address: 214 Massachusetts Avenue, N.E., Washington, D.C. 20002. Tel.: (202) 546-4400; FAX: (202) 546-8328; e-mail: info@heritage.org; website: www.heritage.org

Hessian (1) paid soldier in the Revolutionary War. (2) slang for mercenary. (3) slang for paid campaign or precinct worker. See also VOLUNTEERS.

highballing boasting of having more votes on a congressional vote or more campaign funds than one really has in order to intimidate the undecided to join your side.

high crimes and misdemeanors one of the bases for removal from office of federal officials, including the president, stated in the Constitution (Article II, Section 4), which lists treason, bribery or "other high Crimes and Misdemeanors." There is no specific definition of "high" crimes and misdemeanors in American law. Many legal scholars believe these mean felonies involving moral turpitude and violating the official's constitutional or legal duties. The phrase was partially tested in the impeachment trial of President Bill Clinton in 1999, as to whether committing perjury in a civil matter not directly relevant to the conduct of government was a "high crime" or "misdemeanor." The Senate answered "no."

Hill, the Capitol Hill in Washington, D.C., where Congress meets.

The Hill a weekly (Wednesday) newspaper that covers the U.S. Congress, daily political and campaign news, Washington restaurant reviews, and columns. Address: 733 Fifteenth Street, N.W., Suite 1140, Washington, D.C. 20005. Tel.: (202) 628-8500; website: www. hillnews.com.

hill rat youngish Capitol Hill staff member whose life and work revolve around Congress, its inner workings, and its gossip mills; and who manages to tiptoe through the congressional maze without getting caught in any job-threatening trap.

hit piece a political brochure, usually mailed, that attacks an opponent with harsh words and innuendo to manipulate voters' thinking, often reaching voters too late for the victim or opponent to respond. A hit piece is intended to destroy the opponent's reputation and credibility and put him or her on the defensive. They have become numerous with development of computer-generated mailing lists.

There have been negative campaign brochures and pamphlets throughout history, such as the "coffin" broadside attacking Andrew Jackson for ordering the execution of soldiers in the War of 1812, Richard Nixon's 1946 and 1950 campaigns accusing representatives Jerry Voorhis and Helen Gahagan Douglas of having communist connections, and Lyndon Johnson's anti–Barry Goldwater campaign television commercial featuring an atomic bomb mushroom cloud while a little girl picked a daisy. Television hit pieces reached their apex during George H. W. Bush's 1988 presidential campaign against Democratic governor Michael Dukakis, implying that Governor Dukakis controlled the Massachusetts judicial system's furloughing of Willie Horton and caused his subsequent rape of a woman.

While Democrats and Republicans publicly denounce hit pieces as disgraceful and demeaning campaign techniques that avoid fair and public discussion of the issues, both parties use hit pieces.

HMO   health maintenance organization. In the 1990s an organization of doctors to provide medical services for varied fees and to deal with health insurance companies. HMOs control what treatment or services they or the insurance companies are willing to provide and pay for.

holdout   a member of Congress or any legislative body who waits as long as possible to disclose how he/she intends to vote. Often holdouts are waiting to deal and extract commitments for their home district from the leadership or the president. Other holdouts seek publicity and attention or both.

homeless   people with no home or shelter who may be found living in cardboard boxes or automobiles, under overpasses, in doorways, over sidewalk grates, and under newspapers. The homeless include Vietnam veterans shunned by society upon their return from the war or who needed drug recovery or psychological help and did not receive it. Others include people with health and mental problems, runaways, addicts, the unemployable, and, in the 1990s, the newly unemployed and single mothers with children. California leads the United States in numbers of homeless, partly due to climate and partly due to the closure of half-way houses for mentally disturbed people by then California governor Ronald Reagan.

Since the 1980s the homeless have been a political issue, with conservatives viewing them as people who arouse unpleasant feelings and should be removed from sight and as people who are not trying hard enough to clean themselves up and get jobs. Liberals criticize conservative administrations for being insensitive to the plight of the homeless. They assert that many of them will never be employable and need help.

The recession in the late 1980s and early 1990s created numbers of new homeless who lost their homes, pride, jobs, self-esteem, hope, and unemployment benefits.

honeymoon   a period after an election during which the media go easy on the new officeholder, gives that person a chance to perform, and gives them the benefit of the doubt. When the honeymoon is over, the press attacks and probes with its normal fervor and pleasure.

honoraria   fees paid for speaking. Some members of Congress and former presidents, vice presidents, and cabinet members receive thousands and millions of dollars for speaking at benefits, political fund-raisers, and business meetings, although recent legislation put a cap on the amount a member of Congress can receive annually.

hoopla   spontaneous or contrived emotion and demonstration.

Hoover Commission (Commission on Organization of the Executive Branch of the Government)   President Harry S. Truman appointed former president Herbert Hoover chairman of the commission, Hoover's first public service following his presidency. The commission reported in February, March, and April 1949, urging reorganization of several governmental agencies, creation of the Department of Health,

Education and Welfare, and removal of the Post Office Department from political appointment. It criticized inefficient government entities. Since the Hoover Commission, local and state commissions on governmental reorganization or efficiency are often called "Little Hoover Commissions."

horse race a real contest, often when it had been expected that one candidate would prevail easily.

horse trading political deal-making such as votes on one legislative bill for votes on another.

hotline a direct communication line between two leaders for use in crises, first established during the Kennedy administration between the president's office and the leader of the Soviet Union.

House Un-American Activities Committee (HUAC) originally called the House Committee on Un-American Activities, it was created in 1938 to investigate both Nazi and communist activities in the United States on the eve of World War II. First chaired by Texas congressman Martin Dies as the temporary Special Committee on Un-American Activities (1938–44), the committee became a vehicle for political intimidation.

Dies and his successor as chairman, Congressman John Rankin (D–Miss.), under whom it became a permanent committee, presided over a vicious chase of their enemies in the name of anti-communism. The committee engaged in character assassination, career destruction, and harassment of intellectual, academic, political, and artistic leaders. Members of the com-

mittee used it to silence liberals and label them as radicals and communists and as a springboard for their own political and financial ambitions.

Then congressman Richard M. Nixon developed his reputation as an aggressive and tough member of the committee by getting Alger Hiss, a former State Department adviser, to apparently perjure himself (1948) regarding his contacts with former communist Whitaker Chambers. At highly publicized hearings in the 1950s, prominent movie industry entertainers and executives accused show business friends and enemies of having communist ties in an effort to save their own careers. California and Connecticut had their own state committees.

Although criticized by Eleanor Roosevelt, President Harry S. Truman, and many other national leaders, the committee used the power of subpoena, citations for contempt, accusations without proof, and professional witnesses to continue its activities until it was abolished by the House of Representatives. Conservatives saw the HUAC as a noble enterprise to avoid potential communist infiltration, whereas liberals saw the committee's activities as intimidation and restraint of free speech. Generally discredited, HUAC became the Internal Security Committee in 1969 and was abolished by Congress in January 1975.

House Ways and Means Committee an extremely powerful congressional committee that oversees expenditures and allocations of funds.

housing legislation, federal New Deal legislation that began with the **Home Owners Refinancing Act** (June

13, 1933) to save people from mortgage foreclosure. More comprehensive was the **National Housing Act** (June 28, 1934), which established the **Federal Housing Administration (FHA)**. Through the FHA the government insured loans, making mortgages easier to obtain and stimulating home purchases and repairs. The **Public Housing Administration** was added (September, 1937) to finance projects for low-income families to be built by local communities and states. Congress began assistance for urban renewal (redevelopment) projects in **Title One** of the **1949 Federal Housing Act**. Other legislation has created secondary financing (mortgage and bond purchasing) and operations such as **Federal National Mortgage Association (Fannie Mae)** and federally assisted urban renewal.

The **Housing and Home Finance Agency** managed housing policies until 1966 when it was replaced by the **Department of Housing and Urban Development (HUD)**.

Housing development carries the social benefits of home ownership and basic shelter, while housing construction and repair carry the great-est impact on the economy of all industries. Generally, Democratic administrations have expanded housing financing and tried new methods of assisting housing development, whereas Republicans have contracted them.

HUD (Department of Housing and Urban Development) a federal agency created by the Department of Housing and Urban Development Act (November 9, 1965) to administer mortgage programs that help Americans become homeowners. HUD encourages and facilitates new housing construction, renovation of existing rental units, aid for low-income families, and it works to prevent discrimination in housing and rentals. On-site problems are handled by regional offices. Headquarters: 451 7th Street, S.W., Washington, D.C. 20410. Tel.: (202) 708-1422; website: www.hud.gov

human rights (1) the rights and privileges supposedly belonging to every man and woman. (2) those rights that cannot be denied by any government entity. Human rights may include the right to be protected against inhumane treatment and punishment, the right to political freedom and beliefs, freedom of speech, freedom of religion, and the right to a fair trial.

The United Nations Charter on Human Rights and the European Declaration on Human Rights are the best sources of definitions of human rights and how they can be achieved and defended in various countries.

As monitored and revealed by Amnesty International and the United Nations, flagrant violations have occurred: apartheid in South Africa, massive killings of alleged communists in Indonesia, and arrests and murders under Philippines dictator Ferdinand Marcos, "Papa" and "Baby Doc" Duvalier in Haiti, and Idi Amin in Uganda, "disappearances" in Chile and Argentina, brutality and rape against Muslim women in Bosnia, arrests, murders, and disappearances under communist control in the former Soviet Union and China, and limited access to rights among the poor in the United States.

Conservatives are often slow to become concerned about human rights, believing that every country has a right to run things the way their people want them to. They also seem to believe that human rights violations only occur in other nations.

Liberals see human rights as a national as well as international concern. They believe that some minorities and homeless people are deprived of their human rights in the United States. Examples include underrepresentation of "undesirables" in American court proceedings, intimidation to cut off free speech, and neglect of America's homeless and mentally ill.

human rights violations mistreatment of people ranging from violent brutality to false imprisonment without regard for their human rights.

The Hundred Days the first 100 days (March 4, 1933–June 16, 1933) of President Franklin D. Roosevelt's New Deal, beginning on his Inauguration Day. It actually consisted of 104 days. Desperate to alleviate the Great Depression, he utilized legislation developed by his Brain Trust, adopted by Congress, and explained to the public in his fireside chats and twice-weekly press conferences, which made this the most productive executive/legislative governmental period in American history. Bills enacted, agencies and services created, and executive orders issued in this period were:

March 5: four-day bank holiday to stop runs on banks and savings and loans;

March 9: Emergency Banking Relief Act passed by Congress in eight hours;

March 20: Economy Act to reorganize agencies and cut salaries;

March 22: 3.2% alcohol beer and wine legalized;

March 27: Farm Credit Administration;

March 31: Civilian Conservation Corps (CCC) with 250,000 new jobs in conservation;

April 19: gold standard abandoned;

May 12: Federal Emergency Relief Act, a federal/state program for unemployed poor;

May 13: Agricultural Adjustment ACT (AAA) to raise prices with subsidies and other means to benefit farmers;

May 18: Tennessee Valley Authority;

May 27: Federal Securities Act, the first registration of stocks;

June 13: Home Owners Refinancing Act, the first federal housing legislation;

June 16 (the day Congress adjourned): National Industrial Recovery Act (NRA) to establish minimum wages and hours and the right to collective bargaining; Public Works administration to provide jobs in public construction; Federal Bank Deposit Insurance Corporation (FDIC); Farm Credit Act; and the Railroad Transportation Act giving regulation of the railroad holding companies to the Interstate Commerce Commission.

idealism philosophy and behavior based on a concept of things as one thinks they should be or as one wishes them to be, based on ideals. Idealism may contrast with some people's perceptions of reality. It is the opposite of materialism, in the sense that one cannot "put a finger on it." Idealism is the subject of profuse writing and theorizing by many 18th-century German, Scottish, and English philosophers, including Immanuel Kant, Johann Gottlieb Fichte, Georg Wilhelm Friedrich Hegel, Thomas Hill Green, William Wallace, Edward Caird, and Bernard Bosanquet.

ideologue a person who tries to impose his/her ideology on others. In politics an ideologue is often considered to be more concerned with policy positions than winning elections.

ideology (1) doctrines or strong opinions based on one's view of how the social world, government, or political system should work and of what it consists. (2) a set of attitudes or moralistic views stating what we should do or should want to do. There can be as many ideologies as there are individuals. See also IDEOLOGUE.

image how a person appears to be, resulting from contrived or perceived public relations efforts. Some candidates and managers believe image is all that counts, while others stress substance.

immigrant (1) a person who enters a new country with the intention of staying there. (2) derogatory term for illegal immigrant.

immigration the act of coming into a new country, region, or environment for the purpose of settling in that country.

Immigration has long been respected in the United States, a country perceived as open to all people who need to leave undesirable or repressive conditions. All but a few American forebears came from other countries.

A series of restrictive statutes has been passed in the United States. The first limitation on immigration was the Chinese Exclusion Treaty with China in 1880, followed by the Chinese Exclusion Act (May 6, 1882), which barred all immigration by Chinese laborers for 10 years and was renewed every decade until 1920. The Chinese Exclusion Act was finally repealed in 1943. When the Irish chief of police of New Orleans was murdered in 1891, it resulted in mob lynching of 11 Sicilian immigrants accused of the crime, a diplomatic confrontation with Italy, and less governmental encouragement of Italian immigration.

The Immigration Act of 1907 gave President Theodore Roosevelt the power to restrict Japanese immigration, and he promptly ordered laborers from Japan excluded. The next year the Japanese government agreed not to issue passports to laborers wishing to come to the United States. A literacy test for all immigrants was included in a bill passed over President Woodrow Wilson's veto (February 5, 1917), which also restricted immigration of all Asians.

The first and basic immigration quota act was passed on May 19, 1921, and went into effect on June 3, 1921. It permitted immigration of three percent of each nationality already shown in the U.S. census of 1910, and a total immigration limit of 357,000 per year. This greatly favored European immigration, and the restrictions on Asian laborers stayed in force until 1942.

Over President Harry S. Truman's veto, Congress passed (1952) the McCarran-Walter Act that further limited immigration, set quotas based on the 1920 census, and abolished racial restrictions, since they were being ruled unconstitutional in court tests. President Truman believed the act was discriminatory.

In the United States, the most recent immigrants are often the worst treated and most oppressed. Often they submit to oppression to avoid discovery and survive in the workplace. Waves of immigrants sometimes oppress the next wave of immigrants, resulting in early 20th-century signs warning "no Irish-Italians-Jews need apply."

Historically, recent immigrants to the United States have been exploited as cheap labor, such as during the 1860s when Chinese men were used inhumanely to build the American railroad system and during the 20th century when Mexicans were used to pick farm crops. Africans pick crops in Europe, and east Indians pick crops in Canada. The jobs and functions new immigrants perform are usually jobs that longer-term residents see as demeaning and refuse to do. A worldwide recession in the 1990s brought unprecedented waves of migration and immigration from depressed countries to countries believed to have better real or imagined economic conditions.

In the United States, increased immigration has prompted deeper discussion of what the U.S. role as a refuge for the world's distressed people should be, but no consensus has been reached. Similar discussions continue in Canada and throughout Europe.

U.S. senator Dianne Feinstein (D–Calif.) proposed a one-dollar toll charge at U.S. borders, and Sen. Barbara Boxer (D–Calif.) advocated use of armed National Guard members to patrol the borders.

Most liberals seem to believe that since nearly all of America's ancestors were immigrants, Americans should remain true to the open door principle. They also dislike the apparent racism of efforts by conservatives to close the borders. Still, some liberals too harbor some resentment when new immigrants receive preferential treatment in low-cost business loans or college admissions.

Some conservatives and some liberals fear that new immigrants take jobs, take advantage of welfare benefits, and are often in America illegally, and, therefore, they should be stopped at the border and sent back (to Mexico). In the 1990s, Republican governor Pete Wilson of California (1991–99) advocated official denial of public programs such as education and health care to illegal immigrants, including children. Attitudes toward immigrants tend to fluctuate with the economic times.

impeachment the right of the House of Representatives to charge a government official (president or judge) with a high crime or misdemeanor. The House votes on the articles of impeachment, and the Senate actually tries the case and requires a two-thirds majority to convict. Several Federal judges have been impeached, convicted, and removed from office.

President Andrew Johnson was the first president to be impeached. The Senate failed to convict him by one vote in 1867. The charges against Johnson were basically political, contending that he dismissed his secretary of war, which was prohibited by the Tenure of Office Act, a statute that was clearly unconstitutional. Richard Nixon resigned to avoid the process, as the House Judiciary Committee charged him with impeachable offenses in 1974, resulting from obstruction of justice in the Watergate scandal. Even Republican stalwarts like Senator Barry Goldwater (R–Ariz.) warned that they would join a majority of senators in voting to convict Nixon. Charged with perjury in a civil matter regarding personal sexual accusations by Paula Jones and with obstruction of justice for alleging suggesting people tailor their stories to match his statements regarding his White House affair with Monica Lewinsky, President Bill Clinton was impeached by the House. Republicans in the Senate fell far short of obtaining enough votes to convict Clinton on any charge.

imperialism the establishment of colonies or extension of a governmental entity's rule or control beyond its original geographic boundaries by invading and acquiring other nations' territories by military or physical force. Motivation for imperialism often includes commercial markets, strategic military bases, or raw materials. Imperialism reached its height in the 19th century during the expansion of the British Empire, which controlled, administered and owned substantial territory in every continent.

Since World War II, American policy has opposed imperialism, while the United States has exercised considerable control over the economies and even governments of some countries in Latin America and in the South Pacific in the last half of the 20th century.

Conservatives prefer holding on to colonies or spheres of economic interest as part of the status quo or acquiring new ones for business reasons, while liberals see imperialism as building an empire by selfishly and insensitively exploiting others against their will. Supporters of both viewpoints oppose other countries' foreign imperialism, such as that of Nazi Germany, the Soviet Union, Japan during World War II, and 19th-century Britain.

implied powers powers believed to be implicit but not expressed in the U.S. Constitution's "Elastic Clause" in Article I, Section 8, in which the government can "make all Laws which shall be necessary and proper for carrying into Execution the foregoing Powers."

Various administrations have taken advantage of this clause to suit their wishes. The greatest breakthrough in use of these powers came with the New Deal's broad legislative programs in the 1930s.

inalienable rights those rights that cannot be given up and cannot be taken away; "among these rights are life, liberty, and the pursuit of happiness." The phrase "pursuit of happiness" was supplied by Thomas Jefferson. John Locke (1632–1704) previously spoke of life, liberty, and the preservation of property.

inauguration (1) the formal induction or swearing in of a president of the United States, on January 20 following a presidential election, and the celebrations that go along with the ceremony. Inaugurations have ranged in recent decades from the modesty of President Franklin D. Roosevelt's fourth in 1944 during World War II at the White House to the splendiferous celebrations of presidents Eisenhower through Clinton. The Republican and Democratic parties now use the many events that go with an inauguration as fund-raisers, ranging from $100 parade tickets to those costing thousands of dollars for preferred seating at concerts and balls featuring major entertainment stars. (2) the swearing in of newly elected governors in each state.

income tax a tax based on a percentage of an individual's or company's income, with a sliding scale of higher rates for the wealthiest earners to the lowest for the poorest.

The first attempt at a legal direct income tax was struck down by the U.S. Supreme Court ruling in *Pollack v. Farmer's Loan and Trust Co.* (1894). The Sixteenth Amendment to the U.S. Constitution (1913) authorized the federal government to levy income taxes. In addition to federal income taxes, almost all states utilize income tax systems.

While revenues raised by income taxes fund social and welfare programs and maintenance of the infrastructure, they also finance defense, weapons, nuclear arms, and atomic bomb testing.

Conservatives often advocate reduction of income taxes and social welfare programs. President George H. W. Bush was elected partly because of his 1988 vow: "Read my lips, no new taxes." As president, Bush approved an income tax increase under congressional pressure, fatally damaging his public credibility. Liberals generally favor the income tax as the fairest revenue producer to pay for necessary programs that help society. Arkansas governor Bill Clinton defeated President Bush (1992) partly by vowing to reduce the middle class's income taxes and increase those of Americans with annual incomes of $200,000 or more. Apparently because the Bush administration's budget deficit was far greater than Bush revealed or Clinton claimed to know, President Clinton gave very few income tax cuts. In the wake of the 1994–2000 economic boom, the inflow of federal income tax revenues created a surplus. What to do with the expected surplus became a major campaign issue in the 2000 presidential election. Vice President Al Gore advocated paying off the national debt and insuring Social Security and enhancing other social programs, while Governor George W. Bush favored giving a national tax cut first and privatizing part of Social Security, while building the military and a few education programs. See also TAX LOOPHOLES.

incumbent   a person who holds an office, either elective or appointive. An office holder may use "Incumbent" or "(Inc.)" following his/her name on election ballots in some states. In the late 20th century, being an incumbent has not always carried a positive identity, since many voters want to "throw the bums out" who, they think, got the country into such a mess. This constituent attitude has led to legislation in some states to limit the number of terms for incumbents.

independent   a person not affiliated with Democrats, Republicans, or any other named parties, who has registered to vote as an Independent or possibly as one who declines to state. Independents usually do not want other people to know their political preferences and want to avoid campaign solicitations.

Former senator Eugene McCarthy (D-Minn.) ran for president as an Independent in 1976, and Congressman John Anderson (R–Ill.) did the same in 1980. In 1992, industrialist Ross Perot ran for president as an Independent, Bernie Sanders, a known socialist, ran successfully for reelection to Congress as an Independent, and former Democrat and California state senator Quentin Kopp ran successfully for reelection. These candidates shared little philosophically except that they knew they were dissatisfied with the two largest parties.

Independents also remain independent from each other and have no unifying organization. Some Independents believe that true independent thinking, not constricted by "Republican" and "Democrat" boundaries, may be what is needed to solve America's 1990s problems. See also AMERICAN INDEPENDENT PARTY.

independent counsel   an attorney responsible to no one, to conduct a specific investigation with few constraints into potentially criminal conduct of high level officials, including the President. The independent counsel was created by legislation which took its appointment away from the president and gave it to the attorney general. Independent counsels were appointed to investigate the late and former President Richard Nixon's connection to Watergate, President Ronald Reagan's involvement in Irangate in which weapons were traded for hostages and funds in Iran, and the money was diverted to the Nicaraguan *contra* rebels (Reagan was exonerated), and to investigate President Bill Clinton's role and truthfulness in Whitewater (Arkansas) development investigation. The political reaction to the use of more than $60 million spent to investigate President Clinton caused the Congress to let the statute die and not be renewed in 2000.

indirect taxation   taxes collected through sales taxes and use taxes, instead of directly from a person in income taxes or property taxes. See also DIRECT TAXATION.

industrial democracy   (1) a theory that workers should have influence and more say in the organization of their working lives, and that profits from their efforts should be divided among them. (2) cooperative management. Proponents favor industrial democracy over representative democracy and would like to see government and industry controlled by workers making democratic decisions on all affairs of the business or government agency. Traditional American business executives regard industrial democracy as unworkable, but it is used increasingly through labor negotiations and by Japanese-owned businesses in America.

Industrial Workers of the World (IWW)   known as "Wobblies," they were "one big union" of unskilled workers founded in 1905 in Chicago in response to the American Federation of Labor's (AFL's) opposition to organizing unskilled workers, and "radical" or socialistic unionism.

Original leaders included William D. Haywood, president of the Western Federation of Miners, Daniel De Leon, leader of the Socialist Labor Party, and Eugene V. Debs, former railroad unionist and a leader of the Socialist Party. Violence dominated their organizing efforts in Rocky Mountain and Pacific Coast states, and they generally mistrusted negotiation settlements favorable to them.

The IWW was the only U.S. labor organization to oppose World War I, resulting in persecution and prosecution by the federal government (1917–19), which drove them underground. Ideological conflicts between socialists and radical communists in the 1920s led to the demise of the Wobblies.

infidelities   sexual escapades with someone other than one's spouse, which became a political term when President Bill Clinton denied that he had ever engaged in infidelities or in extramarital affairs. He has since admitted to some.

inflation   (1) a natural loss of value in currency, resulting in an increase in prices, followed belatedly by wage increases and a drop in interest rates. (2) an increase in the amount of currency in circulation.

Moderate inflation is favored by debtors who can pay longterm debts with cheap money. Severe inflation takes the value out of increased income and can ruin economic stability. Runaway inflation in many nations has caused complete collapse or extreme devaluation of their currencies. Contraction of the money supply by the Federal Reserve is a classic method used to fight inflation.

influence peddler   a person who sells his/her ability to communicate with or influence legislators or other officeholders.

information   (1) knowledge people acquire by various means. (2) all that people are allowed by their government to know.

Information Superhighway   a high-tech term for a network of communication lines to carry voice, video, data, graphics, and other information fast enough for video telephone calls and two-way television on fiber optic lines. The superhighway would carry communication 30,000 times faster than the copper wire used currently for telephone calls. Those involved estimate that it will take $100 to $200 billion and 10 to 15 years to complete the superhighway. The Clinton/Gore administration considered this superhighway's construction to be as important to the future of U.S. business as was the construction of the nation's highway network after World War II.

In former vice president Al Gore's presentation to the "Superhighway Summit" (January 11, 1994), sponsored by the Academy of Television Arts and Sciences at the University of California at Los Angeles, comedian and actor Lily Tomlin asked if this superhighway was just for the "electronically elite." Good question. A "digital divide" has developed between "haves" who have access to computers/the Internet, and "have nots" who don't.

No one has said the Information Superhighway will be a freeway. It could turn out to be a toll road, possibly limiting accessibility in the early years, and, like most computer world developments, coming down in costs after the initial release.

infrastructure   (1) a substructure or underlying foundation. (2) the American network of highways, bridges, rail systems, and anything else that connects parts of the vast United States, its utilities, and economies.

Presidents Ronald Reagan and George H.W. Bush allowed America's infrastructure to disintegrate into disrepair in favor of not creating what they considered to be "make work" jobs.

initiative   a process by which voters offer a measure, usually through petitioning, for a vote on an election ballot at the local or state level. The initiative process began in Wisconsin under progressive Republican Robert La Follette's leadership in the first decade of the 20th century, was followed by Republican California Governor Hiram Johnson, and became a principled goal of the progressive movement of both parties. Most cities and countries provide for initiatives. Several proposals for federal initiatives have died aborning.

in-kind contributions   gifts of goods and/or services such as free rent, airline tickets, food, or printing to campaigns or candidates. In-kind contributions are supposed to be reported, but they are easier to hide and harder to trace or prove than checks.

inner circle a small group of friends or supporters who believe, along with those outside the inner circle, that they have special influence on or access to an officeholder. Sometimes the officeholder is unaware of this group's belief in its standing.

inoperative statement Republican president Richard Nixon's White House press secretary Ron Ziegler's words for "lie."

insider a person who is part of "the group," the decision makers, or the power wielders. An insider is presumed to know secrets of how things really work and may be, in the eyes of some people, part of "the problem." In a time when the public views insiders as the enemy, any candidate who can distances him/herself from the insiders. See also OUTSIDER.

insurgent a personal or group mentality advocating radical change in the policies of a government or organization and/or desiring to take over the power or control of that entity.

Traditionally, insurgents inspire fear in conservatives because they challenge and threaten to upset the status quo. Liberals may attempt drastic changes and power grabs, rarely succeed, and do not see themselves as insurgents. Extreme conservatives such as Patrick Buchanan considered their own moves within the Republican Party as making them insurgents, and they were proud of it. Buchanan eventually left the Republican Party for the Reform Party.

integration the bringing together of different racial groups (such as white and African-American) to achieve equality through reconstruction of a society of many races after abolishment of segregation of races.

intelligence (1) secrets and spying. (2) a national security system involving secrets and spying. (3) the gathering of secret political, military, or diplomatic information. In the United States, the civilian intelligence agencies are the Central Intelligence Agency (CIA), which collects and analyzes foreign information, and the Federal Bureau of Investigation (FBI), which does the same thing for domestic information.

Supposedly professional, technical, and apolitical, both agencies have been used for political purposes, including providing back-up and rationale for administration policies and investigations and gathering files on opponents. Under Director J. Edgar Hoover, the FBI collected information and spied on war resisters and protesters as well as homosexuals and liberals, implying that these interest groups engaged in illegal acts.

Conservatives and some liberals "went along" and rationalized that this spying and information collection on Americans was in the country's best interest. Others saw these intelligence activities as threats and unconstitutional attempts to silence the opposition. Apparently Hoover's lust for information on gays was an overreaching cover-up of his own alleged homosexuality.

The FBI has returned to its more traditional role as a provider of professional investigatory services to the federal government.

The cold war's end raised the issue of the high cost, free from public accounting, for the giant American intelligence operation overseas. Because of its clandestine nature and the scope of its operations, the CIA remains a difficult agency for even members of the U.S. Senate and House to investigate and analyze, including any effort to recommend reductions or improvements.

interest group (special interest group or pressure group) people organized around a central, common interest. Often these organizations develop simply as support groups, but many are also formed to espouse ideas and promote them before those in powerful political decision-making positions. Examples include trade unions, veterans, environmentalists, parent-teacher associations, industries, farmers, educators, organized ethnic groups, women's organizations, and the military-industrial complex. Techniques of communicating an interest group's positions range from campaign contributions or withholding of same, marches and mass demonstrations, slick mailings, publicity disguised as news, and direct lobbying of legislatures and government agencies. Almost every American, knowingly or not, belongs to a special interest group. See also PACS.

intergovernmental lobby lobbying and deal-making between government agencies, officials, committees, and branches, such as the Defense Department lobbying Congress for funds.

interim commission a commission made up of legislators, public officials, and private citizens to study or manage a specific issue or problem between regular legislative sessions.

Internal Security Committee the Senate version of the House Un-American Activities Committee. Officially named the Senate Subcommittee to Investigate the Administration of the Internal Security Act and other Internal Security laws, it was a Judiciary Committee subcommittee, enjoying its heyday in the late 1940s and 1950s. The act creating the committee was found unconstitutional by the U.S. Supreme Court in 1966.

In the guise of ferreting out communists, it used its hearings, subpoena power, charges by paid informers (some of whom, like Harvey Matusow, admitted lying), and a lack of constitutional protections to harass, intimidate, and "expose" people whose opinions some senators wished to suppress. Senator James O. Eastland, a conservative pro-segregationist from Mississippi, chaired the committee during most of its life.

Another Senate version was the Subcommittee on Investigations of the Government Operations Committee, headed by Senator Joseph R. McCarthy, whose charges of communism terrorized public officials, academics, and liberal thinkers between 1949 and 1954. See also MCCARTHYISM.

international community those people actively involved in diplomatic relations around the world.

International Longshoremen and Warehousemen Union (ILWU) a highly political labor union of dock workers on the Pacific Coast and in Hawaii, which arose out of the 1934 San Francisco waterfront strike. Its most prominent president was Australian-born Harry Bridges, who survived government claims that he had lied about communist associations when he entered the United States.

The ILWU welcomed minorities and developed health plan protection, pensions for those automated out of jobs, and other innovations once considered radical. With automation and the accompanying decline in membership, the ILWU's political potency also waned. The ILWU still takes good care of its members and allows a father to pass his "book" or job on to his son.

International Monetary Fund (IMF) specialized agency of the United Nations that began operations on December 27, 1945. An organization that emerged from one of the proposals that came from the Bretton Woods Conference (1944). Created to stabilize international currencies and give financial aid during crises, the IMF is governed by a Board of Governors, made up of one governor from each of 182 member nations. Members vote and have influence according to the size of their nation's initial deposit and governments, in a currency crisis, can withdraw more funds than they hold in deposits. The IMF can provide technical assistance to improve management and impose economic restrictions on members requesting loans or currency devaluations. Address: 700 19th Street, N.W., Washington, D.C. 20431. Tel.: (202) 623-7000; FAX: (202) 623-4661; e-mail: publicaffairs@imf.org; website:www.imf.org

internment detention or confinement in a country or in a designated,

limited space, usually for political reasons, including as enemy aliens.

The most famous such action in the United States was the internment of Japanese citizens or anyone of Japanese ancestry on the West Coast as urged by General John L. de Witt, commander of the 6th (West Coast) Army during World War II, as a military measure after the bombing of Pearl Harbor by the Japanese. The order was signed by President Franklin D. Roosevelt on February 19, 1942.

One hundred thousand people of Japanese ancestry, both American citizens and noncitizens, were interned at inland "relocation camps," losing jobs, homes, property, and dignity in the process. Initially, some were held in race track horse stalls, and most were confined behind chain-link fences in encampments. Two-thirds of those interned were U.S. citizens in the effort endorsed by then California attorney general and later U.S. Supreme Court Chief Justice Earl Warren, as well as California governor Culbert Olsen. Internment was opposed as unconstitutional by Secretary of War Henry L. Stimson and U.S. Attorney General Francis Biddle.

The most famous camp was Manzanar in rural northern California, and there were camps in Arkansas, Utah, and other states, usually in inhospitable geographic areas. Opportunists bought up truck farms and other property left behind and owned by the uprooted citizens. A similar relocation program was invoked in Canada.

Fifty years later, after the internment action was declared unconstitutional by the U.S. Supreme Court, reparations of $20,000 were paid by the U.S. government in 1990–91 to each person interned and still living. Upon hearing the news, some American blacks wondered aloud where their reparations were after centuries of enslavement.

interposition a theory promulgated by some southern U.S. politicians to block integration of schools and facilities by "interposing" state segregation laws. In the 1940s and early 1950s, southern states used interposition often, carrying states' constitutional "police powers" rights to an extreme. See also NULLIFICATION.

interstate commerce movement of goods or money from one state to another, regulated by the federal government. The government can regulate commerce within a state when it may impact interstate movement of goods and services.

intervention involvement by a third person or party into a legal or diplomatic case to try to bring about a desired result.

in-the-loop a condition of ego-imagined privilege, often meaning that one is invited to all the "important" parties and receives press releases and secret information and gossip. Occasionally egos shatter when people find they were left out of a decision-making process or gathering. President George H. W. Bush said he was not "in-the-loop" on Iran-Contra decisions when he was Ronald Reagan's vice president.

intrastate commerce movement of goods or money and general conduct of business within the borders of one state.

invasion an attack from the outside on a country, body, or rights.

investment (1) paying to buy things or putting money into a business in hopes of making a profit. (2) as used by President Bill Clinton, a euphemism for government spending on social or business development programs, or spending money to buy education and jobs for the underprivileged.

invisible primary fund-raising that goes on before campaigns begin. The invisible primary was particularly evident in the 2000 presidential primary, in which media coverage focused on how much money candidates had raised and had in the bank as if that was the central concern, instead of concentrating on their positions on issues. Winning or losing the invisible primary has a large psychological influence on candidates and contributors.

IRA (1) Irish Republican Army, which campaigns and employs some terrorism in its fight for reunification of the six counties of the North, also known as Northern Ireland, with the Republic of Ireland. (2) Individual Retirement Account, into which individuals or couples may deposit tax-free funds annually if their combined incomes do not exceed certain limits. Legislation adopted in 1994, sponsored by five of the then seven female U.S. senators, permitted housewives or househusbands to invest in IRAs independent of their spouses or partners, supposedly acknowledging that homemaking is a job.

Iran-Contra affair an incident in 1987 in which President Ronald Reagan's administration arranged clandestinely for American businessmen to sell military hardware to Iran, whose fundamentalist Muslim government had held the American embassy staff and others as hostages (1978–81). In turn, national security official Lt. Col. Oliver North and several top military and diplomatic officials close to the president arranged for the sales profits to be funneled to the *contras,* a guerrilla army fighting the left-wing government of Nicaragua. Such payments expressly violated American law. At the same time, President Reagan insisted repeatedly that the United States would not deal with terrorists and contended that no money was going to the *contras.* North had his secretary help him shred all the pertinent documents when the scheme became known. He and his superior—presidential military adviser Admiral John Poindexter—were both convicted of violations of law in supporting the president's claim that he was unaware of their actions. Their convictions were reversed and ordered dismissed on appeal.

The activity reached scandalous proportions and affected the final years of President Reagan's administration, as well as that of President George H. W. Bush. Later revelations (October 1992) of Secretary of Defense Caspar Weinberger's meeting notes, showing George Bush's knowledge of specific criminal events, possibly contributed to Bush's reelection loss to Democrat Bill Clinton.

The implication was that President Reagan and Vice President Bush either condoned violations of the law or were out of touch and had little knowledge of what key members of their administration were doing. The scandal grew with revelations of "security" improvements (paid for by arms profits) made to North's home and the attempted suicide by one of the alleged top-level government participants.

Later, Oliver North changed his story and claimed that President Reagan really did know what had transpired and did not object.

Many conservatives and Republicans see Iran-Contra and White House officials' activities as a patriotic, noble activity necessary in the defense of freedom. Liberals and Democrats see it as a scandalous abuse of power endangering Americans' lives and principles.

Irangate a reference to alleged crimes committed by members of President Ronald Reagan's administration and concealed in a manner similar to the Watergate scandal and cover-up. See also IRAN-CONTRA AFFAIR.

Iraqi War (President Bush's War or Gulf War) an originally undeclared war and military attack orchestrated by President George H. W. Bush in 1991 to "restore democracy" by driving Iraqi forces out of Kuwait, which they had invaded successfully and which Iraqi leader Saddam Hussein declared as his. In support of multiple United Nations resolutions approving military force to drive Hussein out of Kuwait, the U.S. Congress voted by a narrow margin to support the war effort. When bombing of Iraqi positions and Baghdad (in which many civilians were killed) did not cause Iraq to pull out, American ground forces (with some allied help) swept out of Saudi Arabia and quickly drove Hussein's army from Kuwait. Iraqi troops suffered enormous losses while U.S. casualties were minimal, mostly from "friendly fire." Ironically, Kuwait, ruled by self-declared royal families, never had democracy and still does not. Saddam Hussein remains in control and power in Iraq.

President Bush's popularity rose to an all-time high during the war. Some liberals, however, protested and advocated negotiations instead of killing for peace in the name of "democracy."

Iron Law of Oligarchy   a theory propounded by German economist and sociologist Robert Michels (1876–1936) in *Political Parties,* his study of international politics of the German Social Democratic Party. Interesting for its portable wisdom, his work suggests that all organized groups are inherently undemocratic. The law states that organization is necessary to accomplish anything, but organization requires and leads to bureaucracy, and bureaucracy ends up with power in the hands of a few at the top. Further, oligarchy exists within political party hierarchy, which may or may not separate its thinking from the masses.

Real-life examples of this theory include the Republican Party's 1990s struggle with factions groping for power at the top, which controls candidate selection, distribution of funds, and philosophical leanings. The religious right has recognized the power that comes from being part of the Republican Party oligarchy and has worked diligently to take over that oligarchy and replace it with its own. However, while this faction listened to

its own zealots, it failed to listen to the larger masses, possibly contributing to the 1992 election of Bill Clinton to the presidency.

Those at the top of a bureaucratic oligarchy, such as city managers, school superintendents, and cabinet secretaries, control information upon which its voting body or chief executive makes decisions affecting its constituency.

Iron Triangle   a term familiarized by Senator John McCain (R–Ariz.) in his 2000 Republican presidential primary campaign referring to the link among lobbyists, money, and legislation.

irrational exuberance   a term coined and used as the title of a book by Robert J. Shiller to describe the wild valuation of the stock market in 2000.

IRS (Internal Revenue Service) (1) the part of the Department of the Treasury responsible for collection of taxes. (2) possibly the most feared and despised agency of the U.S. government.

"is"   the word President Bill Clinton employed in saying that his guilt in lying to a grand jury depended upon "what the meaning of the word 'is' is."

Islam   a religion of which Mohammed (570–632) is the prophet. Adherents are referred to as Muslims and include nearly 500 million people worldwide. According to Mohammed's message embodied in the Koran, the state or government is a religious institution, meaning they are one and the same, providing believers with a complete socioeconomic theory and structure in which all (men) enjoy economic equality. Usury is prohibited, and women must wear veils and absent themselves from active participation and decision making. Islam and Islamic beliefs and studies have enjoyed a resurgence in popularity since World War II, with thousands of new conversions within the United States from the 1970s through the 1990s.

isolationism   international theory and foreign policy position that a nation chooses not to participate or only participate in a minimal way in international affairs or the affairs and interests of other nations.

President George Washington warned against "foreign entanglements" in his farewell address. The United States deepest period of isolationism began in 1919, after President Theodore Roosevelt's jingoism, World War I, and the failure of the United States to join the League of Nations. Leading isolationists in that era included U.S. senators Henry Cabot Lodge (who led the Senate fight against joining the League of Nations), Hiram Johnson, and William Borah.

The most prominent late 1930s isolationist organization was America First, whose chief spokesman was popular aviation hero Charles A. Lindbergh. America's post–World War I isolationism played a contributing role in enabling dictators to assume power, knowing the United States would not interfere. American isolationism ended abruptly when Japan attacked Pearl Harbor, Hawaii, on December 7, 1941. Bipartisan

internationalism followed and has continued since the end of the war in 1945. The end of isolationism led to U.S. membership in the United Nations, enactment of Truman Doctrine and the Marshall Plan to rebuild Europe, technical assistance to underdeveloped countries, a permanent system of foreign aid, funding of the World Bank, and creation of the Peace Corps.

More ardent conservatives remained isolationist, bemoaning giving up any authority to international agencies ("Get the U.S. out of the UN and the UN out of the U.S."), and spending tax dollars to help foreign peoples.

Liberals see isolationism as shortsighted, selfish, discriminatory, and a failure to recognize that the world is now small and issues must be dealt with on a global basis.

In 1992, conservative Republican presidential primary candidates Patrick Buchanan and David Duke called for "America First," referring to isolationism as well as protectionism of American industry and business. The economic recession in the early 1990s led to the conservative belief that making importation of foreign (especially Japanese) goods difficult, curtailing foreign aid and spending the money at home, and barring immigration from third world countries would help the economy.

issue   a matter or question to be discussed and decided, sometimes by voting.

issue ads   political advertisements that supposedly discuss only issues without reference to a candidate. Issue ads have become dodges of post-

Watergate campaign spending limits, by which well-financed supporters can spend unlimited dollars directly for the creation and airing of ads, without contributing their money to a candidate or party or having any public record of their spending.

issue paper a carefully researched and written paper that develops background information and opinion and states a candidate's position on an issue.

Jacksonian Democracy a period of government and political reform begun by Andrew Jackson's election to the presidency (1828) and continuing through Martin Van Buren's administration (1837–41). Jackson appealed directly to the voters and worked to allow every white man to vote, both of which constituted unprecedented and radical steps. Up to that time property ownership usually had been a requirement for voting. Until 1832, some presidential electors were chosen by legislatures rather than by popular vote. Jacksonian Democracy also witnessed new developments in education, prison reform, labor relations, and early humanitarian efforts, using common reason as the best judge. Jackson opposed debtors' prisons and fought the power of large banks while supporting slaveholders. Some people viewed him as a spokesman for slaveholders, while others considered him as a spokesman for populism and the development of democracy.

Granting the vote to women, blacks, and Indians was not even considered by Jacksonians, resulting in new feminist movements in which Dorothy Dix, Susan B. Anthony, and Amelia Bloomer worked for woman's suffrage.

In 1831 and 1832, Jackson diverted from Jeffersonian states' rights by defeating nullification, the theory that a state could vote to "nullify" application of some federal laws. South Carolina believed it could select which federal laws superseded state laws and which South Carolinian laws could replace federal laws. President Jackson obtained congressional authority to use the army to collect import taxes and enforce federal law.

Japanese American Citizens League (JACL) the oldest Asian-American organization for the protection of ethnic civil liberties, the JACL dates back to 1929. It was greatly responsible for lobbying to secure $20,000 recompense for each surviving Japanese American interned by the federal government during World War II. It is a low-key but effective political force with 112 chapters in 25 states. Address: 1765 Sutter Street, San Francisco, Calif. 94115. Tel.: (415) 921-5225; FAX: (415) 931-4671; e-mail: jacl@jacl.org; website: www.jacl.org/

Jeffersonian Democracy a movement led by President Thomas Jefferson in the early 1800s to inject stronger democratic features into American government. Considered to be less radical and less liberal than later Jacksonian Democracy, Jeffersonian Democracy stressed the need for leadership by those most capable, individuals who would naturally be chosen by the people. The question is, what did "capable" mean? Certainly it meant white, male, and popular.

Jefferson believed in the "yeomen"—small independent farmers, artisans, and proprietorship businessmen—as the stalwarts of a stable democracy. He was fearful of urban financiers' and large industries' power to corrupt democracy by self-interest. This position put Jeffersonian Democracy in opposition to Alexander Hamilton, a spokesman for a strong central government and large financial interests.

Jehovah's Witnesses members of an evangelical Protestant religion and sect founded in the United States (1872) by Charles Taze Russell, a former Congregationalist. Followers were originally called Russellites. The crux of Jehovah's Witnesses' beliefs is their expectation that the second coming of Christ is about to occur and will destroy Satan's rule and firmly establish God's theocracy. Each member or witness considers him/herself to be a minister of God. They also believe that when Christ comes, everyone who is not a Jehovah's Witness (and is therefore part of Satan's scheme) will die, leaving only Jehovah's Witnesses on earth. At that time, they will, by rights, divide up and distribute the wealth among them.

Jehovah's Witnesses do not vote in elections or participate in the political/governmental processes in the belief that their first duty is to God. Therefore Jehovah's Witnesses do not pay tribute to lay government, although they use government-run courts, schools, and hospitals and pay taxes to support the government.

Ironically, Jehovah's Witnesses have had considerable impact by bringing successful legal appeals to the Supreme Court against mandatory flag salutes in schools and for religious liberties, including the right to evangelize door-to-door.

Jim Crow slang name for blacks that comes from a minstrel song title popularized by T. D. Rice (1835): "Wheel about and Turn about and Jump, Jim Crow."

Jim Crow laws laws passed in many southern states following withdrawal of federal troops after the Civil War requiring segregation of the races (blacks from whites), including bars to voting, compelling demeaning use of "colored only" facilities, and forcing blacks to sit in the back seats of buses. Eventually many such laws were challenged successfully, such as *Brown v. Board of Education* in 1954.

jingoism a policy of boastful patriotism favoring an aggressive, warlike foreign policy, particularly exemplified by that of Theodore Roosevelt (1901–1909).

Jingoism's characteristics were favored by Vice President George H. W. Bush in his 1988 presidential campaign when he toured flag factories, talked about patriotism as a campaign issue, and criticized actress Roseanne Barr for her national anthem rendition.

Jingoism's defenders believe America has a "manifest destiny" to control world affairs, often by force.

Liberals assume that patriotism is understood, that it has meanings besides flag waving and bombing, and that flag waving is a phony campaign issue. They claim to prefer negotiation to war.

John Birch Society founded in 1958 by wealthy candy manufacturer Robert Welch (1899–1985) as a semisecret conservative organization that was prominent in the 1960s and 1970s. An organization obsessed with the dangers of communism, it was named for a missionary killed by Chinese army soldiers. Members generally favored isolationism, accused both Republicans and Democrats of leaning toward communism, and published lists of supposed communist sympathizers.

Liberals saw Birchers as extremist, dangerous, and neo-fascistic, while many conservatives viewed them as patriots spreading the truth. Republican leaders usually feared association with John Birchers, even when they agreed with them. In the early 1960s a few officeholders openly identified themselves as "Birchers." As it gained a reputation for irresponsible anticommunism bordering on paranoia, the John Birch Society fell into general disfavor, especially among moderate Republicans. The collapse of the Soviet Union robbed the society of its primary reason for existence.

Address: P. O. Box 8040, Appleton, Wisc. 64912. Tel.: (920) 749-3780; FAX: (920) 749-5062; website: www.jbs. org

joint session a legislative session in which both houses participate. The U.S. Congress holds joint sessions to listen to the president's State of the Union address and to welcome some foreign heads of state or diplomats. Joint sessions are held in the House chamber.

judicial activism situations in which judges affect and make new public policy through their decisions. Judicial activism raises difficult questions regarding judges' roles in creating, interpreting, or defining constitutional policy and determining the boundaries among the judicial, executive, and legislative branches and their responsibilities. Critics contend that judicial activists usurp the legislative branch's authority. Defenders argue that the courts act only to interpret the laws so as to make them relevant to modern times. Charges of judicial activism are usually made by people who do not agree with a judge's decision.

judicial branch (of government) the part of the government which contains the system of courts and judges that interpret laws and decide lawsuits. It is one of the three branches of government, along with the executive and legislative. At the federal level there are district courts that try cases, circuit courts of appeal, and the Supreme Court as the final arbiter of the constitutionality of laws and governmental actions. Federal judges are appointed by the president for life, with the advice and consent of the Senate, and can only be impeached for violations of law.

judicial review   the power held by appeals courts to determine the legality of a trial court's decision. At the federal level, the appeals courts and ultimately the Supreme Court reviewing a lower court ruling can determine the constitutionality of laws passed by the legislative branch or actions taken by the executive branch. If the courts decide they are not legal or constitutional, the law or action is nullified. This authority was confirmed by the U.S. Supreme Court in *Marbury v. Madison* in 1803.

judiciary   (1) all the courts in the United States (both state and federal) that form, as a whole, the judiciary or judicial branch of the government. It joins the executive and legislative branches. (2) total body of judges.

juice   political influence or power to get things done when asked.

Junior Tuesday   primaries held on the first Tuesday in March, beginning "March Madness" (See p. 180), caused by "front-loading" (See p. 115) of primaries earlier and earlier in a presidential election year.

junket   a pleasure trip taken by legislators or public officials and paid for with public funds under the guise of research or study of an issue or problem.

Some members of Congress used to consider junkets part of their fair take or as a perk. Usually the public looks scornfully on those officials who still take junkets, particularly during a recession. A constituency's recourse if displeased with an official who takes junkets is to vote him/her out of office.

junta   from Spanish, meaning council or board. *Junta militar* means military council. A junta is usually made up of military officers who take over the government and form the ruling hierarchy after a militaristic overthrow of the previous government in a coup d'état. The core group of a junta is often made up of men from each of the country's military services, with each man's power relative to his rank in his own military branch, as well as to that branch's power in the total military force. Rival military leaders spend much time jockeying for power within the junta, based on their presumed personal or branch strength. Juntas are most common in Latin America but also have occurred in Greece, Myanmar (Burma), and other countries.

justice   (1) the use of authority and power to uphold what is right, just, or lawful; the administration of law; procedure of a law court. (2) procedural justice in the execution of constitutional due process, fair trial, and equality before the laws and courts. (3) social justice: giving people what they have a right to, which may include due process, such as social or human rights, the right to subsistence, right to shelter, clothing, food, fair treatment, and equal rights to employment and enjoyment. (4) the executive department charged with enforcing the nation's laws, headed by the attorney general. (5) a member of the Supreme Court of the United States or of a state's top appeals court.

K

Kennedy-Nixon debates the first televised debates between presidential candidates, held on September 26 and on October 7, 13, and 21, 1960. It was the first presidential campaign during which a majority of American families owned television sets. The debates drew nearly 70 million viewers, the highest number to that date of any event besides the World Series. To make the debates possible, Congress passed legislation suspending the rule requiring broadcasters to give "equal time" to candidates of minor parties. At the time there were at least 14 lesser political parties, including Conservatives, Socialists, and National Vegetarians.

Due to his charm, demeanor, and ability to answer tough questions, John F. Kennedy seemed to "win" the first debate over Richard M. Nixon. Nixon appeared to be edgy, uncertain, nervous, and pale in contrast to Kennedy's youth, confidence, and vigor. The first debate often receives credit for providing Kennedy

with his narrow margin of victory over Nixon in the November election. The latter three debates were rated "even."

The debates' popularity led to similar broadcasts between final election presidential candidates Jimmy Carter and Gerald Ford (1976), Ronald Reagan and Jimmy Carter (1980), Ronald Reagan and Walter Mondale (1984), George H. W. Bush and Michael Dukakis (1988), Bush, Bill Clinton, and Ross Perot (1992), Clinton and Robert Dole (1996), and Al Gore and George W. Bush (2000).

President Ronald Reagan's "There you go again" responses to Democrat Jimmy Carter's 1980 verbal attacks helped Reagan immensely. Governor Michael Dukakis's pedantic, unemotional answer to a reporter's question about the death penalty for a hypothetical killer-rapist of his own wife hurt him badly. Al Gore's apparent changes of personality from one debate to another, coupled with George W. Bush doing better than expected, seemed to hurt Gore and help Bush in the 2000 election.

One prior radio debate took place in 1948, in which Republican presidential contenders Thomas E. Dewey and Harold Stassen met before the Oregon Republican primary. Dewey's dulcet tones and sharp delivery carried the debate, leading him to defeat Stassen in the primary and, effectively, eliminate Stassen's chances for the nomination.

keynoter   a person who makes a keynote speech at a gathering or convention to build up excitement and set a positive tone or theme for the delegates.

At political conventions the keynoter is often someone who has a reputation as an orator and whose career can be enhanced by giving the speech. Sen. Alben Barkley's (D–Ky.) stirring speech to the 1948 Democratic Convention helped make him a popular choice for vice president. New York governor Mario Cuomo's 1984 keynote address was a powerful performance that catapulted him into consideration for a future presidential nomination. Although she was little known outside Texas before the speech, Texas state treasurer Ann Richards was famous throughout the country after she delivered her lines "George Bush was born with a silver foot in his mouth" and "That dog won't hunt." In 1990 Ms. Richards won the Texas governorship in an upset, but she was later defeated for reelection by George W. Bush.

Many keynoters have disappointed their selectors, including Democratic governor Frank Clement of Tennessee who repeated "How long, oh God, how long?" at least 10 times in 1956,

Senator John Glenn (D–Ohio) who droned his way out of consideration for the vice presidency in 1988, and Senator Phil Gramm (R–Tex.) who bored his television audience to near death with a repetitious and nasty diatribe against the Democrats in 1992.

keynote speech   an address usually given early in a political convention to unify and inspire delegates and set the tone at a convention. See also KEYNOTER.

kickback   giving or paying back part of money received as a commission.

Kickbacks have been required in some states and countries as a part of doing business with government entities. In Indiana political patronage employees of the state were required to kickback 3 percent of their state salaries to the Indiana Democratic Party as late as the 1970s. Such kickbacks went on openly and possibly illegally for years.

Former Republican vice president Spiro Agnew demanded a kickback of five cents for every pack of cigarettes sold in Maryland in vending machines within state buildings when he was governor. Agnew's sophisticated kickback system on state construction contracts included 25 percent to the state official who arranged the deal, 25 percent to the official who brought it to Agnew, and 50 percent to Agnew himself. His kickbacks were secret, illegal, and unreported on his income tax returns. Agnew continued to collect Maryland kickbacks when he was vice president, resulting in his resignation (1973) as part of a plea bargain by which he would not go to jail for income tax evasion.

kinder, gentler nation   phrase used by Vice President George H. W. Bush in his 1988 presidential nomination acceptance speech at the Republican National Convention and in his inaugural address. Bush supporters believed he created a kinder, gentler nation following Ronald Reagan's presidency. Bush detractors saw his bombing of Iraq and tax increases as less than kind and gentle.

kingmaker   a political maneuverer who is so powerful and/or so highly respected that his or her blessing or nod toward a particular candidate for office can make or break that person's career. A kingmaker's power is built on donations, shrewdness, expertise, and, perhaps, intelligence. Reputation is the most important asset, since party leaders often wait to see which aspirant the kingmaker supports. Few kingmakers actually exist, although large contributors, known as "fat cats," come close. Kingmaking is really a state of mind held by both the maker and the makee.

Queenmakers lack recognition, partly because of their newness to politics. Emily's List became a powerful force in researching, supporting and financing female candidates that produced results beginning in 1990.

KISS (Keep it simple, stupid.)   a political and sales saying meaning one should keep one's use of English simple so that the uninformed can understand one's points.

kitchen cabinet   close friends or informal associates of a president in whom he/she has complete trust and confidence and with whom he/she meets regularly or in crisis. The kit-chen cabinet may or may not include official cabinet members. Membership and influence is completely at the subjective will of the president.

"Kitchen cabinet" was first used during Andrew Jackson's presidency (1829–37) and applied to a small group of his closest friends whose advice he deemed to be more important than that of the official cabinet. Jackson's friends met in the White House kitchen, which was intimate and warm.

kitty   cash in a bank account.

knee-jerk liberal   a snide term referring to a liberal who responds to issues, buzz-words, or certain political leaders automatically without thinking.

Knights of Labor   the first important nationwide labor organization in the United States. Formally named the Noble Order of the Knights of Labor in 1869 by its founder and first leader, Uriah S. Stephens, it was a secret organization to protect its members from their employers' reprisals. Eventually it proposed workers' cooperatives to replace capitalism.

After Terrence V. Powderly's election as its Grand Master Workman (1879), the group abandoned its secrecy and mysticism and removed "noble" from its title. Powderly decentralized power, allowing regional leaders to take control and make decisions about methods and means themselves.

Membership of the Knights of Labor reached its peak (700,000) in 1886, the year of 1,600 strikes, but the so-called Haymarket Riot in Chicago tarnished the Knights' reputation. The resultant antiunion feeling led to the Knights' swift decline and its replacement as the leading American labor organization by the American Federation of Labor (AFL), founded in December 1886.

Know-Nothing Party

also known as the American Party, Order of the Star-Spangled Banner, and the Native American Party, it was one of the first "third party" movements in the United States. Founded in the 1850s, it functioned primarily to oppose immigrants, especially Roman Catholics from Ireland. Know-Nothing meetings were held in secret. When members were asked what was discussed, they replied, "I know nothing."

In its one national election effort, the party's 1856 platform included anti-Catholic and anti-alien planks. Its presidential candidate, ex-Whig president Millard Fillmore, carried only the state of Maryland, after which the party soon disappeared. Later other "American parties" surfaced in the 1870s and 1880s, including one in California that worked to exclude Chinese and other Asians from employment.

Know-Somethings

Know-Nothings who left that party because they could not get the Know-Nothings to abandon secret meetings in favor of public meetings or secure their opposition to slavery. A minority within the Know-Nothing Party from 1855 to 1857, the Know-Somethings then joined the Republican Party.

Koreagate

a 1976 scandal in which Korean businessmen were accused of trying to peddle influence through gifts and campaign contributions to U.S. officials and members of Congress. House Speaker Carl Albert (D–Okla.) stepped down soon after the accusations.

Ku Klux Klan

a secret political terrorist organization formed in southern states after the Civil War and dedicated to establishing white racial supremacy.

Originally the Klan was a social club in Pulaski, Tennessee (1866), and later moved its center to Nashville to form "The Invisible Empire of the South." It was led by a Grand Wizard with a pyramid of descending hierarchy of Grand Dragons, Grand Titans, and Grand Cyclopses. Klan members wore white robes and sheets to disguise themselves and to scare and terrorize blacks and others from voting or seeking social, political, and economic equality.

Its membership declined following passage of the Force Bill of 1871, by which the federal government attempted to outlaw secret organizations. The Klan revived itself in 1915 as a national organization to limit the rights of blacks as well as new immigrants, Catholics, and Jews. By 1924, it was a major political force in southern states as well as border states such as Missouri (where it defeated anti-Klan county judge Harry S. Truman) and some northern states, particularly Indiana. That year the Republican and Democratic conventions declined to condemn the Klan, but Republican vice presidential candidate Charles G. Dawes attacked the Klan as un-American.

During the Great Depression the Klan retreated to its southern base, as anti-black bands of night riders beat and lynched "uppity" blacks. With integration came antimask laws even in southern states, thereby reducing membership demonstrations to those men willing to show their faces.

In 1990, David Duke, a former Ku Klux Klan Grand Wizard and American Nazi, made a serious run for the governorship of Louisiana as a Republican. President George H. W. Bush finally denounced the Klan, as personified by Duke, when it appeared Duke actually had a chance to become governor and the Republican Party status quo might be threatened.

In the South and Midwest a few youths are organizing new Ku Klux Klan chapters to keep minorities out of their towns.

labor unions organizations of unskilled and skilled manual workers and some professionals, from auto workers and food servers to professors and doctors, advocating higher wages and better working conditions for their members.

In the United States unions existed in the early 1800s in skilled trades (often called craft unions) joined together in 1886 by the American Federation of Labor (A.F.L.). Industry-wide unions grew in the 1930s, leading to formation of the Congress of Industrial Organizations (C.I.O.) Unions reached their peak membership in the early 1950s, but they have lost both members and clout since. The A.F.L. and C.I.O. merged in 1955. Major unions include the Teamsters, United Auto Workers, American Federation of Teachers, United Mine Workers, International Federation of Ladies Garment Workers, and unions representing carpenters, plumbers, boilermakers, transportation workers, steelworkers, and electrical workers.

For many decades labor unions were thought to lean toward liberalism, but by the 1970s many members, reaching economic security and fearing loss of that security, became increasingly conservative to protect their jobs and their neighborhoods from minorities and their incomes from taxes. They helped elect Republican presidents Richard Nixon, Ronald Reagan, and George H. W. Bush. With the election of Bill Clinton, labor unions again looked, although with some skepticism, to the Democratic Party as favoring working people and promising more jobs.

Reagan and Bush both viewed labor unions as the causes and culprits of inflation and the American recession through their demands for higher wages, which increase manufacturer's costs, and ultimately the retail prices of goods. Liberals and Democrats see labor unions as a means to assure workers a reasonable wage on which to live and support their families.

laissez-faire French for "let do." Noninterference by a person or a government, allowing the people to do as they please, in economic, business, political, and private matters. In government relations, laissez-faire sometimes connotes letting business owners determine labor relations, working conditions, wages, and cutthroat competition their way, without regulation or control.

Laissez-faire originated in 19th-century Europe and America with liberal opposition to semifeudal monopolies in which government or the state controlled all aspects of business relations.

In the United States the trend developed into extreme opposition to any controls or regulation of business by government. In the 1980s and 1990s conservative Republican presidents Ronald Reagan and George H. W. Bush advocated and implemented laissez-faire policies, including deregulation of savings and loans and loosening of environmental regulations.

Liberals and some moderates feel laissez-faire is a rationalization for rapacious practices of robber barons and unscrupulous businesses. Conservatives yearn for the government to take its "hands off" business, believing overregulation limits expansion and adds to costs.

lame duck an officeholder, legislature, or administration who/which either lost the last election or chose not to run again and still holds office for the rest of the elected term. The outgoing officials possess diminished power since no one owes them anything and can get little from them. As a result, lame ducks have little persuasive powers in their legislative bodies.

The public's attention has moved on to their successors.

landslide (1) an overwhelming, irresistible majority of votes for a candidate, political party, cause, or position in an election. (2) an election that is not close.

It is in the interpretation of "not close" that definers disagree. Presumably a landslide might be 60 percent of the vote. But winners by margins of only 4 percent have declared their victories landslides or mandates, while losers in those same elections see their opponents' triumphs as squeakers.

The Last Hurrah (1956) (1) a popular political novel by Edwin O'Connor revealing the often humorous tale of Boston ward politics. It focuses on the final campaign of Frank Skeffington, a character based on James Michael Curley (1874–1958), Massachusetts governor, congressman, and Boston mayor, who was elected once while imprisoned for mail fraud. The book was made into a John Ford movie (1958), starring Spencer Tracy and several top character actors playing Boston pols, and into a television movie (1977) featuring Carroll O'Connor. (2) a term referring to an old politician's last ego-feeding campaign or public effort when the odds are against him/her and the race or comeback attempt seems to be in vain.

late-term abortion an abortion done in the third three months of pregnancy, also called a partial-birth abortion by anti-abortion activists.

laundered money money passed by those giving or receiving it through other people's bank accounts to disguise who gave it.

laundry list a legislator's, lobbyist's, or executive's list of goals.

law all the rules of conduct established by a society through legislation or custom to govern the behavior of citizens. Codified law is written or organized law and may include enacted statutes. English laws that are not written but based on established practice and/or precedents are called the common law. The first known set of laws were the Code of Hammurabi of ancient Babylonia. Other early examples are the Ten Commandments and the Roman Justinian Code.

law and order (1) the state of society in which civil and criminal law processes exist and where law enforcement agencies take responsibility for maintaining a peaceful condition. (2) a concept and pretense used by law enforcement agencies and conservatives to use police forces to suppress expression of free speech, free assembly, and potential crimes. Occasionally law and order is a euphemism for enforcement of criminal law without due process, particularity against minorities.

Leader of Her Majesty's Loyal Opposition the leader of the party with the second highest number of members in the parliament.

leadership the ability to motivate or inspire others to follow a particular course of action while making them believe it is the appropriate one. Leadership is thought to be a good quality except when it is abused, as it has been by leaders such as Adolf Hitler, Benito Mussolini, Ferdinand Marcos, corrupt televangelists, union leaders, or political machine bosses.

Quality leadership involves worthy goals, organization of effort, and the ability to delegate authority, impart imagination, and instill inspiration.

League of Conservation Voters (LCV) a leading voter persuasion organization whose members believe in and are part of the environmental movement. Founded in 1970 as a political action committee (PAC) of Friends of the Earth, LCV raises money door-to-door and by telemarketing, gives contributions of money and skilled campaign management to favored candidates from local assembly to the presidency, holds press conferences, and buys commercial media time for candidates. LCV has chapters in most states. Address: 1920 L Street, N.W., Suite 800, Washington, D.C. 20036. Tel.: (202) 785-8683; FAX: (202) 835-0491; e-mail: lcv@lcv.org; website: www.lcv.org/

League of Nations the first major worldwide organization created to prevent war. The precursor to the United Nations, the League of Nations was first announced as one of President Woodrow Wilson's Fourteen Points (1918) and appeared as a clause in the Treaty of Versailles (1919). It was always weak because it lacked the membership of the United States and, for a time, Germany and the Soviet Union and had no means to enforce its mandates.

League of Women Voters founded in 1920 by Mrs. Carrie Chapman Catt, who called for such an organization at the 1919 convention of the National American Woman Suffrage Association. Her intention was to move into the field of nonpartisan political education and maximize women's votes, at which the league has become masterful. Due to their reputation as even-handed researchers and information disseminators, the league is often asked to moderate and host political debates from local to national levels. Its leaders are prohibited from partisan political activity. The league now has chapters in all 50 states, the District of Columbia, Puerto Rico, and the Virgin Islands. Address: 1730 M Street, N.W., Suite 1000, Washington, D.C. 20036. Tel.: (202) 429-1965.

leak a news item or information released secretly and intentionally before the official announcement time to: (1) try out a concept on the public and get a response before the whole program is released; (2) beat an opponent to the punch; or (3) damage an opponent. A leak may be planned by the perpetrator and be seen as unplanned by the person targeted. In that case the latter is often caught off guard and finds him/herself without a response or with the impact of his/her grand announcement effectively muted.

left (left wing) (1) from a French tradition begun in 1789 in which those members of the French National Assembly who supported the king sat on the right of the Estates-General and opponents sat on the left. (2) any place on the political spectrum from moderately liberal through socialist to communist. Franklin D. Roosevelt said "I am a little left of center." (3) amorphous political category of voters who generally favor changing things in favor of the largest number of people possible and away from the status quo, calling it progress. The left may favor nationalization of certain industries, nationalized medicine, higher taxes on the wealthy, elimination of tax loopholes for the wealthy, closer income equality, elimination of nuclear weapons, equal education and employment opportunities, child care, and "choice" on abortion. (4) ironically since 1986, in Marxist countries, the left consists of those who want change or reform toward democracy and away from "right" or conservative, strict, Marxist doctrine, once considered the most "left" of all political philosophies.

leftist a person who holds leftish or left-wing political views, generally favoring social and economic change toward greater equality.

legislation written measures or potential laws developed by members of a legislative body and presented to the whole body for discussion and voting to create a new law.

legislative branch (1) the branch of government created to make laws, and usually made up of elected representatives such as Congress in the United States. (2) one of the three branches of American government, along with the executive and judicial.

legislature a group of persons or representatives, usually elected, who are empowered to write, vote on, and make laws for a democratic government entity. In many countries the legislature is called *Congress,* as in the United States. It is called *Parliament* in England and Canada, the *Diet* in Japan, the *Duma* in Russia.

Lend-Lease Act   an act passed by Congress (1941), allowing President Franklin D. Roosevelt to supply (by lending or leasing) war materiel to countries that seemed vital to the United States's welfare, including Great Britain and later the Soviet Union then fighting against Germany and Japan. By the end of 1945, the United States sent $50,000,000,000 to its Allies: 60 percent to Great Britain, 22 percent to the Soviet Union, half in munitions and half in petroleum products. Eventually Lend-Lease turned into just plain subsidies of those countries. The "reverse lend-lease" provided American troops abroad with raw materials, food, and lodging valued at $17,000,000,000. One does not need a calculator to see the imbalance.

Leninism   (1) first Soviet Russian dictator (1918–1924) V. I. Lenin's interpretation of Marxism. (2) a political philosophy that espouses strong, authoritarian, undemocratic political leadership and assumes that the masses are not equipped and cannot know what is best for them, therefore cannot become revolutionary on their own, and so must be led by a group of elite (self-appointed) wise men, known in Lenin's scheme as "intellectual revolutionaries." While Lenin argued that the state (his dictatorship) would "wither away" and leave a people's democracy, it never did.

let the dust settle   wait for a while to let reactions or fallout calm down before bringing up a topic, legislation, or nomination again.

levee   Canada: a morning coffee to which constituents are invited either publicly or by invitation, usually given by an elected or public official. An earlier version of a soiree.

level playing field   (1) a term popularized in 1990s campaigns to mean fairness, with everyone starting the game, business, political campaign, or debate with equal rights and the same rules. (2) fairness and equal chance at education and jobs.

liberal   (1) a person who subscribes to liberalism, showing concern for human rights and needs, open to new ideas. Conservatives, such as President George H. W. Bush, succeeded in convincing some followers that liberals were dangerous. See also LIBERAL-ISM. (2) member of the Liberal Party in Canada.

liberal democracy   a philosophy of indirect majority rule (in Britain) in which the public elects representatives to a legislative body in which each delegate or representative is not required to represent or reflect his/her constituents' views. This is a system in which voters entrust their elected representatives to make decisions for them. During the 19th-century liberal democracy stood in juxtaposition to the danger of the "tyranny of the majority" (de Tocqueville and John Stuart Mill) on the basis that the true majority's rule could be worse than other tyrannies.

Liberal Party   (1) a small New York City–based and New York State–operated political party created as a 1944 spinoff from the American Labor Party, which, in turn, had split to the left from the local Democrats. The Liberal Party has supported Democratic and Republican reform candidates for statewide office. It also provides a legal "line" (or designation) on the ballot for candidates who have lost to "organization" candidates for New York City mayor or city council. After losing a three-way race for the Republican nomination for Mayor, John Lindsay won the final election in 1969 on the Liberal ballot line. Address: 381 Park Ave. South, New York, N.Y. 10016. Tel.: (212) 213-1400; website: www.liberal-party.org (2) In Canada, a middle-of-the-road party, which often has led the government. Address: 81 Metcalfe St., Suite 400, Ottawa, Ontario K1P 6M8. Tel.: (613) 237-0749; FAX: (613) 235-7208; website: www.liberal.pe.ca. (3) In Great Britain, the Liberal Party slipped into third place behind Labour and Conservatives in the 1920s, and today most of its members are in coalition with the Socialist Democrats to form the Social Democratic Liberal Party (SDLP).

liberalism   a political concept and attitude whose definition has changed over the centuries and has different meanings depending on one's position in the political spectrum. Originally liberalism developed in the late 18th and early 19th centuries as a bourgeois movement of the merchant class in quest of freedom from the vestiges of feudalism and control by the nobility and royalty. Features that continue today in the United States include espousal of freedom of all kinds, including basic civil liberties, advocacy of independence of the individual against a powerful body, advocacy against war and in favor of peaceful

negotiation, and commitment to equality for all. Liberals usually favor openness to new ideas and honor human rights and needs. They generally hope to peacefully change the way things are in order to benefit the largest number of people.

Liberals tend to hold feminine (nurturing) values, including working to develop interdependence and relationships, such as a "global economy," and working toward consensus and compromise. Liberals do not look for an enemy and are more likely to honor differences and diversity without needing to make anyone wrong. Everything is personal, and they often identify and empathize with other people's suffering. Conservatives may interpret these characteristics as weakness or waffling.

Conservatives and many Republicans see liberals as frightening leftists who want government to solve every problem and spend other people's (taxpayers') money. Republican presidential candidate George H. W. Bush called Massachusetts Democratic governor Michael Dukakis a "liberal" during the 1988 final election campaign, believing it was the nastiest pejorative word he could apply to his opponent. Needing an enemy against whom to rally his political troops, Bush continued to use the "L word" through his first four years in office as if it condemned anyone to whom he applied it. And often it did. In 1992, after 12 years of presidentially instilled fear and timidity, liberalism or its principles seemed to be on the rise again in the wake of conservative-led recession, racism, and division.

Far left radicals, Marxists, and communists ridicule liberals as "sellouts" coopted by "the system," who will not fight for radical reform. A few liberals see themselves as radicals, but most see themselves as mainstream, correct, and principled, while viewing radicals as unrealistic dreamers.

libertarian a person who believes all men (and supposedly women) have birth rights that cannot be taken away by any government body or in deference to anyone else's rights. Libertarians often hold a distrust of government intervention because, by its nature, it reduces individual rights. They also believe in full civil rights for the individual. In the 1970s American libertarians organized as a political party with committees in several states but elected no public officials at the state legislative or executive levels. Libertarians use their network and public relations talents to express their concern with "too much government" and to promote a general conservatism combined with a belief in broad individual autonomy. Address: 2600 Virginia Ave., N.W., Suite 100, Washington, D.C. 20037. Tel.: (202) 333-0008; FAX: (202) 333-0072; e-mail: hq@lp.org; website: lp.org

Liberty League a small organization conceived by conservative Democrats in the summer of 1934 in opposition to Franklin D. Roosevelt's New Deal and in favor of defeating him in 1936. Claiming FDR's programs were too radical, the Liberty League received tremendous news coverage due to its shrill attacks and financing by the DuPont family. Among the league's leading members were John Raskob, former treasurer of the Democratic Party, and an embittered and increasingly conservative Al Smith, 1928 Democratic presidential nominee.

The Liberty League supported Republican Alf Landon for president (1936) and so embarrassed the Republican Party by distributing a brochure picturing Eleanor Roosevelt with two blacks that the Republican National Committee asked it to stay out of the campaign.

It emerged again to oppose Roosevelt's ill-conceived "court packing" scheme in 1937, but it disappeared by 1940.

Liberty Party an abolitionist political party that appeared on a few state ballots in 1840. Its presidential candidate, James G. Birney, received only 7,069 votes that year and 62,000 in 1844. The Liberty Party marked the first anti-slavery political effort, and it led to the Free Soil Party (1848) and eventually to the Republican Party (1854).

libs a pejorative nickname for liberals used by someone who dislikes or opposes their views.

lieutenant governor (1) the second-highest elected official in a state. Some states' lieutenant governors have specific governmental departments to oversee and others have very little to do except in emergencies when the governor is out of the state. (2) Canada: the monarch's representative in each province, appointed by the governor general on the recommendation of the prime minister, with mostly ceremonial duties.

lily white a term that refers to an organization or community in which all members are Caucasian, often intentionally excluding minorities, specifically African Americans.

limited nuclear war a war employing only a few small nuclear weapons.

limited war usually a localized, two-party war whose escalation is believed by those perpetrating it to be under control and in no danger of leading to nuclear war. A "limited war" may be "controlled" in the eyes of some people, but devastatingly ruinous to the involved nations.

limousine liberal a wealthy Democrat or liberal who espouses modest living (for others), equal rights, peace, equal housing, equal pay, supports environmental causes and liberal candidates and lives a showy lifestyle in contrast to that which he/she advocates for others. The term is used by those who are not rich as a critique of wealthy liberals. Inherent in the term is the suggestion that limousine liberals should practice what they preach by giving away their money to the beneficiaries of liberalism.

line-item veto a privilege advocated by Republican presidents Ronald Reagan and George H. W. Bush that would allow the president to cross out or eliminate an entire program from the federal budget in order to cut the budget without the need for congressional approval. When the Republicans gained control of both houses in the 1994 election, line-item veto legislation was enacted. President Bill Clinton began to use the line-item veto, the state of New York challenged its constitutionality, and the Supreme Court later ruled it was unconstitutional because it delegated legislative powers to the president. The Republican Congress had not expected Democrat Clinton to use the line-item veto. Some states allow the governor to strike items from the budget after it is adopted.

little old ladies in tennis shoes conservative older women who support conservative causes with money, usually in small contributions.

Howard Jewell, then assistant attorney general of California, coined the term in a study on right-wing organizations. Jewell's superior, then California attorney general Stanley Mosk, used the term publicly and is often credited with its invention.

litmus test (1) a test conducted by dipping a strip of paper treated with litmus into a substance to measure content by the reaction of the litmus—red for acid, blue for alkali; (2) an issues "test" vice presidential candidates may have to pass to be on a (Republican) presidential ticket. The term was used in the 2000 election referring to a potential running mate's or appointee's position on abortion.

lobby (verb) to try to get a legislator to vote for or against a measure by persuasion, providing information, cajoling, entertainment, or payoffs, subtle or blatant.

lobbyist a person who lobbies. Industries, special interests, and causes often have highly paid lobbyists to influence legislators, prepare legislation, appear at hearings, and develop a favorable public relations campaign. The name comes from the fact that representatives of specific interests would gather in the Willard Hotel lobby, frequented by congressmen in the 1800s, to buttonhole members of Congress and try to persuade them to vote their way.

Many activists believe that lobbyists wield increased power in states where residents have approved term limits to control the time period legislators may serve. Their theory is based on suspicions that, with increased turnover and constant influxes of new legislators, the new lawmakers rely on lobbyists for information and guidance.

lockout action taken by an employer to keep workers out of the workplace and off the job because of management-worker disagreements, union membership, or a strike. A lockout amounts to management punishing workers by not allowing them to work during or because of disputes, in an effort to force workers (unions) to give in to management's position.

Locofocos the liberal wing of the New York Democratic Party in the 1830s. Locofocos believed in equal rights and were known for their reformist zeal.

Locofocos acquired its name after Tammany Hall meeting at which the regular Democrats turned out the gas lights to quiet and stifle the liberals. The liberals then struck friction matches called Locofocos to light the room.

logrolling (1) voting for each other's bills as an exchange of favors. (2) mutually beneficial aid among politicians. (3) mutual backscratching. (4) giving help and praise with a hint of overdoing it.

loophole See TAX LOOPHOLE.

loose cannon a pejorative term for a person who is independent, not controlled by anyone or any discernible principles, and whose actions are unpredictable. An office-holder who is called a loose cannon often acts outside of his/her party's expectations and does not conform to his/her party's guidelines, directives, or legislative platform.

loose construction also known as "liberal construction," loose construction refers to interpreting or construing the U.S. Constitution in a "loose" way to meet changing times and conditions. It stands in contrast with "strict" construction, which theoretically follows the language of the Constitution without reference to a new social context. Historically the U.S. Supreme Court has tacked back and forth between the two concepts.

Los Angeles Times the largest regional newspaper in the country with 1,196,000 readers, trailing only the *Wall Street Journal* and *USA Today* in circulation. For the entire 20th century, the *Los Angeles Times* has dominated political editorial power in the Los Angeles basin. Staunchly conservative and Republican until the early 1970s, the paper has broadened its editorial outlook and policy and expanded its reportage. The *Times* was recently sold to the *Chicago Tribune*.

love fest an overdone bipartisan agreement, meeting, or effort.

lower house (1) the U.S. House of Representatives, created as the "people's house," proportionally representing the general population instead of the states. The lower house is often referred to as "Congress," although the Congress also applies to the combined House of Representatives and Senate. (2) in some countries with parliamentary governments the lower house represents the general population as opposed to the aristocracy. In Great Britain and Canada the House of Commons is the lower house.

loyal opposition   those who do not agree with an incumbent administration's policies or with those of a legislature's majority and who take the role of making their opposition views known.

The term originated in England and applied to members of parliament who opposed the King's policies but remained loyal to him. Currently in England it refers to the parliamentary opposition to the prime minister. In a multiparty system like Canada's and Britain's the loyal opposition constitutes the party that holds the second largest number of members of parliament.

loyalty oath   (1) an oath swearing one's loyalty or faithfulness to a country, including willingness to defend and support the government. A loyalty oath is required to obtain an American passport, serve in elected public office or on commissions, and in the military. (2) a controversial sworn declaration that included the statement: "I am not now and never have been a communist (or member of a communist organization)," which was required by federal statutes (1947) and in several states (most notably California) to hold a federal or state job, including as a teacher or professor.

The so-called noncommunist oath was opposed by civil libertarians when it was adopted, and it caused considerable campus unrest in the early 1950s. The oaths were used to threaten perjury prosecutions and FBI investigations and were attacked as "thought control" by the few Americans who were not intimidated. What constituted "communist organizations" was determined by the attorney general and included many which were obviously not communist. Numerous Americans refused to sign or swear to this restrictive oath on principle and were barred from government employment. It was declared unconstitutional in 1967.

Some partisan and philosophical groups have refused to take any loyalty oaths because they oppose taking oaths created by governments, do not believe in government policies, or believe they can only swear such allegiance to God.

L-word   a term used by President George H. W. Bush in his 1988 presidential campaign as an emotionally venomous reference to his opponent, Massachusetts governor Michael Dukakis, stemming from Dukakis's membership in the American Civil Liberties Union.

machine politics See POLITICAL MACHINE.

maiden speech a newly elected legislator's first speech before a legislative body.

majority government in parliamentary governments, the governing party, which by nature has a majority of the parliament.

majority leader a majority party member of a legislative body chosen by his party to be its spokesperson and leader. The majority leader in the U.S. Senate is that body's most powerful and influential person. These have included Democrat Lyndon B. Johnson (1955–60) and Republican Robert A. Taft (1953). In the House of Representatives the majority leader is second in power to the Speaker of the House. The Senate majority leader usually decides who sits on what committees, party policy, what bills will come before the full legislature, and when they will come up, and the House majority leader assists the Speaker in those functions. See also SPEAKER OF THE HOUSE.

majority party the party that has more than half the votes (members) in a legislature.

majority system a system in which 50 percent + 1 vote is required to win an election, pass a bill, or accept a motion.

male chauvinism primarily a women's expression for the male attitude that men are superior to women and that women are not worthy of equal rights and equal pay for equal work.

Interpretations of male chauvinism vary by the sex of the interpreter and according to political perspective. Many men do not recognize such chauvinism and deny it exists, while others are so sensitive to it that they are embarrassed. Many women acknowledge male chauvinism, resent it, and may use the expression "male chauvinist pig." Other women do not acknowledge it and deny its existence. Some women see it as a dominating factor in their lives, and still others submit to it believing it is the appropriate order of male-female relationships.

Conservatives tend to acknowledge male chauvinism's existence the least, believing that it is appropriate behavior, and conservative women often do not see it as offensive. Liberal men are slightly more sensitive to the phenomenon's role in society, and liberal women created the term and fight for the syndrome's termination.

In politics, many women see male chauvinism exemplified by beliefs that women are the volunteers who put on parties and low-cost fund-raisers, command little policy influence, and get low-level jobs, while men make the big contributions, buy power, determine issues positions, and get most of the high-paying "think-jobs."

managed care according to the Clinton White House's "Health Care Update" (August 1993), "General term for any system of health care delivery—such as an HMO—organized to enhance effectiveness." "Managed care networks . . . are usually organized by insurance carriers, but also can be organized by employers, hospitals, or hospital chains. Payment is made on a fixed basis, which provides incentives to control costs. Translation: a system that gives everybody the care they need, keeps cost down and improves quality." Managed care appears to provide for coverage for everyone as long as they can pay for it through insurance or employment, which obviously leaves out millions of people.

managed competition an economic theory espoused by Hillary Rodham Clinton as part of the Clinton health care reform package, "that organizes health care delivery and financing in an attempt to combine the best elements of government regulation and freemarket competition. Those paying for care are organized into large groups, and providers then compete for their business." The Clinton White House's "Health Care Update" (August 1993) stated further that managed competition is "a way to give individuals and businesses bargaining power so that they can get the health care they want at an affordable price." The program was blocked in the House of Representatives.

managed news information selected, organized, and disseminated by the government or officeholders to bring about a specific public reaction, usually favorable to the government. Managed news affects what information the public receives and uses to make its decisions.

mandate the wishes of a political electorate expressed to a representative, from town council to president, usually by giving the candidate a handsome majority in an election.

Many elected officials interpret broadly the presumed command handed them by their constituents through electoral victory. The mandate is seen differently by the winner and his/her supporters and by the loser and his/her supporters. Often winners elected by small pluralities after bitter campaigns psychologically believe and verbally declare that the public has given them a firm mandate or right to carry out what might turn out to be an unpopular decision. Winners with large victory margins rarely need to proclaim the strength of their mandate, because they usually have one. Often losers in close elections believe, and sometimes rightly so, that their points of view were supported by a near majority of the voters and that, therefore, the winner does not have a clear mandate even though he/she declared one.

Republican senators often reminded Democratic president Bill Clinton that he gained only a minority (43%) of the 1992 vote in a three-way presidential race and, therefore, lacked a strong mandate. Presidents Abraham Lincoln and Woodrow Wilson did not let the fact that they both won far less than 50 percent of the vote keep them from claiming clear mandates.

The broadest interpretation of the word "mandate" is one that affirms that, if one wins by any margin at all, one has an enthusiastic command and support from the public to do what one wants to do as well as to put into effect everything he/she promised.

mandatory option   a self-canceling phrase meaning you have several choices but you have to choose one of them.

manifest destiny   an accepted tenet of most Americans of all parties from the Mexican War (1846) up to the Spanish-American War (1898) proclaiming that Americans were a people chosen by God to create a model society and absorb all of North America. It was used as a psychological rationalization to expand America from the Atlantic Ocean to the Pacific Ocean to include acquisition by conquest of Texas, New Mexico, and California, and Oregon, Washington, and Alaska by negotiation. Southerners saw manifest destiny as a reason to acquire more land (states) and expand slavery. The phrase was coined by John L. Sullivan in U.S. *Magazine and Democratic Review* (1845).

man on a white horse   sometimes, simply "a man on horseback," this term is a euphemism for savior, a person who will arrive strong, pure, honest, and holy to save people—from constituents, misguided leaders, and even themselves. White symbolizes cleanliness, peace, holiness, purity, virginity, and simplicity. Horse symbolizes masculinity, boldness, strength, and mystery.

The term originated in France in 1888 during a recurrent crisis. The Third Republic was in turmoil and many French citizens advocated a dictatorship led by General Georges Boulanger, who liked to appear on horseback. The general was later charged with conspiracy and fled the country.

In the depths of the Great Depression (1931), some conservatives secretly planned a take over the U.S. government on behalf of general and chief of staff Douglas MacArthur, whom they called the "Man on the White Horse." General MacArthur, however, had nothing to do with the planned cabal and it died aborning.

MAPA   Mexican-American Political Association, an Hispanic political action organization that evolved during John F. Kennedy's 1960 presidential campaign. Strongest in California, the group endorses candidates, develops Hispanic candidates for public office, holds statewide and national conventions, conducts grass-roots organizing, and generally works to increase Hispanic-American political awareness and participation. Address: unknown.

Marbury v. Madison   In this U.S. Supreme Court case Justice John Marshall ruled (February 24, 1803) that the Supreme Court could strike down statutes it found to be unconstitutional, making the Supreme Court the final arbiter of constitutional interpretation.

In the final hours of John Adams's presidential term, he appointed judges of the Federalist Party to help ensure that the judicial branch would remain out of the hands of president-elect Thomas Jefferson's Democratic-Republicans. Some of the commissions were not delivered until after Adams's term expired, and Jefferson's secretary of state, James Madison, refused to present them to the judge-designates. Appointees William Marbury and three others asked the Supreme Court for a writ of mandamus by which the Supreme Court would order Madison to deliver their commissions to them.

Much to everyone's surprise, Federalist Marshall dodged the political bind of favoring Federalists over Republicans by ruling that the Judiciary Act, which created the judgeships, was unconstitutional. Most important, Justice Marshall used the case to establish that the Supreme Court has the right as well as the obligation to resolve constitutional questions, which was Marshall's real aim.

March madness   the abundance of primary elections front-loaded into the month of March, causing presidential candidates to travel madly in those states holding these primaries, together with a frenzy of spending on advertising in those states.

March on Washington   a term used for a massive public march in the nation's capital to draw attention to issues the demonstrators believe should be considered by legislators and the president.

The August 28, 1963, march on Washington is the march against which all modern demonstrations at the capital are measured. Named the Freedom March by the civil rights leaders who called the event, this march on Washington drew more than 200,000 participants and 10 major speakers, including the Rev. Martin Luther King Jr., who made his classic and emotional "I have a dream" speech. A cross-section of Americans walked peacefully to the Lincoln Memorial to express their feelings and positions, including white and black federal workers, including white daughters of southern members of Congress.

marijuana   a hemp plant smoked in cigarette form for psychological and other effects and for relief of pain caused by diseases, including some cancers. Smoking marijuana is largely prohibited in the United States, and its potential legalization for medical or recreational use is a recurring political issue.

Marshall Plan (European Recovery Program)   U.S. program to provide relief and rehabilitation to devastated European countries after World War II. The plan was first proposed (1947) in a speech by U.S. Secretary of State George Marshall with President Harry Truman's approval. The U.S. Congress established the Economic Cooperation Administration and appropriated $13,000,000,000 in economic aid. The U.S.S.R. objected to the plan on the basis that it was an American plot to gain undue influence over Europe and refused to participate. Sixteen nations formed the Organization for European Economic Cooperation (OEEC) to administer the funds, which helped rebuild and rejuvenate war-ravaged Western Europe, including France, West Germany, Britain, Italy, Belgium, and the Netherlands. This working alliance led to the North American Treaty Organization (NATO) and countered the influence of Communist parties in some European countries. Former secretary of commerce and diplomat Averell Harriman was named to direct the program.

martial law a declaration by a civilian government (or dictator) to empower the military forces (army, national guard, police) to govern, control, or even rule with absolute authority. Usually civil rights and legislative processes are suspended, curfews are imposed, and movement of individuals is curtailed. Martial law control is sometimes called a state of siege or state of emergency. Ferdinand Marcos's declaration of Martial Law in the Philippines (1973) is a prime example.

Martial law can also apply to temporary military rule by invading or liberating armies, such as the Allies in France, Italy, Germany, and Japan in the final years of World War II.

Martin v. Hunter's Lessee (1816) a U.S. Supreme Court ruling that sustained the Judiciary Act of 1789. In this decision written by Justice Joseph Story, under the leadership of Chief Justice John Marshall, the Supreme Court imposed its own power of judicial review over the states' highest courts and extended its power to determine constitutionality on appeals from state and federal courts. The ruling is an extension of *Marbury v. Madison* in that it broadens the power of interpretation.

Marxism the economic, social, and political philosophy and methodology developed by Karl Marx (1818–83) and laid out in his three-volume work *Das Kapital* (primarily 1867, and completed by Friedrich Engels in 1885 and 1895) and the *Communist Manifesto* (1848). Marx, writing in London after expulsion from Prussia, set out several theories: (1) that the value of all capital is based on the labor of those who created it; (2) that there is a constant "class struggle" between the wealthy, allied with the middle-class "bourgeoisie," and the "proletariat" (the working class); (3) that the course of history follows the Hegelian theory of thesis, antithesis, and synthesis, of which the class struggle is an example ("dialectical materialism"); (4) that capitalism is doomed as an economic system since it diverts unearned capital to the wealthy from those who labored to create it; and (5) that religion is an "opiate" to distract people from rectifying their material inequality. Basically an analysis of history during the industrial revolution, Marx's theories became an international political force following the Russian Revolution in 1918, which used Marxism as the basis for Soviet communism as interpreted by V. I. Lenin. It became the philosophical foundation for several other socialist and communist regimes in the 20th century, including governments established in the People's Republic of China, Cuba, North Korea, Vietnam, and several states of the now defunct Soviet Bloc. It constituted the basis of doctrines espoused by some revolutionaries in Africa as well as Western European Communist parties. See also MARXIST LENINISM.

Marxist Leninism Marxism as interpreted and employed by V. I. Lenin (1870–1924), founding leader of the Soviet Union (1918). Lenin propounded his version of Marxism in *The Development of Capitalism in Russia,* which he finished in 1899 while exiled in Siberia, and in his program of organization and action presented to a congress of international Marxian Socialists in 1903. Lenin gave philosophical Marxism a strongly political structure "resting on an economic foundation" in which the dictatorship of the proletariat would be temporary until "all the springs of collective wealth flow with abundance" when communist society would "[Take] from each according to his abilities, [and give] to each according to his needs." See also BOLSHEVIKS; LENINISM; MARXISM.

mass media (or media) communications with the masses via television, radio, newspapers, magazines, or computer ostensibly to report the news and other information.

In the United States the mass media (plural of medium) have moved beyond serving simply as reporters of information and now can greatly influence politics and society's decisions and development by selecting and controlling information relayed to the public. By limiting the range of words to which most Americans are exposed, the mass media can control the number of words American use, either to think or to speak. Therefore, the mass media can affect the public's thinking and action, as much by the information it chooses not to present as by what it does present. It can, for example, influence election results by declaring winners before voting polls close.

Many conservatives view mass media reporters as liberals overly critical of them. Liberals complain that some newspapers and magazines are owned by conservatives who control the news (excluding them or coloring stories) and editorial endorsements.

Mass media in dictatorships have been used to disseminate outright, one-sided propaganda, as a result of control of the media by the person or administration in power. Many American presidents have manipulated the mass media by playing favorites, releasing information to reporters whom they trust to reveal only what the presidents want known. In May 1992, members of the mass media argued over how much brutality in the southcentral Los Angeles riots was appropriate to show the public. Some argued that they had a duty to mirror every detail while others believed they had a responsibility to select the number and brutality of beatings and fire settings. Protection of the newsmakers and the public's right to know are always conflicting issues.

matching funds (1) government program funds (usually federal) that are granted to states, counties, or municipalities if those entities provide an equal contribution, thus guaranteeing local participation. Granting of these funds usually requires adherence to standards of use set in Washington. Redevelopment (urban renewal) funding for cities is a good example. Imaginative recipients often try to make their contribution from financing for local improvements, which they would have received with or without the federal funding. (2) a component of public financing of presidential campaigns. See also PUBLIC CAMPAIGN FINANCE.

materialism (1) putting higher values on material possessions than on morality, religion, philosophy, custom, or culture. (2) a Marxist theory that one's social consciousness is the result of one's material and economic condition or status, and therefore all social and political conditions are dependent upon material or physical things.

maverick (1) a label created in reference to Samuel Maverick who refused to brand his Texas ranch cattle. They roamed, stampeded, mixed, and bred with other ranchers' branded cattle. Eventually Maverick claimed all unbranded cattle as his. (2) a person who cannot be labeled correctly as belonging to one particular party, faction, or perspective and who acts independently and somewhat unpredictably.

McCain-Feingold Bill a campaign finance reform bill jointly authored by Senator John McCain (R–Ariz.) and Senator Russell Feingold (D–Wisc.), which basically would prohibit most "soft money" contributions.

McCarran Act (McCarran Internal Security Act) required registration of all communists with the attorney general, barred communists from employment in government or defense plants, denied passports to communists, barred former communists from entering the United States, authorized the attorney general to name communist-front organizations (also required to register), and set up the Subversive Activities Control Board.

The McCarran Act, authored by Senator Pat McCarran (D–Nev.), was enacted September 23, 1950, by overriding President Harry Truman's veto, on a vote of 291–48 in the House and 57–10 in the Senate. Truman contended that the act was aimed at controlling opinions and not activities. No one registered, and the attorney general brought noncompliance charges against 44 individuals and 22 organizations. None of these charges stood up on appeal.

An important side effect was the use of the act in the 1950s as the rationale for "investigations" by the House Un-American Activities Committee, the Senate Internal Security Subcommittee, and the Senate Subcommittee on Investigations ("The McCarthy Committee") to embarrass or intimidate persons accused without due process.

In 1965 the U.S. Supreme Court ruled the passport restrictions unconstitutional and in 1966 it declared that registration violated the ban on self-incrimination contained in the Constitution's Fifth Amendment.

McCarthyism term used to describe the methods, the collective mental set of the supporters of Senator Joseph Raymond McCarthy (R–Wisc.), and the fearful political atmosphere created by McCarthy's unsubstantiated charges against the Truman administration and anyone he suspected of communism or he wanted "to get" in the early 1950s. His principal tactic involved waving papers he claimed contained lists of communists in various government departments in time for evening news deadlines. He never showed the names.

Using paid witnesses willing to say anything, Senator McCarthy accused numerous officials and experts of participating in a communist conspiracy against the United States or of being blind dupes to communism. Many of those he attacked had expressed dismay with Chiang Kai Chek's government, which had left mainland China for Taiwan. Much of the funding for Senator McCarthy's political activities came from Chiang's "China Lobby."

Government officials and academics panicked in fear that their careers would be ruined if Senator McCarthy accused them and so they refused to complain about McCarthy's demagoguery, resulting in a form of self-censorship. Republican strategists, including Richard Nixon, enjoyed McCarthy's trashing of Democrats as the party of traitors.

Eventually newscaster Edward R. Morrow exposed some of McCarthy's tactics on national television, cartoonist Walt Kelly in his comic strip *Pogo* parodied him as a sleazy swamp cat, and Congressman Eugene J. McCarthy (D–Minn.) bested Joe McCarthy on a national radio debate. By 1954 Republican president Dwight D. Eisenhower tried to disassociate himself from Senator McCarthy and the tactics he employed in his attack on the army as a nest of communist sympathizers.

McCarthy's supporters saw him as a dedicated patriot and guardian of "Americanism." His opponents saw him as an irresponsible, self-promoting witch hunter undermining civil liberties and ruining people's careers and lives. Targets of McCarthyism included General George Marshall, China expert Owen D. Lattimore, diplomat Philip Jessup, Secretary of State Dean Acheson, and most of the Staff of the State Department. McCarthyism ended abruptly when the Senate censured him in 1954. He died three years later, in part due to his alcoholism. See also ARMY-MCCARTHY HEARINGS.

McNary-Haugen bills (1924–1928) congressional bills meant to keep farm prices high, enabling farmers to make greater profits on crops such as wheat, cotton, and tobacco. The McNary-Haugen bills resemble many of those benefiting America's farmers today.

The bills included a provision to establish a federal farm corporation to purchase and store surplus crops until demand and prices rose or sell them abroad at local prices, which were below the American market value. The government corporation's losses were covered by an equalization tax levied on growers.

The plan was criticized as being socialistic and bills were defeated in the House of Representatives (1924) and in both houses (1926). New versions passed in 1927 and 1928, but both were vetoed by President Calvin Coolidge. Eventually the concept was adopted by President Franklin D. Roosevelt in his New Deal.

means test   a requirement that government benefits paid to a citizen must be based on the recipient's income and financial status. Student loans, food stamps, and Aid to Families with Dependent Children (AFDC) are means-tested programs.

measured response   calculated, careful response to negotiations or provocation, made with the hope that problems can be resolved without war.

media   (1) communication vehicles and their representatives or reporters, such as newspapers, magazines, radio, television, and the Internet. (2) the plural of *medium.*

media event   an event organized or staged solely and explicitly to gain exposure to the media (particularly television news) for the person or subject. When photographs or television coverage is possible, it may be called a "photo-op," for photo opportunity with little news content.

Medicaid   federal program of matching-fund grants to the states to provide medical care for the needy (particularly children of the poor), enacted on July 30, 1965, along with Medicare for senior citizens. Each state's entitlement is based on its per capita income. Since 1972, the state programs have required a small premium for enrollment. Criticisms of overuse, double billing and unnecessary examinations by doctors, hospitals, and clinics have been met in part by computerization of the patient profiles. Medicaid is administered on the national level by the Health Care Financing Administration under the Department of Health and Human Services, and in each state by a similar administrative body. In most states the program is called Medicaid; in California it is called MediCal.

Medicare   a federal government insurance system signed into law by President Lyndon B. Johnson on July 30, 1965, to provide most Americans over 65 with basic health insurance to cover medical and hospital care with funds from Social Security and other sources. Presidents and Congress debate potential cutbacks or increases in social security and Medicare payments perennially. Generally conservatives favor limitations on funds expended and liberals object. Little change generally occurs since the recipients constitute large voting blocs.

Me Generation   critical reference to those young people who came to maturity in the 1970s and 1980s, a time of relative affluence, after the national struggles over civil rights, the Vietnam War, and cultural change in the 1960s. The Me Generation's elders saw them as selfish, inconsiderate, little concerned with social change, highly materialistic and for "me first"—hence the pejorative designation. Some people find this attitude reflected in what they saw as the rapacious nature of politics and business in the 1980s. See also POLITICS OF GREED; YUPPIES.

mending fences making peace with one's opponents after an election or with one's critics to facilitate governance and to get reelected. Mending fences may include compromising formerly strong positions on issues or personalities.

merchants of death (1) *Fort Worth Star-Telegram* columnist Molly Ivins's term for the United States as the "number-one arms merchant in the world." (2) pejorative term popular after World War I for manufacturers of military weapons.

merit system a civil service promotion system developed so that employees advance on the merits of their work instead of on patronage and longevity.

To some liberals "merit system" constitutes buzzwords for abandoning enforcement of equal rights and affirmative action to offset minority hiring and promotion.

Conservatives, as well as many moderates and liberals, endorse the merit system as the only truly fair system, even though its tests may put minorities, the unemployed, the undereducated, and the undertrained at a disadvantage.

message theme of a campaign or candidacy. A candidate has to strive to get his or her message across to the voters.

Mexican American Legal Defense and Education Fund (MALDEF) an organization formed in 1968 to promote and protect the "civil rights of Hispanics in the United States." Pete Tijerina decided that Hispanics in the Southwest needed an organization similar to the NAACP to protect and

advance their civil and legal rights. Jack Greenberg helped Tijerina secure major funding from the Ford Foundation. Tijerina recruited then-Texas assistant attorney general Mario Obledo, who eventually became president and general counsel. MALDEF has advocated for Hispanics on bilingual education, voting rights, reapportionment, fair employment and payment, governmental appointments and immigration issues. Address: 634 South Spring Street, 11th Floor, Los Angeles, Calif. 90014-1974. Tel.: (213) 629-2512; FAX (213) 629-0266; e-mail: maldef@azteca.net; website: www.maldef.org

Middle America a term first used by syndicated columnist Joseph Kraft in 1968 to describe "the great mass of some 40 million persons who have recently moved from just above the poverty line to just below the level of affluence." In the 1990s, the term more aptly applies to millions of Americans who are one paycheck away from poverty or homelessness. The attitudes of Middle America change with religious, economic, and political waves.

middle of the road a political position that suggests a position on the middle line between two extremes, but may in fact constitute no position at all. Middle of the road used to imply a moderate position in the total political spectrum, but in the 1990s Republicans have employed the term to describe positions in the middle of the Republican perspective.

Conservative Republican presidents Ronald Reagan and George H. W. Bush tried to polarize American political thinking between liberal and conservative, with little true middle-of-the-roadness left. In the 1990s the Democratic leadership moved distinctly to the right to aim at the middle of the road so as to avoid Bush's designations of "liberal."

midnight basketball   a controversial program that began in New York City as a program to keep inner-city youth occupied in participating in sports activities within the community during long summer nights.

mid-term election   (1) an election that takes place midway in any president's four-year term. Mid-term elections may seem mid-term for the president, but for a member of Congress, who is up for election every two years, so-called midterm elections are full-term elections. The party in the White House often looses seats in mid-term elections. (2) Canada: an election held between federal elections, usually called to fill a vacancy. See also BY-ELECTION.

militant   the condition of being ready and willing to fight for one's principles because of one's strong, active commitment to a cause or belief. Conservatives often use "militant" to describe Democratic activists, while liberals consider the Ku Klux Klan and some right-to-life organizations' tactics as militant.

militarism   (1) ready use of the military to solve problems. (2) glorification of militaristic trappings. (3) a country's threat to use military force to gain its ends, thereby threatening world peace and encouraging stockpiling and brandishing of armaments.

military-industrial complex   "military" refers to all the armed forces, and "industrial" refers to the businesses and manufacturers that benefit from the military, often by producing and selling them arms, nuclear weapons, and aircraft. The term may include congressional armed forces committees and was coined by general and president Dwight D. Eisenhower in a January 18, 1961, speech in which he warned against the dangers of the influence of this power base. The "industrial" sector influences the military's decisions by means of well-placed campaign contributions and through less visible support, while the "military" scratches the "industrial's" back by making procurement decisions, which increase "industrial's" business.

Conservatives, always concerned about national security, favor preservation of the military-industrial complex's status quo, often benefit from it, and sometimes are part of it. Liberals worry about the combined power of the military-industrial complex and its influence on congressional and executive branch policy making. They also see two dangers: (1) if this entity is allowed to produce weapons almost with abandon, the government will want to use them and, (2) diversion of the national economic base and expenditures from social programs to armaments and an increased national debt can result.

military intelligence   a collection of information about other countries' military activities, thought also to be a contradiction in terms or a self-canceling phrase.

military regime   a group of people (men) controlling a government with military force, often following a coup d'état. The military regime often suspends civil rights and legislative processes, and rules without checks and balances. Sometimes factions within a military regime war with each other, resulting in a coup within a coup. In many countries, particularly in Latin America, the military's assumption of power is often facilitated by the right wing to declare martial law, a state of emergency, or a state of siege during military proclamations of national emergencies. See also JUNTA.

ministerial accountability session
Canada: a political party convention or parliamentary session in which department ministers (cabinet members) answer questions from delegates or legislators.

minority   (1) less than half of a public. (2) a group united by a common identity, usually ethnic, racial, religious, or political, that differs substantially from the majority that dominates, wins elections, and overpowers the minority. Political minorities may exist on single issues or be short term, while ethnic, racial, religious, and national minorities are established social groups. Minorities are often mistreated by the dominant majority. To make up for past transgressions, the American majority has instigated "affirmative action" through legislative mandate to help minorities recover from discrimination, an effort seen as "reverse discrimination" or "quotas" by many conservative whites. (3) in the United States, a term used to define African-American,

Asian, Hispanic, or Native American racial groups, and homosexuals.

Statistically women make up America's majority, but they are treated like a minority. In California (1990) "minorities" combine to make a disparate majority, with whites in the minority.

minority government   Canada or United Kingdom: usually a coalition government in which the governing political party has less than a majority of the members of parliament.

minority leader   a minority party member of any legislative body whose peers select him/her as spokesperson and leader. The minority leader is usually an experienced member who has the ability to lead and unify party members to vote for legislation and develop issues and publicity for his party members. In the House and Senate he is often a spokesman for his party's position and responds to the majority's program proposals.

minority report   a legislative communication presented by the minority in a vote to state their position for public knowledge and for the record.

Miranda Decision (*Miranda v. Arizona*)   the U.S. Supreme Court decision (1966) establishing the rights of a criminal suspect ro be told by arresting officers that he/she has the right to remain silent, the right to legal counsel, and the right to be told that anything he/she says can be used (in court) against him/her. Further, if the accused person confesses, the prosecution must prove that he/she knowingly waived these rights. These rights must be read or recited to the accused, and are also known as "Miranda Rights" or "rights."

mislead   a word used by U.S. politicians instead of the word "lie" to describe untruths they have spoken.

mission   (1) the sending out of people to persuade or force others to adopt one's or a government's thinking, perspective or position. (2) a special function, task, or purpose that someone is sent out to accomplish.

mission creep   the changes in a mission, purpose, or task that evolves while the mission is in progress, for example, peacekeeping forces sent to another country who eventually end up bombing the country.

Mississippi Freedom Democratic Party   a civil rights organization that sent 64 black and four white delegates to the 1964 Democratic National Convention demanding to be seated in place of the lily-white segregationist Mississippi delegation.

The Freedom Democrats, led by Fannie Lou Hamer and Aaron Henry, claimed that the official party had fought registration of black voters, that delegates had been selected undemocratically, and that the segregationist delegation did not intend to support the national party platform. The televised credentials committee testimony forced a compromise (worked out by Hubert Humphrey and Walter Mondale) that seated the Freedom Democrats as an "at large" delegation, but did not unseat the "regulars," who then staged a walkout.

At the 1968 Democratic Convention, the Mississippi Freedom Democratic Party, backed by delegates for both Eugene McCarthy and Hubert Humphrey, unseated the all-white "regulars." The event was a major triumph in the fight to end segregated politics in southern states.

moderate   a person holding a political position in the middle philosophically between conservative and liberal and without die-hard commitment to a position. Many Republicans consider themselves to be moderates, usually within their own party, and do not hold militant views in any extreme. Moderate Republicans struggled in the late 1980s and 1990s to retain even minor control of their party against the strength of the religious right and other conservatives.

Democrats range from moderate to liberal, but rarely use the word relative to themselves. On occasion they use it in reference to certain Republicans, usually with a congratulatory tone that the individual does not line up with the extreme wing of the Republican Party.

monarchy   a system of government in which a single individual of royal or noble heritage rules a country from the top of a pyramid of authority. Succession is based on inheritance from the royal family. In a constitutional monarchy, such as the United Kingdom (or Canada), the monarch's power is limited, and elected and voting entities generally control governmental functions. In this case there remains a reverence and respect for the monarch as a head of state who has the power of moral suasion. In Great Britain the monarchy recognizes a new government following elections and grants that government the authority to dissolve parliament, when it lacks legislative support or when mandated by law, and call a new election, beginning the whole cycle again.

Following World War I, monarchies in Germany, Russia, Austria-Hungary, and the Ottoman Empire came to an end. A few monarchies remain, including Great Britain, Japan, Norway, Sweden, the Netherlands, Belgium, Denmark, Spain (restored), Monaco, Saudi Arabia, Jordan, and Nepal. See also CONSTITUTIONAL MONARCHY.

money   currency that pays for political campaigns, buys influence, and corrupts the greedy. The late California state treasurer and state assembly speaker Jesse Unruh used to call money "the mother's milk of politics."

money laundering   See LAUNDERED MONEY.

Monroe Doctrine   a declaration of principle written by John Quincy Adams and announced by President James Monroe in his 1823 message to Congress. Under his doctrine the United States ostensibly assumed responsibility for the defense of the Western Hemisphere. The original intent was to fend off European colonization, but more recently (1962) President John F. Kennedy invoked the Monroe Doctrine to resist the Soviet Union's placement of missiles in Fidel Castro's communist Cuba. Kennedy employed a blockade to force a Soviet withdrawal. President Lyndon B. Johnson used the Monroe Doctrine to rationalize the U.S. "intervention" in the Dominican Republic (1965).

At its founding conference (1945) the United Nations recognized the Monroe Doctrine as a doctrine of regional sphere of influence, and it still does.

Moral Majority   an alliance of New Right and New Christian Right (Religious Right) formed in 1979, so designated by President Richard Nixon.

The Moral Majority worked to elect conservative candidates who shared their beliefs that current office-holders and Supreme Court justices did not reflect their morals, which they presumed to be those of the majority of Americans. They crusaded for Christian prayer in public schools, against abortion, and against homosexual activity or even association with homosexuals whose sexual orientation they judged as contrary to the precepts of the Bible.

The Moral Majority was instrumental in the elections of President Ronald Reagan and Vice President George H. W. Bush, in which adherents employed a clever merging of church and state interests. Leader Jerry Falwell kept and issued his "moral report cards" on Congress and espoused "pro-God, pro-family" programs.

Conservatives accepted the Moral Majority's power, votes, campaign contributions, and principles, all of which resulted in President George H. W. Bush's revised position on "choice" in which he moved from favoring the right to choose to opposing it and withdrawing the rights of federally funded health clinics to disseminate information on abortion. This latter act was reversed by President Bill Clinton on his first day in office, restoring the rights of clinics to distribute abortion information to all clients. (2) a term applied by some anti-abortionists to describe themselves or people with the same opinions.

mossback   an unrelenting conservative who moves or changes so slowly that moss can grow on his/her back.

Most Favored Nation (MFN)   a diplomatic and trade status designation with and by the U.S. government. Most Favored Nation (MFN) status can result in lowered tariffs for goods imported to the United States from the designated country as well as cooperative trade and tariff agreements.

MFN can be used to bring economic and diplomatic pressure against nations lacking the status. MFN status had been withheld from the People's Republic of China due to its abuse of human rights. The Tiananmen Square massacres (1990) against pro-democracy activists brought China's abuses to the American public conscience, resulting in public and congressional demands, led by Representative Nancy Pelosi (D–Calif.), that MFN status be withheld until human rights violations cease. President George H. W. Bush favored giving China MFN status without demanding improvement of human rights violations.

President Bill Clinton extended MFN status to China (1993 and 2000) with the stipulation mandating review of China's human rights activities and MFN status at the end of one year. With prodding from President Clinton, Congress gave China MFN status without restrictions, such as annual review, despite opposition

from organized labor, some environmentalists, and human rights advocates.

motion   a proposal to discuss or vote on a suggestion.

Motor Voter Bill/Act   a bill and then an act passed by Congress and signed by President Bill Clinton (1993) allowing voter registration with driver's license applications. The bill was generally opposed by conservatives who feared that, if the process were made easier, more Democrats would register to vote. It probably benefits both parties equally.

mouthpiece   paid spokesperson.

movers and shakers   activists with influence on decisions, appointments, and favors given.

MTV   a successful cable music television network that features music videos, humor, and hip news broadcasts to appeal to young Americans. Occasionally criticized for showing videos espousing sexism, abuse, and violence, MTV is watched my millions of Americans and influences much of America's youth on commercial purchases and social issues. MTV has brought young Americans who do not read newspapers or magazines in touch with current events and politics. MTV's Tabitha Soren interviewed candidates Bill Clinton and President George H. W. Bush during the 1992 presidential campaign, opening the sessions to questions from the audience and bringing presidential politics close to young voters for the first time.

muckraker a person, often a reporter, who digs persistently to uncover and expose details of news and investigates difficult stories involving scandal, corruption, and business activities against the public good.

Theodore Roosevelt first used the term (1906), alluding to the character in John Bunyan's *Pilgrim's Progress* who was too busy raking muck to consider his heavenly crown. Roosevelt applied it to journalists, novelists, and historians who published shocking accounts and revelations of corporate and governmental activity, including unhealthy work conditions, government corruption, and industry control by monopolies.

Sometimes used pejoratively, the term is now often used respectfully for those who engage in the business of revealing inequities and injustices.

mudslinging making outrageous, malicious, wild, and derogatory verbal attacks or charges against an opponent, usually political.

mugwump (1) from a Native American word meaning "Big Leader" or "Big Chief." (2) a leader or person who sees her/himself as a leader but who really is not. (3) a term first used in 1872 to describe liberal Republicans who deserted the Ulysses S. Grant ticket in thinking they were more influential than the party. (4) a Republican who refused to support the 1884 nomination of James G. Blaine and supported Democrat Grover Cleveland while denouncing Blaine. (5) a person registered in one political party but who often votes for candidates of another party. (6) a person who has his mug on one side of the fence and his wump on the other.

multiculturalism a policy or custom of supporting several national origin or ethnic cultures side by side with appreciation, respect, preservation, and nurturing for all.

multilateral (1) having many sides. (2) having participants representing more than two sides. (3) when two or more nations participate in a discussion, an event, a war, or an agreement. (4) in nuclear arms negotiations, multilateral means that a country is ready to reduce its nuclear arsenals while another country does the same, as: "I will throw one away if you will throw one away first." By contrast, unilateral nuclear disarmament means getting rid of all nuclear arms irrespective of what an opponent does or does not do: "We are going to throw ours all away and hope that you do too," or "we are all going to throw ours away at the same time."

multilateralism diplomatic and trade relations among more than two separate nations.

multinational state a state made up of several nations, such as the United Kingdom.

multiparty system a political system with more than one political party, although "multi" suggests more than two major political parties. "Major" commonly refers to a party whose members consult and participate in forming a new government or administration after an election, runs second, or constitutes a large segment of the voting public. In the United States, Republicans and Democrats, as the only major parties, tend to ignore other parties, hoping to wish them away. In multiparty systems it is more difficult for one party to gain a true majority, forcing existing parties to work with the others toward mutually agreeable compromise to form a government. Great Britain and Canada have at least three parties, Germany has three including the Green Party, France has more than 100, Italy has dozens, and Argentina has at least 24. Parliamentary systems support multiple parties because of proportionality and the need to "form" a government, requiring consensus and agreement on leadership.

Mutual Assured Destruction (MAD) a theory prevalent from the mid-1950s to the late 1980s to describe a situation in which at least two countries stockpiled competitive amounts of nuclear arms that were so great that no party could use them to inflict damage on the other because any usage would mean mutual and, possibly, total destruction of both contesting nations (as well as the rest of the world). MAD thinking played a major role in the arms race and cold war with the inherent need or desire to keep up with and outpace the other country. During the 1950s to the 1980s, some thought MAD was the sole consideration that kept the United States and the U.S.S.R. from war.

NAACP See NATIONAL ASSOCIATION FOR THE ADVANCEMENT OF COLORED PEOPLE.

NAFTA (North American Free Trade Agreement) a complex proposed trade agreement to facilitate trade between Canada, the United States, and Mexico by reducing import tariffs and increasing sales and improving economies throughout North America.

Proponents believe the agreement will enhance the purchasing power of Mexican and Canadian residents and thereby improve American production, sales, and employment. Opponents fear that manufacturers will take advantage of the agreement to open plants in other countries to skirt the power of unions and avoid the payment of higher wages in the United States, thereby reducing American jobs and contributing to rampant pollution, particularly in Mexico. Unions and 1990s presidential candidate Ross Perot vehemently opposed the NAFTA. It passed both the House and Senate in November 1993, with unions vowing to defeat representatives who voted for it, but they failed to do so. It is still unclear what the effect of NAFTA has been.

Nannygate a controversy that arose early in President Bill Clinton's administration (1993) in which his first two nominees for attorney general, corporate lawyer Zoe Baird and Judge Kimba M. Wood, withdrew their names from consideration after it was discovered that they had employed illegal aliens as nannies and had not paid their Social Security taxes in violation of existing law. Even though Wood's offense ostensibly occurred before the 1986 law existed, presidential advisers insisted she withdraw to avoid embarrassment to the president among voters. Other cabinet-level presidential appointees Ron Brown as secretary of commerce and

Bobby Ray Inman as Clinton's second secretary of defense also failed to pay Social Security taxes on domestic help. Brown was confirmed by the Senate, but Inman withdrew his name from nomination (January 18, 1994) citing, in part, his Nannygate problems. Both paid their back taxes upon nomination.

narrow construction   a theory of constitutional interpretation that holds that all decisions by the U.S. Supreme Court and lower courts should be based on the exact words of the Constitution, and/or on what historians believe was the framers' intent, without subjective analysis. Of course, statements of what the framers' intent might have been are highly subjective and will vary based on the interpreter, what the person knows, the source of his/her knowledge, and his/her personal background and perspective. Opposite of "broad construction."

The Nation   one of the oldest intellectual opinion magazines in the United States, a liberal periodical read by a relatively small but influential audience of opinion leaders. E. L. Godkin founded the magazine (1865) to help freed African Americans adjust to their new lives. Under the editorship of Paul Elmer Moore (1909–1914), the magazine turned toward general discussions of progressivism and muckraking (of union practices), civil liberties, liberalism, and socialism. Address: 33 Irving Place, New York, N.Y. 10003. Tel.: (212) 209-5400; FAX: (212) 982-9000; e-mail: info@ thenation.com; website: www.thenation.com

nation building   an effort by a developed nation to assist an underdeveloped country to grow in a way the helping nation would like, with hopes of developing a physical and governmental infrastructure and an improved economy.

national anthem   a country's patriotic song. The U.S. national anthem is "The Star Spangled Banner," written by Francis Scott Key while watching the British bombardment of Fort McHenry (1814) during the War of 1812. Sung to an 18th-century drinking tune, it did not become the official American national anthem until named as such by an act of Congress in 1931.

Controversial renditions of the Star Spangled Banner include those of Jose Feliciano and Roseanne Barr, whose interpretations were deemed unpatriotic at the times they were sung.

Other national anthems include Great Britain's "God Save the King/Queen," Canada's "O, Canada," and France's "Marseillaise."

National Association for the Advancement of Colored People (NAACP)   America's largest (500,000 members) antidiscrimination organization, founded (1909) by the merging of the Niagara Movement, a W. E. B. DuBois–led band of young blacks, and a group of concerned conscientious whites. Founders William E. Walker, Garrison Villard, Jane Addams, John Dewey, and Hamilton Holt created the organization to work toward abolition of segregation and discrimination in transportation, socialization, voting, housing, employment, and education. The NAACP engages in political action, education, and public information, and of direct action (sit-ins). In 1939 the NAACP Legal Defense and Education Fund was established. It carried the case of *Brown v. Board of Education* to the U.S. Supreme Court, where Thurgood Marshall successfully argued for the school desegregation decision (1954). Although it does not endorse candidates, presidential hopefuls and presidents, particularly Democrats, usually speak to NAACP conventions. Republican candidate George W. Bush made a 2000 conciliatory speech to the NAACP in which he admitted to prior Republicans' neglect of the NAACP and its goals. Senator Robert Dole, 1996 Republican presidential nominee, refused to speak to them. Address: 4805 Mount Hope Drive, Baltimore, Md. 21215-3297. Tel.: (410) 521-4939; website: www.naacp. org

National Committee committees maintained nationally by both the Democratic and Republican parties. Until 1972 both major parties' national committees consisted of one national committeewoman and one national committeeman from each state. In that year the Democrats changed their system to one of proportional representation from each state. The Republicans still send one woman and one man to their national committee. National committees set party policy between national conventions and select their own officers and chairs, except when a U.S. president names the chair. They plan party strategy, raise funds between elections, run the parties' national conventions, and centralize power by enabling the national chair to pass out the funds for campaigns.

National committees believe they have power in determining public policy, when, in reality, that is determined by an incumbent president and/or Congress. Members of the national committee enjoy prestige principally among party activists.

Gaps often exist between national committees' policies and candidates' positions and beliefs. Addresses: Democratic National Committee: 430 South Capitol Street, S.E., Washington, D.C. 20003. Tel.: (202) 863-8000; website: www.democrats.org Republican National Committee: 310 1st Street, S.E., Washington, D.C. 20003. Tel.: (202) 863-8500; FAX: (202) 963-8820; e-mail: info@rnc.org; website.rnc.org

National Committee for an Effective Congress a group formed in 1948 to support candidates by effecting face-to-face encounters between members of Congress, congressional candidates, and the voting public. Claiming to be completely impartial and not aligned with any interest group, its first chairman was James Roosevelt and its longtime director was Maurice Rosenblatt.

The Committee for an Effective Congress generally supports liberal candidates with money and informs contributors of sympathetic candidates' needs. It also attempts to provide voter and precinct target marketing, demographic targeting, polling, and general advice. It keeps a close watch on Congress with particular concern for effectiveness, hard work, and progressive outlook. Address: 122 C Street, N.W., Washington, D.C. 20001. Tel.: (800) 547-5911; e-mail: info@ncec.org; website: www.ncec.org

national conventions quadrennial meetings of the two principal political parties held to nominate presidential and vice presidential candidates and to adopt a party platform. First held by the Anti-Masonic Party (1831), national conventions give delegates the power to nominate, but, in fact, delegates are usually already bound in differing degrees to vote the way they are pledged since most are now chosen in primaries or caucuses as slates for particular candidates.

Delegate selection methods vary by state and range from gubernatorial or party appointments of favorite, loyal supporters who can deliver money or votes to self-consciously democratic systems electing delegates by district caucuses open to the public.

The victorious nominees are usually known well before the conventions and most business is decided by select insiders on special-interest committees prior to the national convention. Today they are staged primarily for televised psychological manipulation of public opinion, and should be called "nomination festivals."

National Council of Churches of Christ in the U.S.A. a social action organization founded on September 29, 1950, by the merger of eight Protestant interfaith organizations. The group has grown to include 31 denominations, representing 40 million members, to educate through the media and publications on such subjects as civil rights, women's rights, and problems of the poor. Address: 475 Riverside Drive, New York, N.Y. 10115. Tel.: (212) 870-2227.

national identity a nation's citizens' collective image of themselves or their country, or the view of that country by outsiders, sometimes based on language, culture, heritage, or experience.

national interest a determination of what is best for a country or its people, which may favor some at the expense of others.

national health care (nationalized medicine, national medical insurance, state medicine, socialized medicine) several terms used to describe or attack a system to provide complete medical care for all citizens of a country, made available by public funding.

While the United States has made some of the most advanced technical discoveries in medicine in the world, it is the only major industrialized nation without some form of universal national health insurance or care.

Historically Republicans and conservatives, bolstered by doctors' professional associations and their hefty campaign contributions, have looked at national health care as "socialized medicine," inflicting upon the concept a semantic blow as a liberal program that smacks of socialism.

Liberals and Democrats have been only slightly more aggressive in exploring the possibilities of a national health program. Led by Senator Edward Kennedy (D–Mass.) for several years, most liberals have advocated a national health care system benefiting all citizens equally. They see national health care as an absolute necessity and personal right. President Bill Clinton's campaign promises tended to fall somewhere between pleasing the doctors and the insurance companies. As President, Clinton made a national health plan a priority and asked his wife, Hillary Rodham Clinton, to develop a health care plan for the country. The resulting proposal focused on "managed competition" in health care delivery for all Americans, paid for primarily by employers, a single form to reduce paperwork and costs, and cost controls. It was defeated in Congress.

Some liberals favor a "single payer" plan funded by taxes and premiums as exists in Canada and Great Britain, while some conservatives offer tax incentives to business owners as motivation to offer health insurance to their employees. Both Democrats and Republicans agree that something must be done to improve the American health system, because it is inadequate, expensive, 40 million children and their parents are without health insurance, and many among the public are demanding action. Party differences focus upon how it should be improved.

National Labor Relations Act (Wagner Act) also known as "Labor's Magna Carta," an act of Congress (1935) that declared that employees working at companies engaged in interstate commerce had the right to organize into unions and to bargain collectively with employers. It also established the five-person National Labor Relations Board (NLRB) to regulate industrial labor relations. The act defines which actions by employers constitute unfair labor practices.

National Labor Relations Board (NLRB) created as part of the National Labor Relations Act (Wagner Act), it is an independent regula-

tory commission with five members appointed by the president with the consent of the Senate. The NLRB is intended to protect employees' rights to unionize, prevent abuses by employers or larger labor organizations, and oversee unions. Address: 1099 14th Street, Washington, D.C. 20570. Tel.: (202) 273-4270; FAX: (202) 273-1789; website: www.nlrb.gov

National Labor Relations Board v. Jones and Laughlin Steel Corporation a case in which the U.S. Supreme Court ruled five to four (1937), in an opinion by Chief Justice Charles Evans Hughes, that the National Labor Relations Act establishing workers' rights was constitutional under the commerce clause of the Constitution. The ruling constituted a triumph for the New Deal after other New Deal legislation had been declared unconstitutional by the conservative majority of the Supreme Court, which President Franklin D. Roosevelt called the "nine old men."

National New Democratic Coalition a national 1980s network of Democratic Party officeholders, activists, and national committee members who shared interest in campaigns, progressive issues, and human rights. The group evolved into the Democratic Leadership Council. See also DEMOCRATIC LEADERSHIP COUNCIL.

National Organization for Women (NOW) a feminist organization formed after the Equal Employment Opportunity Commission refused to enforce a Civil Rights Act (1964) clause prohibiting discrimination on the basis of gender. NOW has

branches throughout the United States and has worked to develop and promote employment opportunities for women, create and support legislation to establish truly equal opportunities, and support women candidates. NOW actively opposed the confirmation of Clarence Thomas for Justice of the U.S. Supreme Court (1991). It now concentrates on "choice" and women's reproductive rights, the proposed Equal Rights Amendment, and support for civil rights, including lesbian and gay rights. NOW's activities are usually seen as "feminist" by some liberals and as radical by many conservatives and moderates and a few liberals. Address: 1000 16th Street, N.W., Suite 700, Washington, D.C. 20036-5705. Tel.: (202) 331-0066; website: www.now.org

National Recovery Administration (NRA) part of the National Industrial Recovery Act (June 1933), which authorized President Franklin D. Roosevelt to institute industry codes to eliminate unfair trade practices, reduce unemployment, establish minimum wages and maximum hours, and guarantee labor's right to collective bargaining. The NRA became a government agency set up to stimulate business recovery from the Great Depression. The codes benefited big business interests at the expense of small business and consumers, although it did allow for development of the labor movement. Companies managed in compliance with NRA codes displayed Blue Eagle emblems in their windows. The NRA was struck down by the Supreme Court in the *Schecter Poultry Corp. v. United States* decision (1935). The *Schecter* case ruling stipulated that setting standards under such codes was an improper delegation of government authority and held that code creation should be the responsibility of the legislative branch. Many of the NRA codes were precursors of legislation on pertinent subjects, such as child labor laws, minimum wages, and industrial safety.

National Review the most prominent journal of American conservatism, founded and still edited by William F. Buckley. Buckley has used the magazine as a platform to espouse and spread his own philosophy and to publish articles that are intellectually and philosophically conservative. Address: 215 Lexington Avenue, New York, N.Y. 10016. Tel.: (212) 679-7330; e-mail: nronline@national-review.com; website: www.nationalreview.com

National Rifle Association (NRA) originally an organization formed in Great Britain (1860) for those interested in the sport of shooting with rifles and pistols. Created in the United States in 1870, and formerly known as the National Rifle Association of America, the NRA by the 1970s claimed a membership of 1,100,000 target shooters, hunters, gun collectors, gunsmiths, and law enforcement officers.

The NRA began to lobby actively against gun control in the early 1960s, making opposition to handgun registration, waiting periods for security checks, and bans on automatic assault weapons their crusades. They actively countered movements for gun control legislation following the assassinations of John F. Kennedy, Rev. Martin Luther King Jr., and Robert F. Kennedy. Claiming that the Second Amendment gives all individuals and state militias the right to bear arms, the NRA created fear among hunters and gun devotees that such controls could lead to loss of legitimate use of guns. This position became a lucrative recruiting and fund-raising tool of the organization.

The association supports members of Congress who oppose gun control with money and votes.

Liberals usually avoid NRA types, detest their militaristic attitudes, favor some gun control, including registering handguns and banning assault weapons with rapid fire capability, and see NRA members as extreme narrow-minded conservatives. NRA members and supporters consider themselves to be sportsmen and defenders of the people's right to protect themselves against criminals. Their favorite slogans are: "Guns don't kill people, people do" and "If guns are outlawed only outlaws will have guns."

The NRA lost some influence in the 1990s after outbreaks of children killing foreign tourists and others with handguns, mass murders and drive-by shootings by mentally disturbed people and gangs with assault weapons, and broader public support for the "Brady Bill." It remains a focused, political force and has begun a new—and somewhat successful—campaign to get women to buy guns to avoid being victims. Under its president actor Charlton Heston, the NRA's rhetoric became increasingly vitriolic and partisan, claiming that President Clinton and Vice President Gore needed some gun deaths to gain support for the Clinton/Gore agenda to ban guns. Address: 1600 Rhode Island Avenue, N.W., Washington, D.C.

20036. Tel.: (202) 828-6000; website: www.nra.org

National Urban League a voluntary service organization of civic, labor, business, and religious leaders established (1910) to eliminate race discrimination and obtain full personal and civil rights for African Americans. First called the National League on Urban Conditions among blacks, it was a coalition of groups that had been working on such urban problems as housing, employment, family breakdown, and juvenile crime. The Urban League originally worked to secure industrial jobs for blacks and to help newly arrived migrant blacks to adjust to urban life. Its current emphasis includes equal job and promotion opportunities, counseling, education, guidance, and greater housing opportunities. The Urban League reached its peak membership of 50,000 in 90 local groups in the 1970s. Address: 120 Wall Street, New York, N.Y. 10005. Tel.: (212) 558-5300; e-mail: info@nul.org; website: www.nul.org

National Women's Political Caucus (NWPC) a group formed in 1971 to achieve equal representation for women at all levels of elective and appointive government positions. NWPC set out to support women candidates, register women voters, and help women acquire decision-making positions and respect. At its inception, NWPC worked to fight "sexism, racism, violence, and poverty," and one of its most visible organizers and supporters was Representative Bella Abzug (D–N.Y.). It welcomes men as members, seeks out potential candidates of both major parties, and supports them with fund-raising and voter registration. Address: 1630 Connecticut Ave., N.W., #201, Washington, D.C. 20009. Tel.: (202) 898-1100; FAX: (202) 785-3605; website: www.nwpc.org

National Youth Administration a New Deal agency (1935–43) formed to promote part-time employment for high school and college students.

nationalism (1) loyalty and pride in one's country. (2) a slightly obsessive devotion to one's nation that allows leaders and followers to believe that national security and national interests (determined by those leaders) are more important than international considerations and cooperation. (3) ideology and emotion that make loyalty to the nation or state the most important consideration in political decisions. (4) sometimes the driving force for independence and self-determination and a demand for equal standing and treatment. The last two elements motivated the various nationalities of the Soviet Union to force its breakup into separate states, as well as leading to the division of Yugoslavia into several Balkan states.

Nationalism puts one's country first above all others and all other considerations and can engender a strong positive identification with a nation's culture, history, and people. It can also lead to isolation and hatred and fear of foreigners (xenophobia). On occasion nationalism has been used emotionally and psychologically by a leader to manipulate a people's support and prey on their fears while obscuring other problems. In 1991, President George H. W. Bush used

nationalism to arouse American fear of Iraqis and Saddam Hussein to garner support for the Gulf War. Bush's efforts distracted American voters' attention away from the country's savings-and-loan scandal and recession, and unified public spirit against Saddam Hussein. Hussein, in turn, used Iraqi nationalism to rouse his people to a fighting spirit and obscure that country's economic weakness, oppressive government, and devastating casualties from the war.

nationalized medicine See NATIONAL HEALTH CARE.

nation-state a country with an established government.

Native American Party See KNOW-NOTHING PARTY.

Native Americans (1) formerly known as American Indians or those people indigenous to North America (called "first people" in Canada), particularly before Columbus' arrival. (2) anyone born in the United States. (3) another self-given name for members of the Know-Nothing Party (1850s) who opposed immigrants, especially Irish Catholics.

nativism the belief that citizens whose ancestors occupied a country first are superior to, or more aristocratic than, newer arrivals. Those who believe in their own nativism often expect to be treated better than other people and recognized for their social position and status.

Many Anglo-Saxon Protestants who arrived in America from England held such an attitude, and each new wave of immigrants to the United States has felt superior to those who follow, resulting in discrimination against people by nationality or ethnicity. American Indians are the ultimate nativists, but their high regard for themselves is largely ignored by white immigrants, who set up their own pecking order exclusive of Indians. Groups who have suffered from nativistic prejudices include Italians, Irish, blacks, Asians, Catholics, and Jews.

Modern nativism couches its contentions in fear for jobs, potential welfare cases, health problems, and radical nationalist rivalries imported by some immigrants.

NATO (North Atlantic Treaty Organization)

an alliance of North Atlantic nations set up to provide a common defense of freedom. Actually, it was established to protect against the perceived threat of communism. The NATO Treaty was signed (1949) by the foreign ministers of Belgium, Canada, Denmark, France, Ireland, Italy, Luxembourg, the Netherlands, Norway, United Kingdom, and the United States. Greece and Turkey joined in 1952, and West Germany in 1955. Eastern European nations in the Soviet sphere formed the Warsaw Pact as a counterweight. France is now only a partial member, since it removed its military forces from NATO's direct control. Originally a cold war entity, NATO created its own defense installations and coordinated air, naval, and ground forces of member nations. Government leaders of many NATO nations have questioned the need for its structure since the end of the cold war while leaders of some Eastern European states plead for membership as they work to establish genuine democratic governments. Address: NATO, 1110 Brussels, Belgium.

natural law (1) laws and standards thought by some to be derived from moral principles and God's law and will. (2) laws derived from nature and reason, embodied in the Declaration of Independence statement that "all men are created equal, that they are endowed by their creator with certain inalienable Rights, that among these are Life, Liberty and the pursuit of Happiness." John Locke had used the phrase "protection of property." (3) opposite of positive law, or those created by the state, namely, by man. Some people rationalize that laws against killing and stealing are natural law, as they interpret God's will. Natural law assumes, falsely, that all people worship the same Judeo-Christian God, and thus share an understanding of natural law premises.

In his Senate Judiciary Committee confirmation hearings for the Supreme Court, Clarence Thomas referred more than once to natural law, expecting people to know precisely what he meant. Americans formed their own conclusions, many held differing views of what he meant, and some criticized him because they did not share his conception.

Natural Law Party a small American political party founded by followers of Maharishi Mahesh Yogi, founder of transcendental meditation and onetime guru to the Beatles. The party's basic doctrine holds that society should be governed by basic ethical and scientific principles that are common to all mankind. The party focuses on disease and crime prevention, reduction of stress by employing transcendental meditation, and promotion of the principle that government should not legislate morality or interfere in private moral decisions. Address: P.O. Box 1900, Fairfield, Ia. 52556. Tel.: (800) 332-0000; FAX: (515) 472-2011; e-mail: info@natural-law.org; website: www. natural-law.org

natural rights (1) rights supposedly endowed by God's will. (2) rights that one would derive from divine law or in a totally natural state, such as rights to life, property, family, and the right to be free to do what one wants as long as the action does not harm another human being or infringe upon another person's human rights. Since natural rights are not given by legislation, they cannot be withdrawn by legislation or man's laws.

naturalized citizen a person born in a country other than the United States who immigrates to the United States, meets the residency requirement (five years), passes a written test, takes the loyalty oath, and becomes a U.S. citizen.

Naziism the beliefs of a fascist German political party named the National Socialist German Workers' Party (Nationalsozialistische Deutsche Arbeiterpartei), generally known as the Nazi Party (1919–45).

Under its leader, German chancellor Adolf Hitler (1933–45), Naziism was the philosophical underpinning of his totalitarian, brutal, and murderous regime. Naziism stressed the superiority of the white, Aryan race and denigration of Jews, blacks, gyp-

sies, other racial minorities, and ethnic immigrants to Germany. It included the systematic elimination of six million Jews and members of the opposition. It was supported by industries anxious to profit from massive military production and millions of middle-class Germans who hoped for full employment and came to believe in the myth of German superiority. Naziism required blind faith in Hitler's absolute dictatorship and the precepts that underpinned it, including militarism, brutality, and aggression.

Near v. Minnesota a case in which the U.S. Supreme Court ruled that "prior restraint" upon publications is a violation of free speech and free press. The 1931 decision struck down a Minnesota statute that had allowed police abatement (removal and destruction) of "malicious, scandalous, and defamatory" or "obscene, lewd and lascivious" newspapers. The *Near* case involved a libelous anti-Semitic newspaper, which had been confiscated under the state statute.

While not part of the ruling, the above attributions require subjective judgments. One person's obscenity may be another person's fine art, and one person's legitimate news is another's libel. In the balance between free speech and noxious statements, free speech is favored.

negative advertising advertising that attacks a candidate's opponent instead of emphasizing the candidate's own positive qualities.

negative campaigning the campaign practice of emphasizing one's opponents' negatives, either actual or imagined, instead of advocating one's own positive positions. Senatorial candidate Richard Nixon took campaigning to a new low in 1950 when he called his opponent, Helen Gahagan Douglas, the "Pink Lady," implying she was a communist. Much of Lyndon Johnson's winning 1964 campaign against Senator Barry Goldwater (R–Ariz.) concentrated on Senator Goldwater's alleged militaristic posture and arch-conservatism. It worked. President George H. W. Bush epitomized negative campaigning in the 1992 presidential race by referring to candidates Bill Clinton and Al Gore as "bozos" and "Ozone Man." Many campaigns have "opposition researchers" looking into the life and personal history of the opponent for negatives such as college pranks, drug samplings, business and financial problems, tax histories, divorces, sexual harassment, health problems, and other potentially embarrassing facts to use negatively against the opponent. See also HIT PIECE.

neo-conservatism (1) a term coined by author and political scientist Michael Harrington in reaction to American politics in the 1960s and 1970s to describe some Republicans and Democrats, mostly in New York and California. American neo-conservatives are anticommunist and pro-Western and have muted their voices since the end of the cold war and the fall of communism in the U.S.S.R. (2) as followers of President Ronald Reagan, neo-conservatives were against government interference in people's lives and favored the federal government's withdrawal from regulation of industries. (3) adherents favor "welfare reform" (read "reduction of serv-

ices") to welfare recipients, including AFDC and assistance to the handicapped on the basis that anyone who wants to can get a job. Some neo-conservatives believe in a few social and aid programs, especially those that help the business and farming communities. (4) neo-conservatives resemble regular conservatives in their attitudes toward sexual practices in that they abhor homosexuality, and have opposed large expenditures for AIDS research. (5) they are pro-Christianity and are often born again. (6) neo-conservatives speak out for "strong morality" but famous televangelists such as Jim Bakker and Jimmy Swaggart have gone to jail for stealing money from their followers. (7) they oppose Affirmative Action and quotas and advocate closing the borders to most immigrants, particularly from third world countries.

neo fascism a new form of fascism that attracts young militants and adult militia members, whose philosophy may include elimination of all non-Aryan races and harsh treatment of certain segments of society.

neo-Nazis supporters of a recent revival of Naziism and extreme conservatism in the United States, Germany, and other countries in the 1980s and 1990s. In the 1980s many young neo-Nazis took on superficial outward signs including shaved heads and black leather clothing with metal decorations, and they espoused disdain for minorities, immigrants (with darker skin than theirs), foreigners, and non-Christians in the name of white superiority and Christianity. They include some survivalists and generally favor carrying weapons or arms as their constitutional right. In the 1990s neo-Nazis discarded identifiable garb (conforming non-conformist outfits) and they included within their ranks extreme conservatives of all ages and some major rock stars in the Soviet dis-union. Even American high school students draw swastikas on their binders, in sympathy to, or misunderstanding or lack of knowledge about neo-Nazis. In a few mid-American cities young neo-Nazis have formed "posses" to keep outsiders (dark skins) from moving into their towns.

Liberals, moderates, and most conservatives see neo-Nazis as inhuman, frightening, not worthy of public and media attention, and certainly not representative of their views. Some liberals, especially Jewish liberals, see them as an intolerable threat to democracy. See also WHITE ARYAN RESISTANCE.

nepotism (1) favoritism shown to relatives. (2) the practice of favoring relatives in making appointments to jobs or political positions over other candidates regardless of qualifications or fitness for the job, office, or task. Finding jobs for relatives strikes many politicians as a family duty. President John F. Kennedy's appointment of his brother, Robert Kennedy, as attorney general was a prime example of a nepotistic appointment and was defended as necessary for the president to appoint someone he could fully trust. Outsiders assume that appointing relatives increases the income or power of the appointer or grantor of the jobs and often look negatively upon nepotism as cheating. Those benefiting from nepotism think it is their due and defend it as perfectly proper.

Nervous Nellies people who lose their nerve, particularly on a position they have taken. President Lyndon Johnson used the term to describe opponents of his Vietnam policy, which involved increasing troops and fighting without a declaration of war by Congress.

neutralism (1) the position of countries who did not align themselves with any major military power, such as the United States or U.S.S.R., during the cold war. Often neutral countries will accept aid from one of these countries without a military commitment. Neutralism allows for communication and trade throughout the world as well as full membership in the United Nations and participation in international affairs. (2) similar to nonalignment. With the end of the cold war, neutralism has diminished in importance since confrontation no longer exists between the United States and the former Soviet Union. Significant rapprochement has also developed between the United States and China. Even traditionally neutral Switzerland is considering joining the United Nations.

neutrality a position of a country that prefers not to take sides in a war or international disagreement between two or more countries. A neutral country lends no help to any warring party or permits them to use its territory for any warmaking activity. Neutral countries are traditionally immune from attack and usually continue trade with warring countries. It was the official policy of the United States between World War I and World War II. (1918–41). Switzerland is a perpetually neutral country, and both Switzerland and Sweden practice "armed neutrality," in which each is politically and militarily neutral but is armed to defend its own borders.

New Deal the domestic programs of President Franklin D. Roosevelt from 1933 to 1939 designed to bring economic relief from the Great Depression and legislation to prevent future paralysis of the capitalist system. FDR first used the term in his 1932 presidential nomination acceptance speech at the Democratic National Convention. It signified the beginning of an activist executive role in American government. The three elements of the New Deal were the Three R's: Relief, Recovery, and Reform.

The WPA (Works Progress Administration) and CCC (Civilian Conservation Corps) hired the unemployed to distribute emergency aid, construct roads and bridges, and work in national forests. The AAA (Agriculture Adjustment Act) helped farmers; the NRA (National Recovery Administration) established minimum wage, maximum hours, and child labor regulations; the FDIC (Federal Deposit Insurance Corporation) created government insurance for bank deposits in Federal Reserve System banks; the SEC (Securities and Exchange Commission) protected the public from fraudulent stock market practices, and the TVA (Tennessee Valley Authority) supplied cheap electricity and worked to prevent floods, improve navigation, and produce nitrates. From 1934 many programs assisted and encouraged artists, writers, actors, and musicians.

In 1935 the New Deal shifted its prime interest from rural to urban and labor problems, enacting the Wagner Act of 1935 to strengthen unions and increase the government's role in labor-management relations; creating the NLRB (National Labor Relations Board) in 1939, which set minimum wages and maximum hours; and establishing Social Security in 1935, which granted old age and widows' benefits, unemployment compensation, and disability insurance.

The U.S. Supreme Court declared some New Deal programs unconstitutional, but, by 1939, FDR could appoint enough friendly justices to get approval of new legislation. Those New Deal programs aimed at relief and recovery ended with America's entry into World War II in December 1941.

New Democratic Coalition See NATIONAL NEW DEMOCRATIC COALITION AND NEW DEMOCRATS.

New Democratic Party (NDP) Canada's most liberal and third oldest major political party. With a strong union base, the NDP has won control of governments in several provinces, but has never won a national election. NDP has offices in each province with separate phone numbers and addresses. National NDP: e-mail: ndpadmin@fed.ndp.ca; website: www. ndp.ca

New Democrats a label created by and for presidential candidate Bill Clinton to separate him from old Democrats, namely, those who had preceded him in prominence and those whom the Republicans labeled "taxers and spenders."

The philosophy of this amorphous group evolved from another effort (New Democratic Coalition) initiated by southern Democrats, founded by Senator Charles Robb (D–Va.), and now known as the Democratic Leadership Council. The New Democrats were never defined by anyone publicly, leaving it to the private and collective imagination to define the term. However, it was no secret that use of the term was meant to shake off the "liberal" and losing image of recent Democratic standardbearers such as George McGovern and Michael Dukakis. The New Democrats strive to be different in leaning toward conservatism, pragmatism, and expediency and away from close association with principles identified with traditional Democrats. Address: 578 C Street, N.E., Washington, D.C. 20002. Tel.: (202) 546-0007; FAX: (202) 544-5002; website: www.dleppi.org. See also DEMOCRATIC LEADERSHIP COUNCIL.

new economy   the economy of the late 1990s to early 2000s invigorated by Internet and high-tech (dot-com) industries that created thousands of new millionaires and jobs, changed wealth and tax bases from industrial production industries to high-tech industries, and introduced globalism. See also GLOBALISM.

new face   a candidate who has not run for office before, carries no scars from previous political battles, and appears to have great, refreshing potential.

New Freedom   President Woodrow Wilson's label for his reform movement from 1913 until World War I (1917). New Freedom reforms included: the Federal Reserve Act (creating the Federal Reserve Bank to control the flow of currency), the Fed-

eral Trade Commission, the Clayton Anti-Trust Act, legalization of income tax by constitutional amendment (1913), and the Federal Farm Loan Act.

New Frontier   a name used by John F. Kennedy in his Democratic presidential nomination acceptance speech at the Democratic National Convention in Los Angeles (July 1960). Kennedy suggested the country needed a new spirit of sacrifice, discovery, and commitment. He never actually delineated the New Frontier program, although he rekindled an old American frontier emotion to always try new things, and a "nothing is impossible" attitude. Kennedy was elected promising more governmental help to stimulate the economy, expansion of the national defense, increased foreign aid, and creation of the Peace Corps. Later he added pledges to send a man to the moon by 1970 and to guarantee real voting rights for southern blacks.

new international economic order   a restructuring of the world's economic system in which wealthier nations give up power and dominance to less developed countries by manufacturing goods and employing locals in countries around the world; also a result of globalization.

New Isolationism   a late 1990s revival of American isolationism based on fear of giving up sovereignty to the United Nations, opposition to spending taxes on aid to developing countries, protectionism to secure American industries and jobs without concern for trade imbalance, and opposition to the use of military forces as an arm of American foreign policy. American isolationism nearly disappeared during and immediately after World War II, and international involvement by the American government was supported by both major parties in the second half of the 20th century. See also GLOBALISM.

New Left a 1960s–1970s movement born in opposition to U.S. Vietnam War involvement and the military-industrial complex. The New Left tried to turn this opposition into an antiestablishment political movement, which advocated improvement of social, living, and economic conditions of blacks and other poor people by radical means. Many supporters believed strongly in participatory democracy (which they did not believe was happening), and claimed there was little hope in the existing system. Some were interested in the philosophy of Chinese Marxist Mao Tse-tung. While influential in radicalizing many young people, the New Left never succeeded as the leaders of an American left-liberal antiwar coalition, which they envisioned.

new media innovative means of communication that include Internet, talk radio, electronic town meetings, and alternative cable television.

new racism (1) a resurgence of disguised racism in the 1980s and 1990s, based upon the depressed U.S. economy and fear of loss of jobs, security, face, and homes by thousands of whites because of competition by inexpensive labor in Asia and Latin America and the willingness of people of color to work at jobs whites are not willing to do. (2) animosity and new proposed restrictions on immigration (implicitly of people of color) to bar welfare absorbers and people willing to work harder for lower wages than are longtime, resident whites. In the late 1990s economic boom, new racism seemed to subside, although the president of the Dallas NAACP was forced to resign due to his comments about Jews following Vice President Al Gore's selection of Senator Joseph Lieberman as his running mate in 2000.

Liberals and some Democrats see this attitude as extreme racism, fear, and danger couched in economics, citing the fact that nearly all Americans have come from immigrant ancestors. Immigration issues conjoin with new racism. See also IMMIGRATION; NAFTA.

The New Republic a magazine of liberal opinion, comment, and information founded (1914) by Herbert Craly with Walter Lippmann as a contributing editor. Based in Washington, D.C., its influence among opinion makers has always been greater than its 100,000 circulation would indicate, mostly because of the quality and reputation of its writers. Editors included Henry A. Wallace in the late 1940s and current owner Martin Peretz. Address: 1220 19th Street, N.W., Suite 600, Washington, D.C. 20036. Tel.: (202) 331-7494; FAX: (202) 331-0275; e-mail: online@ tnr.com; website: www.tnr.com

New Right (Religious Right, Hard Right, Christian Right, Christian Conservatives) a vague term blending Republican conservatism with born-again Christian fervor, conviction, and intolerance. Leaders and followers rant against socialism, communism, materialism, abortion, sex education, and sometimes against Jews and immigrants. The New Right also connotes an attitude of superiority of America, whites, Christians, and fundamentalists who believe in a literal interpretation of the Bible. In general the New Right is anti-equal rights, opposes the "liberal press," and regards the rest of Americans as being obsessed with sex, pornography, and self-indulgence. They are usually outspoken opponents of members of the American Civil Liberties Union, National Organization for Women, National Education Association, the "establishment," unions, the "lenient" courts, and academic institutions.

The New Right became an active force in the 1980 election of President Ronald Reagan and Vice President George H. W. Bush, and they worked hard for the Rev. Pat Robertson in his 1988 quest for the Republican presidential nomination. The group now includes the most reactionary of the "Moral Majority." Commentator Bill Moyers dubbed the New Right as the "Hard Right."

In the 1992 presidential campaign Vice President Dan Quayle created a new target for the New Right: "the cultural elite." By 2000, religious right leadership moderated their tone to separate themselves from the far right, but they did not change their positions on many issues. Conservative Rev. Pat Robertson called for a moratorium on executions in criminal cases until an evaluation of the conviction process can be done.

New South an attitudinal region rather than a geographic one, which has two ironic characteristics: the liberalization of traditional conservative Republicans and Democrats, while urging a more conservative or centrist position upon liberal Republicans and Democrats who live in the South.

New York Post a tabloid newspaper in New York characterized by splashy front pages. With a history of exposés such as the secret Nixon fund (1952), the *Post* has set trends but suffered under absentee ownership in the 1990s, losing 200,000 readers. Ranking 14th in the nation with slightly over 500,000 readers, it is fourth in the New York City area, trailing the *New York Times, Daily News,* and *Newsday.* Address: 1211 Avenue of the Americas, New York, N.Y. 10036. Tel.: (212) 930-8000; FAX: (212) 843-9300; e-mail: feedback@nypost. com; website: www.NYPost.com or www.NYPostonline.com

New York Times America's most influential newspaper, the *Times* is both the oldest and largest circulation newspaper in New York City (1,108,447) despite eschewing large headlines and comics. Noted for thorough reportage, including international coverage, excellent writing, and incisive editorials, the *Times*'s opinions are valued by political, business, and editorial leaders around the nation. The *Times*'s publication of the *Pentagon Papers* (1970) helped discredit American participation in the Vietnam War.

Fiercely independent in editorial policy, in recent years the *Times* has leaned toward Democratic policies and officeholders, causing conservative Republicans to refer to it as the "liberal press," in an attempt to discredit the publication and its Jewish editorial leadership. The *Times*'s potency has increased through purchase of several local newspapers around the country, publication of a western edition, and creation of a syndication network. Address: 229 West 43rd Street, New York, N.Y. 10036. Tel.: (212) 556-1234; e-mail: info@ nytimes.com; website: www.nytimes. com

NIMBY (Not In My Back Yard) a phrase often used in reference to people who claim they are not reactionary or racist, but who do not want racial, economic, or housing integration or development in their neighborhoods. It is okay somewhere else, but not next to them. Such integration would lead NIMBYs to say "There goes the neighborhood."

NIMBYs may want to help the homeless but they do not want a homeless shelter or mental health clinic in their neighborhood out of fear or prejudice. They include new school advocates who do not want the new school in their neighborhood. The term may also apply to conservatives who advocate nuclear power but do not want the plants near their homes.

"no controlling legal authority" language used by Vice President Al Gore after being caught making allegedly illegal fund-raising calls from the White House and from his office across the street to mean that he had not violated a federal law against raising money on federal property.

No New Taxes a phrase employed by 1988 presidential candidate George H. W. Bush, as in "Read my lips: no new taxes!" He did raise taxes, damaging his credibility.

NOK short for "not our kind", a phrase used by former representative Pat Schroeder (D–Colo.) to express military men's view of women in the armed forces.

nomenclatura the old Soviet Communist Party's membership list from which selection was made of government appointees and employees at all levels from town and regional management up to the Central Committee in Moscow. Getting one's name on the list was hard to achieve and brought status, including one's children getting to spend summers at select "Young Pioneer camps," and it created a political elite that became the financial elite as well. Listing and appointments were demanding and tightly controlled, resulting in personal stress, paranoia, competition, alcoholism, and an elitist hierarchy.

nomination (1) the naming of a person to office or as a candidate for political office. (2) a political party's designation of a person as its candidate for partisan office, usually by primary elections or district, state, or national conventions.

nomination papers the papers most candidates have to obtain from a city or county clerk to fill out and obtain sponsors' signatures in order to officially run for office and have their name placed on the ballot.

nonbinding primary a "beauty contest" primary election in which delegates to national conventions are elected, resulting in a popularity poll whose victorious delegates do not have to vote for the candidate they were elected to represent.

nonpartisan (1) not supporting any specific party or identified with any party or its positions. (2) an election in which candidates are not officially identified with a political party, and no party designations appear by candidates' names on election ballots.

Historically, Republicans have been able to organize on a partisan basis on behalf of their candidate in an officially non-partisan race when the undesignated party affiliation is known to them. At the same time Republicans have claimed that nonpartisan races are nonpartisan for Democrats. In recent years Democrats have become just as aggressive as Republicans, though, especially after watching the Religious Right conservative Republicans organize, support, and win "nonpartisan" local school board and city council elections in 1992.

nonperson a person who is completely ignored by the group or political entity with which he/she used to be an active part as if he/she did not exist. Governments may actively encourage people to ignore a "nonperson" by insinuating a form of guilt by association. This was a technique commonly employed by the Soviet regime to destroy the effectiveness of critics by ostracism.

The late vice president Spiro T. Agnew became a nonperson in the Republican Party after he pled guilty to tax evasion (on money taken as bribes) and resigned. The Republican National Committee claimed not to have his telephone number. Former president Gerald R. Ford, who was a neighbor of Agnew's in California, told the authors: "He travels a lot. We never see him."

nonviolence: (1) a method to gain popular support employing tactics without force, such as passive resistance, fasting, and blocking entrances to buildings, and without answering physical attacks or arrest. (2) the refusal to obey a law one considers to be unjust.

Mahatma Gandhi advocated, practiced, and demonstrated nonviolence in his peaceful revolution to win India's independence from Great Britain. American civil rights workers in the South (1960s) practiced nonviolence advocated by Rev. Martin Luther King Jr. by engaging sit-ins at segregated lunch counters, refusing to resist arrest and attacks, and using peaceful demonstrations. Vietnam War resisters practiced nonviolence at Berkeley and elsewhere until they were violently routed by police and deputy sheriffs. Benigno Aquino practiced nonviolent and peaceful rebellion in the Philippines until he was assassinated by President Ferdinand Marcos's military aides upon his return to Manila (1983) to run against Marcos.

normalcy normal conditions, whatever those might be. The word was coined inadvertently by Republican presidential candidate Warren G. Harding during the 1920 campaign. He misread his speech, which said "normality," and declared the nation wanted to "return to normalcy."

Norris-LaGuardia Anti-Injunction Act (1932) U.S. legislation that restricted the use of court-ordered injunctions in labor disputes. The act rendered unenforceable "yellow dog," contracts, which had required potential employees to pledge not to join a union. It also prevented employers from getting injunctions or restraining orders to prevent strike action. (The Pullman Strike had been broken this way.)

The act was co-authored by Senator George W. Norris (R–Nebr.) and Congressman Fiorello H. LaGuardia (R–N.Y.)

Norris v. Alabama   On the appeal of one of the Scottsborough Boys (young black men falsely charged and convicted in Alabama of raping a white woman), the U.S. Supreme Court ruled in 1935 that the organized exclusion of blacks from jury panels was a violation of due process for black defendants. The American Civil Liberties Union provided the lawyers for this case.

notwithstanding clause   Canada: Section 33 of the Charter of Rights and Freedoms that allows the federal parliament or provincial legislatures to simply declare that their legislation is overriding a provision of the Charter of Rights and Freedoms.

NRA   See NATIONAL RECOVERY ACT; NATIONAL RIFLE ASSOCIATION.

nuclear disarmament   the policy that calls for all nations (but particularly the United States and the Soviet successor states) in possession of nuclear weapons to abandon them as a war tool or a source of destruction and to commit to no further develop-ment of nuclear weapons.

Traditionally most conservatives favor keeping nuclear weapons, while liberals generally favor nuclear disarmament.

nuclear-free zone   a geographic area where the pertinent political/public agency (city council, board of supervisors, legislature, etc.) has voted to prohibit production, storage, or transportation through their jurisdiction of nuclear arms, components, or materials. Examples in California include Sebastopol and Berkeley.

Conservatives tend to view a nuclear-free zone as something devised by left-wing radicals to be defied, denigrated, or ignored, contending that enforcement is impractical and nuclear issues are national ones. Liberals created the designation, advocating it as a symbol that the whole world should become a nuclear-free zone.

nullification   the states' rights position delineated by vice president and then South Carolina senator John C. Calhoun in the early 1830s that state governments were empowered to set aside and declare void federal laws, acts of Congress, or Supreme Court decisions. President Andrew Jackson vigorously opposed nullification, and threatened military action against nullifiers, who attempted to block collection of import duties, as violators of federal law. More than 170 years later nullification lingers in the minds of states' rights advocates.

October surprise a presidential or campaign act or tactic to catch the opposition off guard without time to reply before an election and win favor with the public. The term was first used in an assertion by former staff of President Jimmy Carter that President Ronald Reagan's campaign had arranged to postpone release of American hostages in Iran until after the 1980 presidential election. In 1992 Democratic presidential candidate Bill Clinton's staff feared that President George H. W. Bush would pull an October surprise by bombing Iraq just before the election to regain popularity, which hit its pinnacle when he bombed the country in the Gulf war. Bush waited until after the election.

official family appointees of a president or governor whom he/she keeps close, relies upon, and trusts both professionally and personally.

Office of Management and Budget (OMB) the office that prepares the president's annual budget requests for presentation to Congress, keeps track of programs and expenditures, and estimates costs of proposed governmental programs. OMB is an outgrowth of the Bureau of the Budget, the one lasting contribution of the Harding administration.

official opposition Canada and the United Kingdom: the political party holding the second largest number of seats in parliament, granted special duties, an official residence for its leader, and offices.

off-shore oil drilling drilling for oil from platforms usually within view of ocean shore-lines and beaches.

Opponents believe the practice ruins natural coastlines and the natural organic balance. They advocate conservation of petroleum and its products to reduce the need for and dependence on oil. Proponents insist offshore oil drilling is necessary as the only way to secure energy independence from Middle Eastern countries. This policy also increases the income of American oil companies, which contribute large sums to current and potential political candidates who support such drilling. Offshore oil drilling holds different meanings and levels of political importance for residents of America's coastlines, inland residents with long driving distances, and residents of oil-producing states. Members of Congress from California may oppose offshore drilling along the California coast but favor it off the Alaskan coast, where they and their constituents do not have to look at the equipment. Residents of Gulf of Mexico states have grown accustomed to offshore oil drilling equipment on the horizon.

off the record   statements made by newsmakers to reporters on agreement that they will not be quoted. Off-the-record statements give reporters background opinions and information and give newsmakers an occasion to vent their feelings without endangering their careers (hopefully).

off-year election   an election held in a year in which there is no presidential election. See also MID-TERM ELECTION.

Old Guard   older, traditional, and occasionally reactionary (male) members of a political party, particularly conservative Republicans and, occasionally, entrenched Democrats. The Old Guard can contribute knowledge if the newcomers appreciate it and ask for it, or they can contribute money to campaigns, but they expect and demand respect. The Old Guard does not easily give up control, or the pretense of control and power.

Old Right   conservatives whose values include economic conservatism, fiscal responsibility, limited government, laissez-faire attitudes, and free trade.

oligarchy   (1) the rule of a few and one of Aristotle's basic forms of government. (2) a political system or government controlled and run by a small, exclusive class or group, many of whom join or form that small group by way of their wealth and/or power, often obtained through patriarchal and patronistic means that hurt the masses while appearing to help them. (3) the people who rule under such circumstances. The Philippines and Haiti have been examples of oligarchies in which political leaders come from a small, elite group of wealthy families.

ombudsman   (1) an official appointed as a watchdog or advocate on behalf of citizens to check on and protect against any infringements upon the rights of those citizens. (2) originally a Scandinavian concept, an ombudsman listens to citizens' complaints about the system or agency, investigates the complaints and evidence, and renders a judgment. Ombudsmen are not usually found in the U.S. federal government, although they exist at the county level and at some universities. They are also common in Canada.

one-man-one-vote   the U.S. Supreme Court ruled (June 15, 1964) that all legislative districts must be based upon population balance, which established what is known as the "one-man-one-vote" rule against diluting an individual's voting power.

Already in 1962, the Supreme Court had declared in *Baker v. Carr* that malapportioned legislative districts were unconstitutional. In the 1964 case of *Reynolds v. Sims,* Reynolds used the *Baker* case doctrine to argue successfully that both houses of state legislatures, including upper houses, had to be apportioned equally, and that unequal population in electoral districts was a denial of equal rights and, therefore, unconstitutional. Until that time the state senates of most states were based on local or county lines.

Lawsuits and legislation followed to cure egregious discrepancies in district size and population, resulting in wholesale reapportionment of state senates in many states (1966). By 1972, state legislative districts of each house were virtually all of equal population. Prior to the one-man-one-vote rule, California offered the most offensive example of malapportionment in Los Angeles County, which was represented by one state senator out of 40 but that contained nearly 40 percent of the state's population.

Eventually city and county representation districts and the Democratic National Committee (which previously had two members from each state) were restructured based on one-man-one-vote representation. (The Republican National Committee still has two members from each state.) Rural areas have lost political clout to the cities as a result of the 1964 ruling. Perhaps the ruling should have been "one-person-one-vote."

one-party system a political system in which one party dominates repeatedly, while other parties are prohibited or so weak they are merely tolerated and on the ballot. Until the upset election of July 2000, Mexico effectively had been a one-party system for 71 years.

open convention a political party convention at which the major decisions are actually made by the delegates, including the individuals who obtain the nominations for president and vice president. See also BROKERED CONVENTION.

open primary a primary election in which voters registered in one party can vote for candidates of any party or as independents and not just for candidates running in the party with which the voter is affiliated.

open shop an industrial plant or business whose employees have a choice of belonging to a union or not. See also CLOSED SHOP.

Operation Rescue (Operation Save America) a militant organization of the religious right (founded in the late 1980s) that uses disruption of clinics and medical offices performing abortions or disseminating information regarding a woman's right to have an abortion. It also uses intimidation at the homes of physicians who perform abortions. The term comes from the group's belief that by preventing abortions, blowing up abortion clinics, and threatening and occasionally shooting doctors who perform abortions, they are saving the lives of unborn children. Hundreds of Operation Rescue members have been arrested. A member of one local group shot and killed a doctor in Florida to press his views against killing unborn babies. Operation Rescue distributed thousands of letters during the 1992 presidential campaign asserting that "to vote for Bill Clinton is to sin against God." The group merged with Operation Save America in 2000. Address: P. O. Box 74006, Dallas, Tex. 75374. Tel.: (972) 494-5316; FAX: (972) 276-9361; e-mail: osa@operationsaveamerica.org; website: www.operationsaveamerica.org

OPO obvious payoff, usually a contract awarded or a vote favoring an industry or union that might be connected remotely to a campaign contribution or other support.

opposition (1) a group of citizens or legislators who do not agree with an incumbent government or its policies and wish to change or influence one or both.

In the United States the opposition is usually the party not occupying the White House, although, as the Democrats move to the center and even right on some issues, a question may arise: is there a single party, and who is the opposition?

In Great Britain and Canada, the opposition is respected and recognized formally, often called the Loyal Opposition, suggesting remaining loyalty and respect for the Crown while offering opposing views, opinions, and positions on issues.

Before its 1990 dissolution, the U.S.S.R. did not allow or recognize formal opposition without exile or death, as in many dictatorships of both the radical right and left. In the Philippines President Ferdinand Mar-

cos imprisoned leaders of the opposition and, in fact, had Benigno Aquino, his opposition contender for president, assassinated as he returned from exile in the United States (1983). Similar suppression of opposition has occurred in China, Chile, Haiti, Indonesia, Myanmar, Libya, Iran, Iraq, and numerous African and Latin American nations. (2) Canada: parliament members belonging to parties other than the party in power. See also LOYAL OPPOSITION.

Opposition Days Canada: 20 days in each parliamentary session when motions offered by the opposition can be debated.

opposition research (1) absolutely limitless investigation of an opponent's personal and public statements, background, and records. (2) dirt digging.

ordinance a law or statute adopted by a city council or town board.

Oregon Citizens Alliance conservative organization in Oregon sponsoring and campaigning for local laws denying minority status or benefits to homosexual organizations and prohibiting government investment in gay organizations or institutions. Gay rights supporters refer to such ordinances as anti-gay rights laws. The Oregon legislature passed a law in 1993 which bars such ordinances and supersedes newly passed local laws. While such laws cannot be enforced, their passage reflects anti-gay attitudes in the 14 cities and six counties where they have succeeded. Address: P.O. Box 9276, Brooks, Ore. 97305. Tel.: (503) 463-0653 (Salem).

organization (1) any structure of people to accomplish goals by working together, including businesses, armies, clubs, institutions, and governments. (2) gathering together of people to work for a common goal, elect a candidate, or pass a proposition. Political organization usually involves careful management, maintenance of lists of names, addresses, and phone numbers, and intensive efforts to motivate people to work together to further the common goal.

Organization of American States (OAS) almost all nations in the Western Hemisphere joined together in a regional support association based on historic Pan-American relationships and supporting the principles of the United Nations. The OAS's charter was signed on April 30, 1948 in Bogotà, Colombia. Its goals were to strengthen peace and security in the Western Hemisphere and encourage interstate cooperation on economic, social and cultural matters. One of its premises is that an attack on one nation is an attack on all. It supported President John F. Kennedy's 1962 quarantine against Russian shipments of missiles to Cuba and U.S. intervention in the Dominican Republic (1965). The OAS expelled Cuba in 1962 at the insistence of the United States. Canada has recently joined the group. Address: 17th Street and Constitution Avenue, N.W., Washington, D.C. 20006. Tel.: (202) 458-3000; e-mail: pimultimedia@oas.org or svillagran @oas.org; website: www.oas.org

organize to enlist, sign up, and gain membership of and commitment by workers in a labor union, special-interest group, campaign or political party. The purpose of labor union organizing is to extend the benefits of union membership to new recruits and enlarge the union and, thereby, its power. The purpose of political organizing include campaigning, registering more members into one's party and getting those registerred out to vote to win elections.

The Other America **(1962)** a landmark book by Michael Harrington, an intellectual socialist, who proved that there was widespread "invisible" poverty in the United States amid apparent affluence. *The Other America* had great impact on policy makers, including such members of the Kennedy administration as Attorney General Robert Kennedy and Vice President Lyndon Johnson. In the short run the book led to the "War on Poverty," and in the long run Harrington's thesis has become a consistent element in modern economics.

outerclass a term used by President Bill Clinton, presumably to refer to Americans who no longer fit into the U.S. economic system. The outerclass do not hold jobs, are not qualified for changing job markets, lack education to adjust to new economic trends, do not receive government benefits or cannot get themselves off welfare, have needs that are not being addressed by legislators, and are seen as a nuisance by many more prosperous Americans.

out front having a known, stated opinion or position without playing coy or dealing for favors before stating the position.

out of the loop (1) outside the group close to a chief executive, leader, or candidate that trades essential, operating information and makes decisions. (2) uninformed.

outsider a candidate who either is or claims to operate outside the seat or center of power. Often candidates portray themselves as outsiders to distance themselves from insider politicians or incumbents whom the public loves to hate. They claim that an outsider is believed to be more pure and honest than an insider. The outsider's lack of experience equates to lack of contamination by the system.

Oval Office (1) the name and description of the president's office in the White House. (2) a term for the center of power of the United States.

overkill (1) to overdo in elimination of opposition. (2) a concept in nuclear weapon stockpiling that a nation or nations possess such an abundance of nuclear weapons that it/they can obliterate their opponent of the moment and still retain an unused nuclear surplus. Collectively, overkill can mean that all nuclear nations possess enough nuclear weapons to eradicate the world and still not use up their nuclear weapons.

override a term used to indicate overcoming a president's veto of congressional legislation, which takes a two-thirds vote of the membership of each house of Congress. An override of a presidential veto means that the bill is enacted.

oversight (1) a power and responsibility of Congress to oversee and check on the functioning of executive branch officials' and agencies' conduct, performance, and expenditures. (2) a feature missed.

overvote votes cast by a voter for more than one candidate for the same office, resulting in no vote being counted on that ballot for that office.

Ozone Man President George H. W. Bush's disparaging name for Senator Al Gore during the 1992 presidential campaign. Bush's name-calling referred to Senator Gore's environmental reputation and highly acclaimed book, *Earth in the Balance: Ecology and the Human Spirit* (Houghton Mifflin, Boston, 1992), and apparently emanated from campaign exasperation and desperation.

PAC See POLITICAL ACTION COM-
MITTEE.

pacifism opposition to all war and
violence as morally unacceptable solutions to conflict. Pacifism includes the
belief that disputes can be solved by
peaceful means of communication
and negotiation. Pacifists include people who are long-term antiwar activists, as well as others who become
pacifists in regard to specific conflicts
such as the American intervention in
Vietnam and Iraq.

American pacifism primarily stems
from religious groups such as the
Friends and Unitarians who philosophically oppose all violence. The
concept in America may have developed from horrors experienced personally or vicariously during the Civil
War, World Wars I and II, and the
Korean and Vietnam wars. Often the
children of those who experienced
such fighting turned against military
violence and killing of other human

beings. Another source derives from
the view of Marxists and other leftist
radicals that decisions to fight wars
are made by an elite leadership for
selfish economic reasons, sending the
average person out to die on the bat-
tlefield. Due to exemptions given college students during the Vietnam War,
poor African Americans, farm boys,
and unskilled workers did most of the
fighting and suffered most American
casualties.

Conservatives generally consider
pacifists to be left-wing liberals and
fanatics and occasionally see pacifism
as sinful, unpatriotic, and even treasonous. They will tolerate those who
occasionally oppose war and violence
for religious reasons. Liberals tend to
be more tolerant of all pacifists.

Some liberals are pacifists and see
pacifism as the only correct moral
alternative. Pacifists whose positions
are based on religious beliefs or long-
term moral opposition to war are entitled to draft exemptions or duty not
involved in fighting.

Packwood diaries thousands of pages of transcribed tapes made by Senator Robert Packwood (R–Ore.) during his tenure in the U.S. Senate. Senator Packwood, once thought to be a champion of equal rights for women, was accused by several female staffers of sexual harassment in the form of unwanted sexual advances. Packwood implied that his diaries told all and implicated other political officeholders. As Senate Ethics Committee members began to probe the case, Packwood claimed the order to produce the diaries violated his right to privacy. One of his assistants admitted that he had altered the tapes. Senator Nancy Kassebaum (R–Kans.) became the first Republican U.S. senator to call for Packwood's resignation (December 1993). Packwood resigned.

pact (1) an agreement between two parties or national governments, usually characterized by both parties doing something for the other or supporting each other simultaneously or reciprocally. (2) journalese for a treaty or official agreement.

pairing votes an arrangement between two members of the U.S. House of Representatives or Senate to balance votes of members on opposite sides of a bill or resolution in case one or both people should be absent. Paired votes are counted and recorded and work when a member on one side of an issue agrees not to vote or to be absent when a member on the other side expects to be absent. Members utilize pairing when they want their position recorded and wish to avoid the appearance of unconcern, which is far different from missing votes entirely.

palace guard the inner circle of influential friends who surround a high-level officeholder, particularly the president, and believe they protect or shield him/her from bad news, the public, or even new ideas that are not theirs. Members of the palace guard regard themselves as powerful, and they are. They are usually most effective at protecting their own positions and keeping challengers from entering the president's inner circle. Palace guards often perform a collective and national disservice by filtering ideas and information from reaching the president and presuming to decide what is best for the country.

The term is most often used by people outside this inner circle, especially those of the opposite party. A palace guard sometimes does exist, but often it occurs only in the minds of outsiders. In Richard Nixon's administration the palace guard was very real and arrogantly powerful.

parachuting Canada: dropping in of a candidate to a district or riding in which he or she does not live at the wishes or selection of a prime minister or party leader. Similar to "carpetbagging."

paramilitary forces groups of men attired in uniform who often exercise power by force in the name of internal security. Usually they handle riots, border patrols, suppress rights with "death squads," and fight insurgents in unofficial domestic wars. They often lack true military discipline, leadership, and any legal control.

France's gendarmerie are paramilitary police who differ from local and national police. El Salvador and Haiti employ large paramilitary forces. In the United States there are militia organizations that train and practice military tactics, claiming a need to protect themselves from the government.

parish (1) a geographic area served by a Christian, especially a Roman Catholic, church thought to have originated by drawing the boundaries of the parish on the basis of the faithful's ability to walk to church. (2) in Louisiana a political and geographic designation similar to a county.

parliamentary government a system of government in which the executive is elected by and responsible to the legislature, as in Great Britain and Canada. The people vote for members of the House of Commons while the upper chamber is the House of Lords in Britain, whose members are appointed or hereditary, and the Senate in Canada, whose members are appointed. The members of the majority party in the House of Commons elect the Prime Minister, who in turn appoints the cabinet from among members of parliament of his or her party. If the executive or prime minister acts in ways the parliament believes are not in their constituents' best interests (and therefore not in theirs), they can remove the executive and elect a new one if he/she loses a vote of confidence on any significant issue.

Many countries with parliamentary systems have several political parties, making a majority difficult to attain. This leads to coalition governments in which minority parties bargain for cabinet posts in exchange for votes for prime minister. Where there are numerous parties, administrations become unstable and may fall at any sign of coalition fragility. Italy is the worst Western example of this condition, with scores of parties and dozens of governments in the past 55 years. In Ireland, the second- or third-place party almost always holds the balance of power while not holding enough votes to form its own government.

Benefits of parliamentary governments are (1) that first-place parties without a majority must listen to other parties' representatives, involve them in policymaking, and truly govern by consensus; (2) administrations must be sensitive to current conditions without holdover executives (like Herbert Hoover in the Great Depression) long after the public becomes disillusioned; (3) a prime minister can be removed when the people are dissatisfied.

Political party service is particularly important in parliamentary systems since leaders such as prime ministers or would-be prime ministers and cabinet members are chosen from among party leaders and veterans. The fact that a dynamic, able outsider has no chance to gain entry can be a weakness of this system.

parliamentary privilege a privilege granted to members of parliament that allows them to speak freely and not be intimidated by others.

partial-birth abortion a term coined by anti-abortionists for emergency late-term abortions done in the third trimester of pregnancy. "Partial birth" suggests that the fetus could possibly live. See also LATE-TERM ABORTION.

partisan a person who supports or advocates a political party's positions, almost without reason or restraint.

partner (1) a co-owner of a business entity. (2) the politically correct term for a homosexual's lover in a committed, monogamous relationship in which the two partners share their lives with each other. (3) to pair up with another person, agency, or company to work on a shared project toward a shared goal.

party caucus a group consisting of all members of a party in a legislature.

party discipline control of legislators of the same party, having them vote as a bloc once a program is decided. Members of the U.S. Congress tend to vote as would their constituents back home, while in Canada party discipline is stronger and constituents elect representatives assuming they will vote the current party line.

party faithful those members of a political party who can be counted on to vote for the party's candidates and/or make regular contributions.

party leader the person elected by members of a party or members of a legislature of one party to lead that party and speak for it and its members.

party line the accepted and articulated party positions and policy on issues that candidates are expected by leaders and followers to espouse, even when those positions are out of date or contrary to popular wisdom or will. Such loyalty was required by Marxist governments, which demanded philosophic and political conformity.

party loyalty strong devotion to a political party, enabling a person to vote in legislatures for party policy or leaders whether that individual believes in them or not. Party loyalty also suggests voting for the party's candidates even when the voter does not like the candidates, just for the sake of the party.

party machine See POLITICAL MACHINE.

passive resistance a nonviolent technique to demonstrate opposition to a government entity's policies or actions by not cooperating with them. Mahatma Gandhi espoused and demonstrated passive resistance in his nonviolent struggle for India's independence from Great Britain.

Examples of the concept used in the United States include sit-ins in segregated restaurants and withholding the portion of a person's federal income taxes estimated to be used for nuclear or war development if the person disapproves of those expenditures. The Rev. Martin Luther King Jr. received the Nobel Peace Prize (1964) as America's leading advocate of nonviolence, which encompassed passive resistance.

Usually because of a lack of understanding of the process, conservatives tend to view passive resistance as a disturbing, traitorous act and often dismiss participants as being left-wing, ideologues. Liberals view passive resistance as a conscientious, positive act of expression of one's viewpoint and often believe that everyone should engage in it. See also NONVIOLENCE.

paternalism   an attitude and relationship between a government, the governors, and the governed in which the governors and government regard themselves as occupying a superior and dominant position over the governed, such as in a traditional father/son or daughter relationship. Some view governmental paternalism as a relationship in which the father (government) provides expected, necessary, and helpful services to the child (the governed) without expectation of responsibility or return of favors, and solely in fulfillment of its role. It is particularly prevalent in nations that were once colonies of Spain.

patriotism   a love for, loyalty to, and zealous support of one's country, particularly in relationship to other countries.

Occasionally patriotism has become controversial in political campaigns. In his successful 1988 presidential campaign, Vice President George H. W. Bush raised patriotism as possibly the most important issue of the year, symbolized by his visit to an American flag factory and the ebullient flag waving by his supporters. President Bush's effort to focus on patriotism and flags was meant to draw an unfavorable contrast to Democratic presidential candidate governor Michael Dukakis who once had vetoed a mandatory flag salute bill that was patently unconstitutional.

In his unsuccessful 1992 bid for reelection, President Bush questioned challenger Bill Clinton's patriotism because of Clinton's demonstrations against the Vietnam War when he was a graduate student in England, even though the U.S. Constitution protects Americans' rights to assemble and speak freely.

English scholar Samuel Johnson called patriotism "the last refuge of a scoundrel" in April 1775, just before the opening shots of the American Revolution at Lexington and Concord.

patronage   appointments, offices, or favors distributed by those in power, usually in return for favors done or campaign contributions, particularly if those favors help to get the person in power elected to his/her position. Favors may include jobs, contracts, and economic and honorary awards such as appointments to commissions, which give the member prestige or income they may not have had before.

pauper's oath   a sworn statement required by some government agencies declaring that the person owns nothing of real value before that person may receive relief or welfare. See also MEANS TEST.

pay your dues   to spend unspecified time as a newcomer learning the ropes at the feet of higher-ups to earn the right to political advancement.

PC   (1) politically correct. (2) Canada: Progressive Conservative Party. (3) United Kingdom: Privy Council.

Peace and Freedom Party   an alternative political party in California that arose in 1967 primarily in opposition to the Vietnam War, government policies, Republicans, and Democrats. It was essentially radical and contended that "the system" had failed. Original leaders included Robert Avakian, Saul Landau, Jack Weinberg, and Robert Scheer. The Peace and Freedom Party never elected any candidates and waned in the 1970s, but in 1990 the party's Congressional candidate drew enough protest votes away from Representative Doug Bosco (D–Calif.), who had alienated environmentalists, to defeat Bosco. Address; P.O. Box 24764, Oakland, Calif. 94623. Tel.: (510) 465-9414 or P.O. Box 741270, Los Angeles, CA 90004. Tel.: (323) 759-9737; website: www. peaceandfreedom.org

Peace Corps   a U.S. government agency of volunteers created by the Peace Corps Act of 1961 (with only Senator Barry Goldwater [R–Ariz.] dissenting in the Senate) on the inspiration of President John F. Kennedy and others. Its purpose is to help underdeveloped countries by providing skilled workers and teachers in education, agriculture, health, trade, technology, and community development. Its goal is to help countries develop themselves to the point where the Peace Corps is no longer needed. Volunteers generally go to a country that has asked for volunteers and live with local residents for two years. Sargent Shriver, husband of Kennedy sister Eunice, served as the first director of the Peace Corps, with Bill Moyers as assistant director. The Peace Corps grew from 900 volunteers in 16 countries (1961) to more than 10,000 volunteers in 52 countries (1966), then dropped to 6,000 in 60 countries in the late 1970s. It became a subagency

of ACTION, an umbrella agency designed (1971) to oversee volunteer efforts both at home (VISTA) and abroad. President Richard Nixon vowed to close down and eliminate the Peace Corps. It survived, possibly due to his forced resignation. Presidents Ronald Reagan and George H. W. Bush attempted to scale down the Peace Corps, preferring to build war tools instead of peace tools. Address: 1111 20th Street, N.W., Washington, D.C. 20526. Tel.: (202) 606-3010 or (800) 424-8580; website: www. peacecorps.gov

peace dividend   a term coined by Dr. Seymour Melman, Columbian University emeritus professor, to suggest that the public can benefit from a reduction in military expenditures by reduction of taxes and increased spending on social programs. Melman contends that high military spending damages the economy since it is nonreproductive, has low labor intensity, is immediately obsolescent, and stimulates inflation, in contrast to productive, socially useful, labor-intensive, and high economic impact spending on housing, health care, highways, and transportation. Thus, economic stability is an element of the peace dividend.

In the short term, some economists and politicians contest the peace dividend concept because they see thousands of layoffs resulting from closings of weapons factories, airplane production plants, and military bases.

peaceful coexistence   the idea that nations which hold ideals that appear to be in conflict can exist and compete together peacefully while tolerating (or ignoring) the others' views.

The concept was first expressed in the late 1950s by then Soviet Union premier Nikita Khrushchev who called on the democratic United States and communist U.S.S.R. to coexist peacefully to avoid nuclear war, claiming that the Soviets would eventually dominate anyway by economic means and not by war. However, both the United States and the Soviets continued to stockpile military weaponry.

peacekeeping (1) a diplomatic and military term referring to the act of sending military forces to another country to mediate, intimidate, and prevent escalation of armed confluce or genocide. (2) bombing one side in a conflict to keep it from killing the other side.

peacekeeping missiles missiles used to threaten and shoot down airplanes and missiles of one country that might harm another if they reach their target.

peace movement the modern American peace movement arose during the 1950s due to concerns and fears about the cold war arms race and desires for nuclear disarmament. In the mid-1960s it focused on American involvement in Vietnam, using techniques such as marches, demonstrations, education, and propaganda. Peace movement activists continue to express concern about the influence of the military-industrial complex. Its membership seems amorphous and unidentified, although its sympathizers tend to grow during threatened or actual war times. The peace movement has generally drawn from middle-class, often intellectual, and occasionally radical-fringe Americans who usually employ nonconfrontational tactics. See also ANTI–VIETNAM WAR MOVEMENT.

peacenik a pejorative term that originated in the mid-1960s and usually used by conservatives to identify people opposed to war, similar to "dove." Peacenik conjures up a Beatnik-type image of dirty clothes, beards, pipes, and poetry.

peak to reach one's pinnacle of popularity. Peaking at the right time supposedly assures victory for a candidate. Some candidates reach the high point of good publicity, name recognition, and popularity too early and lose momentum before the election. Others appear to peak too late and come to believe that "if we just had one more week we would have won the election."

pecking order a term originating in barnyard protocol to refer to the hierarchy existing in Congress or any governmental office or agency that means the biggest and most powerful chickens get their feed first, with newer, less powerful chickens chasing around for the remains.

Pentagon (1) the five-sided building in Arlington, Virginia, in which the Department of Defense and military offices are located. (2) a term used to refer to the U.S. military establishment that makes military decisions.

Pentagon Papers officially entitled *History of the U.S. Decision-Making Process on Vietnam Policy,* the once-secret Pentagon record of the development of the Vietnam War under presidents Truman, Eisenhower, Kennedy, and Johnson without public knowledge of the buildup. The Pentagon Papers were commissioned by then secretary of defense Robert S. McNamara (1967). The 47 volumes cover American involvement from World War II to May 1968.

Many of the papers were published first in serial form by the *New York Times,* commencing on June 13, 1971. The Defense Department obtained a federal court order halting publication on the ground it endangered national security, but the U.S. Supreme Court reversed the order on June 30 as an unconstitutional prior restraint. The *Times* won a Pulitzer Prize for the publication, which appeared in both hard and soft cover books. Dr. Daniel Ellsberg, former Defense Department Far East specialist who gave the papers to the press, was charged with espionage and theft. The case was dismissed on free speech and free press guarantees and, in part, due to an illegal break-in at Dr. Ellsberg's psychiatrist's office by agents of the Nixon White House.

The *Pentagon Papers* revealed much about policies and actions previously kept secret from the American people and established the definitive right of the media to expose such chicanery.

people of color politically correct term for black, Hispanic, Asian, or any other people of skin pigmentation other than white; initiated by those whom it describes.

People's Park a piece of property in Berkeley, California, that belongs to the University of California and has been taken over as a residential park where homeless people, drug addicts, and counter-culture enthusiasts hang out. In the 1960s People's Park received major media attention due to political demonstrations, protests, and riots.

per capita income the total income earned in a country divided by persons living in that country.

perestroika (1) originally a Russian word for restructuring Soviet and Russian government and political systems. (2) monumental restructuring of any system.

perk short version of "perquisite," which means financial or other benefits generally unknown to the public and available to public officeholders or public servants outside of itemized salary or published benefits. Perks may include free lunches, a free house, airplane tickets, a car and chauffeur, a parking space, or group health insurance. Sometimes the value of perks adds substantially to the base, publicly known salary. The public usually looks upon perks suspiciously.

persona non grata a Latin term employed to mean a person who is not welcome in a particular country, usually due to an unfriendly act such as spying, revealing unseemly details of an official's life, or simply telling the truth about an official who does not want that truth known. The term usually results in refusal of entry into or expulsion from a country.

personal party a party set up by an individual whose personal beliefs dominate that party's philosophy, such as John Hagelin's Natural Law Party in the United States and Preston Manning's Reform Party (now Canadian Alliance) in Canada.

petition (1) a document requesting a legislative or decision-making body to place a political position, issue, person, or measure on an election ballot, signed by registered voters. This is a right guaranteed by the First Amendment to the U.S. Constitution. (2) a list of signatures gathered in support of a particular position to be presented to decision makers.

photo op short for photo opportunity, usually a set up action pose contrived to look natural and in the act of doing something significant. Photo ops are announced as such to the press by press staff of the candidate or officeholder with the suggestion that the candidate or officeholder is doing the press a favor. The favor is, at most, mutual.

picket a person who stands or walks outside a factory, store, business, office, corporate headquarters, or government building to protest policy, work conditions, wages, or other conduct or issues, usually carrying a sign of protest, discontent, or information derogatory to the picket's target.

picket line an organized group of pickets, which can be limited by court order prohibiting blocking entrances or causing disturbances. The right to picket is constitutionally protected as an expression of free speech and free assembly.

pinko a pejorative slang term commonly used politically from 1946 to 1980, usually applied by conservatives to liberals to link them with communist ideology. The term is rarely used since the Soviet Union disbanded.

Most liberals view the term as one to be feared if applied to them and a label they would prefer to avoid, while some consider it an honor to have incited conservatives to the point where they will use the inflammatory expression. Of course, what was considered to be "pinko" in one decade may not be in another.

In the 1970s American television situation comedy series *All in the Family,* character Archie Bunker (played by Carroll O'Connor) called everyone with whom he disagreed a pinko, a usage somewhat common among conservatives at the time. Senator Joseph McCarthy used the term with abandon to describe those with whom he disagreed (1949–56).

plank one provision, article, or principle in a platform of a political party. The allusion is to a wooden platform, made up of many planks.

planning a systematic and quasi-scientific method of designing developmental growth of a geographic area, usually attempting to balance business, industrial, housing, and recreational interests. The key tool to enforce public planning is zoning, which establishes areas of use, size of parcels, heights, buffer areas, and other limitations and controls.

Generally conservative developers, builders, and homeowners regard planning as a restrictive infringement upon their personal and constitutional rights. Liberals tend to believe in planning as a means to control and balance growth and environmental protection.

plant (1) a person sent into a rival campaign to spy and learn strategy, report it, and occasionally foul it up. (2) to conspire to get a particular question asked at a press conference.

platform a set of principles, ideals, and potential policies adopted by a party at a convention or by a political candidate.

Platforms (and their composite planks) are supposed to state positions for which the party stands. In reality candidates often ignore platforms, particularly if they do not agree with them. In the United States candidates often ignore their national party platform, particularly controversial planks. In Canada the party platform and positions are the heart of most campaigns.

player a powerful political insider who participates in decision making and candidate selection. The term is used in the context: "He's or she's a player," meaning he or she is part of the political game and not just an onlooker.

plebiscite an expression of the people's will by direct vote on an issue, question, or resolution. Plebiscites have been used to settle questions such as to which country disputed territory should be awarded. The word got a bad name when Nazi Germany organized rigged plebiscites (electors could only vote "Ja") on border areas with France and Czechoslovakia.

Pledge of Allegiance a verbal commitment of loyalty to the United States, recited usually while facing the American flag. Text: "I pledge allegiance to the flag of the United States of America and to the republic for which it stands, one nation, under God, indivisible, with liberty and justice for all." The pledge was written by Francis Bellamy and published in the magazine for which he worked, *Youth's Companion,* on September 8, 1892. Mr. Bellamy's original version said "my flag" instead of "the flag of the United States of America," a change which was made in the early 1920s. "Under God" was added by an Act of Congress in 1954. The Pledge of Allegiance has raised controversy in two regards intermittently throughout American history. The phrase "one nation, under God" brings up questions of separation of church and state according to the U.S. Constitution. The mandatory recitation of the Pledge of Allegiance has been contested in some public school districts and states by those with religious or ethical reservations against such pledges. The Supreme Court has ruled that a student can remain seated and/or silent. The Pledge of Allegiance should not be confused with the Loyalty Oath.

PLO (Palestine Liberation Organization) an organization of Palestinians formed in 1948 when the state of Israel was established and 1.5 million Palestinians were displaced. Palestinians settled in United Nations camps in the Gaza Strip, Jordan, and Lebanon. Hopes of returning to their homeland have been dashed both in various violent losses, such as Israel's defeat of Syria and Egypt in the Arab-

Israeli wars of 1956 and 1967, and at failed talks, such as at Camp David (United States) in 2000. Many political groups emerged from among the migrating Palestinians, including al-Fatah, led by Yasir Arafat. Al-Fatah was the largest and wealthiest group and was dedicated to remaining independent of control by any Arab regime. In 1970, Arafat emerged his group with Christian-Arab George Habash's Popular Front for the Liberation of Palestine (PFLP), resulting in the current PLO.

Arafat recommended cessation of violence in 1973, and in 1974 the United Nations recognized the PLO as representing all Palestinians wherever they lived. The PLO became the first nongovernmental organization to address (by Arafat) a plenary session of the United Nations (1974), and was admitted to the Arab League in 1976. In 1982, Israel invaded and attacked PLO–controlled southern Lebanon and surrounded the Palestinian section of Beirut. Some Palestinians were interned in refugee camps and others scattered. This defeat led to the rise of younger Palestinians advocating violence in Israel.

In September 1993, the PLO entered into an agreement with Israel to recognize Israel in return for Palestinian autonomy in the Gaza Strip and parts of the West Bank, including Jericho, together with negotiation of future accommodations.

plum   political payoff of a job for work performed or donations contributed.

plum book   the nickname for a publication containing a long list of presidential appointments and high-level civil service jobs, officially called *Policy and Supporting Positions*. The plum book is available in paperback and on computer discs, the latter being more expensive, detailed, and difficult to use.

plumbers   staff members of President Richard M. Nixon who tried to block information from reaching the press.

pluralism   a political system that has more than one source of power or influence.

In the United States, the executive, legislative, and judicial branches of government all have power and influence, but so do special interest groups, their lobbyists, PACS, unions, industrial associations, political parties, and legislatures, all of whom share in the total power of governance. A pure pluralistic government consists of interest groups participating equally and sharing in decision-making processes.

Pluralism also refers to the right of religious groups with strongly differing views to equal consideration, such as with reference to the issues of birth control and abortion rights. In a pluralistic society partisans holding one view cannot impose their views on others by domination.

plurality   the margin of electoral victory by gaining the most votes whether or not the winning candidate obtained a majority (50 percent plus one). In a race in which there are several candidates the winner with only a plurality may not represent the views of the majority. This can occur when several candidates who share a persuasion split the vote and lose to a single candidate with another view and thus frustrate the public will. To guard against this type of result several states (particularly in primaries), and many cities and countries hold run-off elections between the two top vote getters if there is only a plurality and no majority. Democratic president Bill Clinton won election in 1992 by a plurality of the popular vote, gaining 43 percent of the vote in a three-way race with Republican president George H. W. Bush and independent candidate Ross Perot.

If the leading presidential candidate wins only a plurality of the Electoral College vote, the House of Representatives elects the president from among the top three vote getters, which has happened once. If no vice presidential candidate gets a majority of the Electoral College vote, the Senate elects the vice president from between the top two candidates, which has also happened only once.

PM an experimental newspaper (1940–48) financed by mercantile heir Marshall Field III. The only major newspaper in modern times to attempt to exist on circulation revenues alone, *PM* was a lively, liberal tabloid newspaper. Field lost $4 million with New York–based *PM*, but he did much better with the advertising-crammed *Chicago Sun-Times* and the Field Syndicate.

P.M. prime minister.

pocketbook issue a political issue that the public believes is important because it affects their income, their ability to buy things, and their lifestyle.

pocket veto a veto by inaction that can occur when Congress or another legislature adjourns 10 days or less after passing a bill and before a president or governor signs a bill, either by bad timing or choice. The executive theoretically puts the bill in his/her pocket without his/her signature, and the bill dies when the current congressional or legislative session expires without a chance to override.

point-of-order a question raised by a participant asking for a ruling on the propriety of a discussion or motion in accordance with the deliberating body's rules of order. Usually a point-of-order demands a ruling by the Chair.

pol a political activist who possesses political skills and thrives on the sport of politics.

polarization setting two extremes of opinion against each other or inciting opponents to expound extreme viewpoints, which discourages communication.

police an official group of people designated and paid to keep order, enforce laws, prevent and detect crimes, arrest alleged violators, and safeguard the health, safety, and welfare of citizens.

In many nations the federal police act at the behest of the incumbent national government. The United States has no official federal police force, and the Constitution gives police powers to the states, although the Federal Bureau of Investigation (FBI), Treasury Department agents, Secret Service, and National Guard all perform some policing functions.

In the United States, police exist at the state, county, and municipal levels. State police often concentrate on highway safety, county sheriffs are elected, and local (city or town) police chiefs are usually appointed.

The question often arises regarding at what point police overstep their duties and violate citizens' civil liberties. Increasingly the public is demanding that police be professionally trained with such lines delineated as clearly as possible.

police powers from the 10th Amendment to the U.S. Constitution, the state governments' rights and powers to protect the welfare, safety, health, and even morals of the public. Controversy often surrounds the question of who is to decide what level of "protection" is appropriate, particularly on morals questions. Police powers include licensing, inspection, zoning, quarantines, setting wages, hours, and working condition standards, and establishing safety regulations in the states. The federal government has similar powers over postal services, taxation, and interstate commerce. Abuses of police powers may include Internal Revenue Service harassment, repeated audits of citizens whose political positions are disliked by an incumbent administration, or excessive use of force in making arrests.

Conservatives generally regard police powers as constituting patriotic controls, including censorship, except when such controls affect them personally in cases such as taxation, stringent zoning controls, or interstate commerce regulation. Liberals and libertarians are often concerned about the abuse of those police powers that

are invasive of civil liberties. All three viewpoints concur on the need for protection against crime and criminals.

police state a political system in which the executive in power ignores or eliminates civil liberties, judicial freedoms, and legislative practices. The executive makes use of the police force and secret police to carry out confiscations, curfews, and military and paramilitary violence to intimidate and overpower a nation so as to extend his/her power. Occasionally unbeknownst to the executive, the police develop their own power and corruption pyramid. Examples of police states include Nazi Germany (Gestapo), Stalin's U.S.S.R. (KGB), Marcos's Philippines, and "Papa Doc" Duvalier's Haiti.

policy a usually agreed upon governing principle, course of action, or plan based on wisdom, learned skill, and developed craft. (2) Canada: position on an issue.

policy papers position papers.

policy wonk a person who is devoted to the research, study, and development of governmental policy, beyond consideration of any other facets of life and often without much practical, political, or life experience.

politbabble (also polibabble) a language composed of most of the words in this dictionary, created accidentally and unofficially but carrying secret meanings to form a political insider's communication code. Until now one would have to serve an active apprenticeship to learn to speak polit-babble in order to understand political statements ranging from conversations in campaign headquarters to presidential speeches.

Politburo the Political Bureau of the former Soviet Union's Communist Party, which actually held more power than the government. The Politburo was continually in session and wielded more power than the U.S. cabinet, presidential administration, and Congress combined. Although technically not part of the government, the Politburo made all everyday and emergency decisions and directed all policy. Politburos also existed in other European Communist parties.

Political Action Committees (PACS) corporate, union, professional, or other special-interest groups formed to lobby officeholders, to contribute to favored candidates, and to avoid maximum campaign contribution limitations. The first major political action committees were formed by organized labor's CIO in the early 1940s. As nonprofit corporations PACS can receive contributions of any size and then direct them to candidates, political party funds, or propositions favoring their beliefs and positions. Some PACS demand and/or bundle contributions from individual employees, and usually withhold knowledge of contributors' names from candidates, reporters, and the public.

Real estate firms, physicians and other health care professionals, pharmaceutical companies, organized labor, farmers and agribusinesses, tobacco companies, defense industries, educators, and home builders contribute the largest amounts of money to political campaigns.

PACS give millions of dollars to candidates and campaign funds, thereby buying influence and drawing attention to their needs, perhaps out of proportion to the needs of citizens not so represented. PACS form a part of power sharing in a pluralistic society.

political asylum a classification by which a host government grants asylum to an individual who requests such status on the grounds that he/she faces substantial danger, including possible loss of life, should they return to their country of origin.

political base a close-knit, loyal, devoted, and hopefully expanding group of supporters upon whom a candidate can count in all circumstances and that a candidate can employ in seeking higher office, bringing those supporters and their enthusiasm along with him/her. Many elected officials and candidates for office believe they must protect their political bases at all costs. See also POWER BASE.

political cartoons originating in the early 1800s, political cartoons portray political figures carrying on conversations with subtle and not so subtle messages that probably would not be written in prose. The caricature of Andrew Jackson sitting sprawled on a throne and labeled "Andrew the First" needed no explanation. Political cartoons deliver a message with a dramatic, illustrative punch.

Thomas Nast, who developed the Republican elephant and the Tammany tiger, drew outrageous pictures of Tammany Hall's Boss Tweed, which helped ruin the bribetaker. Most American newspapers have their own political cartoonist, many of whom are syndicated.

Some political cartoons have actually affected the nation's thinking, such as Walt Kelly's depiction (1948) of presidential candidate Thomas E. Dewey as a robot on railroad tracks, Herblock's Nixon coming out of a sewer and asking if he can be of any help, or a miniature Harry Truman sitting in a large presidential chair with the query: "Little man, what now?"

political consultant   a person who gives political campaign advice and organizes campaigns for a fee on a freelance basis.

political correctness   a form of psychological censorship that disallows mentioning political thoughts or positions or words that may offend another person, group, or officeholder. The concept includes intimidation by the insinuation that reprisals will follow offensive statements. Communications ranging from movies to political speeches are tailored not to offend religious, ethnic, gay, and other political minorities as well as majorities.

Efforts to achieve political correctness may endanger rights of free speech and thought, lessen sensitivity about others' perspectives in the use of words, and limit discussion of real-life issues. Each faction of a political party or any special interest-group sees words used differently. Political correctness therefore varies according to perspective and group.

Political correctness is particularly acute on American college campuses where faculty and students are urged, forced, or humiliated into maintaining awareness of the concept to avoid the appearance of bigotry, whether the speaker harbors such attitudes or not. Political correctness requires a conformity to speech neutrality, which does not necessarily breed attitudinal neutrality. Political correctness leads people to use occasionally absurd phrases in order to avoid saying what they really mean.

political culture   the political art, concepts, practices, customs, and institutions of a party, government, country, region, or planet.

political economy   (1) the combination of politics and economics and how they relate and affect each other. (2) the economics of a government. (3) a one-time name for political science.

political junkie   a person who lives for politics, collects political information, watches and listens to political speeches, examines vote returns, and loves to discuss and analyze politics.

political machine   an amorphous organization made up of elected officials, government appointees, and political helpers in neighborhoods to deliver votes to an officeholder in return for which the officeholder or political leader ("boss") delivers patronage, services, favors, building permit approvals, and even coffee, donuts, and beer to helpers.

Examples of political machines were those of the late Chicago mayor Richard Daley (1950s–1970s) and a modern liberal version, San Francisco's Burton family, led by Congressman Phil Burton, assisted by his brother, Representative and then state senator John Burton, Congresswoman Sala Burton (Phil's widow), and brother Robert Burton (1960s– 80s).

Political machines, which are particularly effective in cities, are often criticized by people outside the machines and by the opposition. The control they wield services the loyal and destroys the disloyal, opponents affirm. A politician's political organization is often called a machine by his opposition. People who are part of a machine often know exactly where they stand, enjoy a certain level of security and employment, and know what to expect. Political machines also turn out the votes of their party or candidates.

political party an organization that attempts to attract and bring together persons who share common beliefs, political positions, and party registration in order to promote those positions, select candidates, and seek power by getting those candidates elected to office. Political parties collect funds for candidates' campaigns, help in campaign work, and, in some states, control and administer patronage. Each of the United States's two major political parties has a national committee made up of representatives from all 50 states. They meet every four years at conventions to nominate presidential and vice presidential candidates, although most decisions are made prior to the meetings, leading to the suggestion that the conventions should be called "nomination festivals."

The official parties are made up of county, state, and national committees but include officeholders, volunteers, donors, as well as all voters registered in the party.

political prisoners persons arrested and imprisoned on usually phony, trumped up charges when their real offense is opposition to the political regime in power. During World War II the United States and Canada detained everyone in the country of Japanese descent as prisoners in fenced camps. Well-known political prisoners have included Eugene V. Debs (United States), Nelson Mandela (South Africa), Benigno Aquino (Philippines), Alexander Solzhenitsyn (Soviet Union), and recent democracy advocates in China, Chile, and Cuba. Amnesty International reports annually on political prisoners in dozens of countries.

political psychology the science and study of a country or region's history, culture, myths, language and its origins, social and migratory patterns, psychology, family patterns, lore, myths, and symbols. Political psychology also studies how these factors influence political thinking, voting, attitudes, prejudices, activity, passivity, and support for leaders, monarchs, and elected officials.

political science a branch of the social sciences that includes the academic study and analysis of politics and governmental affairs and is a major department of study in most American universities. Aristotle called political science the "Queen of Sciences," although it disappeared as an individual academic discipline until it reemerged in the 19th century. In the interim, journalists, political philosophers, and a few theologians examined the subject. Academic subdisciplines include political theory, comparative government, politics, international relations, political sociology, and political parties. Particularly in the early 20th century, it was called "political economy."

political sociology a subfield of political science that concentrates on behavior, beliefs, and political and electoral behavior of the masses. Political sociology is one of the most theoretical of the political sciences due to the impact of innovative theories that treat of political sociology by Karl Marx (1818–83) and Emile Durkheim (1858–1917).

political suicide an act by an elected official that is drastically contrary to the wishes of his/her constituents, from a vote on a bill they see as against their best interests to flaunting a companion other than his/her spouse.

political theory a philosophical approach to discover the meaning and values of politics and that seeks to discover and develop theories of political behavior combining empirical and supposed moral truths to create ideal political institutions. Plato (427?–347 B.C.E.), Aristotle (384–322 B.C.E.), Thomas Hobbes (1588–1679), John Locke (1632–1704), and John Stuart Mill (1806–73) were original and classical political theorists.

politician a person involved professionally or as an avocation in politics either as officeholder, candidate, campaign manager, or manipulator. Application of the word to anyone involved in politics often carries a derogatory meaning, implying such a person is someone who schemes or seeks personal gain or opportunism.

Because of this negative connotation and resulting lack of respect in the United States for many politicians, many candidates run for office as nonpoliticians, claiming they are not what they are doing. A first-time candidate often runs as a nonpolitician or outsider. Once he or she is elected, the voters almost immediately regard him/her as a politician.

politico (1) a fan of or participant in politics, including activists, candidates, and officeholders. (2) slang for politician. See also POL.

politics (1) the art and science of political government and governance, political affairs, methods, opinions, and principles. (2) the art and science of bringing a person to public office through campaigns and elections. (3) a necessary function in democracy to govern by the people's will. As distinguished from government, which is the operation and management of the state after election, politics is the way and means by which people and parties get into elective office.

politics of meaning a somewhat vague slogan of President Bill Clinton (1993), which he said would replace the "politics of greed" of the 1980s during the administrations of Ronald Reagan and George H. W. Bush. A prime example under President Clinton would have been a guarantee of health insurance for every American instead of high insurance premiums and price gouging by pharmaceutical companies and physicians.

politics of personal destruction the practice of verbally ripping apart a person's history, dignity, and character with dual goals of defeating the person and destroying the person's political career.

polity   the recognized form or principles on which a political entity is based, such as a political organization, government, constitution, or institution.

poll   (1) the place where you vote. (2) Canada: precinct. (3) survey of opinion or attitudes. (4) to ask people their views.

poll, exit   See EXIT POLL.

poll kits   materials assembled to help those working to get out the vote, which may include a voters' list, brochures, and pens.

poll tax   a tax or fee charged in some southern states levied on everyone who registered to vote in an election. The tax was cumulative, that is, if you failed to vote or pay at one election, you might have to pay that tax plus the current tax to vote in the current election. The poll tax originated to discourage poorer citizens, especially blacks, in the South from voting. The 24th Amendment to the U.S. Constitution abolished poll taxes and made them illegal when Congress adopted the amendment on August 27, 1962. It was ratified by two-thirds of the state legislatures on January 23, 1964.

In the early 1990s British prime minister Margaret Thatcher raised her country's hackles by proposing a head tax on all adult citizens, which amounted to a poll tax since one could not vote without paying the tax.

poll, tracking   See TRACKING POLL.

poll watcher   a person who spends election day at a designated polling place, usually representing a particular candidate or party, to make sure all election laws are followed and usually to mark off those who have already voted on a campaign's voting list.

polling place   an official government-selected and government-designated place to vote. Polling places are supposed to be marked by an American flag hung flat on an exterior wall and should be accessible to all voters. Voter lists, marked regularly to show who has voted, are supposed to be posted at every polling place.

polls   place to vote. See also EXIT POLL, POLLING PLACE, PUBLIC OPINION POLL, TRACKING POLL.

pollster   a person who takes polls by surveying voters' opinions.

polyarchy   a form of government run by many persons representing many interest groups. In Yale University political science professor Robert Dahl's theory, government is run by competing special-interest groups with the government functioning as mediator or broker.

popular front   political alliances of convenience or expediency, usually between left-wing or revolutionary parties in a political system. A Popular Front organization may include small centrist, radical, and communist factions that, without such coalitions, would lack a real voice or clout. Sometimes they evolve in response to crises, depression, or a foreign threat. Popular fronts have changed politics and government in several countries, such as France, Spain, and Chile.

populism (1) a political theory based upon the concept of acting in the interests of the masses and enjoying their support, usually used in opposition to incumbents. (2) a term used occasionally misguidedly, particularly when it is applied to a mass movement in which the leadership is from an elite sector of the populace and not strictly from the common people.

Populism sometimes appeals to the masses as an alternative to oppressive institutions, in some instances leading to more oppressive ones when people follow charismatic leaders such as Adolf Hitler and Argentina's Juan Peron, who used populism to mask dictatorship. American populists have ranged from sincere, positive activists, such as unsuccessful Democratic presidential candidate William Jennings Bryan (1896, 1900, 1908) and President Jimmy Carter (1977– 81) to demagogues, such as Louisiana governor and then senator Huey Long in the 1930s.

Populist Party a late 19th-century American political party (also called the People's Party) centered on the existing economic discontent in the South and West and dissatisfaction with both the Democratic and Republican parties. The Populists' demands included circulation of more printed money, a graduated income tax, and nationalized railroads. As Populist Party presidential candidate James B. Weaver from Iowa gained 1,040,000 popular votes and 22 electoral college votes (1892). The Democrats absorbed some of the Populists' programs by 1896, and the Populist convention endorsed Democratic presidential candidate William Jennings Bryan. Bryan lost the final election to William McKinley, and the Populists disappeared as a separate political party.

pork an opponent's negative word for programs or money a legislator obtains for his/her a district or state to benefit his/or constituents. Members of an opponent's party see the other person's successes as pork, while what they bring home to their own district is "bacon." See also PORK BARREL LEGISLATION.

pork barrel legislation legislative bills passed that fund sometimes superfluous projects in the districts of prominent and dominant legislators to pump up the economy and his/her reelectability. Pork barrel projects might include dams, highways, duplicate bridges, federal office buildings, and military bases. The term originated from barrels of pork meat given to American slaves as a reward for docile behavior.

porkers legislators or lobbyists who campaign to have their special program for their district included in the budget, even if at the expense of another district's needs.

position paper a written statement of a candidate's position on a specific issue. Campaign workers pass out position papers to interested constituents, contributors, and the press. Some campaign managers do not think position papers are important, but voters who want to know a candidate's positions before they decide how to vote believe they are extremely important.

positive discrimination   See RE-VERSE DISCRIMINATION.

positive law   a term used by English philosopher Thomas Hobbes in his work *Leviathan* (1651) to refer to legislative rules created by people and enforced in and by a society, in contrast to so-called laws of nature or natural law. The latter two laws may include rules of a tradition or religion and the concept of morality. Statutory law and common law can be compared in the same way.

pot   marijuana, of which the legality of smoking is a perennial political issue. One argument for legalization is its medical benefits in relieving cancer or AIDS pain.

Potomac fever   a nearly irrepressible desire to work in Washington, D.C., usually based upon experience of the supposed excitement, power, and importance of the work done there. The worst case of Potomac fever results in a fierce desire to run for president.

power   (1) the right to command others, backed up by coercion, bribery, persuasion, or dominance. (2) the influence to get things done, to have others do things for you, to have officeholders respond to your requests and opinions, and to have others support your positions.

Power includes the ability to enlarge the number of people influenced.

The larger the group gets the more power the leader holds because of the increased number of people he/she can influence.

Political power is often elusive and can be lost suddenly.

power base   a candidate's or office-holder's natural or developed support group on which he/she can count. See also POLITICAL BASE.

power broker   a person who exerts political power or influence, usually behind the scenes, either in a legislative body or in parceling out appointments or other help in return for favors.

power of the purse   a power held by legislators who vote on whether a president's or legislator's pet projects get approved or included in the budget, often resulting in the rise or fall of that president's or legislator's popularity.

power tactics   methods by which individuals translate power bases to specific actions.

precinct   a geographic region designated as a voting unit with a polling place on election days, reporting results to a city or county, that forwards the results to the state. Precincts also provide a handy unit for political organizing and getting out the vote. Precinct lists of voters are usually available at county clerk's offices.

precinct captain   a person who oversees registration and gets out the vote in a specific precinct for a political party. In some cities where political machines enjoy true power and control, precinct captains can also wield great power. They may be consulted for appointment recommendations or even favoritism for services rendered.

precinct list   a list of all registered voters in a precinct, including names, addresses, phone numbers, and party affiliations of those voters who wish to reveal them. Precinct lists are usually available from county clerks and should be posted for public inspection outside each polling place. Candidates' campaigns and party organizations use them for door-to-door campaigning and get-out-the-vote efforts.

pregnant chad   See CHAD.

premier   See PRIME MINISTER.

president   (1) a head of state in a republic. (2) United States: the chief executive who holds both great power and symbolic importance. According to the Constitution, the president is the commander in chief of the armed forces, signs treaties, appoints cabinet members, government leaders, and ambassadors to foreign countries, grants pardons, and ensures that laws are enforced. In some countries the president's position is ceremonial (Italy, Germany, Israel) with the prime minister holding the real power.

presidential pardon   unlimited power given to the president by the Constitution to pardon a person convicted of or potentially facing charges for crimes. Most famous presidential pardons include President Gerald Ford's pardon of resigned president

Richard Nixon and President Bill Clinton's controversial pardon of fugitive Marc Rich, who was on the FBI's 10 most wanted list, and whose ex-wife had given more than $1 million to Clinton campaigns and the Clinton library.

presidential succession   a question incompletely answered by the U.S. Constitution, which left presidential succession to Congress in the absence of a vice president. Absence of a vice president could occur if the vice president died, resigned, became too disabled to govern, or succeeded to the presidency.

The first succession law was signed by President George Washington on March 1, 1792, naming the president pro tempore of the Senate and the Speaker of the House of Representatives next in line of succession to the presidency.

When President James A. Garfield was shot (1881) and Vice President Chester Alan Arthur became president, the United States had neither a president pro tempore in the Senate nor a Speaker in the House. When Grover Cleveland's vice president, Thomas Hendricks, died in 1885, a similar vacuum existed. As a result, Congress made the secretary of state the successor (1886).

President Harry S. Truman proposed that the Speaker of the House come first in succession since he was an elected official, resulting in a 1947 law creating the succession as follows: Speaker of the House, president pro tempore of the Senate, secretary of state, and down through the cabinet offices. However, due to death and succession, periods when there was no vice president have totalled 34 years.

Senator Birch Bayh (D–Ind.) introduced and pushed through a constitutional amendment ensuring: (1) if there were no vice president, the president would nominate a successor to be approved by a majority of both houses of Congress; (2) a system to establish, in the event of the disability or incapacity of a president, that for the duration of the term the vice president would become "acting president"; (3) the old 1947 order of succession would apply until a new vice president is approved. Senator Bayh's legislation became the 25th Amendment to the Constitution, adopted by Congress on July 6, 1965, and ratified by sufficient states on February 10, 1967. Gerald R. Ford became the vice president in 1973 under the 25th Amendment. When Ford became president in 1974 upon Richard Nixon's resignation, Ford nominated Nelson A. Rockefeller as vice president, and Rockefeller was approved by Congress.

presidential timber a person deemed by his/her party's leaders to qualify for and possess the potential to be elected and, incidentally, qualified to be president. A person who is presidential timber may have the following qualities: good looks, a clean record, good fund-raising ability, malleability to the views held by party leaders, public acceptance and following, electability, good personality, and respect among party regulars.

press newspaper and magazine reporters and the newspapers and magazines themselves.

press corps group of journalists recognized and credentialed to cover a specific candidate, activity, or location, such as the White House.

press gallery (1) the group of journalists in Canada assigned by their newspapers, television, or radio stations to cover the government's and legislature's activities. (2) a section above the floor of a legislature set aside for journalists.

pressing the flesh shaking hands and assiduous mingling by candidates among voters, often in crowds.

pressure group an organization or a group of organizations which attempts to influence government decisions and policy by exerting pressure on a variety of points in the political system. Pressure methods may include staging strikes, printing fliers, advertising in local, mass, or special interest media, hiring lobbyists to represent their views, and withdrawing support from elected officials who fail to comply with the group's wishes. Many such pressure groups are now called Political Action Committees (PACs) and are subject to limitations on financial contributions.

Primary Colors a novel vaguely based on the 1992 Clinton-Gore campaign by "Anonymous" (Joe Klein), who covered the campaign for *Newsweek*.

primary election a public election held to determine who will be the parties' candidates in the final election, either as top vote getters of their parties or as the top two vote-getters in nonpartisan races. The primary election developed to rectify a system whereby candidates were chosen by party leaders and at conventions. An open primary is one in which all voters can vote for candidates of any party. A closed primary is one in which one must be registered to vote with the party for whose candidate one wants to vote. Primary election dates vary by state, and several states vie to compete to hold the first quadrennial presidential primary, mostly due to the media attention and commercial spending the primary brings to the state with the first primary.

Early presidential primaries and their ensuing media coverage may exert undue influence over voters in other states, which is precisely what early victorious candidates count on. Since 1968, in a majority of states, primaries have become the means to choose most national convention delegates pledged to presidential candidates.

prime minister a politician and government leader who is usually selected by the country's legislature to lead the cabinet or government and communicate between the legislature and the country's monarch, if one exists. Sometimes subordinate to the president (France) or monarch (Saudi Arabia), the prime minister may be the leader of the majority party. In Canada and Great Britain the prime minister is chosen by House of Commons members belonging to the majority party.

priming the pump spending government money to stimulate the economy. A concept comprising an element of Keynesian theory of economics used first by Franklin D. Roosevelt as part of the New Deal in 1933.

prison reform a perennial political issue that began with attempts to make prisons more humane and livable. Prison reform developed to include programs for rehabilitation, retraining, and education for postprison life. Other prison reform issues include overcrowding, bad food, medical assistance, heat, activities, access to legal assistance, and safety from abuse by guards or predatory inmates. The effort also encompasses the right to conjugal visits, fair and effective sentencing, and limitations or abolition of the death penalty.

The first organization to advocate prison reform was the Philadelphia Society for Alleviating the Miseries of Public Prisons, founded in 1787. Prison reformer and nurse Dorothea Dix (1802–87) led the effort before the Civil War, and church groups and others took up the cause afterward.

privacy a state or condition constituting removal and seclusion from others with the implication of secrecy and solitude.

The legal right to privacy was first delineated in an 1890s Harvard Law Review article by Professor "Bull" Warren and young Louis D. Brandeis, who eventually served as a U.S. Supreme Court justice. From this work flowed numerous court cases, usually challenging the media's invasion of people's privacy when there was no apparent newsworthiness of the investigation or report.

Rights of privacy generally protect a citizen from (1) intrusion into one's seclusion or solitude or into one's private affairs, (2) public disclosure of embarrassing private information, (3) publicity that puts one in a false light before the public, and (4) appropriation of another's name for personal or business advantage. "The right to be left alone" is personal to each individual.

One's right to privacy in the United States has been controversial, particularly since J. Edgar Hoover's reign of intimidation at the FBI during which spy files were compiled on his political opponents, incumbent presidents, people who crossed him, or people who exhibited strong leadership in directions of which he did not approve. Americans have the right to see their own files following passage of the Freedom of Information Act (1966). Privacy became a major issue in the early 2000s because of Internet information sources that make available everything from individuals' Social Security numbers to medical records.

private bills bills that would give special privileges, benefits, or changes in law to specific individuals, corporations, groups, or organizations.

private enterprise (1) businesses operated by private owners, as opposed to government nationalization of ownership. (2) a conservative buzzword for the catch-all panacea for solving America's economic, unemployment, and health care problems—a rationale that apparently has not always worked.

private member's bill a bill sponsored by a single member of a legislative body.

private sector business, as opposed to government (public sector).

privatization the return of government functions to the private sector based on the theory that private business can perform a job the way the people want it done, more efficiently, and at less cost to the public or government. During the 1980s privatization became a fashionable rationale for private management companies taking over public enterprises, such as hospitals. Many public hospitals were in trouble and became convinced that private companies could manage them better. Often better management meant reduction of services.

Privy Council (1) advisers to a ruler. (2) Canada: a ceremonial organization comprised of former and current cabinet ministers, which may mean the governor general. (3) United Kingdom: a group of advisers to the Queen, which includes members of the cabinet and other leaders of the Commonwealth.

pro-choice an attitude favoring a woman's right to choose what happens to her body, particularly choosing whether or not to have an abortion or a diseased breast removed without religious or governmental interference.

Conservatives tend to be anti-choice and "pro-life." Liberals tend to be pro-choice.

progressive (1) a person who favors and works for political progress and reform. Change and improvement are inherent in a progressive's beliefs. (2) a member of the Progressive Party. (3) buzzword for liberal. See PROGRESSIVE PARTY.

Progressive Conservative Party (Canada) a political party also called Tories, which generally believes in somewhat progressive social policies and fiscal conservatism. The PCs last led a majority government in 1993 under Prime Minister Kim Campbell. In 1993 its members of the House of Commons dropped to two, but PCs still head some provincial governments. Under the leadership of former prime minister Joe Clark the Progressive Conservatives had enough members of parliament in 2001 to be a recognized party. Address: 601-275 Slater Street, Ottawa, Ontario K1P 5H9. Tel.: (613) 238-6111; FAX: (613) 238-7429; e-mail: pcinfo@pcparty.ca; website: www.pcparty.ca

progressive education an educational theory, experiment, and movement in the United States and Europe beginning in the late 19th century centered on the individual child. Progressive education developed in reaction to the narrowness and formalism of traditional education and aimed at educating the whole child. Theorists included A. B. Alcott, Henry David Thoreau, and John Dewey, whose goal was to impart knowledge to children while helping them develop their own talents. Thoreau also saw progressive education as a microcosm of democracy.

Progressive education's roots can be traced to Jean-Jacques Rousseau's novel *Emile* (1762). Other important names in the movement include Johann Bernhard Basedow, Friedrich Froebel, and Elizabeth Rotten (Germany), Johann Pestalozzi and Adolphe Ferriere (Switzerland), Horace Mann (United States), Maria Montessori (Italy), and Ovide Decroly (Belgium). John Dewey's Chicago Laboratory School and Rudolf Steiner's Waldorf Schools were pioneering institutions.

Progressive education in public schools became popular in the 1930s when topical work "units" and projects appeared as the norm in many schools. However, traditional educators and parents feared that the basics of reading, writing, and arithmetic were being neglected in such programs.

Progressive Movement an early 20th-century organization formed within the Republican Party to advocate reforms such as open primaries, recalls, referenda, initiatives placed on ballots, clean government, conservation, and control of monopolies and trusts. The movement's leader was Wisconsin governor and senator Robert La Follette ("Fighting Bob") who wanted to become the Republican candidate for president as a Progressive. La Follette became sick in 1911, and former president Theodore Roosevelt assumed the leadership. President William Howard Taft, La Follette, and Teddy Roosevelt all ran for the Republican nomination for president. Roosevelt lost, pulled out of the Republican Party, and formed the Progressive Party (Bull Moose Party). See also PROGRESSIVE PARTY.

Democrat Woodrow Wilson and many other Democrats co-opted the name by calling themselves progressives, and they adopted many of the same issues in their programs.

Progressive Party an alternative political party that surfaced in three separate presidential elections, considerably reconstituted.

1911–12: the political wing of the Republican Party, organized by Senator Robert M. La Follette (R–Wisc.) to oppose President William Howard

Taft's conservative control of the party. This group formed a party to support Theodore Roosevelt for president after he lost the regular Republican Party nomination. The Progressives of 1912 (nicknamed "Bull Moose") advocated direct primaries, extension of the vote for women, and electoral reform (progress) to include initiatives, recall, and referenda. With the Progressive Party split off from the Republican Party, both Teddy Roosevelt and Taft lost to Democrat Woodrow Wilson. Teddy Roosevelt won more than 4,000,000 votes and 88 electoral votes, far more than President Taft's eight electoral ballots.

1924: a new American political party formed by dissident liberals, Midwest farmers, progressive Republicans, socialists, and some labor unions—all of whom were disenchanted with what they viewed as conservative domination of both the Democratic and Republican parties. The party nominated Senator Robert La Follette for president and favored a "housecleaning" of entrenched executive branch departments, public control of natural resources, public (national) ownership of railways, and reduction of taxes. Even though La Follette won nearly 5,000,000 votes and 13 electoral votes, the Progressive Party fell apart upon La Follette's death in 1925.

1947–48: political party founded by former vice president and secretary of commerce Henry A. Wallace, who had left Democratic president Harry S. Truman's administration. The supporters of this progressive effort believed the Democratic and Republican parties were too conservative. Essentially a protest movement, this Progressive Party focused on foreign issues rather than domestic ones, advocating a conciliatory attitude toward the U.S.S.R. Wallace won more than 1,000,000 popular votes and no electoral votes in the 1948 presidential election, losing substantial support in the final month of the campaign due to the Soviets' increased bellicosity and Truman's vigorous campaign. By 1952 it was a fringe political party of the far left, abandoned by Wallace.

1984: Vice President Walter Mondale called his supporters within the Democratic Party the Progressive Branch.

progressive tax   a graduated tax that features a lower rate of taxation for persons of lower incomes but demands a higher rate for persons of higher incomes.

Prohibition   a movement begun in the second half of the 18th century to outlaw or prohibit the manufacture, sale, and transportation of intoxicating beverages, culminating in the Eighteenth Amendment to the U.S. Constitution (June 19, 1919).

Upon the amendment's adoption, thousands of Americans guzzled their "last drinks," and prohibitionists poured liquor down the streets. The Roaring Twenties followed, during which the public bought liquor from bootleggers, gangsters, illegal importers, and each other. Everyone knew someone who made his own liquor, sometimes called "bath tub gin."

Prohibition failed as a national policy. Herbert Hoover called it a "noble experiment." Public protest, President Franklin Delano Roosevelt, and the Democrats all contributed to the amendment's repeal with passage of the Twenty-first Amendment (1933). Nevertheless, some states granted "local option prohibition" to counties and cities.

Prohibition Party   the oldest minor political party in the United States, formalized in 1869 after more than 70 years' efforts at temperance organizing. The party's main goal was to gain prohibition of the sale of alcoholic beverages through appeals favoring "moral" and religious thinking. It reached an electoral high tide in garnering a steady 250,000 votes from 1888 to 1916. Its real success resulted from its tough lobbying to pass the Eighteenth Amendment to the U.S. Constitution, which ushered in Prohibition (1920–33). Since repeal of that amendment, the Prohibition Party's support has been negligible.

proletariat   the working class of any society, usually not owning property, and in juxtaposition to propertied classes, the bourgeoisie, middle class, and, in some countries, the nobility. The word was popularized by Marxists who glorified the working class.

pro-life   a buzzword for favoring the rights of the unborn child (fetus) and the beliefs of active anti-abortionists who are against women controlling their own choice of whether to have abortions on the basis that a life starts at conception and abortion is murder. It is the official doctrine of the Catholic Church, but many American Catholics are privately pro-choice even if they would not personally have an abortion. Many pro-lifers are conservative Christians, or part of the Religious Right, including millions of people who helped elect Ronald Reagan, George H. W. Bush, and George W. Bush to their presidencies. Ironically, many pro-lifers favor the death penalty. See also PRO-CHOICE.

propaganda   the systematic, widespread dissemination of information with a goal of conversion and indoctrination, possibly involving deception or distortion of fact. Many propagandists believe they are spreading the truth and that the truth they are spreading is the real and universal truth.

Propaganda is used by most governments to influence their own people and the people and governments of other countries. It reached its zenith with Joseph Goebbel's Nazi propaganda machine in Germany (1933–45) and Stalin's iron-fisted control of all media in the Soviet Union (1928–52). The Voice of America and the United States Information Agency (USIA) perform this function for the U.S. government in an effort to influence overseas opinion.

proportional representation   a system of representation in which all political parties and factions gain seats in a legislative body in proportion to their percentage of the popular vote. Protagonists of the system believe it contributes to and encourages alternative parties because they know they can secure a place in the legislature and that they will be included in the process of negotiation and conflict resolution. Proportional representation does not exist in the United States, where representatives are elected by district and usually by the two dominant parties. The most complex system of proportional representation exists in Ireland, which recounts ballots to determine the second, third, and fourth choices of voters if their first choice loses.

Proposition 13 a California ballot proposition passed in 1978 as part of a taxpayers' revolt that cut the state property tax from 3 percent to 1 percent of assessed market value and froze the assessment of real property until it was sold. This effectively devastated local tax support for California's educational system. The brainchild of Howard Jarvis, Republican businessman and executive director of the Los Angeles Apartment Association, the initiative secured a place on the ballot following collection of 1.3 million voters' signatures. It was supported by Paul Gann and Nobel Prize–winning economist Milton Friedman. While great disparities exist on taxes for homes purchased after 1978, the U.S. Supreme Court upheld Proposition 13 in *Nordinger v. Hahn* (June 18, 1992).

protectionism a belief in protecting a country's industries and manufacturers, and thereby jobs, from foreign competition by tariffs and other restrictions on imported products.

A popular concept before the Great Depression, protectionism regained popularity in the United States in the late 1980s and early 1990s due to the American economy's decline, monumental job losses, the international trade imbalance, and importation of goods produced less expensively in countries outside America during that period.

The opposite of free trade, protectionism prevails among NAFTA (North American Free Trade Agreement) opponents in the United States and Canada.

protesters people who oppose policies or legislation by verbalizing, marching, and waving signs to get the attention of legislators or decision makers and media.

protocol (1) a system of diplomacy that implies polite terms of respect, conduct, and procedure by which political and international discussions, ceremonies, etiquette, and general affairs are conducted. (2) a draft of a diplomatic document or negotiation.

proxy (1) a person delegated to act for or vote on behalf of another person. (2) the piece of paper officially designating one person to act or vote on behalf of another.

public campaign finance a concept that government finance of a large portion of political campaigns would reduce the influence of campaign contributors on policy and candidate selection. The Campaign Finance Reform Act (1974) provided for a campaign fund created by taxpayers who check a box on their income tax forms indicating they want to contribute to the matching fund. The Federal Election Commission administers the presidential campaign fund, and candidates must raise the equivalent to demonstrate their viability.

Public campaign finance and the resulting multimillion dollar fund has led to increased television advertising, reduced volunteerism and grass-roots politics, and it has kept weaker presidential candidates in races even after doing poorly in early primary elections.

To obtain the subsidy candidates must adhere to certain limitations on campaign contributions and expenditures and strict (and expensive) reporting procedures. Candidates can refuse the public financing and avoid these strictures, but only Governor George W. Bush declined federal campaign funds in 2000 primaries, which allowed him to raise and spend limitless funds in hard and soft money during the primary election season.

public domain (1) an area of land owned by the general public. (2) the state of patents and copyrights when they pass from private ownership to public ownership, usually due to the lapse of time, approximately 70 years from the death of the author under present legislation.

public interest (1) the common welfare of a society, supposedly shared and understood by all citizens equally, regardless of race, sex, national origin, creed, status, or power. (2) that which thought to be in the best interest of society as a whole, and the opposite of selfish or personal interests of individuals or special pleader groups.

Legislators often apply a test to legislation, asking themselves, "Is it in the public interest?" What is in the public interest is a subjective judgment and will vary according to the experiential exposure of the evaluator.

Conservatives and liberals usually differ on what the public interest is, partly because their publics differ. When an officeholder has lost touch with what the people view as the public interest, that is, their interest, the public becomes disenchanted with that representative and replaces the person with another who seems to understand their perception of what the public interest is. Usually the new person has learned the current local language, enabling him/her to understand and to be understood. Keeping in touch with the ever-changing and evolving language of a public is key to understanding what it regards as the public interest.

public interest law a form of legal practice begun in the 1960s and 1970s, in which lawyers represent individuals or groups in lawsuits about issues they deem to be in the public interest. Operating originally out of storefronts, often in low-rent neighborhoods, public interest lawyers represented a minor revolution by charging fees much below the norm. Most public interest lawyers discovered how to make large incomes in this specialized practice, often through "class action" lawsuits representing many plaintiffs similarly situated, perhaps as victims of price fixing or overcharging by a public utility.

public opinion poll a survey of public opinion done by telephoning supposedly random names and asking supposedly objective, unslanted questions. Usually the goal of public opinion polls is to gauge the public's attitudes toward an issue (abortion, death penalty, universal health care), a product, or a political candidate or issue.

Polling practices and questions can distort the results favoring the position on issues or the candidate supported by those commissioning the poll, with varied intentions ranging from discouraging other candidates from running to influencing voters. Polls can also sway elections by psychologically manipulating the public opinion of those who prefer to follow leaders or winners and ditch apparent losers. See also EXIT POLL; GALLUP POLL; TRACKING POLL.

pump priming the concept that government spending to put people to work in industry and trade can prime the pump of economic stagnation. Based on British economist John Keynes's economic theory, it formed the basis for much of President Franklin D. Roosevelt's New Deal and the effort to pull the United States out of the Great Depression. The term derives from the effort to get water to flow into a pipe and create natural suction to start the pump flowing.

pundit a person who is seen by the media and/or himself or herself as an expert or an authority, particularly in politics and who believes other people rely on his/her opinions and judgments about politics and politicians. Often pundits are wrong, a fact enjoyed humorously by political junkies who do not enjoy such tenuous stature.

Pure Food and Drug Acts a series of laws passed by Congress to control adulteration of foods and drugs transported in interstate com-merce beginning in the early 1900s. Practices and situations improved by these acts ranged from meat slaughterhouse and plant inspections, correct labeling and grading of meats and packaged foods as well as narcotics in medicines, identification of drugs' healing powers and diagnostic and therapeutic devices, and contents labeling.

purge (1) the organized removal or killing of a person or persons holding views contrary to those in power. Stalin, Hitler, Marcos, the Indonesian government, and Serbs are all well known for purging their enemies or ethnic groups they believed to be undesirable. In the United States purging usually occurs at election polls, by recall election, or by subtle exclusion from political inner circles or cut-off of communication. (2) removal of names from voter lists of those who have died, moved away, or failed to vote in a presidential election or to re-register.

purse strings control of expenditures of federal money.

push polling giving highly negative information about an opponent in the guise of taking an opinion survey. Example: "Do you favor 'candidate Jones proposal that income taxes be raised 10 percent?," when Jones has not made such a proposal.

Q.C. Canada: Queen's Counsel.

Queen's Counsel a lawyer who has been appointed counsel to the Crown, meaning they can wear a silk robe. During the reign of a male, it becomes King's Counsel.

question period a period (each weekday) during which opposition members in the House of Commons in Canada and the U.K. can ask questions of government ministers, bring up discussion topics, and criticize policies.

quid pro quo (1) from Latin meaning something for something. (2) one thing done in return for another. (3) promising or doing something in return for someone doing or promising to do something for you. Members of Congress trade support for bills on a quid pro quo basis.

quorum the minimum number of members of a legislative or other voting body required to be present to conduct business. Often it is a simple majority, as in the U.S. Congress.

quorum call (1) an official counting of those present to determine if there is a quorum. (2) a request that the chairman (Speaker) determine if a quorum is present and, if not, that the members be required to attend, as in the House of Representatives or Senate.

quota (1) a share or proportion of a whole. (2) a designated part required to represent a constituency. (3) a number set for employment or immigration below or above which numbers may not fall. (4) a usually negative buzzword for employment or university admission goals that favor minorities and appear to discriminate against whites, usually used by conservative whites. In reality, quotas have been the basis of "affirmative action" to give employment, promotions, and equal pay to members of minorities or women who are under-represented. This system has been criticized as setting "quotas" without regard for equal or superior training, experience, or merit.

Quotas have been used by the government to control imports, exports, and immigration. Quotas were first used to favor immigrants from northern Europe, England, and Ireland. Recent special immigration bills have increased Irish immigration beyond the normal proportion allotted to all immigrants. Congress has passed similar bills to allow larger than usual numbers of immigrants from Vietnam and Cambodia following the Vietnam War on the basis that those desiring entry into the United States needed political asylum.

In the early 1990s, there were calls for new immigration quotas by some conservatives, such as California governor Pete Wilson, based upon the belief that recent immigrants were making use of government services and welfare without paying taxes and by some liberals who feared immigrants were taking jobs from Americans. Other liberals viewed such quota efforts as a form of racism.

In the 1980s and early 1990s, American universities made efforts to extend equal opportunities to potential students of all races, admitting more Asians, African-Americans, and Hispanics than their population proportion to rectify past unequal educational opportunities. White conservatives whose children were not admitted to universities as a result shouted that unfair "quotas" were being set, which discriminated against their qualified children.

Many liberals see such efforts as constituting equal opportunity, unless their college-age children are affected negatively.

R

racial profiling reaction to or categorization of a person according to pre-conditioned stereotyping of behavioral expectations based on race. Examples include: arrests of black people because they are black instead of for what they did and stopping cars for suspicion of wrongdoing just because the drivers or passengers are black or Hispanic.

racism a political or social practice based on prejudice against an individual's racial origin, including hatred of or discrimination against others because of their physical, ethnic, and sometimes cultural differences from oneself.

Racism exists worldwide. Some Filipinos exhibit racism toward Chinese and Samoans, many Germans demonstrate racism against Turkish and Vietnamese immigrants, "foreigners," and non-Aryans, English against blacks, Indians, and Irish, French against North Africans, Italians against Chinese and Turks, and Chinese against Vietnamese and vice versa. In India racism exists in the country's caste system, based on the original Tamils' resentment of "Aryan" invaders. In the United States racism often pits whites against all minorities, especially blacks, but it also exists against Hispanics and Asians. Some blacks and other minority members hold prejudices against whites.

Racism is often grounded in economic competition, envy, or fear, in addition to the arrogant claim that one's race is superior to others. Often racism is practiced by those who occupy the next step up the ladder from the victims, such as poor southern whites against blacks or unskilled white workers against highly motivated Mexicans and newly arrived Asians. Stereotyping is a common element in most racism, such as the assumption that expected negative traits of one group apply to all people of a certain race, much of which is based on unfamiliarity, ignorance, contempt, or fear.

Conservatives may engage in what others call racism but may not see it as such themselves. They tend to see it as the natural order of things. Liberals are more inclined to claim avoidance of racism, acknowledging its existence but espousing nonparticipation in its perpetuation. Many liberals actively work to end racism, although it pervades politics in both blatant and covert appeals to fears of other races. Standout examples include anti-integration oratory in the South through the 1970s, references to "our kind of people" and "he's one of us" campaign slogans in the 1980s and 1990s, and Republican vice president George H. W. Bush's 1988 presidential campaign commercial featuring paroled African-American convict Willie Horton, who committed new crimes while on a prison furlough program in Democratic opponent governor Michael Dukakis's state of Massachusetts.

radical   a person who favors fundamental or extreme change, often by attacking a political or social problem by delving into the root of the problem and devoting time and energy to correcting an alleged basic wrong. Radicals sometimes are so strongly opposed to an existing political, economic, or social system that they will use riots, subversion, or violence to upset or destroy that system in order to replace it with something—sometimes anything—"new."

Radicals at both extremes attack liberals. The radical far left sees liberals as willing to "sell out" a cause and as cowards, because liberals believe in steady progress in a series of incremental improvements. Right-wing radicals attack liberals as radical leftists (communists) in disguise and are intolerant of moderate conservatism. Liberals, in turn, usually view radicals as demanding the impossible by unsocial methods that cannot develop public support and, therefore, are irrelevant to practical or consistent improvement of society.

Individual definitions of what is "radical" are totally subjective, but usually mean the extreme opposite of one's own views.

radio commentators   radio news broadcasters who comment on political news and opinion.

Radio commentary on the news began in the mid-1930s with 15-minute programs that became popular and influential. Well-known commentators ranged from liberals such as Raymond Gram Swing, John B. Hughes, William Winter, Edward P. Morgan (sponsored by labor unions), and Daniel Schorr to conservatives such as Fulton Lewis Jr., Boak Carter, and H. V. Kaltenborn. They also included nonaligned newsmen Lowell Thomas, Gabriel Heatter, James Abbey, and Chet Huntley, and newspaper columnists Walter Winchell and Drew Pearson. Radio commentary's popularity waned with television news' development, but enjoyed a resurgence in the 1990s with conservative commentators' call-in shows such as those of Rush Limbaugh and Dr. Laura Schlesinger.

railroad   (1) to rush through quickly preventing, and designed to prevent, careful consideration and debate of an issue. (2) to push a candidate through to nomination at a convention using pressure from the top and developing a "stampede" based on a claim that this is the inevitable nominee, so you had better "get on board." (3) to cause to go to prison on phony charges without a chance to secure true justice.

rainmaker (1) a member of a law firm whose principal role in that firm is to attract and bring in new clients and who may be a former government official with connections to agencies and legislatures. (2) a lobbyist who delivers legislative support for his/her clients and increases their profits and income by his/her actions.

rally (1) an up-beat public event to increase emotion, enthusiasm, and support for a candidate or cause. (2) to help gain support for a candidate or cause.

random sampling survey or poll conducted by asking questions or searching results supposedly without a plan or pattern.

rank and file ordinary members of an organization, military unit, or labor union, as opposed to executives or officers.

ranking member the member of a legislative body or committee who belongs to the majority party and has the most seniority among the members, thereby ranking first after the committee chair.

ranking minority member the senior or selected leading member of a legislative body or committee who belongs to the minority party.

rap a shortened form of "rapping" or talking to mean initially African-American poetry chanted to scratching records, electronic music, and occasional "acoustical" (real) instruments. Rap has become a medium through which some young African Americans and others express and reveal their social and political concerns. Rap artists often forecast public and societal problems and unrest ignored by other segments of society. "Gangsta rap" allegedly advocates brutal and criminal means of dealing with these problems as well as abuse and mistreatment of women. Many African-American leaders decry "gangsta rap."

rapid response team an organized group of campaign workers, first identified in the 1992 Clinton/Gore campaign, that devised a system to quickly answer in detail claims or charges by the opposition, to acquire information on President George H. W. Bush's and Vice President Dan Quayle's plans, research points in advance of their speeches, and inform Clinton and Gore so that they could make statements on the topics before Bush and Quayle did. Rapid response is used by both major parties to anticipate candidates' statements and hopefully embarrass them in front of the media.

reactionary (1) a person who wants to reverse political progress, occasionally to return to a simpler time (when he/she profited more) and felt safer. (2) a pejorative term for an extreme American conservative. (3) a person who reacts negatively to or resists proposed real change in government or society, often because such changes threaten that person's status quo. (4) in the states of the former Soviet Union reactionary applies to those who oppose democratic change and favor return to the old ways (communism).

The term was first used by 19th-century liberals to refer to those determined to impede progress or a new plan or program.

Reaganauts vehement supporters of Ronald Reagan's presidency and philosophy. See also REAGANOMICS.

Reaganomics President Ronald Reagan's advocacy of tax reductions, government spending reductions (except for the military), reform (decrease) of government regulations, and "sound" economic and monetary policy. Reaganomics also included his espousal of supply-side economics, a theoretical stimulation of an economy by aid to business.

realignment a shift of sociopolitical groups to new party affiliation or loyalty after parting with their long-term, traditional identifications that one acquires with one's parentage or peer group. The original affiliations once led to predictable voting patterns.

Realignment occurs occasionally in the United States, such as liberal Republicans support of President Franklin D. Roosevelt's New Deal coalition following the 1929 financial "crash" or the departure of labor's rank and file from the Democratic Party and support of conservative presidents Ronald Reagan and George H. W. Bush in the 1980s. The most significant long-term realignment in recent times was the shift of southern conservatives from the Democratic

Party to the Republican Party, beginning in the 1960s. In Great Britain realignment occurred during the 1920s and 1930s when the Labour Party attracted working-class voters away from the Liberal Party in support of more socialistic policies.

Realignment also takes place among nations. Since World War II, various nations have shifted from support of the Soviet bloc to that of the West, and to nonalignment and vice versa, depending upon internal politics and national interest.

realpolitik (1) a 19th-century German political concept meaning the "politics of realism" in which one must stay focused on the target and not be distracted by emotion, idealism, or sentimentality. Such distractions might lead to loss of power. (2) newer usage implies constant and vigilant cynicism looking for the hidden agenda or ulterior motives behind candidates' and officeholders' statements and proposals, and constant search for the truth or real-life political intentions.

reapportionment redrawing of legislative district lines every 10 years following the U.S. census for congressional district lines, and at the same or other times for state legislature and county districts.

Originally reapportionment only altered congressional district lines, beginning with 65 members and districts in the first House of Representatives. After the 1790 census the number increased to 106 members and increased after that only by addition of new states until 1910, when the number was fixed at 435 by an act of Congress. Reapportionment of congressional, state, and local districts was controlled entirely by state and local laws until the U.S. Supreme Court ruled (1962 and 1964) that imbalanced districts were unconstitutional. It also ruled that reapportionment of congressional districts and both houses of state legislatures must be based on population parity and established the "one-man-one-vote" rule for all electoral districts. As a result, all congressional and state legislative districts must have equal populations within a state and cannot be structured unnaturally to favor or shut out representation by political or ethnic groups.

Districts are still usually drawn to favor the party in power in the state. This is accomplished by lumping together voters of the opposition party in one district, allowing them to win that one seat and thereby creating several districts favoring the majority party with narrow but winnable registration margins. When a legislature cannot agree or its plan is vetoed by a governor or found to be unconstitutional after legal challenge, the state supreme court may be required to draw and adopt "impartial" district lines. Of course, if the majority party is the party of the governor, his/her court appointees may draw the lines slightly more equal to some than to others. Some states employ non-partisan commissions to draw the districts impartially.

reasonable people pejorative phrase used often in insults traded by both Republicans and Democrats as during President Bill Clinton's impeachment in the House of Representatives, referring to those who agree with you, and suggesting those who do not are unreasonable or lacking in power to reason or understand the law (your way).

recall an elective process by which voters can remove an elected official from office before his/her normal term expires. In the United States, states that allow recalls often require a percentage of voters in the elected official's constituency to sign petitions demanding the recall before it is put on a ballot. Usually a recall petition cannot be circulated until an officeholder has been in office for a designated period. Some states allow recalls of judges and legislators. Recall was one of the reforms promoted by progressive Democrats and Republicans in the first two decades of the 20th century, along with initiatives, referenda, and direct primaries.

recession an economic downturn characterized by several factors, including depressed sales, slowed investment, increased unemployment and individual debt, fewer housing starts, decreased tax revenue, lower production, and a contraction of business activity, lasting two consecutive quarters. A recession is frequently accompanied by a drop in prices due to decreased demand, lower interest rates, and a fall in stock market prices. A prolonged and deep recession is a "depression."

Conservatives may not describe an economy that evidences these factors as a recession. They may call it an economic adjustment, or part of the natural ebb and flow of economics. Conservatives also tend to garner earnings at the top end of the income scale and are not affected by the first waves of a recession.

Liberals often work at the low end of the scale and feel the recession's effects early. While liberals may vigorously voice warnings about recession's effects, conservatives either do not hear them or agree because the recession is not yet a part of their experience. As late as December 26, 1991, President George H. W. Bush said he could not understand why there existed so much public worry despite the fact that millions of American workers were losing their jobs and homes only days before Christmas and Chanukah.

recount   a repeated or second count of votes following a close election and usually requested by a loser who suspects votes were counted unfairly, inaccurately, or dishonestly. In most jurisdictions, the party requesting the recount must pay the costs of the recount unless the original results are overturned.

One danger in recounts is that ballots disappear between counts. Almost always recounts produce different numbers than the original count, but they rarely reverse the outcome. In 2000, in the crucial battle for Florida's 25 electoral votes, when the candidates were only a couple of hundred votes apart, demands by Al Gore's campaign and others for a hand recount, in several counties, were rejected in a case that was decided by the U.S. Supreme Court.

recycling   an effort and process popularized beginning in the late 1960s and early 1970s to collect used paper, aluminum, and glass products to reconstitute and reuse them in order to conserve natural and national resources.

Originally some conservatives saw recycling as a liberal, pinko, environmentalist plot to undermine (their) businesses. Liberals viewed recycling as the right thing to do for survival. Today people of most philosophical outlooks generally recognize the importance of recycling.

red baiting   calling an opponent a communist or hinting that the person has communistic leanings or associations, usually without factual foundation.

red herring   a false issue or false charge to divert or mislead people. The term comes from the folkloric notion that if you are being traced by a bloodhound and you draw a red herring across the path, the dog will follow the smell of the herring instead of the path he was following.

Originally a tactic used in politics to divert attention from issues in a campaign and cast doubts on an opponent's character. One candidate might call another a communist, as did Richard Nixon in his congressional race against Helen Gahagan Douglas and as did many other politicos in the McCarthy era. George Smathers called the sister of Senator Claude Pepper (D–Fla.) a thespian (creating confusion with lesbian in an unaware public) and defeated him. President Harry S. Truman labeled the claim that communists were in the government as a "red herring."

In the 1988 presidential campaign, Vice President George H. W. Bush threw out Willie Horton as a red herring in a television commercial. Horton was an African-American man who committed rape when on furlough from a Massachusetts prison while Bush's opponent, Michael Dukakis, was governor. While Dukakis had nothing to do with the case, as a red herring it diverted attention from other issues and incited fear.

redistricting a process by which state legislatures redraw state and congressional districts following each 10-year census. See also REAPPORTIONMENT.

redlining the practice of either actually or theoretically drawing a red line around inner-city or ghetto neighborhoods by insurance companies who either refuse to insure homes and automobiles in redlined districts or charge exorbitantly more than for equal services in other neighborhoods and by mortgage companies, banks, and other lenders who refuse to make loans on homes in redlined areas.

redneck (1) originally a hard-working rural man who got a "red neck" from bending over in the fields. (2) a pejorative term meaning politically narrow, racist, and bigoted man who is usually from the South or who migrated elsewhere from poor southern rural areas.

Reds (1) communists. (2) a term used pejoratively by conservatives to refer to opponents, liberals, communists, union members, and even artists, or, basically, anyone more liberal than the name caller. (See PINKO.) The term derived from the fact that communist countries throughout the world used red flags as their symbols, the best known of which was the Soviet Union's red flag bearing a hammer and sickle.

red tape (1) paperwork and apparent requirements and obstacles to getting something done. (2) bureaucratic impediments to governmental action by burdensome regulations, delays, and exhaustive paperwork.

Red Tory Canada: name for Progressive Conservatives (Tories) including leader Joe Clark, who are liberal on social programs and conservative on management matters.

redundancy a euphemistic term for a person who has been laid off from work.

referendum a method by which citizens can make a decision directly by voting, rather than indirectly through legislators, to approve or disapprove of state or local laws. Some states require certain matters and propositions to be submitted to referendum. Most referendum statutes require a percentage of voters to sign petitions to put propositions on the ballot. Referenda were one of the progressive reforms of the early 20th century along with recall, initiatives, and direct primaries.

reform (1) an improvement or correction of faults in government or political processes, hopefully by stopping abusive practices and replacing them with better procedures. (2) to correct corruption.

Reform became a cause in the United States in the 1880s after revelations of corruption in federal, state, and municipal governments. It was revived by President Franklin D. Roosevelt as one of the "three R's" of the New Deal. Today advocacy of some type of "reform" is a required tenet of most politicians.

Conservative Republican president Ronald Reagan believed that reform of the system to get government off people's backs entailed deregulating industries such as savings and loans, which resulted in disaster in that industry.

Reform is seen differently from varied political points of view, with the common denominator of correcting or changing what an incoming party believes the incumbent party did wrong.

Year 2000 Republican presidential primary candidate senator John McCain (R–Ariz.) campaigned as a reformer, based on his co-sponsorship of the McCain-Feingold Bill to reform campaign finance practices. Since the reform became fashionable, former governor George W. Bush of Texas also claimed he was a reformer and later a "reformer with results." Some politicians call any change they favor as a "reform."

Reform parties in both Canada and the United States, new conservative parties that aim to "reform" policies and management style of governments, generally favoring "Christian values," the death penalty, less government, lower taxes, school vouchers, private health care, and eliminating gun control and abortion. They stress national self-sufficiency over international cooperation. In Canada now called Canadian Alliance, the party currently holding the second largest number of parliamentary seats. In the United States, Reform Party founder H. Ross Perot received 19 million votes as an independent in 1992 and 9 million as the

first Reform candidate for president in 1996. In 2000 the party split in two, and the old Perot supporters nominated physicist John Hagelin, whereas the new conservative members nominated Pat Buchanan.

Ross Perot founded the Reform Party in the United States in 1992. Preston Manning founded the Reform Party in Canada in 1987. He was unseated as its leader by Stockwell Day after renaming it several times, ending up with the Canadian Alliance. Address: Reform Party USA, P.O. Box 9, Dallas, Tex. 75221, e-mail: webmaster@reformparty.org; website: www.reformparty.org

refugee a person who flees from his/her native country to another due to religious, economic, or political persecution. Many French people fled to the United States and neighboring European countries after revocation of the Edict of Nantes in 1685; Irish left Ireland by the millions during the potato famine of the 1840s, which many believed to be rooted in religious and political persecution by the British; Vietnamese fled to the United States after the Vietnam War and communist takeover in 1975; Cubans still flee to the United States to escape Fidel Castro's communism; and Haitians attempt to flee their oppressive, poverty-stricken homeland for the United States. All are refugees. The United States is a nation of refugees and immigrants, except for American Indians.

regionalism the real or theoretical division of a country or continent into parts or administrative regions to maximize and economize uses of resources, interests, products, and knowledge. Each region supposedly has common characteristics and interests and has discernible geographic delineations.

registration the process by which a person signs up to vote after establishing his/her residency and other qualifications. Most states require a person to register only once per residence as long as the person votes in presidential elections. In some states registration is cancelled if a person fails to vote in two successive elections or in a presidential election. Voters who register are sometimes given a receipt, which they are obliged to keep to present at the polls if their registration is challenged or if an election official says they did not register.

Time limits and registration deadlines vary greatly from several weeks before an election in some states to the day before elections in a few. Most states require the elector to state a political party preference or declare "decline to state." Some states have "open" registration, which does not require registration in a political party, allowing voters to vote in any party's primary election.

regressive tax taxes that burden lower-income people more than higher-income people. For example, the sales tax is a regressive tax because it requires a larger percentage of a poor person's income than of a wealthy person's income to be paid when purchasing the necessities of life.

regulatory agency a government agency that enforces rules and regulations in a particular field, such as the Federal Communication Commission and the Environmental Protection Agency.

reinventing government a concept promoted by a task force headed by Vice President Al Gore (1993) to reorganize government by finding imaginative solutions to new problems to serve people more efficiently. Such reinvention includes turning over to private business some jobs that were previously performed by government, with an expected outcome of reducing employees and costs.

repatriation sending a person back to his or her original country of birth, citizenship, or allegiance.

representative (1) a member of the U.S. House of Representatives. (2) a person sent by election or appointment to act for the people or his or her superior.

representative democracy a governmental system in which the public elects representatives to make political decisions for them, often by designated geographical districts. A representative democracy contrasts with a direct democracy in which the people themselves, and not representatives, make decisions and make laws, such as in New England town meetings.

reproductive rights initially a politically correct term for a woman's control over her own body and what happens to it, from willingness to engage in sexual acts to the right to choose whether or not to have an abortion or give birth to a child, take birth control pills or hormone pills, use contraceptives, and have hysterectomies. Reproductive rights now also include some men's pleas that they have rights to participate in a woman's decision to either bear or abort their child.

republic a state or nation in which leaders are elected and which has an elected president or prime minister as leader, as opposed to a monarchy or oligarchy, and similar to a representative democracy. The word "republic" is often misused to mean nation, particularly by dictators who disallow elections.

Republican (1) a person who believes in and advocates republics. (2) a member of the Republican Party, usually more conservative than a member of the Democratic Party.

Republican Party one of two major American political parties. Its origins derive from opposition to slavery. The Republican Party was founded as a liberal movement in 1854 at Ripon, Wisconsin, by abolitionist Whigs, Democrats, and Free Soilers. Since the late 19th century it has been characterized by support of free enterprise and individual initiative, and general suspicion of big government. It generally favors limited government intervention in social welfare. The Republican Party tends to support offshore oil drilling, nuclear arms, the death penalty, and a conservative foreign policy. Members of the Republican Party are often, but far from exclusively, business people, Protestants, professionals, members of the middle and upper classes, and farmers.

The Republican Party became more conservative than the Democratic Party by the 1870s, and throughout its history it has endured tugs- of-war between its moderate and conservative wings.

The first, and probably greatest, Republican president was Abraham Lincoln (1861–1865) who successfully preserved the Union. The moderate to liberal faction of the party included the 19th-century presidents, particularly Chester Alan Arthur who pushed civil service reform.

In the 20th century, moderate Republicans included President Theodore Roosevelt (1901–09), presidential candidate Wendell Willkie (1940), California governor and Supreme Court Justice Earl Warren, President Dwight D. Eisenhower (1953–61), and New York governor and vice president Nelson Rockefeller. Conservatives included Herbert Hoover (1929–33), Richard Nixon (1969– 74), and Ronald Reagan (1981–89). Both Hoover and Reagan migrated politically from liberal to conservative. George Bush shifted from moderate to conservative to please Presi-dent Reagan and the religious right of the Republican Party, while Gerald Ford eased from conservative to moderate.

Between 1860 and 2000, Republicans occupied the presidency for a total of 84 years, compared to the Democrats' 56 years. Since 1932, however, they have been basically a minority party, holding the presidency 28 years to the Democrats' 40 years and seldom dominating either house of Congress. In 1994 the Republicans captured both houses of Congress and continued to control Congress through the Clinton administrations.

The Republican Party is known as the "Grand Old Party" (GOP), and its symbol is an elephant. Address: 310 First Street, S. E., Washington, D.C. 20003. Tel.: (202) 863-8500; FAX: (202) 863-8820; e-mail: info@rnc.org; website: www.rnc.org

resolution   a statement of opinion or principle agreed upon by a legislative body or other group of people. In the case of the U.S. Congress, resolutions are submitted to Congress for adoption to express a joint sense of agreement on an issue. Resolutions are not binding acts of law and do not require the president's signature.

Respect Life   a buzzword for born-again Christian and Catholic anti-abortion movements used to distinguish themselves from the negative images of identification with Operation Rescue violence of the early 1990s. Respect Life attempts to turn anti-birth control and anti-abortion efforts to a psychological and semantic positive.

responsible government   Canada and United Kingdom: the concept that a government, meaning prime minister and cabinet, are responsible and accountable to their parliament and serve as long as parliament approves of what they are doing. Parliament can vote "no confidence" in the prime minister and cabinet, which means the prime minister must call an election. Parliament can also show its "confidence" in the prime minister and cabinet by voting approval of the leaders' conduct.

revenue   money used and collected from the public and spent by a government. Means of collection include

taxes, borrowing (particularly through issuing bonds), import duties, and occasionally operating some state-controlled enterprise. Fines and license fees are important sources of revenue in some smaller jurisdictions.

revenue enhancement   Bill Clinton's term for increased taxes or other ways of bringing more money into the government's coffers.

reverse discrimination   the condition in which the majority feels it is discriminated against in order to favor or make amends to the minority, who had been victims of discrimination in the past.
  Charges of reverse discrimination have been made against university admission policies and public employee hiring practices in which minorities whose opportunities and employment had been previously limited now enjoy preferential treatment.

revisionism   redefining or modifying old historical or political theories once thought to be sacred to meet current or personal needs or views.

revolution   (1) a drastic change of any kind. (2) overthrow of a governmental or social system and replacing it with another. A revolution often involves the support of a large segment of a country's population, as differentiated from a coup d'état, which can involve only a few people who take power from the existing leadership by threat or force. Revolutions, usually fueled by class conflicts, can occur by three means: violence, election, and destabilization of the existing government. The American Revolution (1775) is an example of violent revolution supported by community leaders. The takeover of Cory Aquino's "People Power" from dictator Ferdinand Marcos in the Philippines (1986) after election results had been falsified and the Bolshevik Revolution in Russia in 1918, a carefully planned use of organization with popular support, were both relatively nonviolent revolutions. Ongoing struggles in certain Latin American countries demonstrate continuing processes of "the revolution" by government destabilization.

In the United States and other stable democracies, peaceful revolutions of both ideas and leadership can be accomplished by election.

rider an attachment or amendment (which would not pass on its own) to a popular legislative bill that will slip in with the principal measure. Often riders are added to get a measure through the legislative process based on knowledge that a president although he opposes the rider, will not veto major favored legislation just to eliminate the amendment.

riding Canada and Britain: a voting district with geographic boundaries for both provincial legislatures and federal parliaments. "Riding" came from a geographic territory a candidate or officeholder could ride around on a horse.

riding association Canada: a party's district organization or club.

right (right wing) (1) term originating with early French parliamentary practice in which the conservatives sat on the right and the liberals and radicals sat on the left in the legislative chamber. (2) persons or political organizations or positions that favor the status quo or a return to the past, and resisting social or political change unless it is regressive. Usually associated with conservatives and Republicans, the right wing often favors unregulated free enterprise and rule by a form of oligarchy. The right wing often believes in authority, hierarchy, and obedience instead of free thought and creativity. The privileged right wing works to protect their position and the system that grants them their privileges. Ironically, the communist right wing in Russia would like to regress from new democratic efforts toward strictly structured communism in which they held firm positions, roles, and privileges.

Right, New See NEW RIGHT.

right of assembly the right guaranteed by the First Amendment (1791) to the U.S. Constitution allowing Americans to gather in groups, often to exchange and voice opinions on topical issues of the day. Occasionally this right conflicts with police powers reserved to the states or "national security." Thus, an assembly may become "unlawful" (and can be dispersed) if it is violent, clearly threatens to become violent, or prevents the exercise of competing rights, such as the ability of people to enter or exit offices, manufacturing plants, schools, or clinics where abortions are performed.

right to petition the right to appeal in writing to the federal government guaranteed by the First Amendment (1791) to the U.S. Constitution, which prohibits creation or existence of any federal law that would abridge the people's right "to petition the Government for a redress of grievances." The Fourteenth Amendment (1868) stipulates that state governments cannot infringe on this right. Like other rights specifically granted in the Bill of Rights, the right to petition had been denied the American colonists by the British government.

right to privacy See PRIVACY.

right-to-work laws laws written supposedly to assure everyone's right to work. Specifically, they ban employer-union contracts protecting the employment and seniority of union members. Realistically, the laws enable employers to hire nonunion workers and to replace unionized workers with nonunion people. From the employer's view, he/she has the chance to pay less than union wages and thereby make more profit. From the organized labor view, the law and open hiring undermine unions and lead, in many cases, to the break-up of unions, which renders them ineffective.

rightist a person who holds right-wing, conservative views, often supporting the status quo or a previous world order that benefited the individual and/or their interest.

rights privileges due a citizen such as an American's right to a fair trial, right to vote, right to free speech, and right to assembly.

Rights of Man a book by patriot pamphleteer Thomas Paine published in England (1791) as a forceful argument for absolute democracy, personal freedom, and civil rights. Defending the French Revolution, it shocked the Federalists and became the philosophical handbook for the most progressive of the emerging Democratic-Republicans, including Thomas Jefferson.

roadshow congressional committee hearings traveling on the road, going to the voters, usually with many well-publicized stops.

Roberts' Rules of Order a handbook of parliamentary procedure by which many organizations and governmental entities run their meetings, written by General Henry M. Robert.

Rock the Vote major media campaign drive to register young Americans to vote, get them involved in the political process, and make sure they vote. Rock the Vote was organized and coordinated mostly by young voters with unprecedented success. It appeals through young adults' media such as MTV and eye-catching posters, and it resulted in large young voter turnout favoring Democratic candidates Bill Clinton and Al Gore in 1992. Address: 10635 Santa Monica Blvd., Box 22, Los Angeles, Calif. 90025. Tel.: (310) 234-0665; FAX: (310) 234-0666; e-mail: mail @rockthevote.org; website: www. rockthevote.org

rogue country a country that the United States believed did not conform to accepted international behavior, laws, or practices. The term was officially abandoned in 2000, but is still used informally.

Roll Call a semiweekly newspaper covering facts, actions, and occasional scuttlebutt of Capitol Hill. *Roll Call* provides information valuable to government agencies, officeholders and staffs, business, and the general public not available in most newspapers. Address: 50 F Street, N.W., Washington, D.C. 20001. Tel.: (202) 824-6800; FAX: (202) 824-0475; e-mail: letters@rollcall.com; website: www.rollcall.com

roll call vote a voice vote taken by reading officials' names and their responding "yea," "nay," or "abstain." Voting by roll call allows for recording of individual votes, which are then made available to the public. Legislators who do not want their votes recorded individually often call for a voice (all at once) vote. In many legislative bodies the roll call is automated by pushing "yes" or "no" buttons.

royal assent Canada: the process by which legislation passed by parliament is approved and given the seal of approval by the monarch and thereby becomes law.

royal commission Canada: a group of people appointed by the Crown to investigate a problem or situation and produce a report and recommendations.

RU-486 a French-origin "morning after" birth control pill, whose approval for use in the United States was tied up with Christian right-wing views that it should not be approved. RU-486 was approved in 2000.

rubber chicken circuit a euphemism for political dinners, not known for their culinary delights unless one favors the infamous lukewarm chicken, peas, and mashed potatoes that are often served.

rubber stamp a person (particularly a legislator), organization, or political entity that will approve a position and will deliver votes and support to the leadership as expected and without question.

rugged individualism buzzwords based on pioneer ideals used primarily by conservatives to describe a belief that anyone can succeed if he/she just tries hard without government assistance or interference. When used by conservatives or racists, the term also subtly implies that those who cannot succeed are lazy, welfare-abusing minorities. "Rugged individualism" was used most prominently by President Herbert Hoover (1929–33), and later facetiously by Democratic presidents Franklin Delano Roosevelt and Harry Truman to tweak the Republicans about the Hoover administration's disasters, namely, the crash of 1929 and the Great Depression.

Rules Committee (Committee on Rules) a powerful committee of the House of Representatives that decides if, when, and under what conditions bills will be considered. Most bills coming from standing committees must be cleared by the Rules Committee for action on the floor of the House, called "getting a rule." A two-thirds vote is required to move a bill to the floor, which enables the majority of members to stall or move for full

House consideration of a bill, a privilege looked upon favorably by the majority party and negatively by the minority party.

rump session a meeting that occurs when one faction, usually dissatisfied about fundamental issues, walks out on its primary group and sets up its own conversation session. While rump sessions are often publicity stunts, occasionally the divisions are so basic that the separation is permanent.

run-off (election) a deciding, second, or final election held when no candidate receives a majority, usually among the two top vote-getters or leading candidates of each party. The purpose of a run-off is to prevent election by less than a majority of votes, particularly in a multicandidate race. Run-offs are used statewide in a few southern states, including Louisiana, Alabama, and Florida. They are common in municipal elections nationwide and in special elections to fill midterm vacancies in several states, including California.

run-off primary a second primary election between two candidates who received the largest numbers of votes in the original primary in which no one gained a majority or whatever percentage of votes is required for nomination.

running mate a candidate for elective public office running on the same party ticket with another person, such as presidential and vice presidential candidates.

sacred cow a term that comes from the deification of cows by Indian Hindus and means an institution (including person) that must be honored and cannot be touched or changed.

sacrificial lamb a candidate running in a hopeless race just to fill a party's ticket.

sales tax a tax levied as a percentage of sales prices or on receipts from sales. Sales tax is levied at each state's discretion, and local jurisdictions may add their own for such needs as public transportation. Some states do not impose sales taxes but collect the revenue by other means. An example is Nevada, which supports its programs by taxing the gambling industry. In 1993 the Clinton administration briefly considered a national sales tax called a "value-added tax" to fund health care plans.

Benefits of sales taxes include the fact that each bite is relatively painless because it is small and retailers are held responsible for collecting and reporting the tax. Negatives include the fact that the sales tax is a regressive tax that collects a larger percentage of revenue from lower-income people's personal income than from that of the wealthy, who pay a smaller percentage of their income on necessities. A national sales tax (GST) in Canada is unpopular with most Canadians.

SALT Strategic Arms Limitation Talks, begun in 1969 between the United States and the Soviet Union to reduce arms stockpiling. See also ARMS CONTROL.

sample ballot ballots mailed to voters before an election on which they can mark their selections and that they can take to the polls to help expedite the voting process. Sample ballots are often accompanied by a voters' pamphlet, which delineates and explains issues and arguments for and against ballot propositions and may include candidates' statements.

sandbag to set up a person, candidate, or officeholder to ensure that they fail before he/she has a chance to advocate or execute a position or plan. The term comes from sandbags used to stop flooding waters before they follow their natural course and cause destruction.

San Francisco Chronicle leading circulation newspaper (562,000) in the San Francisco Bay area, the 10th largest newspaper in the United States and serving a heavily Democratic area. Owned since 1865 by its founding family, the *Chronicle* was sold in 2000 to the Hearst chain, also once a San Francisco–based newspaper family. Address: 901 Mission Street, San Francisco, Calif. 94103-2988. Tel.: (415) 777-1111; FAX: (415) 512-8196; website: www.sfgate.com/ chronicle

San Francisco Examiner originally the flagship of the Hearst publishing empire, the afternoon *Examiner* trails the morning *Chronicle* in circulation and tends to be slightly more liberal with more coverage of San Francisco activities. With the Hearst chain's purchase in 2000 of the *Chronicle,* the *Examiner* was sold and re-issued as a faint shadow of the old *Examiner.* Address: 110 Fifth Street, San Francisco, Calif. 94103. Tel.: (415) 777-5700; FAX: (415) 243-8058.

sanitize to clean up a written statement by deleting offensive or revealing language, sometimes after its first exposure.

scab slang term for (1) a scoundrel or low, contemptible person; (2) in labor union terms, a worker who takes the place of a striking worker, and crosses picket lines, a worker who refuses to join a labor union or works for less pay under worse conditions than a union member, or a worker who refuses to join a strike.

The conservative/liberal dichotomy on scabs is exemplified in the 1981 air traffic controllers' strike at American airports. President Ronald Reagan encouraged hiring of nonunion workers to fill the federal jobs of unionized air traffic controllers who went on strike to protest low pay and unsafe flying conditions. Union members, liberals, and many Democrats saw the new hires as scabs. Conservatives and Republicans saw the strikebreakers as patriotic Americans taking advantage of an economic opportunity opened for them by overreaching union members. Scabs are often the subject of harassment and violence by displaced workers.

scalawag (1) a white southerner who was a Republican during post–Civil War Reconstruction (1865–76) and took political advantage of the disenfranchisement of confederate officials with "carpetbaggers" from the North. (2) a reproachful and contemptuous term for conservative southern Democrats. (3) a tricky, crafty, slightly deceiving or worthless person ("loser").

scrutineer a person who records voters as they arrive for a candidate and assists or observes vote counting.

secession the withdrawal of a region from a country or other government entity to become independent and self-governing.

Examples of secession attempts include the Confederate States from the United States, which led to the Civil War (1861–65). The U.S.S.R.'s Stalinist constitution technically gave all republics the right to secede, however, no observers expected any to do it. Bangladesh seceded from Pakistan in 1971. In the early 1990s, secessions and break aways occurred within the U.S.S.R. and Yugoslavia, and the Slovak Federal Republic parted from Czechoslovakia. Quebec "sovereignists" seek secession or separation of the province from Canada.

second-class citizen   in a supposedly classless society, American second-class citizens comprise those people who do not enjoy the economic benefits, political influence, or, occasionally, voting rights of the decision makers. Minorities, particularly African Americans, often believe they are treated as second-class citizens.

second house   the upper house of a legislature, including the Senate in the United States, Canada, and France and the House of Lords in Great Britain. Unlike the elected U.S. Senate, which has tremendous power, many second or upper houses have only veto power or the power of moral suasion.

second-strike capacity   nuclear-missile–military-industrial complex term for having a stockpile of nuclear weaponry sufficiently large to be able to respond to a nuclear attack with enough force so as to deter an attacker from launching an original (first strike) attack because it would not be worth the cost. The whole concept of

second-strike capacity seems to be purely macho virility symbol talk, since mutually assured destruction and the end of the world would result from such events. Second-strike capacity exemplifies cold war build-up which benefited few except for the industries developing and building the weapons.

Second World   between 1945 and 1990 the communist bloc nations. First World nations comprise those in North America and Western Europe and certain other industrialized nations such as Australia and New Zealand, and the Third World consists of emerging nations.

sectionalism   supposed unwarranted or undue concern for or interest in a particular section (usually yours) of a country. Stereotypical sections of the United States such as the industrial Northeast, the agricultural South and West, the developing West, the "sun belt," the "rust belt," the Northwest, and the mountain states all contain competing sectionalist interests. Southerners' fierce promotion and defense of their section of the country typifies sectionalism.

secular state   a government which has no official ties to any religion.

In the United States the First Amendment to the Constitution requires separation of church and state, creating a theoretically secular state. Religion has crept into American secularism with "one nation, under God" in the Pledge of Allegiance, and with issues ranging from Christian prayer in schools to posting the Ten Commandments in schools and other public buildings, both of which were declared unconstitutional by the courts. Some conservatives claim that the United States is a "Christian" nation. Governor George W. Bush declared "Jesus Day" in Texas in 2000.

Examples of nonsecular states include Great Britain and its Church of England and Scandinavian countries and the Lutheran Church. The governments of Italy, the Philippines, and most Latin American countries (except Mexico) have strong ties to the Roman Catholic Church. Japan gives official obeisance to its native Shintoism, Israel is theocratic in its relationship to Judaism, and most Muslim countries (particularly Iran and Sudan) have close ties to Islam.

Securities Act of 1933 (Federal Securities Act) a law passed by Congress to protect investors by requiring that information be provided to them about new securities. It required a company offering securities to file all information with the Federal Trade Commission, and send a prospectus to potential purchasers listing the names of officers, a description of the securities offered, and the offering company's financial status report. Upon meeting these demands, the company could offer securities for sale. The act failed to provide control over stock markets and stockbrokers, which was remedied by the Securities Exchange Act (1934) that transferred regulation and receipt of prospectuses to the Securities and Exchange Commission.

Securities and Exchange Commission a commission created by the Securities Exchange Act in 1934 to administer and enforce the act. The commission is made up of five members who are appointed by the president with consent of the Senate for staggered five-year terms. The commission's mission is to protect the public against deception, fraud, and malpractice in securities and financial matters. It has the additional responsibility to regulate utility holding companies. Address: 450 5th Street, N.W., Washington, D.C. 20549. Tel.: (202) 942-7040; e-mail: help@sec.gov or publicinfo@sec.gov; website: www. sec.gov/

Securities Exchange Act (1934) a congressional act meant to supplement the Securities Act of 1933, establishing the Securities Exchange Commission. The act requires registration of all stock exchanges and aims to regulate securities and exchanges to prevent fraud and recurrence of the crash of 1929.

sedition the stirring up of civil discord, discontent, resistance, or rebellion against a government. It can include incitement in speechmaking at meetings or in informal conversations, usually with the goal of overthrowing a government by force.

In the United States sedition is a federal crime if it involves overt acts beyond mere advocacy, including conspiracy. In the three years prior to America's entry into World War II (December 1941), the German-American Bund and other pro-Nazi groups shrilly claimed the United States should not aid Great Britain and France and some adherents spied for Germany. Several members were convicted of sedition.

segregation (1) setting apart, isolating, or separating one group from another or of a minority from the majority. (2) the practice of keeping members of different races apart by forcing them to use separate facilities such as restrooms, restaurants, parks, beaches, swimming pools, and to occupy separate sections of public transportation vehicles or housing. After *Brown v. Board of Education of Topeka* (1954), segregation is no longer legal, although it is still practiced in subtle forms such as ghetto housing.

Conservatives, particularly in the South, have thought of segregation as a natural, good, and appropriate practice. Liberals everywhere see segregation as a negative, sinful, and inappropriate practice, although some engage in it clandestinely.

Select Committee a temporary committee of a legislative body appointed for a limited period to investigate and report on individual, unusual, or special problems or incidents. Examples include the rackets committee (Select Committee to Investigate Improper Activities in Labor-Management Relations) in the 1950s and the House committee set up to investigate the assassination of President John F. Kennedy.

sellout (1) to compromise previous convictions to please a constituency; (2) a person who so changes.

Senate in the United States the upper house (chamber) of the Congress or state legislatures. The U.S. Senate is made up of 100 senators, two senators elected from each state for six-year terms. Besides its legislative duties, the Senate holds hearings on and confirms presidential appointment nominations, has a strong role in foreign affairs and must ratify treaties by a two-thirds vote. A senator is considered to be a more prestigious official than is a member of the House of Representatives since senators represent more voters than do members of Congress, do not have to campaign as often, and receive more notoriety than most House members. In some countries the Senate serves more as a debating society whose members can only veto or delay rather than initiate legislation. In Canada senators are appointed by the prime minister.

seniority (1) status, rank, or precedence obtained by length of service in a job or appointment. (2) a tradition favoring members of legislative bodies who serve longest with special privileges such as committee chairmanships, mayorships, and priority office and parking space assignments. Newer members of bodies, those of the minority political party, and representatives from districts with high turnover consider the seniority system unfair and stifling to advancement by merit. Others see it as undemocratic on the basis that longevity does not necessarily mean competence. Those who favor it (usually those benefiting from it) claim it saves a lot of time and trouble. The late House Speaker Sam Rayburn used to tell freshman members of Congress: "The longer you're here the better you'll like it."

senior White House official anyone working in the White House who holds authority that puts the individual in direct communication with the president. The term is often used by the press when the individual does not want his/her name used as a source of information. It refers to status, rather than to age or experience.

separate but equal doctrine (1) a ruling by the U.S. Supreme Court in *Plessy v. Ferguson* (1896) that segregation of railroad facilities was not an infringement of Fourteenth Amendment rights as long as equal facilities were provided for "Negroes" and "Whites." (2) a ruling unanimously overturned by Chief Justice Earl Warren and the U.S. Supreme Court in the case of *Brown v. Board of Education of Topeka* (1954), which said that "separate but equal" facilities were "inherently unequal," followed by a separate ruling that equal facilities and conditions must be established and utilized equally by blacks and whites "with all deliberate speed."

separation of church and state provision in the First Amendment of the U.S. Constitution that "Congress shall make no law respecting the establishment of religion. . . ." enacted in part to sever the linkage between the Church of England and the government against which American founding fathers and mothers rebelled. Furthermore, the churches established in the American colonies included Roman Catholic, Baptist, Lutheran, Methodist, Presbyterian, and Anglican (Church of England), as well as Jewish congregations, and none wanted any other to become the official American church.

Questions of separation of church and state arise in use of public property for religious displays, such as crèche scenes at Christmas, and Christian prayer in public schools. Some conservatives tend to want a limited mixing of church and state as long as the religion is Christian. Liberals favor the constitutional separation and oppose the mixture, partly because they represent a variety of religions. Claims that the United States is a "Christian nation," used as a rationale for such a mixture, are inaccurate and inappropriate in light of the Constitution, particularly since Jews, Muslims, Buddhists, other religious people, and those with no religion comprise a significant part of the population.

separation of powers plans to divide governmental powers devised by both John Locke and Baron de Montesquieu and proposed by James Madison as part of the Virginia Plan for the U.S. Constitution in 1787. The American government is divided into three branches: the legislative branch to make rules and laws, the judicial branch to provide law courts and interpret the Constitution and the laws, and the executive branch to oversee department administration and application of rules and policies. Realistically some of these separated functions overlap: the executive and the Congress both make policy. Separation of powers theoretically provides for "checks and balances" and prevents a totalitarian system in which a ruling group controls all three branches.

session a formal meeting or series of meetings of a legislative body, such as the U.S. Congress, with fixed beginning and ending dates.

sex (1) defined in *Webster's New Universal Unabridged Dictionary*: "anything connected with sexual gratification or reproduction or the urge for these, especially the attraction of individuals of one sex for those of another." (2) a principal topic in President Bill Clinton's congressional impeachment, in part because he had lied to the American people and to a grand jury in saying, "I did not have sex with that woman." Clinton and his lawyers claimed that oral copulation did not amount to sex for him, only for Monica Lewinsky who performed the act on him.

sexism   social, economic, and political exploitation, domination, and favoritism of one sex over the other —usually men over women—including discrimination by one sex against the other. Some consider that feminism, which developed in reaction to male sexism and discrimination against females, is a form of sexism, favoring women over men.

sexual harassment   buzzwords for the practice of making unwanted sexual approaches to employees with the implied suggestion that their employment status depends upon their response and/or cooperation. Professor Anita Hill's accusations of sexual harassment by U.S. Supreme Court Justice nominee Clarence Thomas in 1991 is a noteworthy example of the issue in a political setting.

Sherman Antitrust Act   U.S. law adopted in 1890 to render illegal restraint of trade between states or with foreign nations. The Sherman Antitrust Act was created in reaction to the growth and power of trusts, which controlled some industries, stifled competition, fixed prices, and enjoyed special rates with transportation carriers.

shoo-in   a candidate who cannot lose, supposedly.

shortfall   late 1980s to early 1990s evasive terminology to say "deficit," meaning "we spent more money than we took in" and used by cagey officeholders to minimize miscalculations or overspending.

short list   the "real" list of usually three to five persons being considered seriously as finalists for a presidential or gubernatorial appointment.

shuttle diplomacy   flying by airplane from capital to capital to negotiate and communicate in person. Secretaries of State Henry Kissinger, Warren Christopher and Madeleine Albright engaged in shuttle diplomacy in the Middle East by carrying personal messages from leader to leader in hopes of bringing about peace.

Sierra Club   an environmental organization founded in Berkeley, California (1892), to preserve the Sierra Nevada Mountain Range. John Muir served as its first president. Its current concerns include exploration, enjoyment, and protection of the wild places of the earth. The Sierra Club lobbies for environmental and conservation positions, publishes books, calendars, and greeting cards, and performs educational and social functions.

The Sierra Club is considered leftist and obstructionist by lumber and oil industry owners and workers and others who favor unlimited growth and development. Liberals generally view it as a vital organization to protect the environment. Address: 85 Second Street, San Francisco, Calif. 94105.

Tel.: (415) 977-5500; FAX: (415) 977-5799; e-mail: webmaster@sierraclub.org; website: www.sierraclub.org Sierra Club Canada's address: 412-1 Nicholas Street, Ottawa, Ontario K1N 7B7. Tel.: (613) 241-4611; FAX: (613) 241-2292; e-mail: sierra@ web.net; website: www.sierraclub.ca

sign-off or sign-on initialing or giving approval to a decision, memo, or policy.

Silent Majority Republican president Richard Nixon's (1969–74) term for all the Americans he believed backed his policies and supported the Vietnam War. He believed that the war's opponents were simply a small, noisy minority and that the silent majority, those who were not speaking out, actually supported him.

silk stocking a term used to describe a neighborhood, election district, or attitude toward wealth in which hardships are unknown and minorities are unfamiliar, except as servants.

silk stocking liberal a liberal who lives a silk stocking life.

single-party system a government and political system in which only one political party is allowed, either constitutionally or unofficially. Elections are rarely held and insurgents demanding second or alternative parties are often eliminated, particularly if they appear to have charisma and leadership.

Such suppression occasionally results in the opposition organizing and growing sufficiently large and powerful to overthrow the single-party elite. Mexico exemplified the single-party system through powerful organization starting in 1934, and continuing until the first truly open and free election in 2000. Most other one-party governments are maintained by dictators, such as the Philippines for 20 years under Ferdinand Marcos's martial law, communist China since 1948, Eastern European nations under the Soviet Union's influence until 1990, Indonesia, Paraguay, Cuba, and Nicaragua for many years, and several African countries into the 1990s.

single-payer system a health care system similar to Canada's that would "designate one entity (usually the government) to function as the only payer" for health care services. Everyone working is taxed for health care and everyone who needs health care gets it at little or no additional cost. Doctors and hospitals are paid by the government and avoid expensive paperwork to bill insurance companies and, ostensibly, unnecessary tests, X-rays, surgeries, and hospitalizations.

single shot voting for only one candidate when there are several offices to be filled. Single shotting means that in an election for city council, with five candidates for three positions, you vote for only one, thereby increasing your candidate's chances and decreasing those of the others. See also BULLET BALLOT.

single tax a taxation theory espoused by Henry George in *Progress and Poverty* (1879) favoring a single tax on all real property at its rental value, whether developed or not, to support government. George believed that this single tax would be fair, since land reflected to the wealth of its owner, pressuring owners to develop their property to its economic potential for the welfare of all. Today the theory is lowly regarded on the basis that land value rarely relates to a person's income or ability to pay taxes, those taxes can be passed on to poorer renters, and some people earn fortunes on which they could pay taxes while owning no real property. The Henry George School of Social Science in New York City still promotes the theory.

U.S. presidential candidates Jerry Brown (1992) and Steve Forbes (1996 and 2000), and Canadian Alliance leader Stockwell Day (2000) all have advocated single taxes. See also FLAT TAX.

sit-down strike   a labor strike technique used frequently in the 1930s whereby workers sat down and refused to work or leave the factory until negotiations were started or agreement was reached.

sit-in   a term that originated in 1960 to describe the action of blacks (sometimes joined by whites) who sat on stools at lunch counters in the South and refused to move until they were served in order to protest and end segregation. Thought to be a variation on "sit-down strike," participants were often arrested by police for violating segregation laws. In the mid-1960s, students also engaged in sit-ins at the University of California at Berkeley, Columbia University, and several other campuses to express their opposition to the Vietnam War by obstructing the passage of university administrators, resulting in arrests, beatings, and teargassing of students by police and sheriff's deputies.

sitting president   a president who is in office, holding down the chair and incumbency.

The address of the White House, official residence and office of the president to the United States in Washington, D.C., is 1600 Pennsylvania Avenue.

skinhead   (1) a person who has shaved his/her head as a symbol of protest of the status quo. (2) 1980s-1990s neo-Nazis who advocate violence against foreigners, blacks, and Jews.

Some young people with shaved heads display more interest in conformist garb than in a philosophical bent or commitment. In the United States true skinheads often terrorize senior citizens, blacks, and Jews, and, in alignment with the Ku Klux Klan, burn crosses on lawns of people they do not like.

slate   a list of all the candidates running for public office or organizational positions that carries the recommendation that a person vote for all of them as a group. Usually all candidates on a slate belong to the same political party or faction of a party and share common views, but occasionally a slate consists of several factions' members.

sleaze factor   a negative characteristic attributed to a candidate or officeholder by reputation for corrupt or near corrupt associations, deals, or immoral personal conduct.

sleeper (1) a problem or piece of legislation whose total impact will not be felt or appreciated until a later date. (2) a candidate whose potential to win is underestimated or unnoticed until he/she succeeds.

slush fund funds collected clandestinely for a single or unspecified purpose such as a potential political campaign, not used for that purpose, and saved for future expenditures, which may include personal expenses or those of friends, employees, or other candidates who might pledge allegiance in return for the slush fund holder's largesse. The term comes from the 19th-century military practice of saving used or changed oil, selling it, and using the profits to buy illegal goods such as liquor.

smoke screen a statement, appearance, or impression created to distract the recipient from the real facts.

smoke-filled room an imaginary but occasionally real "back room" where male political leaders supposedly smoke cigars and decide who runs for office. The term originated at the 1920 Republican National Convention where leaders gathered in a room at the Hotel Blackstone to select Warren G. Harding as their compromise presidential candidate. Harding's manager had predicted that late at night "in a smoke-filled room" Harding would emerge as the favorite.

Smoke-filled room is a term used pejoratively and primarily by people not included in it to imply that supposed democratic process deals are made by a few select men for the whole country without a vote or press coverage.

While the actual smoke may have diminished, the function still exists in some states, with few women participating. Possibly for the first time in American politics, a woman, Pamela Harriman, organized the "smoke-filled room" atmosphere with leaders who preselected Bill Clinton as the chosen 1992 Democratic presidential candidate.

smokers' rights "rights" advocated by smokers and the tobacco industry and its lobby in response to the anti-smokers' rights movement.

Anti-smokers claim that non-smokers have a right to be in public places such as buildings, airplanes, and restaurants with air free of smoke. Smokers' rights advocates claim that smokers have an equal right to smoke. The tobacco industry has funded some smokers' rights clubs in southern, tobacco-growing states. California was the first state to outlaw smoking in airplanes flying through airspace over California, and smoking is prohibited in public places, including restaurants, throughout California, as well as in several other states.

smoking gun (1) through the traditional suspicion that where there is smoke, there is fire, a smoking gun supposedly proves there was fire or it was fired. (2) an act or story about an act that may create proof of wrongdoing. Evidence in the nature of a smoking gun suggests that an act or suspicion may represent a problem or crime yet to be revealed. In the Watergate scandal President Richard Nixon's tapes of conversations referring to the cover-up of the crime were the smoking gun.

snipe   to post political signs, usually in the dark of night, on fence posts, utility polls, vacant walls, and other usually unnoticed visual points. Snipers have to work fast, place signs out of reach, and replenish signs removed almost instantly by the opposition.

soapbox   a real or imagined box or personalized platform on which an occasionally unorthodox speaker stands to deliver his/her message to a crowd, either real or not. "He's on his soapbox" refers to a person who irritates others by speechifying in a situation in which such behavior is not welcome.

SOB   Senate office buildings in Washington, D.C., which house the offices of senators and their staffs.

soccer mom   originally a 1992 term for a supposed voting bloc of suburban, fairly affluent, and educated women who stereotypically drove their kids to soccer in Volvos or SUVs, where they socialized and discussed everything from shopping to politics.

Social Darwinism   a social/political theory derived from Darwin's evolutionary theory of survival of the fittest and popularized by Herbert Spencer (1820–1903), who equated social evolution with progress. Social Darwinism rationalized that those who financially and socially dominated society were "naturally selected" through tough competition. Yale sociologist William Graham Sumner (1840–1910) suggested that American millionaires gained their positions by this natural selection. Conversely, one could theorize that

the poor find themselves in their economic position because of natural selection. Extreme versions of Social Darwinism include the Hitlerian view of Aryan superiority and political domination in Germany and the belief by Japanese in their racial, political, and industrial superiority.

Social Democrats   individual who holds left-leaning beliefs and who may favor nationalization or socialization of certain industries that are believed to be in the social or public interest, such as utilities, transportation, and health care. Social Democrats also usually favor higher taxation of the wealthy to help the needy. Current examples include the British Labour Party, the German Socialist Party (SPD), and the French Parti Socialiste.

Social Democratic Party   a minor American political party formed in 1898 by Eugene V. Debs and others after they left the Socialist Party. In turn, Debs, Victor Berger, and Jesse Cos quit the SDP after it repudiated Debs's plan to "colonize" Colorado. These dissidents renamed themselves the Social Democratic Party of America, electing two members to the Massachusetts legislature. Party members included some American railroad union officials, prominent writers like Upton Sinclair, and political thinkers and activists. Eventually they merged with the Socialist Labor Party's moderate wing to form the new Socialist Party of America (1901).

social programs   term used to refer to those programs that provide services for the entire population. Social programs include financial support to pregnant mothers for home leave following birth, and provision of medical care for all citizens. Countries with strong commitments to social programs include Canada, Sweden, France, and Germany. In the United States, liberals often favor social programs while conservatives may see them as socialistic practices using the money of the wealthy to support people who do not make the effort to better themselves.

social safety net a network of social programs people can fall back on in times of need, especially in Canada, and which offer progressive health care, unemployment insurance, assistance to the disabled, aid to dependent children, and social security.

Social Security a major social welfare program created by the Social Security Act (August 14, 1935) during President Franklin D. Roosevelt's New Deal era. It provided primarily: (1) a federal public assistance program by which the federal government grants funds to help pay for welfare to help the aged, needy, blind, disabled, and dependent children; (2) a system of guaranteed old-age financial assistance from federal funds collected as a percentage from workers' paychecks and employers' contributions. The federal government also assumes responsibility for unemployment compensation.

President Dwight D. Eisenhower created the Department of Health, Education, and Welfare (HEW) that took over the Social Security Administration. Benefits and groups of beneficiaries expanded for years, but were cut back by conservative Republican presidents Ronald Reagan and George

H. W. Bush. For years the late representative Claude Pepper (D–Fla.) championed nonreductions of benefits.

Beginning in the 1990s there was concern that the Social Security fund would be depleted before current workers would reach an age to collect their old-age benefits.

Conservatives generally see social security "welfare" benefits for disability or surviving children as a bad influence on those who do not try hard enough to help themselves and "pull their own weight," although few wealthy conservatives turn down their old-age benefits. Liberals usually see social security and welfare as a matter of conscience and a necessity to help the needy. In the 2000 presidential campaign, preservation of Social Security and the means to fund it constituted a key issue, and both candidates promised to save it. George W. Bush suggested individuals should have the right to invest some of their potential social security deductions in the stock market.

social stratification the hierarchical ordering by class, race, religion, and national origin.

socialism (1) a political theory or system by which the community, society, or state owns major means of production and distribution in place of private owners. The theory is to carry out public production of what people need (which someone must presume to determine) since they will share in the work and production goods instead of producing to make money or profit by convincing people they need the products. Idealistically socialism produces an egalitarian society in which the government fulfills some of peoples' needs, resulting in no poverty, hunger, or homelessness. (2) a political movement to establish such a government. (3) in communist theory socialism is a stage between capitalism and communism. (4) what many communists believed they believed in.

Socialist parties generally differ from communist ones in that they support small business, family farms, and democratic forms of government.

Some moderate forms of socialism often exist in basically capitalistic societies, such as social security, medicare, and workers' compensation.

Socialist Labor Party an American political party organized originally as the Workingmen's Party of the United States (1874). It renamed itself the Socialist Labor Party (1877), becoming the first national socialist party in the United States. The party leaned strongly toward Marxism under revolutionary agitator Daniel De Leon in the 1890s. He hoped to overthrow capitalism with socialism led by trade union members and sympathizers. The Socialist Labor Party was strongest in 1896, but many of its members joined the Socialist Party. It still exists but has had little influence in the last 60 years.

Socialist Party a minor or "third" American political party originally organized by Eugene V. Debs in 1897. A year later Debs and other members withdrew and formed the Social Democratic Party, which then merged with the more moderate Socialist Labor Party to form the Socialist Party of America, which became "the" Socialist Party.

Prominent members included many middle-class intellectuals such as Debs, Morris Hillquit, Victor L. Berger, Charles Edward Russell, Upton Sinclair, William J. Ghent, J. A. Wayland, and Norman Thomas, who was the party's presidential candidate five times between 1928 and 1944. Many of the party's reforms were adopted as part of President Franklin Delano Roosevelt's New Deal, including social security, greater control of stock transactions, unemployment insurance, and guaranteed home loans. Address: 339 Lafayette Street, New York, N.Y. 10012. Tel.: (212) 982-4586; e-mail: socialistparty@sp-usa.org; website: www.sp-usa.org

socialized medicine See NATIONAL MEDICAL INSURANCE.

Socred Social Credit Party, which began in Alberta, Canada, in the 1930s based on economic theories developed originally by Major C. H. Douglas, and extended into British Columbia and led by Premier William A. C. "Wacky" Bennett (1952–72) and his son, Premier William "Bill" Bennett, and Premier Bill Van der Zalm. After losing in 1993, the Social Credit Party disappeared.

soft money money donated to national or state political parties, instead of to candidates, to avoid campaign limitations and reporting of direct contributions to candidates. State or national parties then spend the collected funds on behalf of the candidates or for general uses such as registration and get-out-the-vote drives particularly in districts with close races. In 2000, the Republican National Committee raised nearly

$100 million in soft money, and the Democratic National Committee raised nearly $50 million in soft money.

soft on crime   a label often aimed at a candidate's opponent in an election campaign when voters' fear of crime is at a peak. Candidates or campaign workers more conservative than their opponent sometimes accuse that opponent of being soft on crime. The term can refer to a position against the death penalty or to a judge who gives a convicted criminal a lighter sentence than some among the public wanted. At the same time, some conservatives who accuse liberals of being soft on crime also favor their own right to bear arms. Those who see themselves as tough on crime prefer the death penalty, longer prison sentences, and construction of new prisons. They rarely believe that rehabilitation occurs in prison.

soft on immigration   term most often used by conservatives to label liberals who espouse their beliefs that the United States is a nation of immigrants and that everyone who wants to come should be admitted. Those conservative officeholders or candidates who see themselves as the opposite, i.e., hard on immigration, would prevent more immigrants (usually with skin darker than theirs) from entering the country and using up America's resources.

soft pedal   to play down an issue or statement, particularly if reaction is negative or controversial, and wait for a more opportune time to slip it through.

solidarity   (1) a binding, complete unity of interests, beliefs, opinion, motivation, and purpose, such as is experienced among workers in unions, citizens uniting to rebel, or any group feeling unity in opposition to a threat from outside. (2) name of the movement in Poland in the 1980s against dictatorial, communist-controlled government and in favor of democracy and free elections.

Solon   a person who uses his/her wisdom to make legislative decisions, from Solon, an ancient Greek lawgiver.

sound bite   a short sentence or group of sentences (about 20 seconds, total) comprised of usually single-syllable words employed to keep the message simple, and to fit into brief television reports. Political statements are rarely longer than sound bites, leading to criticism that public political thoughts and statements are neither long nor deep. If the public receives most of its information through television news sound bites, its information and vocabulary become limited to the words in the sound bites. If people think in words, their thoughts will be limited to those words they pick up from sound bites.

Southern Christian Leadership Conference (SCLC)   a nonsectarian Christian organization established by its president, the Rev. Martin Luther King Jr. and his followers in 1957 to help and coordinate local groups working through nonviolence methods for truly equal rights for blacks. The organization worked primarily in southern and border states in running leadership training programs, education projects, and voter registration drives, and in offering counseling on civil rights direct action projects.

The SCLC (sometimes called "Slick") helped organize the 1963 "March on Washington" and voter registration and antidiscrimination drives in Albany, Georgia, and Birmingham and Selma, Alabama. These actions contributed to quick passage of the 1964 Civil Rights Act and the 1965 Voting Rights Act.

At its peak in the 1960s, the SCLC budget was $1,000,000 per year with 150 staff members and 1,000 volunteers. After Rev. King's assassination in 1968, Rev. Ralph David Abernathy became president. Rev. Abernathy lacked Rev. King's charisma, and the organization never again mounted highly effective nationwide campaigns. In the 1970s the leadership divided, and King followers such as Rev. Jesse Jackson broke away. Rev. Jackson set up his own Chicago-based Operation Push (People United to Save Humanity.)

southern Democrat a person living in the southern states who is registered to vote as a Democrat but whose political views are more conservative than the majority of other Democrats. While there is a new strain of political southern liberal emerging, most southern Democrats' views on the separation of races, often founded in fear and competition for jobs, are seen as conservative. Those southern Democrats who are part of the religious right tend to vote conservatively, but they see their opinions as the only correct ones, regardless of political labels such as conservative or liberal.

Conservative Republicans welcome the collaborative thinking and votes of southern Democrats, while liberals and Democrats from outside the South sometimes disparage their votes and thoughts. "New Democrats," who are based in the South, draw on an unusual combination of southern Democrat and liberal views, positions, and followers. Many traditional southern Democrats, such as Senator Strom Thurmond of South Carolina, have switched to the Republican Party.

sovereign (1) a king or queen. (2) a governor or government that rules everyone or runs everything with supreme control.

sovereign state a country that is a totally independent state, which has complete control of its own affairs, unlike a colony.

sovereignty the supreme, unquestioned, or independent right and authority to govern or rule.

Soviet Bloc before 1990, the Eastern European states governed by Communist parties under Moscow (capital of the U.S.S.R. and ideological center of Marxist communism) control and direction. Before the move toward independence and democracy, the Soviet Bloc consisted of the Soviet Union and East Germany, Hungary, Poland, Czechoslovakia, Romania, Bulgaria, and, prior to the 1960s, Albania. Socialist Yugoslavia was independent of the Soviet bloc, but cooperated with it. Cuba was included economically. As former Soviet and Yugoslavian states struggled in the 1990s to develop their own sovereignty, the former Soviet Bloc became history.

Soviet dis-Union   slang term for all the states affiliated before 1990 with the Soviet Union.

Soviet Union   (1) a shorthand name for the Union of Soviet Socialist Republics (U.S.S.R.). (2) group of soviet states that functioned as a nation run from Moscow, Russia, formed between 1918 and 1920 and disbanded in 1990 following demands for democracy and free market enterprise. Technically the word "soviet" meant "council," which in Leninist terminology referred to the "council of workers and peasants."

Speaker of the House   presiding officer of the U.S. House of Representatives elected by his/her peers who is the legislative leader of the majority party. The Speaker holds tremendous power, including making all committee assignments, recognizing and controlling speakers on the floor of Congress, and controlling presentation of bills and pressure for bills he/she favors or dislikes. The Speaker of the House would succeed to the presidency upon the death of the president and the vice president.

Special Committee   See SELECT COMMITTEE.

special prosecutor   a supposedly independent attorney who cannot be influenced and who is appointed by the attorney general to investigate alleged wrongdoing by highly placed government officials. Usually one party is quick to demand appointment

of a special prosecutor to pursue the other party's mistakes. See INDEPENDENT PROSECUTOR.

spellbinder   a political orator who excels in making speeches to such a degree that he/she wraps his/her audience in a spell, and who can incite enthusiasm by his/her manner or cause.

spin   a public relations twist given to words or facts to turn a possibly negative incident into a positive one, or at least to give the impression of a minimal problem.

spin doctor   a person whose role or job it is to manipulate words to turn a potentially bad political situation into a positive one or minimize bad news.

splinter group   a group that has split from the main organization, usually over differences on issues. The term comes from the image of splinters flying from a split board or chopped tree.

split government   a condition that exists when the executive and legislative branches of government are dominated by different political parties, which makes it difficult for the two to agree on very much. More commonly known as divided government.

split ticket   the chance to vote for candidates of different parties on the same ballot.

spoiler   a candidate who enters a political race knowing he/she has no chance to win but who aims to prevent another candidate from winning or winning easily by drawing away some of his or her supporters and votes.

spoils system   the practice of a triumphant candidate or officeholder to "clean house" or fire his/her predecessor's staff and appoint his/her supporters or faithful party people, without regard to the qualifications or abilities of the employees going or coming. It is based on the old adage: "to the victor belong the spoils." Presidents John Adams and Thomas Jefferson began the practice, and Andrew Jackson accelerated its use. The civil service system has limited the spoils system by making non-political government jobs (the bureaucracy) based on merit and not subject to removal upon changes of administration.

Square Deal   President Theodore Roosevelt's label for his philosophy of America's needs, which became a program of his administration (1901–09). His ideas included his idealistic views on labor, citizenship, ethics, and parenthood, which developed into anti-monopoly, pro-consumer, and pro-conservation efforts. These concepts were also later incorporated into the Progressive Party's (Bull Moose Party) 1912 platform when Teddy Roosevelt was its presidential candidate.

stack the court   the opportunity a governor or president has to appoint judges and justices who hold beliefs and legal and political viewpoints similar to his/her own.

staffer   a person paid to work for a candidate or officeholder.

Stalinism   the most conservative, that is, hard-line, conformist, and undemocratic version of communism, as employed and enforced by Soviet dictator Joseph Stalin (1879–1953) in the 1930s and 1940s. Stalinism demanded subservience to the party hierarchy, discouraged and punished political and social debates, and required strict adherence to pronouncements and orders from communist leadership in Moscow. From 1957 to 1964 Soviet premier Nikita Khrushchev denounced Stalinism, thereby ending the Stalin cult. During Stalin's rule, the people had been afraid to complain about or criticize his excesses, including the imprisonment and murder of many dissidents.

stalking horse   a candidate with no chance to win who enters a political contest as a front for another unnamed but presumed candidate or to divide opposition so that a chosen candidate can walk through to triumph or at least come in first. The term comes from hunters using decoys or a horse to sneak into range of their target. As Senator Eugene McCarthy (D–Minn.) once pointed out: "Sometimes a stalking horse forgets to stop running and wins."

stampede   mad rush by legislators to be on the right side of an issue or vote, or of convention delegates to back the winning nominee.

standard-bearer   the person leading a political party's ticket, such as the presidential, gubernatorial, or mayoral candidate.

stand for election   to offer oneself as a candidate or run for office.

stand pat   to refuse to change one's position.

standing committee   an official, permanent committee of a legislative body.

Star Wars   President Ronald Reagan's copycat name (from the movie) for a Strategic Defense Initiative (SDI) aimed at developing outer space weapons to counteract the Soviet Union's Intercontinental Ballistic Missiles. Opponents contended it was a cold war one-upmanship program primarily to benefit the defense industry, which proved to be unworkable and based on false testing information.

state   (1) an amorphous state of mind, like Hollywood. (2) a total, neutral political system including traditional institutions and fixed roles, synonymous with "country" or "nation." (3) one of the United States. (4) nickname for U.S. Department of State.

state of nature   an idealistic, anarchical fantasy of how socialization and interpersonal relations were before government and organized politics arrived in society.

State of the State Message   an annual message delivered by some governors to update the public and to boast of the government's accomplishments during the past year.

State of the Union Message   an annual address the U.S. Constitution requires the president to make to Congress to "give Congress information on the state of the nation, and recommend to their consideration such measures as he shall judge necessary and expedient."

State of the Union speeches are given to a joint session of Congress early in the year and are usually bland except in election years when presidents use the message as a reelection campaign speech with a nationwide captive audience to try to inspire the public's confidence in him and his accomplishments. Until President Woodrow Wilson's presidency (1913), the State of the Union Message was always read by a clerk to the joint session. In 2001 newly-elected president George W. Bush substituted a more limited budget message for the State of the Union address to Congress.

states' rights   The U.S. Constitution's Tenth Amendment states: "The powers not delegated to the U.S. by the Constitution, nor prohibited by it to the States, are reserved to the states respectively, or to the people."

Arguments rage as to the true intentions of this vague language. Originally grounded in Thomas Jefferson's fear of central government, the argument shifted toward a rationalization for slavery, and eventually for segregation laws. South Carolina senator John C. Calhoun (1782–1850) used states' rights to defend the rights of southern states to maintain slavery and to protect the southern agricultural economy from northern industrial and financial power. Despite the Civil War, states' rights survived as the basis for southern segregation statutes and practices until the 1960s.

Conservatives generally favor a smaller federal government, giving greater states' rights powers to the states or local governments. While they prefer certain guarantees by the federal government, they believe the controversy also includes the possibility that states will be less strict in regulation of business and safety practices. Presidents Ronald Reagan and George H. W. Bush favored giving decisions and responsibilities to state governments through the appeal of "states' rights" principles, effectively also dumping the fiscal responsibility on the states while ostensibly cutting federal spending.

Liberals believe in limited states' rights, but they regarded Presidents Reagan's and George H. W. Bush's actions in the name of states rights as an effort to dismantle federal programs in order to undermine social benefits for the poor and educational benefits for all.

States' Rights Democrats See DIX-IECRATS.

statistical dead heat a poll result showing that candidates are within the poll's margin of error (3percent–5 percent), meaning nearly tied.

Statistics Canada Canada's federal agency that provides statistical material on almost any matter that might be of interest to the general public or government, including socioeconomic, political, and criminal facts. Address: Tunney's Pasture, Ottawa, Ontario K1A OT6. Tel.: (800) 263-1136; website: www.statcan.ca

status quo (1) from Latin meaning "state of which." (2) the existing state of affairs, usually in which those who hold money and power determine what is appropriate behavior and customs.

People who have money and power often vote conservatively and are usually content with and want to preserve the status quo. They enjoy the circumstances in which they currently live without regard for others' suffering or needs, including a need to change the status quo.

Liberals accuse conservatives of preserving the status quo to protect their interests and advocate societal and economic changes that conservatives often see as threatening their positions. Conservatives accuse liberals of trying to upset the status quo, which is precisely what they are trying to do.

statute a law written and passed by a legislative body, which has become law.

steamroller a name given to the political convention tactic by which a candidate is made to appear to possess early strong support so as to add to the impression of the inevitability of a candidate's ability to run over the real or potential opposition. Key to the psychology of steamrolling is to convince delegates that they will miss out on backing a sure winner if they do not go along. See also RAILROAD.

stemwinder a captivating, powerful speech.

stepping stone an office for a which a person runs to gain credentials, experience, and a reputation in order to run for a higher office.

stock market (1) the totality of publicly held stock traded at all exchanges. (2) prices quoted on stocks and bonds at a stock exchange.

Stock prices rise and fall somewhat unpredictably. Analyses and rationalizations follow each dramatic rise or fall. Factors affecting the stock market may include a U.S. president's health, his/her standing in political polls, employment rates, war, peace, psychological and emotional trends, good or bad news or rumors about a company or industry, or a change in diplomatic relations between or among the United States and other countries. Stock market prices also can be affected by manipulation, such as "dumping" stock, bidding up prices through massive purchases, or false promotion. The stock market's status can affect a president's reelection chances. In the United States the principal stock market is the New York Stock Exchange. There are also the American Exchange, NASDAQ, and specialized and regional exchanges.

stockpile   to produce and accumulate goods not yet needed as a prudent device or as an attempt to demonstrate greater strength than one's opponent, such as nuclear weapons.

stonewall   to refuse to speak about a subject by talking about other trivial matters or refusing to comment. The term gained popularity in 1973–74 with the revelation that President Richard Nixon had suggested that his aides "stonewall" investigations and questions about the Watergate break-in. See also FILIBUSTER.

Straight Talk Express 2000 Republican primary candidate senator John McCain's campaign buses in which he traveled to many states. McCain became famous for his conservative straight talk on most issues,

regardless of whether or not one agreed with him.

straight ticket   the candidates of one party. One votes a straight ticket by voting only for candidates of one party or on one slate. On some voting machines a voter can pull one lever once and it will register the votes for all the candidates of the voter's party ticket. In some southern states there are circles on the ballot with symbols in them, such as a rooster for Democrats. Stamping the symbol of a party casts one's vote for all candidates of that party, or a straight ticket.

strange bedfellows   part of the saying, "Politics makes strange bedfellows." The inference is that people involved in politics, who normally would not be attracted to each other or have any interests in common, form associations and friendships of expediency. Outside observers often cannot imagine the people involved getting into the "bed" of friendship together.

strategic   long-term military or conflict planning to achieve a particular end. Strategic bombing is part of a long-term plan and goal, compared to tactical bombing, which involves short-term, on the scene, decision making.

straw poll   a poll in which people are asked to vote informally as they might in a real election to find out how they feel about issues or candidates.

straw vote   an unofficial, preliminary, nonbinding trial vote among members of a legislative body or organization to discover how a vote might go and what the results could be. Straw votes are sometimes used to set political campaign strategy according to responses and information gained.

strict construction   refers to interpreting the U.S. Constitution narrowly and literally (as they see it), with little or no reference to the differences between conditions in 1787 and today. Strict constructionists might be rigid in their interpretations and believe that others' views are wrong or that judges who interpret the constitution differently from the way they do are engaging in judicial activism. See also JUDICIAL ACTIVISM.

strike   the usually planned refusal to continue to work until certain worker demands such as improved hours, wages, work and safety conditions, and benefits have been met. After the adoption of the National Labor Relations Act, strikes worked effectively, at least bringing about discussions and negotiations of the issues. Before this legislation (1935) many industries responded to strikes by refusing to recognize unions and using private armies of toughs (called "goons" by union members) to attack strikers in the guise of protecting the factories. Police and/or the National Guard were often used to help break strikes as "unlawful assemblies" between the 1880s and 1935.

In a rare antistrike move by the government, President Ronald Reagan took advantage of a strike of air traffic controllers (1981) to "bust" their union when he approved hiring of nonunion, mostly untrained workers to replace the striking union members.

Strikes are only effective if they are supported by the membership, there are funds sufficient to give minimal aid to striking families, and the cause is viewed as being worth the sacrifice. Public employee (teachers, police, firemen) strikes, once illegal, have become frequent in the 1990s.

A general strike is one in which all union workers in a city or other geographic area refuse to work in support of striking workers. They have not been successful in the United States but occur more frequently in Europe.

strip calling   the act of calling an opposing candidate's supporters list to bash their candidate and speak favorably of your own candidate.

structure   the offices, titles, and jobs that shape a political party or campaign. The structure may exist without people and should not be confused with organization, which requires people's involvement and participation.

Student Non-Violent Coordinating Committee (SNCC—pronounced Snick)   an offshoot organization of the Southern Christian Leadership Conference (SCLC). Formed out of frustration with nonviolent attempts at integrating public facilities at Albany, Georgia, Stokely Carmichael and Rap Brown were among SNCC's prominent presidents. SNCC originally organized nonviolent demonstrations and sit-ins at parks, transportation depots, restaurants, theaters, and lunch counters. It also engaged in freedom rides and voter registration drives, and under Rap

Brown involved itself in international human rights.

In the late 1960s SNCC became more militant, leading to its own offshoot, the Black Panthers. Carmichael's and Brown's revolutionary comments made SNCC an easy target for racists and conservatives, which made it difficult for liberals to support and work with the organization.

Students for a Democratic Society (SDS)   an organization of liberal to far left students formed in June 1962 at a meeting in Port Huron, Michigan, and by the late 1960s reaching membership of several thousands on 150 campuses. Originally committed to the civil rights movement and students' rights, SDS participated in the mid-1960s "free speech movement" and in anti-Vietnam War activities. Some SDS branches turned militant, resulting in violent demonstrations on a few campuses, such as Columbia University, and politicizing many students. SDS faded in the 1970s after the war ended.

stuffing   putting illegal ballots into a ballot box, sometimes forged for dead citizens or people who have already voted at least once.

stump   (1) to campaign and make speeches in different places. (2) the locale of a campaign and the speeches a candidate makes, coming from the fact that political candidates used to stand on tree stumps to make speeches.

subsidy   money given at no cost to the recipient by the government either to individuals, agencies, or other levels of government to accomplish a project. One well-known subsidy is that given to the farming industry, whereby the federal government pays some farmers not to farm and pays others part of their expenses so they can sell at prices the public can afford. Some farmers actually buy more land so that they can receive more subsidies for leaving the land fallow. Other businesspeople may wonder why the government does not subsidize their business.

subversive   (1) a person or act considered to be aimed at ruining or overthrowing the leadership of a government or organization by weakening its structure and capability, or inciting detraction from support of a government. (2) a term used like "pinko" and "fellow traveler" to paint liberals and leftists as un-American, usually without proof.

subversive organizations   groups that support undermining the U.S. government. These have included pro-Nazis just before the attack on Pearl Harbor in 1941, and occasionally communists and far leftists who claimed to be revolutionary. See also ATTORNEY GENERAL'S LIST OF SUBVERSIVE ORGANIZATIONS.

suffrage   the right to vote in political or public elections, often associated with woman suffrage.

suffragette   a woman who militantly advocated woman suffrage, particularly those who campaigned for women to have the right to vote in the United States in the late 19th and early 20th centuries.

suffragist a woman or man who believes in broadening suffrage, especially for women.

suicide by cop committing a crime, threatening police, or shooting law enforcement officers to provoke them to kill you.

suits white men who wear dark suits, appear to represent the supposedly unfeeling, status quo establishment, and presume to make decisions for the rest of the world.

sunset law a law or law provision that allows or forces a program to end on a specified date unless it is reauthorized.

sunshine law a law that requires government meetings to be open to the public, such as California's "Brown Act."

Super Tuesday a Tuesday in March 2000 on which presidential primaries were held in 14 states with 362 Electoral College votes at stake, the result of front-loading. See also FRONT LOADING.

superdelegate a person who is named a delegate to a national party convention because he or she serves as an elected or party official, or is a celebrity, who does not have to go through the normal elective or appointive processes.

superpower (1) state or country that has politicial power over other states or countries. (2) country whose citizens or leaders believe it has influence or power to tell other countries how they should conduct their relations with other countries and what kind of governments they should utilize. A superpower's power derives from economic and military strengths, that is, healthy business and employment conditions, natural resources, and stockpiled arms and armed forces all of which produce diplomatic influence and ability to "police" the world. American leaders refer to the United States as "the only superpower," while the U.S.S.R. claimed to be one before it fell apart. Countries that possess the qualities outlined above and dominate a region have the potential to become superpowers, creating the possibility that China may become the world's next superpower.

supply-side economics an economic theory favoring the supply side of the supply/demand theory by claiming that inflation can be controlled and the economy will be stimulated by lowering taxes on corporations, which will then invest their savings in industry. According to the theory, this will result in increased production, goods, jobs, and income. The theory also suggests that with more goods produced, prices of those goods would decrease and the public's purchasing power would increase. Its principal advocate was Arthur Laffer, a young economist adviser to candidate Ronald Reagan when he was running for president.

President Ronald Reagan espoused supply-side economics, claiming that demand-side only works when the economy is stimulated by government subsidies, which they generally opposed. Supply-side economics also involved deregulation of major industries to allow them the freedom to create and "invest," resulting in higher salaries for executives, bankruptcies, little reinvestment, and the 1980s and 1990s recession/depression.

Supreme Court, U.S. the highest court in the United States.

Article III, Section 1 of the U.S. Constitution provides: "The judicial power of the United States shall be vested in one Supreme Court, and in such inferior courts as the Congress may from time to time ordain and establish."

The Supreme Court's jurisdiction covers appeals on constitutional issues, cases in which the government is a party, cases between citizens of different states, and some other types of cases. The Court's most significant power is to test laws for constitutionality, as established in *Marbury v. Madison.* The landmark decision in the case was written by Chief Justice John Marshall in 1803.

Originally made up of five members, the Court was later increased to seven and then ten, and finally in 1869 the number was established at nine justices. Members are appointed for life by the president with confirmation by the Senate. Confirmation denial became more frequent in the past 25 years. The Senate rejected two of President Richard Nixon's nominees, one because of racist statements made by him and the other because of apparent incompetence. President Ronald Reagan's nomination of Robert Bork was turned down (1987) primarily because Bork's personal interpretation of the Constitution differed from that of the public, many senators, and most law professors. Bork was also not forgiven for having fired Watergate special counsel Archibald Cox at the request of President Nixon. President George H. W.

Bush's nominee, Clarence Thomas, gained confirmation after lengthy hearings on Professor Anita Hill's charges of sexual harassment.

The Supreme Court has changed in notable ways: the Marshall Court (1801–35) established, defined, and expanded the Court's power, including taking jurisdiction over interstate commerce; the "nine old men" of the 1930s declared several New Deal programs unconstitutional; in 1938, a frustrated President Franklin D. Roosevelt proposed "packing" the Court by adding members for each elderly justice who refused to retire, resulting in a public outcry of tampering with the judicial process. Under Chief Justice Earl Warren (appointed 1953), the Court took liberal stands on numerous issues, including desegregation of schools in *Brown v. Board of Education* (1954). Conservatives accused the Court of "social engineering." *Roe v. Wade* (1973) supported a woman's right to choose abortion under certain circumstances, and later the Court restricted use of the death penalty.

Nixon's, Reagan's and George H. W. Bush's appointments resulted in a more conservative Court, coming within one vote of overturning *Roe v. Wade.* President Bill Clinton's appointment of Ruth Bader Ginzberg and Stephen Breyer established a narrowly balanced Court.

surtax an extra tax added on to some goods or taxed on a certain group of citizens. It may be a tax on a tax.

sweetener additions to language of legislation to make it more appealing to legislators.

sweetheart contract   most often a labor-management agreement that is particularly favorable to one or more of the employing companies. Such "contracts" are often criticized as union-owner schemes to promote unfair business monopoly (free of union interference) in exchange for often secret special favors for some union leaders. Outstanding examples were Teamster deals with certain trucking, trailer, and beer companies under union presidents Dave Beck and Jimmy Hoffa (1950s and 1960s). Such under-the-table transactions are not confined to labor-management contracts, but may exist between manufacturers and suppliers or transportation companies and shippers, for example.

sweetheart deal   extraordinary arrangement by which a person or persons benefit, with investment of money, time, or work at levels lower than those required of ordinary participants. The person on the sweetheart end of the deal gets special favors in anticipation of or repayment for other favors, considerations, influence, or power. The person or persons originating the deal benefit by association with the influential person receiving consideration for their involvement.

swing vote   (1) voters in a legislative body whose votes cannot be predicted and who wait until the end of voting to consider all possibilities and make the most of opportunities presented by both sides of an issue before they vote. In close votes swing votes make the decision. Swing voters sometimes hope to attract attention for their districts, their constituencies, or themselves in order to take credit from those who have it to give. (2) blocs of voters who may "swing" one way or another and decide an election.

swinging chad   See CHAD.

sympathy strike   a work stoppage by a category of workers who are not affected by negotiations but who strike in sympathy with and to help striking workers to increase the impact of their efforts and demonstrate solidarity of purpose.

table a bill (1) United States: removal of a measure or bill from consideration or voting by setting it aside in accord with a majority vote to do so. In effect, the vote lays it aside (on the table) for possible consideration later. When the body votes to bring the bill back up again, it is called taking it "off the table." (2) Canada: to offer, present, or propose a motion or bill to parliament for consideration.

tactical short-term military or political planning to achieve an end. Tactical nuclear weapons have smaller warheads than strategic ones do, causing less damage than the latter. By contrast, strategic planning involves broad, long-term planning and action.

talking heads (1) television news anchors, reporters, analysts, and commentators. (2) candidates who simply read cards in campaign commercials without involvement or emotion.

talking points organized, chosen subject messages in sound-bite single syllable words on issues of public interest. Bill Clinton's campaign and the Democratic Party used talking points to inform campaign workers, the press, and the public of important information to be conveyed to and considered by the public. Talking points help message relayers to pass on information in the desired form.

Tammany Hall (1) popular name (from "St. Tammany," a 17th-century Delaware Indian chief) for the old Democratic organization in New York City, founded in 1789, incorporated in 1805 by Revolutionary War veterans as a beneficial society, and dominating New York State Democratic politics until the 1880s. Governor Alfred E. Smith's "new" Tammany soon became corrupt and scandalous, resulting in the resignation of New York mayor James J. Walker (1932). Also known as the Tammany Society,

Tammany Hall's symbol or totem was a tiger, originated by political cartoonist Thomas Nast. Tammany worked against reform Democratic leaders such as Samuel J. Tilden, Grover Cleveland, and Franklin D. Roosevelt. (2) the building where the New York Democratic machine met and made their headquarters. Tammany Hall as an organization dissolved during the mayorship of John V. Lindsay (1966–74).

target voters   those voters whom you believe will be most likely to vote for your candidate if you do a good job of getting out the vote.

task force   a group of people gathered to research and solve a problem or accomplish a specific task.

tax   money demanded and collected by a local, regional, state, or federal government to fund government agencies and services, programs, the military, and other government costs. Forms of tax include percentages charged on income, sales, real estate, personal property, capital gains, business income, imports (tariffs), and inheritance. Taxes have existed in some form since the first governments.

Conservatives blame taxes for most wrongs such as reducing their take-home incomes, financing programs for the poor (read minorities), raising prices, and stifling business. Rarely do they object to their taxes spent for "good programs" such as military weapon production and (their) industry subsidies. They also contend that high taxes hurt businesses and wealthy individuals who would, ostensibly, invest saved money in business expansion and job creation.

Liberals also do not like taxes but see them as necessary to fund needed programs such as infrastructure maintenance, social benefits such as Aid to Families with Dependent Children, food stamps, and assistance for the blind and disabled. Many liberals object to their taxes being spent on military weapons production and war.

Promises to raise or lower taxes have dramatically affected presidential candidates' election results. Democratic presidential nominee Vice President Walter Mondale admitted during his 1984 campaign that, truthfully, he would have to raise taxes. Conservative Republican candidate Ronald Reagan swore he would not raise them, as did his successor, George H. W. Bush. Reagan and "Read my lips" Bush pledged "no new taxes," won and then reluctantly raised taxes. Mondale and Bush's first opponent, Michael Dukakis, told the truth about tax increases and lost. Presidential candidate Bill Clinton campaigned on a promise to reduce taxes for the middle class and raise them for the wealthy. He won the election and succeeded in passing a deficit reduction/tax increase package by two votes in the House and Vice President Al Gore's tie-breaking vote in the Senate. President George W. Bush in 2000 campaigned for across-the-board tax cuts.

tax loopholes   small openings or gaps in the U.S. tax laws that happen to favor those who can find them, either through their own investigative efforts or by their ability to pay someone else with expertise to understand and use them. Swarms of tax accountants and lawyers prosper by finding tax loopholes for people who can pay them. These holes in the tax laws enable some people to make deductions or write-offs to escape paying the level of taxes they would normally pay without the loopholes.

Conservatives see tax loopholes as their just due and available to anyone who can find them. Liberals see tax loopholes as unfairly favoring the wealthy at the expense of the middle class and the poor, who lack the resources to find the loopholes or the second and third homes to write-off their taxable income.

It is not uncommon for wealthy Americans to take advantage of loopholes through careful tax "planning."

Teamsters' Union (International Brotherhood of Teamsters, Chauffeurs, Warehousemen and Helpers)   the largest major labor union not affiliated with the AFL-CIO that primarily represents truck drivers who deliver America's produce and products across the country.

Accusations of imprudent practices and corruption, which burgeoned in the 1950s, led to the Teamsters' departure from the AFL-CIO in July 1968. After Teamsters' president David Beck was indicted for failure to pay taxes on stolen union funds, his successor, Jimmy Hoffa, took over in 1957. Dogged by Senate Rackets Committee counsel and later attorney general Robert F. Kennedy, Hoffa and the teamsters fought corruption charges while increasing the size and power of the union. Convicted of corruption in 1964, Hoffa went to prison in 1967. After his release he remained the power behind the throne until he disappeared on July 31, 1975. He is believed to be dead and is rumored variously to be buried in cement at the bottom of a river or under Meadowlands Stadium in New Jersey. The movie *Hoffa* was based on his life. The Teamsters have been trying to reform the union and its internal democracy.

The Teamsters' political power rests in its huge membership (1.4 million in the United States, Canada, and Puerto Rico) and ability to swing from supporting one major political party to the other, unlike most unions, which favor the Democrats. The Teamsters played an important role in providing the margin of victory in Republican president Richard Nixon's 1968 election.

The current president of the Teamsters is James Hoffa Jr., elected in March 1994. On March 29, 2000, Hoffa testified before the House Subcommittee on Oversight and Investigations claiming to have initiated reform and pledging to continue open reporting, audits, and other reforms, including cleaning out organized crime's influence on local unions. Address: 25 Louisiana Ave., N.W., Washington, D.C. 20002. Tel.: (202) 624-6800; e-mail: feedback @teamster.org; website: www.teamster. org

technocracy   a theoretical government system in which technicians, scientists, and engineers run everything, including society, government and business, in a "Technological Age." Technocrats' goals include solving industrial "underproduction," maximizing productivity, and eliminating manual labor.

Technocracy traces its roots to French philosopher Claude-Henri Saint-Simon's book *Du Système Industriel* and enjoyed special popularity as a modern movement and word between 1930–39, particularly in France and the United States at the end of the Great Depression. It seems to have become American reality in the 1990s. The American "bible" of technocracy was James Burnham's *The Managerial Revolution* (1941).

Teflon (1) a nonstick coating of surfaces. (2) a reference to Ronald Reagan as the Teflon President, suggesting nothing bad would stick to him but only to his associates, who were accused and/or convicted of crimes, including the Iran-Contra Affair.

telephone canvassing using the telephone to take a poll of voters' views, to convince voters of your point of view, or urge them to vote on election day.

televangelist a usually born-again Christian religious preacher who reaches and develops his audience or congregation by television. The term was coined by sociologist Jeffrey K. Hadden. By 1989 there were 336 television ministries watched by 27 percent of the American public.

Most televangelists began in the South following Billy Graham and developed a financially profitable system of preaching, soliciting, and collecting followers' money. Televangelists' flocks and funds grew faster through television than they had in churches, resulting in televangelists owning cable television channels, radio stations, publishing companies, and amusement parks. The most prominent include Jerry Falwell, Oral Roberts, Pat Robertson, Jimmy Swag-

gart, and Jim and Tammy Faye Bakker.

Some televangelists fell into ill repute after soliciting prostitutes, sexually harassing employees, and absconding with donors' contributions. Swaggart and Bakker went to prison for embezzling church funds.

By preaching politics and political endorsements, televangelists played important roles in the elections of Presidents Ronald Reagan and George H. W. Bush, primarily in return for the candidates' newfound anti-abortion positions. Televangelists are partly responsible for the development of the Religious Right.

Jerry Falwell developed the "Moral Majority," which supported Ronald Reagan in the 1980 presidential election. Pat Robertson ran for the Republican presidential nomination in 1988, defeating George H. W. Bush and Senator Robert Dole (R–Kans.) in some states.

Ten Downing Street Official residence and office of the prime minister of Great Britain in London, England.

term limits a 1980s–90s concept passed by voters in several states to limit the number of terms an elected official, particularly state legislators, can serve. Motivation behind term limits is to "get the bastards out" on the basis that entrenched incumbents lose contact with the people, have too many advantages (newsletters, staffs, name recognition, campaign slush funds) over challengers with new ideas, and run government to help themselves and their cronies. Opponents claim that the normal voting process can accomplish that: all voters have to do is "vote out the bastards" they do not like and vote in those they do like.

Conservatives tend to favor term limits, while liberals usually object to them. However, antiprofessional politician sentiment crosses party lines and has helped pass term limitations.

While term limits will limit the time an elected official can serve and may curb entrenched self-interest, they will also prevent legislators from developing expertise through experience. A side effect may be that legislatures subject to term limits will be run by permanent, experienced staff who will provide the only continuity, along with the increased influence of lobbyists who will help "educate" each new crop of legislators.

An effort to limit the number of terms that a member of the House of Representatives may serve (passed in the state of Washington) has been ruled unconstitutional since the House determines the eligibility of its own members.

terrorism   the use of fear and/or violence to bring about quick and dramatic political change by destabilization and intimidation. Motivations for terrorist acts may include ultimate frustration with the system, intimidation, nationalism, anti-colonialism, or the desire to produce changes that are deemed necessary in the national political system. Terrorism is often committed anonymously, demonstrating the terrorists perceived needs to hide their identities and a lack of courage of their convictions.

The 1993 bombing of the World Trade Center in New York exemplifies the anonymity of terrorism: bombs were placed in secret, set off with great destruction, injury, and deaths

and were followed by 14 written and telephoned claims of responsibility. Probably only one organization committed the acts, hoping to effect their political goals while the others lacked even the courage to set the bombs to accomplish theirs.

Other international examples of terrorism include: Italy's Red Brigades, West Germany's Baader Meinhoff group, Uruguay's Tupamaros, Shi'ite Moslems who took hostages in the Middle East, rightwing anti-Semitic terrorist groups in France and the United States who blow up temples and synagogues, and the more militant members of the Irish Republican Army (IRA), who have planted bombs in Northern Ireland and England.

test the waters   explore whether a person can have a chance of winning an election if he/she decides to run for office.

that dog won't hunt   a southern phrase from Texas meaning the proposal will not work. Then Texas state treasurer and later governor Ann Richards introduced the rest of the nation to the term and her humor in her keynote address to the 1988 Democratic National Convention.

theocracy   a government or political system run by clerics, priests, or any head of a religion in accord with the religion's principles and doctrines. Examples of theocracies include Brigham Young's Mormon state of Deseret (now Utah) and Ayatollah Khomeni's Iran.

theorist   (1) a person who studies, forms, and espouses theories. (2) in politics a theorist is someone who studies, writes, and discusses other people's political thoughts and writings, as opposed to a doist who practices the art form.

A theorist talks about other people's experience, and a doist participates in politics, organizes, walks door to door, raises funds, gets the vote out, registers voters, and generally "walks his/her talk." Both theorists and doists form political thought.

theory the branch of political science that emphasizes knowledge of principles and methods instead of practice, that is, its pure, intellectual form rather than its application in campaigns and hands-on conduct of the government.

think tank an organization that coordinates and organizes scholarly research on public policy, often funded by public and private grants and endowments.

Think tanks explore ideas and proposals from the left, right, and center to improve government's effectiveness. Participants usually hope to effect change in public policy by publishing their issues, findings, and proposals, increasing public awareness, influencing government by lobbying, and changing public sentiment.

third parties more appropriately called minor parties, because more than one alternative cannot all be third parties. The two principal U.S. parties are the Democrats and Republicans. Other efforts are called "third parties."

Third parties in the United States have usually been single election or single-issue parties that either collapse or fold back into the two major parties. American third parties include: Anti-Masonic (1830–40), Liberty (1840–44), Free Soil (1848), Native American or Know Nothing (1850–58), Constitutional Union (1860), Greenback (1870–90s), People's or Populist Party (1890s), Socialist Labor and Socialist (ongoing), Progressive (1912, 1924–38, 1948–52), Communist (1920 and continuing), Prohibitionist (1900–1950s), American Labor Party of New York (1930s–1952), States Rights or Dixiecrat (1948), American Independent (1964–present), Peace and Freedom (1968–present), Farm Labor (1930s–44 and part of Democratic Party now), Liberal of New York (1940s to present), and, recently, Libertarian, Reform, Natural Law, and Green.

third rail Social Security or any matter that can prove difficult for a politician. The third rail on electric trains provides power to the train, but if touched could electrocute you.

third way (1) President Bill Clinton's term for a means to think and govern based on collaboration rather than on liberal or conservative terms or divisiveness. (2) an alternative to traditional thinking that things are black or white, right or wrong in which participants look for a new central view or approach to a problem. This method of thinking is popular among some New Democrats in the United States, and in the United Kingdom and Canada. See also COMMUNITARIANISM.

Third World developing nations of Africa, Asia, and Latin America, although some of these, such as

Argentina, are highly developed industrially. The term emerged early in the cold war following World War II, with the United States and its Western European and British Commonwealth allies ("the West") as the First World, and the Soviet Union and its satellites in Eastern Europe as the Second World. Many Third World countries were European colonies before 1939 and remained underdeveloped and exploited as a matter of convenience and expediency for the colonists and colonizers.

thousand points of light an attempted buzzword phrase coined by speechwriter Peggy Noonan for Vice President George H. W. Bush and used by him in his 1988 presidential nomination acceptance speech at the Republican National Convention. Few people understood what Noonan and Bush meant. Apparently the phrase refers to the many ways in which Americans help each other voluntarily.

Three Mile Island the Pennsylvania location of a nuclear power plant that partially melted down (March 28, 1979), causing unknown permanent physical damage to people and the environment. Some radiation leaked into the atmosphere, resulting in local panic, widespread criticism, and protests against nuclear power plants and projects. No one died immediately from the radiation. Along with Chernobyl, Three Mile Island has become a symbol of danger from nuclear reactors.

Three Strikes You're Out an umbrella term, created by Mike Reynolds of Fresno, California, following the murder of his daughter, for 1994 federal and state legislation that makes life prison terms mandatory for criminals who have already been convicted twice of molestation, rape, murder, and certain other crimes, and them commit a third crime. The California three strikes law has been criticized for including nonviolent crimes.

ticket (1) a list of candidates nominated by one political party as they appear on the ballot. (2) a reference to the presidential and vice presidential candidates of one party, who usually run as a team.

tinhorn politician a person who claims to have influence, position, lines of communication to the powerful, and ability, but who, in reality, possesses none of the above.

tokenism (1) a minor concession to appear to give in to or go along with another person's demands or position. (2) Inclusion or appointment of a minority person or a woman as a symbol of supposed openness to their interests.

Tolerance Language Addendum 1996 Republican presidential candidate Bob Dole's attempt to insert language into the Republican Party platform that would allow for tolerance of diverse opinions on choice.

Tonkin Gulf Resolution a congressional resolution that President Lyndon Johnson employed to justify massive American military intervention in the Vietnam War.

Following an August 2, 1964, report that North Vietnamese patrol boats had fired on American destroyers *Maddox* and *Joy* in the Tonkin Gulf, the Johnson administration requested a joint resolution to approve a military response. Congress passed the joint resolution on August 7, 1964, but 64 American air sorties against Vietnamese patrol bases had actually already occurred on August 4. The resolution passed unanimously in the House, and only senators Wayne Morse (D–Ore.) and Ernest Gruening (D–Ark.) voted against it in the Senate.

President Johnson and the Defense Department used the resolution as a "blank check" to involve the United States in nearly all-out military warfare without a congressional declaration of war and instead of America's former role as "advisers and suppliers."

During 1968 Senate hearings new information was revealed: (1) American destroyers had actually fired first; (2) there was great doubt as to whether North Vietnam had fired torpedoes at all; (3) the resolution had actually been prepared in rough draft several months before the alleged incident.

Senator William Fulbright (D–Ark.) carried the original resolution for President Johnson, but later renounced it and supported its repeal in March 1966, along with senators Morse, Gruening, Eugene McCarthy (D–Minn.), and Stephen Young (D–Ohio). Eventually it was repealed in May 1970, at the suggestion of Senator Robert Dole (R–Ks.) on the basis that it was "obsolete."

In the meantime, tens of thousands of Americans had died in the fighting.

Tories (1) United Kingdom: Conservative Party members. (2) Canada: Progressive Conservative Party members. See RED TORY.

tort reform buzzword for limiting the amount people can recover in lawsuits from injuries, medical malpractice, or other torts (civil wrongs).

totalitarianism a system of government by which one political party exclusively controls the government and political processes and ignores or actively refuses to recognize other or opposition parties. Such refusal results in suppression of the opposition, and is often characteristic of dictatorships. Totalitarian rule prevailed in German Naziism, Italian Fascism, and Soviet Stalinism, in addition to many forms in Latin America, wartime Japan, Iran, South Africa, China, and the Philippines under Ferdinand Marcos.

town meeting an assembly of all the people in a town to act as the town's legislative body in voting on policy for the town. This is the only example of direct democracy in the United States. Town meetings are still the means of governance in some parts of New England.

tracking poll a group of questions and public opinion surveys asked of the same people on a planned, timed basis with specific intervals between interviews, such as daily, weekly, or monthly. The purpose of a tracking poll is to ask the same questions repeatedly to gauge changes of opinion on issues or candidates.

trade association an organization of business owners or professionals involved in the same kind of business or profession, such as doctors, dry cleaners, realtors, and liquor producers. Trade associations usually function for their members as lobbyists, educators, and public relations representatives.

trade-off a compromise or deal by which a politician or other person does a favor in return for another favor or gives up on a principle in a bill as a trade for another person giving up something.

trade unions See also LABOR UNIONS.

transparency openness in government, including making facts, functions and processes easily understandable and straightforward for the public. Transparency also includes offering easy access to information, easy opportunity to seek redress for misconduct, and the opportunity to challenge governmental actions.

Travelgate a would-be Clinton White House scandal in which First Lady Hillary Rodham Clinton was accused of firing employees of the White House travel office, to make room for a travel agency run by Clinton friends. No criminal acts were found.

treason a conscious act against one's country in violation of one's expected allegiance to that country. The U.S. Constitution says: "Treason against the United States shall consist only in levying War against them, or, in addressing to their Enemies, giving them Aid and Comfort."

Interpretations of treason vary and they arise in a political context. Senator Joseph McCarthy (R–Wisc.) used the term with abandon, calling the Democrats the "party of treason." In the 1992 presidential election campaign President George H. W. Bush likened candidate Bill Clinton's protests in England against America's involvement in Vietnam to treason. The public reacted negatively to Bush's insinuation.

Actual convictions for treason are rare and, in most cases, involve people who have sold military or scientific information to other countries. Since World War II, the one major U.S. treason case was that of Julius and Ethel Rosenberg, who were convicted of sending atomic secrets to the Soviet Union. Both of them were convicted in 1951 and executed on June 19, 1953.

trial balloon releasing a potential appointment, candidacy, or policy to the media to see what public reaction to the person or concept is before actually making the appointment or proposing the policy or legislation.

triangulation former White House adviser Dick Morris's positioning of President Bill Clinton philosophically somewhere between Republicans and liberal Democrats in Congress.

trickle-down theory an economic premise, used most recently by President Ronald Reagan, that helping big business will help the little people. Assistance and subsidies to corporations will "trickle down" through cracks in the economic floorboards to the masses. Republicans suffered embarrassment at the theory's failures. Democrats reject it whenever it resurfaces, on the basis that the "investment" trickles down only as far as upper executives' salaries and never really gets into the broader economy.

triggered compensation bonuses handed out usually to executives when a corporation makes a windfall profit or sale.

Trojan horse delegate candidate a candidate running to be a delegate to a convention on the expectation of voting for a particular candidate when the delegate really intends to vote for a different candidate at the convention.

Trotskyism the revolutionary beliefs, doctrines, and methods of Leon Trotsky (real name Leib Bronstein) (1879–1940), who lost a power struggle to Joseph Stalin after the death of V. I. Lenin. An early leader of Russian communism, Trotsky was expelled from Russia in 1929 and murdered in Mexico. Trotskyism held two primary principles: (1) the need for "permanent revolution" by which Trotsky is thought to have meant that a people could avoid the interim bourgeois capitalist period after a completed revolution and go straight to an urban proletariat, and (2) there need not be a strict, authoritarian party with hierarchical control, which Lenin and Stalin preferred. This idea supposedly had more appeal in the West where extremely hierarchical party structure was feared. Anti-Stalin communists and radical socialists were often labeled Trotskyites.

Truman Doctrine a pronouncement by President Harry S. Truman (March 12, 1947) that the United States should give financial aid to countries thought to be threatened by encroaching communism. The first $400,000,000 was given to Greece and Turkey for military and economic aid. The Truman Doctrine became the first concrete step in the assumption by the United States of worldwide responsibility outside of formal U.S. foreign policy, as well as America's first active cold war response to the Soviet Union.

truth that which is true or real and matches actual facts. "Truth" came up often during investigations into President Bill Clinton's affair with Monica Lewinsky, about which he did not tell the truth to his cabinet, some members of the Congress, and to the American people.

truth in advertising a legal responsibility to tell the truth in advertisements, including about opponents' and your own statements and positions on political issues and personal backgrounds. The official watchdog in the United States is the Federal Trade Commission, but its powers are limited.

truth squad a group from a political party, campaign, or special-interest organization who follow opposition speakers and tell their side of the story, which is supposed to be the "the truth," and, undoubtedly, is the truth as they see it.

turfed out thrown out or voted out of office.

turnout   the people who actually turn out to vote in an election, often measured by neighborhood or ethnic origin.

Tweed Ring   the New York City Democratic political machine of William M. "Boss" Tweed (1823–78), the boss of Tammany Hall, who specialized in graft and stealing millions of dollars from New York taxpayers from 1869 to 1877, bringing New York to the brink of bankruptcy. The Tweed Ring also included A. Oakley Hall, Richard B. Connolly, and Peter B. Sweeney. They bribed legislators, judges, journalists, Republican opponents, and city workers who might be inclined to squeal.

Hall became mayor, Sweeney became city and county treasurer, and Tweed became superintendent of the street department, positioning themselves for even greater opportunities to steal and receive bribes for city contracts and jobs.

Public opposition to the Ring, its control, and practices developed through articles in the *New York Times,* attacks by Democratic reformer Samuel Tilden, and Thomas Nast's political cartoons. Tweed was convicted of embezzlement (1873) and died in jail. The others all fled the country.

24 Sussex   address of the official residence and office of the prime minister of Canada in Ottawa, Ontario.

two-bit politician   a politician who sells out quickly, prostitutes his/her votes, or compromises too easily for personal expediency without regard for his/her constituents.

two-fer   a person who gets counted as two quota notches, such as an African-American woman.

two-party system   a political system in which there are principally two major political parties. The United States and Great Britain are examples of two-party systems, although, in the latter especially, minor or third parties thrive.

tyranny of the majority   a phrase from John Stuart Mill's *Essay on Liberty* (1859) that became popular among so-called liberals such as Alexis de Tocqueville. Essentially the messages are (1) to guard against insensitive total majority rule, and, (2) the majority has a duty to protect the rights of the minority and not stifle or suffocate them.

Ugly American (1) the title of a novel by Eugene Burdick and William J. Lederer that portrayed stupid, tactless, tasteless, arrogant, and insensitive American officials in an imaginary southeast Asian country. (2) a pejorative term for Americans who travel abroad, typically wearing Bermuda shorts and bright Hawaiian shirts, and loudly judging everything they see or experience by their American standards. Usually such individuals prefer to remain ignorant of local customs and culture, probably out of an insecurity about their own origins and lack of a national culture.

un-American a term used occasionally by conservatives to attack the principles of those with whom they do not agree or who hold values different from their own.

Uncle Sam symbol of the U.S. government, represented by a tall white man with white hair, red and white striped pants, and a blue jacket.

Uncle Tom an expression used to label African Americans who are thought to sell out to, or act subserviently toward, whites. The name comes from the title character of Harriet Beecher Stowe's *Uncle Tom's Cabin* (1852) who tries to please his brutal white master, Simon Legree. Tom suppresses his feelings and even forgives his master/tormentor until Legree beats him to death.

In the 1960s, particularly, the term was used for blacks who worked with conservative whites to get along within the system instead of holding out for true equal opportunity. In 1992, African-American Supreme Court nominee and Republican Clarence Thomas was accused of being an Uncle Tom for becoming a conservative out of expediency.

unconstitutional in violation of the constitution of a state or country. In the United States, this can include criminal behavior, or laws, statutes, and regulations passed by state or federal governments.

underclass an old and resurrected term for the poor, underprivileged people whose incomes are below poverty or subsistence level, and who appear to have little chance to change their economic status. "Underclass" is often used instead of the politically incorrect term "lower class" in a supposedly classless society.

President Bill Clinton said that "it is no longer the underclass, but it is the outerclass" (*Meet the Press*, NBC News, November 7, 1993). His implication appears to be that a large segment of American society lives completely outside the economic system.

underdog a candidate in a political race who is expected to have the least chance of winning, with the implication that there is a glimmer of hope. Underdogs often attract support from people who are less ideologically driven and enjoy supporting the person with the least chance out of sympathy, empathy, or just for the sport of it.

undervote vote not counted because of a deficiency of the ballot, failure by the voter to mark or punch through the ballot, or failure of the vote counting machine.

undue influence more influence or power than others think one should have; in politics usually due to large campaign contributions.

unemployment insurance the federal-state system that enables the federal government to pay laid-off workers fixed amounts of money per week for a certain number of weeks after termination of their employment. As part of the Social Security Act, employers pay a percentage of an employee's wages into the fund.

unicameral legislature a legislature with only one body whose members all vote at the same time and represent constituencies of relatively equal size. Nebraska has the only unicameral legislature in the United States.

union busting declaring striking union workers' jobs vacant and hiring nonunion workers to replace them. Before the existence of the National Labor Relations Board (1935), union busting included hiring toughs to beat up union members, provoke trouble and then call in police help, and other rough methods of intimidation. Republican president Ronald Reagan busted the air traffic controllers' union (1981) by approving the hiring of nonunion and, sometimes, untrained controllers while the union controllers were on strike for public safety improvements and work and pay grievances.

union shop an industry, business, or manufacturing plant where employees are organized into unions, and owners will hire nonunion workers only if they agree to join the union.

unions See LABOR UNIONS.

unit rule a legislative or political convention rule requiring that all members of a voting body must be cast as a unit the way the majority determines.

Used by some state delegations at national conventions and some district delegations at state conventions, the unit rule was thought to give a unit more clout by delivering votes as a bloc. The rule also was criticized as a device to deprive minority voices and as a mechanism to allow choice of a candidate without a mathematical majority. The Democratic Party prohibited it by reform rules in 1972. Southern delegations had used the unit rule extensively at Democratic National Conventions, but until 1976 some states, such as California, had "winner-take-all" presidential primaries. Following adoption of the one-man-one-vote principle, the unit rule has been outlawed by the Democrats but kept in use by the Republicans.

United Nations (UN) a worldwide organization of 188 nations (in 2000) committed to promoting world peace, maintaining obligations to treaties and international law, and furthering social and economic progress for all member nations. The UN was created on June 26, 1945, in San Francisco, California, when 50 nations signed the United Nations Charter to replace the League of Nations. In 1993 the UN had 179 member nations. There are only a few nations that are not members, including Switzerland. While Switzerland wishes to remain nonaligned, however, it does serve as a headquarters for several UN agencies.

The UN's primary bodies include the Security Council, the General Assembly, the Secretariat, the Trusteeship Council, and the Economic and Social Council. A number of specialized agencies exist that are affiliated with the United Nations, including the United Nations International Children's Fund (UNICEF) and the Uni-ted Nations Development Program (UNDP). Addresses: United Nations, New York, N.Y. 10017. United Nations Association of the United States of America, 485 Fifth Avenue, New York, N.Y. 10017–6104. United Nations, Palais des Nations, 1211 Geneva 10, Switzerland. United Nations International Center, A-1400 Vienna, Austria. Public inquiries: Tel.: (212) 963-4475 or (212) 963-9246; FAX: (212) 963-0071; e-mail: inquiries@un.org; website:www.un. org

universal coverage a 1990s buzzword for health care insurance coverage for everyone. Use of the term suggests private insurance company coverage supplemented by governmental coverage for those lacking private health insurance. Many questions arise: if you cancel your health insurance do you get governmental coverage? If an insurance company cancels you due to illness or nonpayment do you get governmental coverage? If you are young and never try to get private insurance do you get governmental coverage? Who pays for your coverage, whether private or governmental? Should Americans strive for "universal coverage" with a Canadian-style "single-payer" (government) health plan with options to use private physicians and facilities?

universal health care a form of health care in which treatment and medicine are made available to everyone, regardless of ability to pay for care or pay for health insurance. See UNIVERSAL COVERAGE.

unofficial record written record made by people who are not official stenographers, court reporters, or clerks of the institution, such as the U.S. Senate. Unofficial records may be made by journalists, historians, or other private individuals.

upper house (1) the Senate in the United States. (2) elsewhere, the legislative body in a bicameral system in which one body supposedly comprises the aristocracy and is selected by heritage or royal appointment (Britain's House of Lords), as opposed to the body elected by the population (Britain's House of Commons.) The U.S. Senate is one of the few upper houses that has power beyond debate, veto, or delay. In Canada senators are appointed by the prime minister can serve until age 75, and have only powers to debate and delay legislation.

Urban League See NATIONAL URBAN LEAGUE.

urban renewal also known as redevelopment, the clearing and rebuilding of slum neighborhoods, using controlled planning, federal funding, and other financial help. Urban renewal was first federally funded in 1949, and is currently overseen by H.U.D., city, county, and state governments and operated by local redevelopment agencies.

While slum clearance and housing improvements are generally regarded as beneficial, concern remains for those—usually poor, minority families—who lose their homes when the slums are torn down for urban renewal as to whether the displaced residents will be able to afford the new units. Subsidies become available for some residents, but they often do not help the poorest. Where do they go?

user fee an amount of money charged by a government agency for use of its services.

User fees are theoretically contrived to lighten the burden on nonusers of some services and increase it on users, forcing users to "pay as you go." Opponents of user fees claim the public has already paid its fees through taxes. In the case of public beaches on American coasts, thought to be public property, user fees are often challenged on the basis that the beach front property is owned by all the people and should be available to all Americans equally and free.

USIA (United States Information Agency) an independent federal agency created to spread good news and information about the United States around the world. Called propagandist by some countries and its detractors, the USIA (known abroad as the United States Information Service) runs the Voice of America international broadcasting service, information centers and libraries, and distributes films, television programs, and magazines throughout the world. It also manages the functions of certain embassy staff positions. Address: 301 Fourth Street, S.W., Washington, D.C. 20547. Tel.: (202) 619-4700; website:www.usinfo.state.gov

U.S.S.R. (Union of Soviet Socialist Republics) between 1918 and December 8, 1991, the nation based on Marxist communism, encompassing the geographical area created by the Russian czars, from the Baltic to the Pacific, and covering 11 time zones. It included Russia, Belarus, Moldova, Ukraine, Kazakhstan, Kyrgystan, Tajikistan, Turkmenistan, Uzbekistan, Lithuania, Latvia, Estonia, Georgia, Azerbaijan, and Armenia.

The U.S.S.R. (also called the Soviet Union) emerged from a two-stage revolution, beginning in 1917 when a violent revolt ousted the czar, and followed in 1918 by a takeover by Marxist Bolsheviks led by V. I. Lenin. Lenin was followed by dictator Joseph Stalin and other dedicated communists. From 1918 to 1991 the U.S.S.R. was the world leader of Marxist communism.

The U.S.S.R. survived through World War II and the cold war in which it controlled much of Eastern Europe and presented an antagonistic and competitive front of the Western capitalist world.

Suddenly in 1989 and 1990 its economy began to unravel. Despite attempts to loosen the bonds of centralized control, introduction of elections, and cooperation with the United States, the communist system collapsed. Lithuania, Latvia, Estonia, and Georgia declared their independence in early 1991, followed by an attempted coup by die-hard, conservative communists against President Mikhail Gorbachev.

In December 1991, the U.S.S.R. was dissolved. Eleven of the republics entered into a loose confederation of independent states that included Russia, Ukraine, and Belarus. Gorbachev soon resigned since there no longer existed a government of which he was president. The republics experimented with democracy and a free market economy somewhat convulsively, with constant hardship, struggles, and coup attempts.

The experiment with authoritarian communism, which had been the U.S.S.R., was dead.

utilitarianism an element of most liberal doctrines and originated by James Mill and refined by his son John Stuart Mill in the 19th century. The theory stresses that the greatest happiness or benefit of the great number of people should be the goal of all action.

Utopianism schemes, thoughts, or experiments aimed at political and social harmony (perfection) and that are, by their nature, impossible to attain.

The name comes from Sir Thomas More's writing (*Utopia*, 1516) about an imaginary island and life in an ideal republic. Sir Thomas More was named Lord Chancellor of England by Henry VIII and who executed by him (1535) for refusing to recognize Henry VIII as head of the Church of England. The Roman Catholic Church has declared him a saint.

values   See FAMILY VALUES.

VAT (value added tax)   a sales tax used in Europe and considered by the Clinton administration for use in the United States. Many politicians and economists see the VAT as a regressive tax because it takes from poor people a proportionately larger portion of spendable income used for necessities than it does from the wealthy.

veep   slang for vice president coined by Veep Alben Barkley (1949–53).

veto   from Latin meaning "I forbid," the right of an executive, ruler, or legislature to reject bills by another branch of the government. A U.S. president or governor can veto legislation that requires the executive's signature to become law by returning it to a legislative body without signing it. Usually the president returns the bill with a "veto message" explaining his opposition.

To override a presidential veto in the United States, Congress must mount a two-thirds vote of those present and voting in each house. If the president does not sign or return a bill within 10 days (excluding Sunday) of receiving it during a congressional session the bill becomes law. If Congress adjourns and the president does not sign a bill within the prescribed 10 days, failure to act is called a "pocket veto."

A veto actually gives one person the power over the majority as represented by Congress, but not over two-thirds of both the House and Senate.

In the United Nations any one of five permanent members of the Security Council has veto power. Those members include China, France, the United Kingdom, Russia, and the United States. See also POCKET VETO.

veto power   a power to veto or stop legislation passed by a state, province, or federal legislative body.

vice president   the second officer in the United States who will succeed to the presidency upon the death, disability, resignation, or successful impeachment of the president.

The position was invented in September 1787, during the Constitutional Convention to provide a successor in case of the death or disqualification of the president. Originally the candidate who received the second highest number of the electors' votes would become vice president, supposedly assuring that he would be the second most popular man in the country. At that time each elector cast two votes without distinguishing votes between president and vice president. Soon candidates began to run on party tickets, resulting in 1800 in a tie between Thomas Jefferson and his running mate, Aaron Burr. The Twelfth Amendment to the Constitution made the votes separate. Should a vice presidential candidate not receive a majority of the electoral votes, the Senate elects the vice president between the two leading vote getters. In 1836, when Richard M. Johnson fell one vote short of an Electoral College majority, the Senate elected him vice president.

The vice president's one official duty is to preside over the Senate, in which he/she only votes if there is a tie. Some presidents have given their vice presidents additional tasks since President Franklin D. Roosevelt asked Henry Wallace to take diplomatic trips and serve as chairman of the War Mobilization Board. Some vice presidents take on diplomatic assignments, attend foreign leaders' funerals, serve on commissions, and direct task forces. Particularly active vice presidents include Dwight Eisenhower's vice president Richard Nixon, Jimmy Carter's vice president Walter Mondale, and Ronald Reagan's vice president George H. W. Bush. President Bill Clinton gave Vice President Albert Gore Jr. more responsibility than any other vice president. Under President George W. Bush, Vice President Richard Cheney is thought to have managed the government and the White House for Bush.

Contrary to historical myth, American vice presidents have not always been obscure figures. Many were prominent senators and governors, two were Speakers of the House, runners-up for the presidential nomination (George H.W. Bush), two Nobel Peace Prize winners (Teddy Roosevelt and Charles G. Dawes), John Adams, and Thomas Jefferson.

The Twenty-fifth Amendment (1967), authored primarily by then senator Birch Bayh (D–Ind.), declares that if the vice presidency is vacant, the president shall nominate a successor who must be approved by Congress. Gerald Ford succeeded Spiro Agnew (1973) under this provision, as did Nelson A. Rockefeller when Ford became president upon Richard Nixon's resignation.

Fourteen vice presidents have become president, eight due to death of the president, five by election, and one (Ford) when the president (Nixon) resigned.

Vietnam War   originally a war between North and South Vietnam that had been stewing and brewing since France's 1954 withdrawal from Indochina.

U.S. president John F. Kennedy first sent "advisers" to help the corrupt and ineffective South Vietnamese government reject communist North Vietnam, and then openly sent soldiers and marines (who were prepared to fight) in 1962. The language was important to avoid letting the American people think they were entering into a war. U.S. involvement escalated under the Lyndon Johnson and Richard Nixon administrations, resulting in approximately 57,000 American deaths. Congress never passed a declaration of war, but Democratic president Lyndon Johnson used the so-called Tonkin Resolution (August 1964) as justification for massive use of U.S. forces.

Beginning in 1966, public opinion mounted against U.S. participation and American deaths in an undeclared and unclear war, forcing President Lyndon Johnson to not run for president in 1968. Senator Eugene McCarthy (D–Minn.) defeated Johnson in the first two presidential primaries, and Senator Robert Kennedy (D–N.Y.) entered the race for the Democratic nomination. Republican Richard Nixon was elected president in 1968 promising a "secret" plan to end the war, but the conflict continued for five more years.

Many young Americans avoided the draft, including thousands who moved to Canada. Even Heavyweight Boxing Champion Muhammad Ali refused induction on religious and philosophical grounds. There were massive demonstrations against the war between 1967 and 1972.

President Nixon's secretary of state Henry Kissinger "negotiated" an end to the "war" (January 1973), which sugarcoated a defeat for the United States. By this time the South Vietnam military and government had proved totally ineffective, most Vietnamese just wanted the war to stop, and the North Vietnamese army was winning the jungle war.

Village of Euclid v. Amber Realty Co.
a U.S. Supreme Court ruling (1926) that zoning ordinances are legitimate exercises of the states' police powers.

violence the use of physical force to damage or injure another or to force an action.

Violence has been used to resolve differences in America since the War of Independence and the Civil War, and can be tied psychologically to American men's needs to fist fight and show supposed strength and power by physical acts, from punching out another man to show turf control at high school to bombing Iraq without attempting negotiation.

Conservatives seem to be more willing to resolve conflict through violence, endorsing the Iraq War in which the United States massively bombed urban centers while opposing abortion as killing and violent. Skinheads and neo-Nazis approve of violence, as did Hitler and Mussolini, to intimidate or eliminate people they do not like.

Liberals claim to oppose all forms of violence and to favor negotiation and peaceful resolution of conflict, but they support a woman's right to choose abortion. Generally, both conservatives and liberals are appalled by violence in the streets, but differ on how to control it.

Violence has become a culture and way of life in the United States, interfering with educational and learning processes. Many students carry guns to school and are constantly distracted by the threat and fear of violence and harm.

visible minority a non-Caucasian racial group whose skin color or facial features distinguish members of that group from Caucasians in a predominantly Caucasian country or state.

VISTA (Volunteers in Service to America) an agency of the federal government created by President Lyndon Johnson as part of the Economic Opportunity Act (1965) to emulate the Peace Corps to educate and train the poor at home in America. VISTA volunteers (over 1,000 by year 2000) served one or two years, usually in urban ghettos or on Indian reservations and in migrant worker camps. VISTA now forms part of the Corporation for National Service (AmeriCorps). Address: c/o Action, 1100 Vermont Avenue., N.W., Washington, D.C. 20525. Tel.: (202) 606-5108; e-mail: vista@AmeriCorps.org; website: www.nationalservice.org

vital interests a country's interests, as determined by legislators, presidents, or prime ministers, deemed to be more important to that country's survival or prosperity than the interests of other countries.

Voice of America originally created on February 24, 1942, during World War II, to broadcast to people in territories captured by the Axis powers (Germany, Japan, and Italy). In January 1948, it became a means to broadcast "objective" programs on American culture and official policy in 53 languages, particularly to countries "behind the iron curtain" during the Cold War. Since 1953 it has been operated by the United States Information Agency (Service) (except for 1978–82), and in 1985 it began aiming broadcasts to Cuba. With the end of the cold war the Voice of America's importance has diminished. It is also on the Internet in 35 languages.

Voice of America should not be confused with Radio Free Europe and Radio Liberty, which were created and operated by the Central Intelligence Agency in the early 1950s and were blatantly anti-communist. Address: 300 Independence Ave., S.W., Washington, D.C. 20237. Tel.: (202) 619-3919; website: www.voa.gov

voice vote a vote in which the chair asks for an oral vote by all those in favor of a proposal and then all those opposed, usually as a group. Members of Congress and state legislatures often call for voice votes so that individual votes will not show.

volunteers people who work on political campaigns and function as staff without pay.

Volunteers do everything in a campaign that the paid staff cannot or does not want to do. Their functions may include: stuffing envelopes, walking door-to-door or canvassing, raising money, writing position papers, forming neighborhood support groups, driving candidates to meetings, and telephoning. Volunteers are especially important in campaigns lacking enormous amounts of money. Volunteers should be managed carefully, because "you can't fire a volunteer."

Volvo voter affluent suburban independent-minded voter.

voodoo economics George H. W. Bush's label for his 1980 Republican presidential primary opponent

Ronald Reagan's plan for "supply side economics," tax cuts, and increased military spending. See SUPPLY-SIDE ECONOMICS

vote to express a preference by ballot or voice on an issue or in favor of a candidate.

vote counter a person who counts or helps watch the counters tabulating votes after an election.

vote early and often a jocular saying and actual practice that originated in various urban political machines, particularly in Chicago, Illinois, where people actually did vote early under their own name and then voted later for people on the voter lists who were out of town or dead.

vote of censure a vote to punish a member or leader for wrongdoing, also known as "a slap on the hand," instead of a more drastic punishment. Many members of Congress favored a vote of censure of President Bill Clinton during his impeachment hearings in the U.S. House and Senate following his affair with Monica Lewinsky and his lies to the cabinet, some members of Congress, and to the American people. A resolution of censure of senator Joseph McCarthy in 1954 ended his attacks in the guise of anti-communism.

vote of confidence a legislative vote that serves as a test of a leader's popularity or of the reflected public support and confidence in his/her leadership. In the United Kingdom, a prime minister may call for a vote of confidence in Parliament when it appears the public lacks confidence in

him/her. If he/she loses that vote, Parliament may vote to replace that prime minister. If he/she wins the vote, he/she will likely stay in office.

voter card an identification card used in some countries with certain unduplicatable identity marks, such as fingerprints and photos, and often with a number used to tabulate when the holder voted.

voter registration See REGISTRATION.

voting machine a mechanical device that registers and tabulates a person's vote when he/she uses it to do so. Machines are used in some places supposedly because they are quicker and allow for fewer "irregularities," that is, cheating. They also break down and get lost on the way to the central counting place. Some voting machines provide computerized results almost instantaneously.

voucher (1) a receipt or paper showing payment made. (2) a piece of paper and buzzword to mean a system by which parents of children who attend or who want to attend private schools could use to pay a part or all of private school tuition. The theory is that vouchers will encourage superior education in alternative private schools, and help students escape public schools that have poor performance records.

Opponents of the voucher system believe that vouchers will allow more affluent parents to remove their children from public schools with which they are dissatisfied either for social (racial) or educational reasons and enroll them in private or religious schools. They also believe that the voucher system will leave schools in which minority students are enrolled at a social and educational disadvantage.

Questions remaining unanswered include: how will the "good" schools hold the new students who will theoretically want to attend them; what will happen to poorer schools that some students choose to leave; what will happen to students who cannot find a "better" school for them?

Conservatives and the religious right favor vouchers. Liberals generally oppose them, except when their children may be destined for an "undesirable" or "unacceptable" school.

waffle to be unable to make a decision, moving back and forth from one side to another to please supporters of both sides, and appearing to lack courage.

Wagner Act See NATIONAL LABOR RELATIONS ACT.

walking-around money (1) cash taken from a campaign fund and slipped to a candidate for small purchases such as meals and drinks. (2) small cash payoffs given to precinct workers to keep or pass on down the ladder to get out the vote on election day. Walking-around money exists in most political campaigns. It surfaced publicly in 1993 when the Republican campaign mastermind Ed Rollins stated, after he chaired New Jersey gubernatorial candidate Christine Whitman's successful campaign, that her campaign gave African-American ministers walking-around money to not encourage their potentially Demo-cratic congregations to vote. Rollins later stated that he had made up the whole story.

walkout (1) a strike of workers who walk off the job. (2) the act of leaving a meeting, conference, convention, or workplace as a protest or expression of disagreement, disapproval, or grievance.

war chest large campaign bank account.

war crimes negative, harmful acts committed by any representatives of a government, including soldiers, before, during, or after a war in violations of war customs. Such crimes include killing prisoners, massacre and maiming of civilians, and raping women left home by soldiers. Examples of war crimes include killing millions of Jews by Nazis in World War II, the My Lai Massacre in Vietnam by American soldiers, mass raping of

Bosnian women by Serbs, and "ethnic cleansing," a euphemism for mass murder and/or displacement of minority ethnic populations in the Balkans and Africa.

The first war crimes trials occurred after World War II when Allied courts tried German and Japanese leaders, commanders, and some lesser officials for "crimes against humanity." Basically these were crimes so massive and inhumane as to violate natural law as well as strict laws of war set out in the Geneva Convention (1864).

War on Poverty a concept originated by Michael Harrington in *The Other America* (1962), adopted by President Lyndon B. Johnson, and expressed in his first State of the Union address (January 1964). Johnson's goal was to eliminate poverty in America, much as President Kennedy had tried to do abroad. Johnson campaigned successfully for a larger food stamp program, more aid to Appalachian Mountain residents, better unemployment insurance, VISTA, and a Youth Job Corps, the latter enacted as legislation by the Economic Opportunity Act of 1964.

Unfortunately President's Johnson's preoccupation with and spending on the Vietnam War blunted the War on Poverty, and many of its remnants were closed down by President Richard Nixon's administration.

War Powers Act an act passed by Congress in 1973 requiring that the president obtain congressional approval before committing U.S. armed forces to a combat zone and notify Congress within 48 hours of committing troops to foreign soil even if there is no combat. The act also requires the president to withdraw armed forces within 60 days unless Congress votes to declare war. The War Powers Act was a response to the ever-deepening and unapproved American involvement in Vietnam between 1964 and 1973 without a federal declaration of war.

Contending that the act was partially unconstitutional since it interfered with the duties of the president as commander in chief and the need for secrecy to save American lives, presidents Ford, Carter, Reagan and George H. W. Bush committed troops to combat zones without congressional approval. President George H. W. Bush got a resolution through the United Nations favoring U.S. intervention in Kuwait to thwart an Iraqi invasion, and then got congressional approval of the UN resolution.

The last U.S. declaration of war was in December 1941, when the United States entered World War II.

ward a geographic and political division or district of a city for electoral purposes. Each ward elects its representative (usually called an alderman) to the city council. Wards also provide the political unit with which statewide and national campaigns deal, utilizing the operational structure and influence of the system to turn out voters on election day.

ward heeler a person who holds a position of minimal but relative power who earns his/her stature working for a political party in a specific precinct, in which he/she becomes an expert and necessary player. Ward heelers pass out literature, register voters, and get out the vote. Sometimes they are paid by officeholders or party bosses.

While ward heelers are often maligned by people outside the system, they perform the function of relaying views and messages both up and down the system's power ladder.

Warren Report   the report prepared and submitted by the Warren Commission to President Lyndon Johnson on its investigation into the assassination of President John F. Kennedy and the subsequent killing of his alleged assassin, Lee Harvey Oswald. Johnson appointed the Warren Commission, so named for its chairman, U.S. Supreme Court Chief Justice Earl Warren, to collect the facts and determine whether President Kennedy was killed by an individual working alone, as part of a conspiracy, or in a combination of the two.

The Warren Report said that the commission concluded that President Kennedy was killed by one assassin and that there was no foreign or domestic conspiracy involved. Before, during, and after the Warren Report, many people have challenged its conclusions after analyzing the angles of bullets' entries, sightings, and other theories. The best known challenge came from Oliver Stone's movie *JFK*. A prominent theory is that the CIA and/or Cuban president Fidel Castro, working with the then U.S.S.R., plotted to kill Kennedy and did so through Oswald, but there is no substantive evidence to support it.

Washington Post   the second most politically influential newspaper in the United States (after the *New York Times*). Its circulation of 780,000 controls a near monopoly of printed information in the nation's capital, making it the sixth largest newspaper in the country. Moderately liberal, the *Washington Post* has exposed many major scandals, including Watergate, and it has featured courageous investigative reporting, hard-hitting columnists, and biting cartoons by Herblock. The paper is owned by Katherine Graham. Address: 1150 15th Street, N.W., Washington, D.C. 20071. Tel.: (202) 334-6000; e-mail: letters@washpost.com or individual writers via website; website: www. washingtonpost.com

WASP   White Anglo-Saxon Protestants, who consider themselves to be the most affluent, comfortable, and powerful people in the United States as part of the establishment. WASPs are thought by minorities and liberals to work to preserve the status quo to retain their positions and to keep others economically inferior.

watchdog committee   a legislative committee that keeps an eye on government agency expenditures and secret activities to make sure such acts are in the public interest.

Watergate   (1) a Washington, D.C., apartment and office complex where the Democratic National Committee rented offices (1972) for the presidential election headquarters, which were broken into and burglarized by men directed by President Richard Nixon's advisers and assistants. (2) the name for that scandal in which the Committee to Re-elect the President ("CREEP") hired a former CIA agent and several Cubans to burglarize the Democratic headquarters to plant a tap on Democratic Party chairman Larry O'Brien's telephone and gain campaign secrets and strategy papers.

The burglars were caught by a security guard.

The subsequent cover-up of the campaign involvement in these crimes and criminals by President Nixon, Attorney General John Mitchell, Chief of Staff Robert Haldeman, assistant John Erlichman, legal counsel John Dean, and others that ultimately resulted in congressional hearings on the break-in and White House involvement. Tapes of President Nixon's partially erased conversations proved he had lied to Congress and the American people and brought about the impeachment charges against Nixon and his subsequent humiliating resignation from the presidency in August 1974. Many of his assistants served time in prison. Nixon was succeeded by Vice President Gerald Ford, who soon pardoned him of any crimes.

watershed election   an election that reflects new public thinking that changes the course of decisions for a long time and whose impact is noticed.

weapons of mass destruction nuclear weapons.

welfare   programs to assist the poor and those unable to care for themselves, operated in the United States by private agencies such as churches and public programs run by local, state, and federal governments. Occasionally the word is used to mean social security.

Conservatives criticize welfare as taking money from the rich and giving it to the poor who could help themselves if they would just try. They see welfare as encouraging dependence of the poor and lazy upon those people who have made their own way, such as themselves. Conservatives also often believe that welfare, welfare cheaters, and unwed welfare (read minority) mothers undermine the economy. Liberals usually advocate welfare as the right thing to do for those in need. Holders of both viewpoints share concern that welfare has become a way of life for too many people and that the system seems to trap many recipients in its rolls.

welfare reform   basic reduction of welfare expenditures to cut welfare costs. Conservatives often see welfare reform as eliminating the undeserving from the rolls while liberals often see it as enabling welfare recipients to work to get off welfare rolls. President Bill Clinton signed a measure forcing and encouraging welfare recipients to take jobs, substantially reducing the numbers of Americans receiving assistance. Clinton also urged employers to hire welfare recipients to get them off the dole.

Whig Party   a major national political party between 1834 and 1854 that grew in opposition to President Andrew Jackson and his "rule." Whig referred to the English parliamentarians who wore "wigs" and whose influence grew parallel to the power of the king.

The Whig Party membership consisted primarily of conservative landowners who were pro–Bank of the United States in the North and pro–plantation owners in the South. Whig Party leaders included Henry Clay, Daniel Webster, and Abraham Lincoln. Whigs elected two presidents, military heroes William Henry Harrison in 1840 and Zachary Taylor in 1848, but they developed no consistent philosophy or strength. The party dissolved over issues including the annexation of Texas, Mexican War, and extension of slavery into the territories. Anti-slavery members joined the new Republican Party founded in 1854, including Abraham Lincoln, who had served one term as a Whig congressman (1847–49). By 1860 the party no longer existed.

whip a member of a legislature who is chosen by his/her peers to serve as assistant to the leader. In the U.S. Congress both the majority and minority parties have their own whips. Whips' duties include making sure members of their party show up for important votes, briefing party members of the leader's plans and intentions, and pairing absent members' votes. The whip position is often a stepping stone to majority or minority leader or even to Speaker of the House.

whistle blower a person working within a government agency or corporation who breaks a code of secrecy and intimidation and who reveals a secret abuse of government procedures, funds, or other people.

whistle stop a relatively fast campaign tour of all towns along a particular route, originally by train. While conversations between candidates and the people who showed up at the stops were superficial, they were exciting and the public got to see and often touch the president or candidate. Harry Truman was famous for his whistle stop campaigning, and Bill Clinton tried to rekindle the spirit and effect with bus tours. Governor George W. Bush used whistle stop tours in some parts of the country in his 2000 presidential campaign.

White Aryan Resistance "a voluntary network of individuals and small groups who cooperate on one issue. That issue is race. We're dedicated primarily to racial separatism. We have no membership dues and no uniforms. We associate, cooperate, and donate time and service."

White Aryan Resistance is led by its founder, Tom Metzger, former California state director (Grand Dragon) of the Ku Klux Klan. Metzger says he quit the KKK to run for Congress (1980), a race in which he won the Democratic nomination in California's 43rd congressional district but lost to incumbent Republican Claire Burgener. Metzger claims that the group survives solely on contributions and publishes a tabloid monthly newspaper, *WAR,* available at $30.00 per year. They also produce a public access television program shown in 15 states called *Race and Reason* and encourage members to get involved at the local political level to change the current system.

The Aryan Nations of Coeur D'Alene, Idaho, led by Richard Butler, received a $6.3 million judgment against them in September 2000 for an incident in which Aryan Nations guards attacked Victoria Keenan and her son Jason outside the white supremacist sect's northern Idaho headquarters.

White Aryan Resistance has been accused of plotting to bomb a prominent African-American A.M.E. Church in Los Angeles in July 1993. Address: P.O. Box 65, Fallbrook,

Calif. 92088. Tel.: (760) 728-9817; FAX: (760) 723-8996; e-mail: warmetzger@aolcom; website: www. resist. com (Note: Information and quotations of Tom Metzger in this entry are from a telephone interview by Kathleen Thompson Hill on July 28, 1993.)

White Citizens Councils   pro-segregation groups that arose in southern states to counteract the civil rights movement in the 1950s. Claiming to follow legal means to prevent integration, they sometimes used violence and appeared to be an unmasked, slightly more respectable version of the Ku Klux Klan. By the 1970s the groups had faded from influence.

white-collar crime   business dishonesty that violates laws against fraud, embezzlement, and deceptive business practices. White-collar criminals generally get lighter sentences than those committing violent crimes, even though their crimes may ultimately affect more people.

white-collar worker   a categorical term referring to office workers and executives who wear white shirts and do nothing in the course of their work that might get them dirty.

White-collar workers, whose professions and incomes vary widely, have not voted as a bloc, but they are generally considered to be more conservative than blue-collar workers, although, in the 1980s, many of the latter voted conservatively also.

white ethnics   whites from eastern Europe, North Africa, or other Mediterranean areas.

white flight   the stampede of whites from big cities to the suburbs to try to escape crime, fear, and the increasing minority and immigrant populations.

white hats   good guys.

White House   the residence and office of the president of the United States. President Bill Clinton has called the White House the "crown jewel of the federal penitentiary system," presumably in reference to his feelings of being imprisoned in his job and "home" without privacy or a real life. The White House was originally painted white to cover up damage from being torched by British troops in the War of 1812. Address: 1600 Pennsylvania Avenue, Washington, D.C. Tel.: (202) 456-1414; website: www.whitehouse.gov

white paper   a thorough study and official government report on a specific subject.

white primary   a primary election in the South where psychological, physical, and economic means were used to prevent African Americans and any other nonwhites from voting. Starting in the 1960s, the U.S. Supreme Court has declared white primaries unconstitutional several times, including rejecting the theory that the Democratic Party was a private club that could set its own conditions for membership.

whitewash   to gloss over or hide faults, malfeasance, defects, or corruption of an office-holder as if they did not exist.

Whitewater   a failed Arkansas land development project that Hillary Rodham Clinton's law firm represented while her husband, President Bill Clinton, served as governor of Arkansas. The U.S. Department of Justice carried out investigations pertaining to the activities of the Madison Guaranty Savings and Loan and its demise, the Clintons' alleged involvement in both entities, and whether any improprieties occurred. Independent counsel Kenneth Starr eventually cleared the Clintons of any wrong-doing.

wholesale politics   going directly to the voters with the goods or candidate.

windbag   a person, candidate, or officeholder who talks too long, pontificates, and says little.

wing nut   a partisan who seems to be out of control and will say almost anything to push his or her cause, often used in the 1990s to refer to James Carville, a Louisiana Democrat and campaign adviser who gained fame for his advice to Bill Clinton, and colorful media interviews.

winner-take-all primary   a presidential primary election in which the winner got a state's entire slate of delegates to a national convention. California used to be the prime example, since beginning in 1960 it sent the largest delegation to national conventions. All its delegates went to the primary winner, leaving candidates who ran close seconds, like Nelson Rockefeller (1964), Eugene McCarthy (1968) and Hubert Humphrey (1972) with no delegates. Since 1976, the principle of one-man one-vote prevails

and winner-take-all primaries are no longer legal.

wire service   a news service that sends out articles to media that reports on and services a large geographic area, for example, Associated Press (AP), Reuters, and United Press International (UPI).

wiretapping   the illegal use of electronic devices to listen to or record other people's telephone conversations.

Republican president Richard Nixon's campaign staff tried to wiretap the Democratic National Committee's headquarters, ultimately resulting in the Watergate scandal and President Nixon's resignation.

Wiretapping may be used legally by government agencies against suspected criminals with court approval and within certain guidelines.

witch hunt   an investigation or prosecution conducted publicly, supposedly to uncover or reveal subversive political activity, but really to harass or discredit an individual or a political group. The term comes from the old practice of eliminating or killing people who someone believed were possessed by witches or the devil.

Wobblies   See INDUSTRIAL WORKERS OF THE WORLD.

woman suffrage   the right of women to vote. In the United States woman suffrage included "women's rights" to speak at public meetings, to own property, and to divorce husbands. The crusade was led by Susan

B. Anthony, Elizabeth Cady Stanton, Lucy Stone, Belva Lockwood, and Carrie Chapman Catt, who achieved woman suffrage by the 19th Amendment to the U.S. Constitution (1920).

Women's Campaign Fund a bipartisan political action committee that helps women get elected to office. The fund provides money and campaign management, planning, and contacts. Women it supports must favor ratification of the ERA, freedom of choice on abortion, and federal funding for abortions for poor women. Address: 734 15th Street, N.W., Suite 500, Washington, D.C. 20005. Tel.: (202) 393-8164; website: www.wcfonline.org

Women's International League for Peace and Freedom an international organization founded in 1915 and dedicated to woman's suffrage, peace, social justice, and feminism. The Women's League achieved its highest membership in the 1930s and lost many during World War II, which was considered a "just" war. Working in the 1990s toward the Women's Peace and Justice Treaty of the Americas, the group's current goals include shifting the federal budget away from the military and toward education, health care, nutrition, and housing, a comprehensive nuclear test ban treaty, eradicating racism, and developing women's empowerment. Address: 1213 Race Street, Philadelphia, Pa. 19107. Tel.: (215) 563-7110; FAX: (215) 563-5527; e-mail: wilpfnatl@ igc.apc.org; websites: www.wilpf.org or in Canada: web.net/-wilpfto

Women's Liberation Movement known pejoratively to those who oppose or deride it as "Women's Lib," a movement beginning in the 1960s to gain and maintain equal economic and social rights for women, including equal pay for equal work, the right to choose whether or not to have an abortion, subsidized or employer-sponsored child care for working mothers, and election of more women to public office. Outspoken original leaders include Betty Friedan, Gloria Steinem, and Congresswoman Bella Abzug.

Women's Strike for Peace also known as the Women's International Strike for Peace, a group founded on November 1, 1961, by Washington, D.C., artist Dagmar Wilson, who organized 60 strikes for peace throughout the country, attracting 50,000 participants. Demonstrators chanted: "End the arms race—not the human race." Principally advocating nuclear disarmament, leaders wrote letters to the wives of President John F. Kennedy and Soviet premier Nikita Kruschev. Widespread favorable publicity ensued and the movement attracted well-known women such as Coretta Scott King and Mrs. Cyrus Eaton to the organization. By 1963 Women's Strike for Peace was the largest peace group in the country, with a mailing list of several hundred thousands.

In 1967 the group focused its energies against the Vietnam War, participated in peace marches, and encouraged its members to support either Senator Eugene McCarthy or Senator Robert Kennedy for president. WSP continued its mixed blend of demonstrations, persuasion, contributions, and political support for campaigns, including the election of Bella Abzug (D–N.Y.) to Congress.

wonk   a person, usually male, who gets his kicks out of nerd-like devotion and intensity of political thought and creative planning. A wonk usually loves all the details of any subject. See also POLICY WONK.

work a room   to meet everyone in a room with the hope of leaving a good impression and encountering the most important people in that room. To work a room most successfully, one should leave with some names, addresses, and phone numbers of the people with whom one wants more contact.

working class   theoretically blue-collar workers or all those who are not white-collar workers, such as industrial assembly-line workers, construction workers, filling station attendants, or food service personnel who may or may not own their own home.

Wounded Knee   (1) a small settlement and creek on the Pine Ridge Indian Reservation in southwestern South Dakota that was the site of two conflicts between Native American Indians and the U. S. Government. (2) the accepted name for one of two massacres and conflicts at Wounded Knee.

In the first massacre (December 29, 1890) the U.S. government, which had drastically reduced the size of the Teton Sioux Indian Reservation, used the army to kill Chief Sitting Bull and 144 other Indians, including women and children running away, in what was supposedly the final defeat of the Indians by whites.

The second battle of Wounded Knee occurred after 200 American Indian Movement (AIM) members, led by Russell Means and Dennis Banks, took over Wounded Knee (February 28, 1973), declared it to be the Independent Ogala Sioux Nation and vowed to stay until the U.S. Government met their demands for new tribal leaders, reviews of all Indian–U.S. treaties, and a Senate investigation of treatment of Indians. Federal marshals surrounded the Indians until May 8, 1973, when the Indians surrendered their arms upon promises of negotiations. Two Indians died, and one marshall was wounded in this confrontation.

writ   (1) a court order. (2) a legal document ordering prohibition or performance of some action.

Writ of Habeas Corpus   a court order to produce a person in court or argue why you are allowed to hold him/her in jail. The judge determines the legality of the detention in regard to the prisoner's rights, often preventing long, illegal detentions.

write-in candidate   a candidate whose name does not appear on a ballot either because he/she missed the filing deadline, was not nominated, or decided too late to run. A write-in candidate often has the confidence (misguided or not) that he/she can win. Write-in candidacies require extensive education campaigns on the issues as well as to get voters to write the candidate's name in on their ballots. They are usually protest efforts to gain publicity and build support with no practical chance of winning. Occasionally write-in candidates win.

write-in vote   the total of write-in votes for people whose names do not appear on the ballot. Only five write-in candidates won election to Congress in the 20th century.

WTO (World Trade Organization)   an international organization of 136 countries, created in GATT meetings in 1994 to facilitate international trade and to set rules of trade and other multilateral economic agreements and all aspects of trade and economic policies. WTO's annual budget is about $83 million (U.S.) as of 2000. The WTO gives legal and economic analyses, provides technical support to developing countries, and helps resolves trade disputes.

When WTO international representatives met in Seattle in 2000, thousands of protesters, including elected officials, demonstrated disruptively against the organization on the basis that the WTO and its members are not elected by member countries and therefore do not represent the will or views of each country's people, yet make trade and labor policies affecting the people of member countries, sometimes favoring the corporations and taking advantage of workers. Helped by relatively violent treatment by Seattle police, protesters gained worldwide publicity and caused reevaluation of the WTO's status, power, and policies.

Address: Centre William Rappard, Rue de Lausanne 154, CH-1211, Geneva, 21, Switzerland. Tel.: (41-22) 739-51-11 or (41-22) 739-50-07 (information); FAX: (41-22) 739-54-58; e-mail: enquiries@wto.org; website: www.wto.org

WWJD   "What Would Jesus Do?", a born-again Christian self-examination question used to help the person decide what to do or how to vote, found on bracelets, signs, and other forms of private and public display.

xenophobia hatred or fear of strangers and foreigners.

While xenophobia can result from many circumstances, recent displays of it seem to be rooted in economic problems in the United States and throughout the world. Loss of jobs and fears of such losses with the possibilities of being replaced by an immigrant worker from another country have motivated conservative officeholders to capitalize on and incite xenophobia. Before and while visiting Japan late in 1991, President George H. W. Bush attempted to arouse fear of Japan and the Japanese as the causes of American economic problems. In the early 1990s, fear of massive immigration spread to more than 60 percent of the population (*Newsweek,* August 9, 1993) as the poor and uneducated teemed legally and illegally across American borders.

Historically refugees from poorer countries migrate to countries where they can find work, often working for lower wages than locals, sometimes displacing local workers by demanding less. Xenophobia develops among the natives, with varied results. Young Irish people travel to England to work in the fishing industry and are absorbed into the local populace. Turks and eastern Europeans migrate to Germany and stand out because they have darker skin and unknown or unfamiliar habits and customs and become targets of prejudice, resentment, hatred, and violence. German thinking is still tainted by the added phobia against any and all foreigners, believing that they are less pure than Germans and lack their pristine Aryan blood. But one needs only to have a pocket picked in Berlin by a Gypsy to begin to comprehend the phobia. French citizens suffer some xenophobia against "North Africans," who come to escape oppression and poverty and work at jobs formerly held by Portuguese, Spaniards, and poor French. Since the late 1800s many Americans have opposed Asian immigration, particularly Chinese, by protest and statute, fearful of job market invasions.

Real reasons to debate immigration policies, open borders, and asylum must be differentiated from xenophobia.

XYZ Affair the inept attempt by French government officials to demand bribes of American envoys John Marshall, John Jay, and Elbridge Gerry in 1798 to obtain access to and influence with French foreign minister Talleyrand (Charles Maurice de Talleyrand-Périgord). The three French operatives were given the code names of X, Y, and Z in communications back to the United States. The case added briefly to anti-French sentiment, but President John Adams overreacted with passage of the Alien and Sedition Acts (1798).

yahoo a politician who tries to overpower others but lacks judgment, experience, sensitivity, or finesse. This use of the word comes from the name of the brutes who lived in trees in Jonathan Swift's *Gulliver's Travels* (1726).

Yalta Conference the last of the wartime conferences among Allied leaders, U.S. president Franklin Delano Roosevelt, Soviet chairman Joseph Stalin, and British prime minister Winston Churchill, held February 4–11, 1945, at Yalta, Crimea, U.S.S.R., to reach an agreement on final strategy in World War II and the period after the anticipated Axis (Germany and Japan) surrender. The leaders discussed topics such as possible Soviet entry into the war against Japan, governing a conquered Germany and four-power (with France) occupation of Germany, control of German industry to stop rearmament, reparations programs, elimination of Nazi influence, and creation of the United Nations.

For decades conservatives criticized the agreements as being too soft on communism by giving Stalin too great an opportunity to force pro-Soviet factions into power in Poland, Hungary, Romania, and other Eastern European countries in return for what became a meaningless declaration of war on Japan (the atomic bomb did not yet exist) and a broken pledge of postwar cooperation.

Defenders argue that the problem was not the agreements, but Stalin's violation of them. The agreements are also defended as reasonable and as being important to Allied victory. Stalin took advantage of Roosevelt's death (April 12, 1945) and of the weakened position of Great Britain to create "satellite" Soviet-controlled governments. He become increasingly uncooperative and belligerent.

Year of the Woman 1992, the year in which more women were elected to the U.S. Congress and to statewide office than ever before.

Some causes for women's electoral successes in 1992 include long-term efforts by the National Women's Political Caucus (NWPC), the National Organization for Women (NOW), disgust with the government as run by men, and the Clarence Thomas U.S. Supreme Court Justice nomination hearings in which sexual harassment was discussed before a national television audience. The makeup of the then all-male Senate Judiciary Committee and its conduct also inspired women to vote for women.

yellow dog Democrat   an expression to describe a Democrat who is so loyal to his/her party that he/she would vote for a "yellow dog" before any Republican.

yellow journalism   a term originating in the 1890s to describe sensationalistic, inflammatory, irresponsible newspaper (and now electronic media) journalism with the aim to incite feelings. William Randolph Hearst engaged in yellow journalism by stirring up hatred of Spain in the months before the Spanish-American War. Yellow journalism originated with the "Yellow Kid," America's first comic strip, which appeared in Joseph Pulitzer's *New York World,* known for vulgar sensationalism.

yellow peril   a late 19th- and early 20th-century term for American fears of and resistance to increasing Japanese and Chinese immigration to the United States, coinciding with Japan's rise as a military power.

Young Americans for Freedom (YAF)   an organization of arch-conservative student activists that devel-

oped from Senator Barry Goldwater's (R–Ariz.) 1964 presidential campaign. Chapters showed up on college campuses in response to liberal and "new left" college student organizations in the 1960s and 1970s. Today there are only three known college chapters.

Young Democrats of America high school, college, and twenty-something Democratic clubs whose members meet to discuss and work for political issues and Democratic candidates. Young Democrat membership reached its pinnacle of activity and influence in the 1960s and is on the rise again. Address: Democratic National Committee, 430 South Capitol Street, S.E., Washington, D.C. 20003. Tel.: (202) 863-8000; website: www. yda.org

Young Republicans National Federation high school, college, and twenty-something Republicans who meet to discuss and work for political issues and Republican candidates. Affiliated with the Republican National Committee, Young Republican membership never reached that of Young Democrats but they, too, still exist. Address: 600 Pennsylvania Ave., S.E., Washington, D.C. 20003. Tel.: (202) 608-1417; FAX: (202) 608-1430; website: www.rnc.org; College Republicans: same address. Tel.: (202) 608-1411; FAX: (202) 608-1429.

Young Turks   (1) originally a young group of Turkish army officers at the time of the Ottoman Empire's collapse who wanted to depose the old leaders and modernize Turkey (1910–1918). (2) newly elected members of Congress who are full of energy and enthusiasm, are not yet broken down by the system, and threaten and plot (usually unsuccessfully) to replace older leaders or eliminate the hierarchical system.

yuppies 1980s term for young, upwardly mobile professionals, meaning twenty- or thirty-something white college graduates who made lots of money quickly in white-collar jobs, engaged in conspicuous consumption, and generally voted somewhat conservatively for candidates and programs they believed would keep them in the comfort to which they had become accustomed. Yuppiedom disintegrated in the late 1980s. See also ME GENERATION.

zero-base budget a budget that starts from scratch every year, with nothing held over from previous years, and requiring justification of every entry.

zinger an unexpected line in a political speech that catches both supporters and opponents off-guard and appears, at least momentarily, to clinch the speaker's success.

Zionism yearning for a homeland or a movement to establish, protect, and advance an independent Jewish state of Israel. Currently the term also refers to the beliefs held by anyone that there should be a separate, protected Jewish state. Some Zionists claim Israeli sovereignty includes the West Bank, Jordan River, Gaza Strip, and Golan Heights. Diplomatic disputes, terrorist killings, rapes, and three wars have occurred in part because of these claims.

Hungarian-born Parisian journalist Teodore Herzl founded the movement in 1895, and it spread rapidly. Many Jews opposed the idea of a Jewish state, citing Jews' progress and some diminishment of anti-Semitism in pre–world War I Europe. World War I, the breakup of the Ottoman Empire, the separation of Palestine, and the British pledge of a Jewish homeland in the 1917 Balfour Declaration gave hope to Zionist leader Chaim Weizmann. Israel was finally founded as an independent nation in 1948, carved out of Palestine, which had been a British protectorate.

In 1993, an agreement of intent was signed by the Palestine Liberation Organization (PLO) and Israel at the White House to give the Gaza Strip and Jerico to the Palestinians as homelands.

zoning the schematic division and labeling of a city or county into areas according to use: residential, commercial, open space, single or multifamily dwellings, recreation, industrial, and light industrial to name a few.

Some conservatives see zoning as an infringement on their personal right to make a profit and on their civil rights, particularly when they want to do something with their land that does not comply with zoning regulations. Liberals generally favor zoning for balanced living, good planning, and ecological protection.

APPENDIXES

THE CONSTITUTION OF THE UNITED STATES OF AMERICA

We the people of the United States, in order to form a more perfect union, establish justice, insure domestic tranquility, provide for the common defense, promote the general welfare, and secure the blessings of liberty to ourselves and our posterity, do ordain and establish this Constitution for the United States of America.

ARTICLE I

Section 1. All legislative powers herein granted shall be vested in a Congress of the United States, which shall consist of a Senate and House of Representatives.

Section 2. The House of Representatives shall be composed of members chosen every second year by the people of the several states, and the electors in each state shall have the qualifications requisite for electors of the most numerous branch of the state legislature.

No person shall be a Representative who shall not have attained to the age of twenty five years, and been seven years a citizen of the United States, and who shall not, when elected, be an inhabitant of that state in which he shall be chosen.

Representatives and direct taxes shall be apportioned among the several states which may be included within this union, according to their respective numbers, which shall be determined by adding to the whole number of free persons, including those bound to service for a term of years, and excluding Indians not taxed, three fifths of all other Persons. The actual Enumeration shall be made within three years after the first meeting of the Congress of the United States, and within every subsequent term of ten years, in such manner as they shall by law direct. The number of Representatives shall not exceed one for every thirty thousand, but each state shall have at least one Representative; and until such enumeration shall be made, the state of New Hampshire shall be entitled to choose three, Massachusetts eight, Rhode Island and Providence Plantations one, Connecticut five, New York six, New Jersey four, Pennsylvania eight, Delaware one, Maryland six, Virginia ten, North Carolina five, South Carolina five, and Georgia three.

When vacancies happen in the Representation from any state, the executive authority thereof shall issue writs of election to fill such vacancies.

The House of Representatives shall choose their speaker and other officers; and shall have the sole power of impeachment.

Section 3. The Senate of the United States shall be composed of two Senators from each state, chosen by the legislature thereof, for six years; and each Senator shall have one vote. Immediately after they shall be assembled in consequence of the first election, they shall be divided as equally as may be into three classes. The seats of the Senators of the first class shall be vacated at the expiration of the second year, of the second class at the expiration of the fourth year, and the third class at the expiration of the sixth year, so that one third may be chosen every second year; and if vacancies happen by resignation, or otherwise, during the recess of the legislature of any state, the executive thereof may make temporary appointments until the next meeting of the legislature, which shall then fill such vacancies.

No person shall be a Senator who shall not have attained to the age of thirty years, and been nine years a citizen of the United States and who shall not, when elected, be an inhabitant of that state for which he shall be chosen.

The Vice President of the United States shall be President of the Senate, but shall have no vote, unless they be equally divided.

The Senate shall choose their other officers, and also a President pro tempore, in the absence of the Vice President, or when he shall exercise the office of President of the United States.

The Senate shall have the sole power to try all impeachments. When sitting for that purpose, they shall be on oath or affirmation. When the President of the United States is tried, the Chief Justice shall preside: And no person shall be convicted without the concurrence of two thirds of the members present.

Judgment in cases of impeachment shall not extend further than to removal from office, and disqualification to hold and enjoy any office of honor, trust or profit under the United States: but the party convicted shall nevertheless be liable and subject to indictment, trial, judgment and punishment, according to law.

Section 4. The times, places and manner of holding elections for Senators and Representatives, shall be prescribed in each state by the legislature thereof; but the Congress may at any time by law make or alter such regulations, except as to the places of choosing Senators.

The Congress shall assemble at least once in every year, and such meeting shall be on the first Monday in December, unless they shall by law appoint a different day.

Section 5. Each House shall be the judge of the elections, returns and qualifications of its own members, and a majority of each shall constitute a quorum to do business; but a smaller number may adjourn from day to day, and may be authorized to compel the attendance of absent members, in such manner, and under such penalties as each House may provide.

Each House may determine the rules of its proceedings, punish its members for disorderly behavior, and, with the concurrence of two thirds, expel a member.

Each House shall keep a journal of its proceedings, and from time to time publish the same, excepting such parts as may in their judgment require secrecy; and the yeas and nays of the members of either House on any question shall, at the desire of one fifth of those present, be entered on the journal.

Neither House, during the session of Congress, shall, without the consent of the other, adjourn for more than three days, nor to any other place than that in which the two Houses shall be sitting.

Section 6. The Senators and Representatives shall receive a compensation for their services, to be ascertained by law, and paid out of the treasury of the United States. They shall in all cases, except treason, felony and breach of the peace, be privileged from arrest during their attendance at the session of their respective Houses, and in going to and returning from the same; and for any speech or debate in either House, they shall not be questioned in any other place. No Senator or Representative shall, during the time for which he was elected, be appointed to any civil office under the authority of the United States, which shall have been created, or the emoluments whereof shall have been increased during such time: and no person holding any office under the United States, shall be a member of either House during his continuance in office.

Section 7. All bills for raising revenue shall originate in the House of Representatives; but the Senate may propose or concur with amendments as on other Bills.

Every bill which shall have passed the House of Representatives and the Senate, shall, before it become a law, be presented to the President of the United States; if he approve he shall sign it, but if not he shall return it, with his objections to that House in which it shall have originated, who shall enter the objections at large on their journal, and proceed to reconsider it. If after such reconsideration two thirds of that House shall agree to pass the bill, it shall be sent, together with the objections, to the other House, by which it shall likewise be reconsidered, and if approved by two thirds of that House, it shall become a law. But in all such cases the votes of both Houses shall be determined by yeas and nays, and the names of the persons voting for and against the bill shall be entered on the journal of each House respectively. If any bill shall not be returned by the President within ten days (Sundays excepted) after it shall have been presented to him, the same shall be a law, in like manner as if he had signed it, unless the Congress by their adjournment prevent its return, in which case it shall not be a law.

Every order, resolution, or vote to which the concurrence of the Senate and House of Representatives may be necessary (except on a question of adjournment) shall be presented to the President of the United States; and before the same shall take effect, shall be approved by him, or being disapproved by him, shall be repassed by two thirds of the Senate and House of Representatives, according to the rules and limitations prescribed in the case of a bill.

Section 8. The Congress shall have power to lay and collect taxes, duties, imposts and excises, to pay the debts and provide for the common defense and general welfare of the United States; but all duties, imposts and excises shall be uniform throughout the United States;

To borrow money on the credit of the United States;

To regulate commerce with foreign nations, and among the several states, and with the Indian tribes;

To establish a uniform rule of naturalization, and uniform laws on the subject of bankruptcies throughout the United States;

To coin money, regulate the value thereof, and of foreign coin, and fix the standard of weights and measures;

To provide for the punishment of counterfeiting the securities and current coin of the United States;

To establish post offices and post roads;

To promote the progress of science and useful arts, by securing for limited times to authors and inventors the exclusive right to their respective writings and discoveries;

To constitute tribunals inferior to the Supreme Court;

To define and punish piracies and felonies committed on the high seas, and offenses against the law of nations;

To declare war, grant letters of marque and reprisal, and make rules concerning captures on land and water;

To raise and support armies, but no appropriation of money to that use shall be for a longer term than two years;

To provide and maintain a navy;

To make rules for the government and regulation of the land and naval forces;

To provide for calling forth the militia to execute the laws of the union, suppress insurrections and repel invasions;

To provide for organizing, arming, and disciplining, the militia, and for governing such part of them as may be employed in the service of the United States, reserving to the states respectively, the appointment of the officers, and the authority of training the militia according to the discipline prescribed by Congress;

To exercise exclusive legislation in all cases whatsoever, over such District (not exceeding ten miles square) as may, by cession of particular states, and the acceptance of Congress, become the seat of the government of the United States, and to exercise like authority over all places purchased by the consent of the legislature of the state in which the same shall be, for the erection of forts, magazines, arsenals, dockyards, and other needful buildings;—And

To make all laws which shall be necessary and proper for carrying into execution the foregoing powers, and all other powers vested by this Constitution in the government of the United States, or in any department or officer thereof.

Section 9. The migration or importation of such persons as any of the states now existing shall think proper to admit, shall not be prohibited by the Congress prior to the year one thousand eight hundred and eight, but a tax or duty may be imposed on such importation, not exceeding ten dollars for each person.

The privilege of the writ of habeas corpus shall not be suspended, unless when in cases of rebellion or invasion the public safety may require it.

No bill of attainder or ex post facto Law shall be passed.

No capitation, or other direct, tax shall be laid, unless in proportion to the census or enumeration herein before directed to be taken.

No tax or duty shall be laid on articles exported from any state.

No preference shall be given by any regulation of commerce or revenue to the ports of one state over those of another: nor shall vessels bound to, or from, one state, be obliged to enter, clear or pay duties in another.

No money shall be drawn from the treasury, but in consequence of appropriations made by law; and a regular statement and account of receipts and expenditures of all public money shall be published from time to time.

No title of nobility shall be granted by the United States: and no person holding any office of profit or trust under them, shall, without the consent of the Congress, accept of any present, emolument, office, or title, of any kind whatever, from any king, prince, or foreign state.

Section 10. No state shall enter into any treaty, alliance, or confederation; grant letters of marque and reprisal; coin money; emit bills of credit; make anything but gold and silver coin a tender in payment of debts; pass any bill of attainder, ex post facto law, or law impairing the obligation of contracts, or grant any title of nobility.

No state shall, without the consent of the Congress, lay any imposts or duties on imports or exports, except what may be absolutely necessary for executing its inspection laws: and the net produce of all duties and imposts, laid by any state on imports or exports, shall be for the use of the treasury of the United States; and all such laws shall be subject to the revision and control of the Congress.

No state shall, without the consent of Congress, lay any duty of tonnage, keep troops, or ships of war in time of peace, enter into any agreement or compact with another state, or with a foreign power, or engage in war, unless actually invaded, or in such imminent danger as will not admit of delay.

ARTICLE II

Section 1. The executive power shall be vested in a President of the United States of America. He shall hold his office during the term of four years, and, together with the Vice President, chosen for the same term, be elected, as follows:

Each state shall appoint, in such manner as the Legislature thereof may direct, a number of electors, equal to the whole number of Senators and Representatives to which the State may be entitled in the Congress: but no Senator or Representative, or person holding an office of trust or profit under the United States, shall be appointed an elector.

The electors shall meet in their respective states, and vote by ballot for two persons, of whom one at least shall not be an inhabitant of the same state with themselves. And they shall make a list of all the persons voted for, and of the number of votes for each; which list

they shall sign and certify, and transmit sealed to the seat of the government of the United States, directed to the President of the Senate. The President of the Senate shall, in the presence of the Senate and House of Representatives, open all the certificates, and the votes shall then be counted. The person having the greatest number of votes shall be the President, if such number be a majority of the whole number of electors appointed; and if there be more than one who have such majority, and have an equal number of votes, then the House of Representatives shall immediately choose by ballot one of them for President; and if no person have a majority, then from the five highest on the list the said House shall in like manner choose the President. But in choosing the President, the votes shall be taken by States, the representation from each state having one vote; A quorum for this purpose shall consist of a member or members from two thirds of the states, and a majority of all the states shall be necessary to a choice. In every case, after the choice of the President, the person having the greatest number of votes of the electors shall be the Vice President. But if there should remain two or more who have equal votes, the Senate shall choose from them by ballot the Vice President.

The Congress may determine the time of choosing the electors, and the day on which they shall give their votes; which day shall be the same throughout the United States.

No person except a natural born citizen, or a citizen of the United States, at the time of the adoption of this Constitution, shall be eligible to the office of President; neither shall any person be eligible to that office who shall not have attained to the age of thirty five years, and been fourteen Years a resident within the United States.

In case of the removal of the President from office, or of his death, resignation, or inability to discharge the powers and duties of the said office, the same shall devolve on the Vice President, and the Congress may by law provide for the case of removal, death, resignation or inability, both of the President and Vice President, declaring what officer shall then act as President, and such officer shall act accordingly, until the disability be removed, or a President shall be elected.

The President shall, at stated times, receive for his services, a compensation, which shall neither be increased nor diminished during the period for which he shall have been elected, and he shall not receive within that period any other emolument from the United States, or any of them.

Before he enter on the execution of his office, he shall take the following oath or affirmation:—"I do solemnly swear (or affirm) that I will faithfully execute the office of President of the United States, and will to the best of my ability, preserve, protect and defend the Constitution of the United States."

Section 2. The President shall be commander in chief of the Army and Navy of the United States, and of the militia of the several states, when called into the actual service of the United States; he may require the opinion, in writing, of the principal officer in each of the executive departments, on any subject relating to the duties of their respective offices, and he shall have power to grant reprieves and pardons for offenses against the United States, except in cases of impeachment.

He shall have power, by and with the advice and consent of the Senate, to make treaties, provided two thirds of the Senators present concur; and he shall nominate, and by and with the advice and consent of the Senate, shall appoint ambassadors, other public ministers and consuls, judges of the Supreme Court, and all other officers of the United States, whose appointments are not herein otherwise provided for, and which shall be established by law: but the Congress may by law vest the appointment of such inferior officers, as they think proper, in the President alone, in the courts of law, or in the heads of departments.

The President shall have power to fill up all vacancies that may happen during the recess of the Senate, by granting commissions which shall expire at the end of their next session.

Section 3. He shall from time to time give to the Congress information of the state of the union, and recommend to their consideration such measures as he shall judge necessary and expedient; he may, on extraordinary occasions, convene both Houses, or either of them, and in case of disagreement between them, with respect to the time of adjournment, he may adjourn them to such time as he shall think proper; he shall receive ambassadors and other public ministers; he shall take care that the laws be faithfully executed, and shall commission all the officers of the United States.

Section 4. The President, Vice President and all civil officers of the United States, shall be removed from office on impeachment for, and conviction of, treason, bribery, or other high crimes and misdemeanors.

ARTICLE III

Section 1. The judicial power of the United States, shall be vested in one Supreme Court, and in such inferior courts as the Congress may from time to time ordain and establish. The judges, both of the supreme and inferior courts, shall hold their offices during good behavior, and shall, at stated times, receive for their services, a compensation, which shall not be diminished during their continuance in office.

Section 2. The judicial power shall extend to all cases, in law and equity, arising under this Constitution, the laws of the United States, and treaties made, or which shall be made, under their authority;—to all cases affecting ambassadors, other public ministers and consuls;—to all cases of admiralty and maritime jurisdiction;—to controversies to which the United States shall be a party;—to controversies between two or more states;—between a state and citizens of another state;—between citizens of different states;—between citizens of the same state claiming lands under grants of different states, and between a state, or the citizens thereof, and foreign states, citizens or subjects.

In all cases affecting ambassadors, other public ministers and consuls, and those in which a state shall be party, the Supreme Court shall have original jurisdiction. In all the other cases before mentioned, the Supreme Court shall have appellate jurisdiction, both as to law and fact, with such exceptions, and under such regulations as the Congress shall make.

The trial of all crimes, except in cases of impeachment, shall be by jury; and such trial shall be held in the state where the said crimes shall have been committed; but when not committed within any state, the trial shall be at such place or places as the Congress may by law have directed.

Section 3. Treason against the United States, shall consist only in levying war against them, or in adhering to their enemies, giving them aid and comfort. No person shall be convicted of treason unless on the testimony of two witnesses to the same overt act, or on confession in open court.

The Congress shall have power to declare the punishment of treason, but no attainder of treason shall work corruption of blood, or forfeiture except during the life of the person attainted.

ARTICLE IV

Section 1. Full faith and credit shall be given in each state to the public acts, records, and judicial proceedings of every other state. And the Congress may by general laws prescribe the manner in which such acts, records, and proceedings shall be proved, and the effect thereof.

Section 2. The citizens of each state shall be entitled to all privileges and immunities of citizens in the several states.

A person charged in any state with treason, felony, or other crime, who shall flee from justice, and be found in another state, shall on demand of the executive authority of the state from which he fled, be delivered up, to be removed to the state having jurisdiction of the crime.

No person held to service or labor in one state, under the laws thereof, escaping into another, shall, in consequence of any law or regulation therein, be discharged from such service or labor, but shall be delivered up on claim of the party to whom such service or labor may be due.

Section 3. New states may be admitted by the Congress into this union; but no new states shall be formed or erected within the jurisdiction of any other state; nor any state be formed by the junction of two or more states, or parts of states, without the consent of the legislatures of the states concerned as well as of the Congress.

The Congress shall have power to dispose of and make all needful rules and regulations respecting the territory or other property belonging to the United States; and nothing in this Constitution shall be so construed as to prejudice any claims of the United States, or of any particular state.

Section 4. The United States shall guarantee to every state in this union a republican form of government, and shall protect each of them against invasion; and on application of the legislature, or of the executive (when the legislature cannot be convened) against domestic violence.

ARTICLE V

The Congress, whenever two thirds of both houses shall deem it necessary, shall propose amendments to this Constitution, or, on the application of the legislatures of two thirds of the several states, shall call a convention for proposing amendments, which, in either case, shall be valid to all intents and purposes, as part of this Constitution, when ratified by the legislatures of three fourths of the several states, or by conventions in three fourths thereof, as the one or the other mode of ratification may be proposed by the Congress; provided that no amendment which may be made prior to the year one thousand eight hundred and eight shall in any manner affect the first and fourth clauses in the ninth section of the first article; and that no state, without its consent, shall be deprived of its equal suffrage in the Senate.

ARTICLE VI

All debts contracted and engagements entered into, before the adoption of this Constitution, shall be as valid against the United States under this Constitution, as under the Confederation.

This Constitution, and the laws of the United States which shall be made in pursuance thereof; and all treaties made, or which shall be made, under the authority of the United States, shall be the supreme law of the land; and the judges in every state shall be bound thereby, anything in the Constitution or laws of any State to the contrary notwithstanding.

The Senators and Representatives before mentioned, and the members of the several state legislatures, and all executive and judicial officers, both of the United States and of the several states, shall be bound by oath or affirmation, to support this Constitution; but no religious test shall ever be required as a qualification to any office or public trust under the United States.

ARTICLE VII

The ratification of the conventions of nine states, shall be sufficient for the establishment of this Constitution between the states so ratifying the same.

Done in convention by the unanimous consent of the states present the seventeenth day of September in the year of our Lord one thousand seven hundred and eighty seven and of the independence of the United States of America the twelfth. In witness whereof We have hereunto subscribed our Names,

G. WASHINGTON: Presidt. and deputy from Virginia

New Hampshire: JOHN LANGDON, NICHOLAS GILMAN

Massachusetts: NATHANIEL GORHAM, RUFUS KING

Connecticut: Wm: SAML. JOHNSON, ROGER SHERMAN

New York: ALEXANDER HAMILTON

New Jersey: WIL LIVINGSTON, DAVID BREARLY, WM. PATERSON, JONA: DAYTON

Pennsylvania: B. FRANKLIN, THOMAS MIFFLIN, ROBT. MORRIS, GEO. CLYMER, THOS. FITZSIMONS, JARED INGERSOLL, JAMES WILSON, GOUV MORRIS

Delaware: GEO: READ, GUNNING BEDFORD JUN, JOHN DICKINSON, RICHARD BASSETT, JACO: BROOM

Maryland: JAMES MCHENRY, DAN OF ST THOS. JENIFER, DANL CARROLL

Virginia: JOHN BLAIR—, JAMES MADISON JR.

North Carolina: WM. BLOUNT, RICHD. DOBBS SPAIGHT, HU WILLIAMSON

South Carolina: J. RUTLEDGE, CHARLES COTESWORTH PINCKNEY, CHARLES PINCKNEY, PIERCE BUTLER

Georgia: WILLIAM FEW, ABR BALDWIN

AMENDMENTS TO THE CONSTITUTION OF THE UNITED STATES

(The first ten amendments known as the Bill of Rights were passed by Congress on September 25, 1789 and ratified by sufficient states on December 25, 1791)

AMENDMENT I (1791)

Congress shall make no law respecting an establishment of religion, or prohibiting the free exercise thereof; or abridging the freedom of speech, or of the press; or the right of the people peaceably to assemble, and to petition the government for a redress of grievances.

AMENDMENT II (1791)

A well regulated militia, being necessary to the security of a free state, the right of the people to keep and bear arms, shall not be infringed.

AMENDMENT III (1791)

No soldier shall, in time of peace be quartered in any house, without the consent of the owner, nor in time of war, but in a manner to be prescribed by law.

AMENDMENT IV (1791)

The right of the people to be secure in their persons, houses, papers, and effects, against unreasonable searches and seizures, shall not be violated, and no warrants shall issue, but upon probable cause, supported by oath or affirmation, and particularly describing the place to be searched, and the persons or things to be seized.

AMENDMENT V (1791)

No person shall be held to answer for a capital, or otherwise infamous crime, unless on a presentment or indictment of a grand jury, except in cases arising in the land or naval forces, or in the militia, when in actual service in time of war or public danger; nor shall any person be subject for the same offense to be twice put in jeopardy of life or limb; nor shall be compelled in any criminal case to be a witness against himself, nor be deprived of life, liberty, or property, without due process of law; nor shall private property be taken for public use, without just compensation.

AMENDMENT VI (1791)

In all criminal prosecutions, the accused shall enjoy the right to a speedy and public trial, by an impartial jury of the state and district wherein the crime shall have been committed, which district shall have been previously ascertained by law, and to be informed of the nature and cause of the accusation; to be confronted with the witnesses against him; to have compulsory process for obtaining witnesses in his favor, and to have the assistance of counsel for his defense.

AMENDMENT VII (1791)

In suits at common law, where the value in controversy shall exceed twenty dollars, the right of trial by jury shall be preserved, and no fact tried by a jury, shall be otherwise reexamined in any court of the United States, than according to the rules of the common law.

AMENDMENT VIII (1791)

Excessive bail shall not be required, nor excessive fines imposed, nor cruel and unusual punishments inflicted.

AMENDMENT IX (1791)

The enumeration in the Constitution, of certain rights, shall not be construed to deny or disparage others retained by the people.

AMENDMENT X (1791)

The powers not delegated to the United States by the Constitution, nor prohibited by it to the states, are reserved to the states respectively, or to the people.

AMENDMENT XI (1798)

The judicial power of the United States shall not be construed to extend to any suit in law or equity, commenced or prosecuted against one of the United States by citizens of another state, or by citizens or subjects of any foreign state.

AMENDMENT XII (1804)

The electors shall meet in their respective states and vote by ballot for President and Vice-President, one of whom, at least, shall not be an inhabitant of the same state with themselves; they shall name in their ballots the person voted for as President, and in distinct ballots the person voted for as Vice-President, and they shall make distinct lists of all persons voted for as President, and of all persons voted for as Vice-President, and of the number of votes for each, which lists they shall sign and certify, and transmit sealed to the seat of the government of the United States, directed to the President of the Senate;—The President of the Senate shall, in the presence of the Senate and House of Representatives, open all the certificates and the votes shall then be counted;—the person having the greatest number of votes for President, shall be the President, if such number be a majority of the whole number of electors appointed; and if no person have such majority, then from the persons having the highest numbers not exceeding three on the list of those voted for as President, the House of Representatives shall choose immediately, by ballot, the President. But in choosing the President, the votes shall be taken by states, the representation from each state having one vote; a quorum for this purpose shall consist of a member or members from two-thirds of the states, and a majority of all the states shall be necessary to a choice. And if the House of Representatives shall not choose a President whenever the right of choice shall devolve upon them, before the fourth day of March next following, then the Vice-President shall act as President, as in the case of the death or other constitutional disability of the President. The person having the greatest number of votes as Vice-President, shall be the Vice-President, if such number be a majority of the whole number of electors appointed, and if no person have a majority, then from the two highest numbers on the list, the Senate shall choose the Vice-President; a quorum for the purpose shall consist of two-thirds of the whole number of Senators, and a majority of the whole number shall be necessary to a choice. But no person constitutionally ineligible to the office of President shall be eligible to that of Vice-President of the United States.

AMENDMENT XIII (1865)

Section 1. Neither slavery nor involuntary servitude, except as a punishment for crime whereof the party shall have been duly convicted, shall exist within the United States, or any place subject to their jurisdiction.

Section 2. Congress shall have power to enforce this article by appropriate legislation.

AMENDMENT XIV (1868)

Section 1. All persons born or naturalized in the United States, and subject to the jurisdiction thereof, are citizens of the United States and of the state wherein they reside. No state shall make or enforce any law which shall abridge the privileges or immunities of citizens of the United States; nor shall any state deprive any person of life, liberty, or property, without due process of law; nor deny to any person within its jurisdiction the equal protection of the laws.

Section 2. Representatives shall be apportioned among the several states according to their respective numbers, counting the whole number of persons in each state, excluding Indians not taxed. But when the right to vote at any election for the choice of electors for President and Vice President of the United States, Representatives in Congress, the executive and judicial officers of a state, or the members of the legislature thereof, is denied to any of the male inhabitants of such state, being twenty-one years of age, and citizens of the United States, or in any way abridged, except for participation in rebellion, or other crime, the basis of representation therein shall be reduced in the proportion which the number of such male citizens shall bear to the whole number of male citizens twenty-one years of age in such state.

Section 3. No person shall be a Senator or Representative in Congress, or elector of President and Vice President, or hold any office, civil or military, under the United States, or under any state, who, having previously taken an oath, as a member of Congress, or as an officer of the United States, or as a member of any state legislature, or as an executive or judicial officer of any state, to support the Constitution of the United States, shall have engaged in insurrection or rebellion against the same, or given aid or comfort to the enemies thereof. But Congress may by a vote of two-thirds of each House, remove such disability.

Section 4. The validity of the public debt of the United States, authorized by law, including debts incurred for payment of pensions and bounties for services in suppressing insurrection or rebellion, shall not be questioned. But neither the United States nor any state shall assume or pay any debt or obligation incurred in aid of insurrection or rebellion against the United States, or any claim for the loss or emancipation of any slave; but all such debts, obligations and claims shall be held illegal and void.

Section 5. The Congress shall have power to enforce, by appropriate legislation, the provisions of this article.

AMENDMENT XV (1870)

Section 1. The right of citizens of the United States to vote shall not be denied or abridged by the United States or by any state on account of race, color, or previous condition of servitude.

Section 2. The Congress shall have power to enforce this article by appropriate legislation.

AMENDMENT XVI (1913)

The Congress shall have power to lay and collect taxes on incomes, from whatever source derived, without apportionment among the several states, and without regard to any census of enumeration.

AMENDMENT XVII (1913)

The Senate of the United States shall be composed of two Senators from each state, elected by the people thereof, for six years; and each Senator shall have one vote. The electors in each state shall have the qualifications requisite for electors of the most numerous branch of the state legislatures.

When vacancies happen in the representation of any state in the Senate, the executive authority of such state shall issue writs of election to fill such vacancies: Provided, that the legislature of any state may empower the executive thereof to make temporary appointments until the people fill the vacancies by election as the legislature may direct.

This amendment shall not be so construed as to affect the election or term of any Senator chosen before it becomes valid as part of the Constitution.

AMENDMENT XVIII (1919)

Section 1. After one year from the ratification of this article the manufacture, sale, or transportation of intoxicating liquors within, the importation thereof into, or the exportation thereof from the United States and all territory subject to the jurisdiction thereof for beverage purposes is hereby prohibited.

Section 2. The Congress and the several states shall have concurrent power to enforce this article by appropriate legislation.

Section 3. This article shall be inoperative unless it shall have been ratified as an amendment to the Constitution by the legislatures of the several states, as provided in the Constitution, within seven years from the date of the submission hereof to the states by the Congress.

AMENDMENT XIX (1920)

The right of citizens of the United States to vote shall not be denied or abridged by the United States or by any state on account of sex.

Congress shall have power to enforce this article by appropriate legislation.

AMENDMENT XX (1933)

Section 1. The terms of the President and Vice President shall end at noon on the 20th day of January, and the terms of Senators and Representatives at noon on the 3d day of January, of the years in which such terms would have ended if this article had not been ratified; and the terms of their successors shall then begin.

Section 2. The Congress shall assemble at least once in every year, and such meeting shall begin at noon on the 3d day of January, unless they shall by law appoint a different day.

Section 3. If, at the time fixed for the beginning of the term of the President, the President elect shall have died, the Vice President elect shall become President. If a President shall not have been chosen before the time fixed for the beginning of his term, or if the President elect shall have failed to quality, then the Vice President elect shall act as President until a President shall have qualified; and the Congress may by law provide for the case wherein neither a President elect nor a Vice President elect shall have qualified, declaring who shall then act as President, or the manner in which one who is to act shall be selected, and such person shall act accordingly until a President or Vice President shall have qualified.

Section 4. The Congress may by law provide for the case of the death of any of the persons from whom the House of Representatives may choose a President whenever the right of choice shall have developed upon them, and for the case

of the death of any of the persons from whom the Senate may choose a Vice President whenever the right of choice shall have devolved upon them.

Section 5. Sections 1 and 2 shall take effect on the 15th day of October following the ratification of this article.

Section 6. This article shall be inoperative unless it shall have been ratified as an amendment to the Constitution by the legislatures of three-fourths of the several states within seven years from the date of its submission.

AMENDMENT XXI (1933)

Section 1. The eighteenth article of amendment to the Constitution of the United States is hereby repealed.

Section 2. The transportation or importation into any state, territory, or possession of the United States for delivery or use therein of intoxicating liquors, in violation of the laws thereof, is hereby prohibited.

Section 3. This article shall be inoperative unless it shall have been ratified as an amendment to the Constitution by conventions in the several states, as provided in the Constitution, within seven years from the date of the submission hereof to the states by the Congress.

AMENDMENT XXII (1951)

Section 1. No person shall be elected to the office of the President more than twice, and no person who has held the office of President, or acted as President, for more than two years of a term to which some other person was elected President shall be elected to the office of the President more than once. But this article shall not apply to any person holding the office of President when this article was proposed by the Congress, and shall not prevent any person who may be holding the office of President, or acting as President, during the term within which this article becomes operative from holding the office of President or acting as President during the remainder of such term.

Section 2. This article shall be inoperative unless it shall have been ratified as an amendment to the Constitution by the legislatures of three-fourths of the several states within seven years from the date of its submission to the states by the Congress.

AMENDMENT XXIII (1961)

Section 1. The District constituting the seat of government of the United States shall appoint in such manner as the Congress may direct:

A number of electors of President and Vice President equal to the whole number of Senators and Representatives in Congress to which the District would be entitled if it were a state, but in no event more than the least populous state; they shall be in addition to those appointed by the states, but they shall be considered, for the purposes of the election of President and Vice President, to be electors appointed by a state; and they shall meet in the District and perform such duties as provided by the twelfth article of amendment.

Section 2. The Congress shall have power to enforce this article by appropriate legislation.

AMENDMENT XXIV (1964)

Section 1. The right of citizens of the United States to vote in any primary or other election for President or Vice President, for electors for President or Vice President, or for Senator or Representative in Congress, shall not be denied or abridged by the United States or any state by reason of failure to pay any poll tax or other tax.

Section 2. The Congress shall have power to enforce this article by appropriate legislation.

AMENDMENT XXV (1967)

Section 1. In case of the removal of the President from office or of his death or resignation, the Vice President shall become President.

Section 2. Whenever there is a vacancy in the office of the Vice President, the President shall nominate a Vice President who shall take office upon confirmation by a majority vote of both Houses of Congress.

Section 3. Whenever the President transmits to the President pro tempore of the Senate and the Speaker of the House of Representatives his written declaration that he is unable to discharge the powers and duties of his office, and until he transmits to them a written declaration to the contrary, such powers and duties shall be discharged by the Vice President as Acting President.

Section 4. Whenever the Vice President and a majority of either the principal officers of the executive departments or of such other body as Congress may by law provide, transmit to the President pro tempore of the Senate and the Speaker of the House of Representatives their written declaration that the President is unable to discharge the powers and duties of his office, the Vice President shall immediately assume the powers and duties of the office as Acting President.

Thereafter, when the President transmits to the President pro tempore of the Senate and the Speaker of the House of Representatives his written declaration that no inability exists, he shall resume the powers and duties of his office unless the Vice President and a majority of either the principal officers of the executive department or of such other body as Congress may by law provide, transmit within four days to the President pro tempore of the Senate and the Speaker of the House of Representatives their written declaration that the President is unable to discharge the powers and duties of his office. Thereupon Congress shall decide the issue, assembling within forty-eight hours for that purpose if not in session. If the Congress, within twenty-one days after receipt of the latter written declaration, or, if Congress is not in session, within twenty-one days after Congress is required to assemble, determines by two-thirds vote of both Houses that the President is unable to discharge the powers and duties of his office, the Vice President shall continue to discharge the same as Acting President; otherwise, the President shall resume the powers and duties of his office.

AMENDMENT XXVI (1971)

Section 1. The right of citizens of the United States, who are 18 years of age or older, to vote, shall not be denied or abridged by the United States or any state on account of age.

Section 2. The Congress shall have the power to enforce this article by appropriate legislation.

AMENDMENT XXVII (PASSED SEPT. 25, 1789; RATIFIED MAY 7, 1992)

No law varying the compensation for the services of the Senators and Representatives shall take effect until an election of Representatives shall have intervened.
When in the Course of human events, it becomes necessary for one people to dissolve the political bands which have connected them with another, and to assume among the Powers of the earth, the separate and equal station to which the Laws of Nature and of Nature's God entitle them, a decent respect to the opinions of mankind requires that they should declare the causes which impel them to the separation.

THE DECLARATION OF INDEPENDENCE

In Congress, July 4, 1776, the Unanimous Declaration of the Thirteen United States of America

We hold these truths to be self-evident, that all men are created equal, that they are endowed by their Creator with certain unalienable Rights, that among these are Life, Liberty, and the pursuit of Happiness.

That to secure these rights, Governments are instituted among Men, deriving their just powers from the consent of the governed.

That whenever any Form of Government becomes destructive of these ends, it is the Right of the People to alter or to abolish it, and to institute new Government, laying its foundation on such principles and organizing its powers in such form, as to them shall seem most likely to effect their Safety and Happiness. Prudence, indeed, will dictate that Governments long established should not be changed for light and transient causes; and accordingly all experience hath shown, that mankind are more disposed to suffer, while evils are sufferable, than to right themselves by abolishing the forms to which they are accustomed. But when a long train of abuses and usurpations, pursuing invariably the same Object, evinces a design to reduce them under absolute Despotism, it is their right, it is their duty, to throw off such Government, and to provide new Guards for their future security.

Such has been the patient sufferance of these Colonies; and such is now the necessity which constrains them to alter their former Systems of Government. The history of the present King of Great Britain is a history of repeated injuries and usurpations, all having in direct object the establishment of an absolute Tyranny over these States. To prove this, let Facts be submitted to a candid world.

He has refused his Assent to Laws, the most wholesome and necessary for the public good.

He has forbidden his Governors to pass Laws of immediate and pressing importance, unless suspended in their operation till his Assent should be obtained; and when so suspended, he has utterly neglected to attend to them.

He has refused to pass other Laws for the accommodation of large districts of people, unless those people would relinquish the right of Representation in the Legislature, a right inestimable to them and formidable to tyrants only.

He has called together legislative bodies at places unusual, uncomfortable, and distant from the depository of their public Records, for the sole purpose of fatiguing them into compliance with his measures.

He has dissolved Representative Houses repeatedly, for opposing with manly firmness his invasions on the rights of the people.

He has refused for a long time, after such dissolutions, to cause others to be elected; whereby the Legislative powers, incapable of Annihilation, have returned to the People at large for their exercise; the State remaining in the mean time exposed to all the dangers of invasion from without, and convulsion within.

He has endeavoured to prevent the population of these States; for that purpose obstructing the Laws of Naturalization of Foreigners; refusing to pass others to encourage their migrations hither, and raising the conditions of new Appropriations of Lands.

He has obstructed the Administration of Justice, by refusing his Assent to Laws for establishing Judiciary powers.

He has made Judges dependent on his Will alone, for the tenure of their offices, and the amount and payment of their salaries.

He has erected a multitude of New Offices, and sent hither swarms of Officers to harass our People, and eat out their substance.

He has kept among us, in times of peace, Standing Armies without the Consent of our legislatures.

He has affected to render the Military independent of and superior to the Civil power.

He has combined with others to subject us to a jurisdiction foreign to our constitution, and unacknowledged by our laws; giving his Assent to their Acts of pretended Legislation:

For quartering large bodies of armed troops among us:

For protecting them, by a mock Trial, from Punishment for any Murders which they should commit on the Inhabitants of these States:

For cutting off our Trade with all parts of the world:

For imposing Taxes on us without our Consent:

For depriving us in many cases, of the benefits of Trial by Jury:

For transporting us beyond Seas to be tried for pretended offences:

For abolishing the free System of English Laws in a neighbouring Province, establishing therein an Arbitrary government, and enlarging its Boundaries so as to render it at once an example and fit instrument for introducing the same absolute rule into these Colonies:

For taking away our Charters, abolishing our most valuable Laws, and altering fundamentally the Forms of our Governments:

For suspending our own Legislatures, and declaring themselves invested with power to legislate for us in all cases whatsoever.

He has abdicated Government here, by declaring us out of his Protection and waging War against us.

He has plundered our seas, ravaged our Coasts, burnt our towns, and destroyed the Lives of our people.

He is at this time transporting large armies of foreign mercenaries to compleat the works of death, desolation and tyranny, already begun with circumstances of Cruelty & perfidy scarcely paralleled in the most barbarous ages, and totally unworthy the Head of a civilized nation.

He has constrained our fellow Citizens taken Captive on the high Seas to bear

Arms against their Country, to become the executioners of their friends and Brethren, or to fall themselves by their Hands.

He has excited domestic insurrections amongst us, and has endeavoured to bring on the inhabitants of our frontiers, the merciless Indian Savages, whose known rule of warfare, is an undistinguished destruction of all ages, sexes and conditions.

In every stage of these Oppressions We have Petitioned for Redress in the most humble terms: Our repeated Petitions have been answered only by repeated injury. A Prince, whose character is thus marked by every act which may define a Tyrant, is unfit to be the ruler of a free people.

Nor have We been wanting in attention to our British brethren. We have warned them from time to time of attempts by their legislature to extend an unwarrantable jurisdiction over us. We have reminded them of the circumstances of our emigration and settlement here. We have appealed to their native justice and magnanimity, and we have conjured them by the ties of our common kindred to disavow these usurpations, which would inevitably interrupt our connections and correspondence. They too have been deaf to the voice of justice and of consanguinity. We must, therefore, acquiesce in the necessity, which denounces our Separation, and hold them, as we hold the rest of mankind, Enemies in War, in Peace Friends.

We, therefore, the Representatives of the united States of America, in General Congress, Assembled, appealing to the Supreme Judge of the world for the rectitude of our intentions, do, in the Name, and by Authority of the good People of these Colonies, solemnly publish and declare, That these United Colonies are, and of Right ought to be Free and Independent States; that they are Absolved from all Allegiance to the British Crown, and that all political connection between them and the State of Great Britain, is and ought to be totally dissolved; and that as Free and Independent States, they have full Power to levy War, conclude Peace, contract Alliances, establish Commerce, and to do all other Acts and Things which Independent States may of right do. And for the support of this Declaration, with a firm reliance on the Protection of Divine Providence, we mutually pledge to each other our Lives, our Fortunes and our sacred Honor.

JOHN HANCOCK, President
Attested,
CHARLES THOMSON, Secretary
New Hampshire
 JOSIAH BARTLETT
 WILLIAM WHIPPLE
 MATTHEW THORNTON
Massachusetts-Bay
 SAMUEL ADAMS
 JOHN ADAMS
 ROBERT TREAT PAINE
 ELBRIDGE GERRY
Rhode Island
 STEPHEN HOPKINS
 WILLIAM ELLERY
Connecticut
 ROGER SHERMAN
 SAMUEL HUNTINGTON
 WILLIAM WILLIAMS
 OLIVER WOLCOTT
Georgia
 BUTTON GWINNETT
 LYMAN HALL
 GEO. WALTON
Maryland
 SAMUEL CHASE
 WILLIAM PACA
 THOMAS STONE

CHARLES CARROLL
OF CARROLLTON

Virginia
GEORGE WYTHE
RICHARD HENRY LEE
THOMAS JEFFERSON
BENJAMIN HARRISON
THOMAS NELSON, JR.
FRANCIS LIGHTFOOT LEE
CARTER BRAXTON

New York
WILLIAM FLOYD
PHILIP LIVINGSTON
FRANCIS LEWIS
LEWIS MORRIS

Pennsylvania
ROBERT MORRIS
BENJAMIN RUSH
BENJAMIN FRANKLIN
JOHN MORTON
GEORGE CLYMER
JAMES SMITH

GEORGE TAYLOR
JAMES WILSON
GEORGE ROSS

Delaware
CAESAR RODNEY
GEORGE READ
THOMAS M'KEAN

North Carolina
WILLIAM HOOPER
JOSEPH HEWES
JOHN PENN

South Carolina
EDWARD RUTLEDGE
THOMAS HEYWARD, JR.
THOMAS LYNCH, JR.
ARTHUR MIDDLETON

New Jersey
RICHARD STOCKTON
JOHN WITHERSPOON
FRANCIS HOPKINS
JOHN HART
ABRAHAM CLARK

THE ARTICLES OF CONFEDERATION

To all to whom these Presents shall come, we the undersigned Delegates of the States affixed to our Names send greeting.

Articles of Confederation and perpetual Union between the states of New Hampshire, Massachusetts-bay Rhode Island and Providence Plantations, Connecticut, New York, New Jersey, Pennsylvania, Delaware, Maryland, Virginia, North Carolina, South Carolina and Georgia.

I   The Stile of this Confederacy shall be "The United States of America".

II   Each state retains its sovereignty, freedom, and independence, and every power, jurisdiction, and right, which is not by this Confederation expressly delegated to the United States, in Congress assembled.

III   The said States hereby severally enter into a firm league of friendship with each other, for their common defense, the security of their liberties, and their mutual and general welfare, binding themselves to assist each other, against all force offered to, or attacks made upon them, or any of them, on account of religion, sovereignty, trade, or any other pretense whatever.

IV   The better to secure and perpetuate mutual friendship and intercourse among the people of the different States in this Union, the free inhabitants of each of these States, paupers, vagabonds, and fugitives from justice excepted, shall be entitled to all privileges and immunities of free citizens in the several States; and the people of each State shall free ingress and regress to and from any other State, and shall enjoy therein all the privileges of trade and commerce, subject to the same duties, impositions, and restrictions as the inhabitants thereof respectively, provided that such restrictions shall not extend so far as to prevent the removal of property imported into any State, to any other State, of which the owner is an inhabitant; provided also that no imposition, duties or restriction shall be laid by any State, on the property of the United States, or either of them.

If any person guilty of, or charged with, treason, felony, or other high misdemeanor in any State, shall flee from justice, and be found in any of the United States, he shall, upon demand of the Governor or executive power of the State from which he fled, be delivered up and removed to the State having jurisdiction of his offense.

Full faith and credit shall be given in each of these States to the records, acts, and judicial proceedings of the courts and magistrates of every other State.

V   For the most convenient management of the general interests of the

United States, delegates shall be annually appointed in such manner as the legislatures of each State shall direct, to meet in Congress on the first Monday in November, in every year, with a power reserved to each State to recall its delegates, or any of them, at any time within the year, and to send others in their stead for the remainder of the year.

No State shall be represented in Congress by less than two, nor more than seven members; and no person shall be capable of being a delegate for more than three years in any term of six years; nor shall any person, being a delegate, be capable of holding any office under the United States, for which he, or another for his benefit, receives any salary, fees or emolument of any kind.

Each State shall maintain its own delegates in a meeting of the States, and while they act as members of the committee of the States.

In determining questions in the United States in Congress assembled, each State shall have one vote.

Freedom of speech and debate in Congress shall not be impeached or questioned in any court or place out of Congress, and the members of Congress shall be protected in their persons from arrests or imprisonments, during the time of their going to and from, and attendence on Congress, except for treason, felony, or breach of the peace.

VI No State, without the consent of the United States in Congress assembled, shall send any embassy to, or receive any embassy from, or enter into any conference, agreement, alliance or treaty with any King, Prince or State; nor shall any person holding any office of profit or trust under the United States, or any of them, accept any present, emolument, office or title of any kind whatever from any King, Prince or foreign State; nor shall the United States in Congress assembled, or any of them, grant any title of nobility.

No two or more States shall enter into any treaty, confederation or alliance whatever between them, without the consent of the United States in Congress assembled, specifying accurately the purposes for which the same is to be entered into, and how long it shall continue.

No State shall lay any imposts or duties, which may interfere with any stipulations in treaties, entered into by the United States in Congress assembled, with any King, Prince or State, in pursuance of any treaties already proposed by Congress, to the courts of France and Spain.

No vessel of war shall be kept up in time of peace by any State, except such number only, as shall be deemed necessary by the United States in Congress assembled, for the defense of such State, or its trade; nor shall any body of forces be kept up by any State in time of peace, except such number only, as in the judgement of the United States in Congress assembled, shall be deemed requisite to garrison the forts necessary for the defense of such State; but every State shall always keep up a well-regulated and disciplined militia, sufficiently armed and accoutered, and shall provide and constantly have ready for use, in public stores, a due number of filed pieces and tents, and a proper quantity of arms, ammunition and camp equipage.

No State shall engage in any war without the consent of the United States in Congress assembled, unless such State be actually invaded by enemies, or shall have received certain advice of a resolution being formed by some nation of Indians to invade such State, and the danger is so imminent as not to admit of a delay till the United States in Congress assembled can be consulted; nor shall any State grant commissions to any ships or vessels of war, nor letters of marque or reprisal, except it be after a declaration of war by the United States in Congress assembled, and then only against the Kingdom or State and the subjects thereof, against which war has been so declared, and under such regulations as shall be established by the United States in Congress assembled, unless such State be infested by pirates, in which case vessels of war may be fitted out for that occasion, and kept so long as the danger shall continue, or until the United States in Congress assembled shall determine otherwise.

VII   When land forces are raised by any State for the common defense, all officers of or under the rank of colonel, shall be appointed by the legislature of each State respectively, by whom such forces shall be raised, or in such manner as such State shall direct, and all vacancies shall be filled up by the State which first made the appointment.

VIII   All charges of war, and all other expenses that shall be incurred for the common defense or general welfare, and allowed by the United States in Congress assembled, shall be defrayed out of a common treasury, which shall be supplied by the several States in proportion to the value of all land within each State, granted or surveyed for any person, as such land and the buildings and improvements thereon shall be estimated according to such mode as the United States in Congress assembled, shall from time to time direct and appoint.

The taxes for paying that proportion shall be laid and levied by the authority and direction of the legislatures of the several States within the time agreed upon by the United States in Congress assembled.

IX   The United States in Congress assembled, shall have the sole and exclusive right and power of determining on peace and war, except in the cases mentioned in the sixth article – of sending and receiving ambassadors – entering into treaties and alliances, provided that no treaty of commerce shall be made whereby the legislative power of the respective States shall be restrained from imposing such imposts and duties on foreigners, as their own people are subjected to, or from prohibiting the exportation or importation of any species of goods or commodities whatsoever – of establishing rules for deciding in all cases, what captures on land or water shall be legal, and in what manner prizes taken by land or naval forces in the service of the United States shall be divided or appropriated – of granting letters of marque and reprisal in times of peace – appointing courts for the trial of piracies and felonies commited on the high seas and establishing courts for receiving and determining finally appeals in all cases of captures, provided that no member of Congress shall be appointed a judge of any of the said courts.

The United States in Congress assembled shall also be the last resort on appeal in all disputes and differences now subsisting or that hereafter may arise between two or more States concerning boundary, jurisdiction or any other causes whatever; which authority shall always be exercised in the manner following.

Whenever the legislative or executive authority or lawful agent of any State in controversy with another shall present a petition to Congress stating the matter in question and praying for a hearing, notice thereof shall be given by order of Congress to the legislative or executive authority of the other State in controversy, and a day assigned for the appearance of the parties by their lawful agents, who shall then be directed to appoint by joint consent, commissioners or judges to constitute a court for hearing and determining the matter in question: but if they cannot agree, Congress shall name three persons out of each of the United States, and from the list of such persons each party shall alternately strike out one, the petitioners beginning, until the number shall be reduced to thirteen; and from that number not less than seven, nor more than nine names as Congress shall direct, shall in the presence of Congress be drawn out by lot, and the persons whose names shall be so drawn or any five of them, shall be commissioners or judges, to hear and finally determine the controversy, so always as a major part of the judges who shall hear the cause shall agree in the determination: and if either party shall neglect to attend at the day appointed, without showing reasons, which Congress shall judge sufficient, or being present shall refuse to strike, the Congress shall proceed to nominate three persons out of each State, and the secretary of Congress shall strike in behalf of such party absent or refusing; and the judgement and sentence of the court to be appointed, in the manner before prescribed, shall be final and conclusive; and if any of the parties shall refuse to submit to the authority of such court, or to appear or defend their claim or cause, the court shall nevertheless proceed to pronounce sentence, or judgement, which shall in like manner be final and decisive, the judgement or sentence and other proceedings being in either case transmitted to Congress, and lodged among the acts of Congress for the security of the parties concerned: provided that every commissioner, before he sits in judgement, shall take an oath to be administered by one of the judges of the supreme or superior court of the State, where the cause shall be tried, 'well and truly to hear and determine the matter in question, according to the best of his judgement, without favor, affection or hope of reward': provided also, that no State shall be deprived of territory for the benefit of the United States.

All controversies concerning the private right of soil claimed under different grants of two or more States, whose jurisdictions as they may respect such lands, and the States which passed such grants are adjusted, the said grants or either of them being at the same time claimed to have originated antecedent to such settlement of jurisdiction, shall on the petition of either party to the Congress of the United States, be finally determined as near as may be in the same manner as is before prescribed for deciding disputes respecting territorial jurisdiction between different States.

The United States in Congress assembled shall also have the sole and exclusive right and power of regulating the alloy and value of coin struck by their own authority, or by that of the respective States – fixing the standards of weights and measures throughout the United States – regulating the trade and managing all affairs with the Indians, not members of any of the States, provided that the legislative right of any State within its own limits be not infringed or violated – establishing or regulating post offices from one State to another, throughout all the United States, and exacting such postage on the papers passing through the same as may be requisite to defray the expenses of the said office – appointing all officers of the land forces, in the service of the United States, excepting regimental officers – appointing all the officers of the naval forces, and commissioning all officers whatever in the service of the United States – making rules for the government and regulation of the said land and naval forces, and directing their operations.

The United States in Congress assembled shall have authority to appoint a committee, to sit in the recess of Congress, to be denominated 'A Committee of the States', and to consist of one delegate from each State; and to appoint such other committees and civil officers as may be necessary for managing the general affairs of the United States under their direction – to appoint one of their members to preside, provided that no person be allowed to serve in the office of president more than one year in any term of three years; to ascertain the necessary sums of money to be raised for the service of the United States, and to appropriate and apply the same for defraying the public expenses – to borrow money, or emit bills on the credit of the United States, transmitting every half-year to the respective States an account of the sums of money so borrowed or emitted – to build and equip a navy – to agree upon the number of land forces, and to make requisitions from each State for its quota, in proportion to the number of white inhabitants in such State; which requisition shall be binding, and thereupon the legislature of each State shall appoint the regimental officers, raise the men and cloath, arm and equip them in a solid-like manner, at the expense of the United States; and the officers and men so cloathed, armed and equipped shall march to the place appointed, and within the time agreed on by the United States in Congress assembled. But if the United States in Congress assembled shall, on consideration of circumstances judge proper that any State should not raise men, or should raise a smaller number of men than the quota thereof, such extra number shall be raised, officered, cloathed, armed and equipped in the same manner as the quota of each State, unless the legislature of such State shall judge that such extra number cannot be safely spread out in the same, in which case they shall raise, officer, cloath, arm and equip as many of such extra number as they judge can be safely spared. And the officers and men so cloathed, armed, and equipped, shall march to the place appointed, and within the time agreed on by the United States in Congress assembled.

The United States in Congress assembled shall never engage in a war, nor grant letters of marque or reprisal in time of peace, nor enter into any treaties or alliances, nor coin money, nor regulate the value thereof, nor ascertain the sums and expenses necessary for the defense and welfare of the United States, or any of them, nor emit bills, nor borrow money on the credit of the United States, nor appropriate money, nor agree upon the number of vessels of war, to be built or purchased, or the number of land or sea forces to be raised, nor appoint a commander in chief of the army or navy, unless nine States assent to the same: nor shall a question on any other point, except for adjourning from day to day be determined, unless by the votes of the majority of the United States in Congress assembled.

The Congress of the United States shall have power to adjourn to any time within the year, and to any place within the United States, so that no period of adjournment be for a longer duration than the space of six months, and shall publish the journal of their proceedings monthly, except such parts thereof relating to treaties, alliances or military operations, as in their judgement require secrecy; and the yeas and nays of the delegates of each State on any question shall be entered on the Journal, when it is desired by any delegates of a State, or any of them, at his or their request shall be furnished with a transcript of the said journal, except such parts as are above excepted, to lay before the legislatures of the several States.

X   The Committee of the States, or any nine of them, shall be authorized to execute, in the recess of Congress, such of the powers of Congress as the United States in Congress assembled, by the consent of the nine States, shall

from time to time think expedient to vest them with; provided that no power be delegated to the said Committee, for the exercise of which, by the Articles of Confederation, the voice of nine States in the Congress of the United States assembled be requisite.

XI   Canada acceding to this confederation, and adjoining in the measures of the United States, shall be admitted into, and entitled to all the advantages of this Union; but no other colony shall be admitted into the same, unless such admission be agreed to by nine States.

XII   All bills of credit emitted, monies borrowed, and debts contracted by, or under the authority of Congress, before the assembling of the United States, in pursuance of the present confederation, shall be deemed and considered as a charge against the United States, for payment and satisfaction whereof the said United States, and the public faith are hereby solemnly pleged.

XIII   Every State shall abide by the determination of the United States in Congress assembled, on all questions which by this confederation are submitted to them. And the Articles of this Confederation shall be inviolably observed by every State, and the Union shall be perpetual; nor shall any alteration at any time hereafter be made in any of them; unless such alteration be agreed to in a Congress of the United States, and be afterwards confirmed by the legislatures of every State.

And Whereas it hath pleased the Great Governor of the World to incline the hearts of the legislatures we respectively represent in Congress, to approve of, and to authorize us to ratify the said Articles of Confederation and perpetual Union. Know Ye that we the undersigned delegates, by virtue of the power and authority to us given for that purpose, do by these presents, in the name and in behalf of our respective constituents, fully and entirely ratify and confirm each and every of the said Articles of Confederation and perpetual Union, and all and singular the matters and things therein contained: And we do further solemnly plight and engage the faith of our respective constituents, that they shall abide by the determinations of the United States in Congress assembled, on all questions, which by the said Confederation are submitted to them. And that the Articles thereof shall be inviolably observed by the States we respectively represent, and that the Union shall be perpetual.

In Witness whereof we have hereunto set our hands in Congress.

Done at Philadelphia in the State of Pennsylvania the ninth day of July in the Year of our Lord One Thousand Seven Hundred and Seventy-Eight, and in the Third Year of the independence of America.

Agreed to by Congress 15 November 1777

In force after ratification by Maryland, 1 March 1781

THE GETTYSBURG ADDRESS

Four score and seven years ago our fathers brought forth on this continent, a new nation, conceived in Liberty, and dedicated to the proposition that all men are created equal.

Now we are engaged in a great civil war, testing whether that nation, or any nation so conceived and so dedicated, can long endure. We are met on a great battle-field of that war. We have come to dedicate a portion of that field, as a resting place for those who here gave their lives that that nation might live. It is altogether fitting and proper that we should do this.

But, in a larger sense, we can not dedicate—we can not consecrate—we can not hallow—this ground. The brave men, living and dead, who struggled here, have consecrated it, far above our poor power to add or detract. The world will little note, nor long remember what we say here, but it can never forget what they did here. It is for us the living, rather, to be dedicated here to the unfinished work which they who fought here have thus far so nobly advanced. It is rather for us to be here dedicated to the great task remaining before us—that from these honored dead we take increased devotion—that we here highly resolve that these dead shall not have died in vain—that this nation, under God, shall have a new birth of freedom—and that government of the people, by the people, for the people, shall not perish from the earth.

Note: Delivered by President Abraham Lincoln on November 19, 1863, at the dedication of the cemetery at Gettysburg, Pennsylvania, which were called "Dedicatory Remarks" in the printed program.

Garry Wills[1] points out there were several reported versions with six relatively minor differences apparently due to how reporters scribbled the words, and last-minute changes in Lincoln's drafts of the address. Printed here is what Wills believed was the actual text.

The address is particularly significant in that for the first time Lincoln declared as a principal aim of the war effort a new birth of freedom in the United States based on the proposition that all men were created equal found in the Declaration of Independence. This was a greater goal than defeating the southern rebels, preserving the Union and freeing the slaves. It is noteworthy that those present reported that President Lincoln stressed the word "people" in his concluding triad. (Imitative orators too often stress "of", "by" and "for.")

---

[1]Garry Wills, *Lincoln at Gettysburg, The Words That Remade America,* Simon & Schuster, New York, 1992.

PRESIDENTIAL ELECTION RESULTS
(1789–2000)

Candidate	State	Party	Popular Vote	Electoral
1789				
GEORGE WASHINGTON	VA	none		69[1]
JOHN ADAMS – VP	MA	none		34
John Jay	NY	none		9
Hanson Harrison	MD	none		6
John Rutledge	SC	none		6
John Hancock	MA	none		4
George Clinton	NY	none		3
Samuel Huntington	CT	none		2
John Milton	GA	none		2
James Armstrong	GA	none		1
Edward Telfair	GA	none		1
Benjamin Lincoln	GA	none		1
1792				
GEORGE WASHINGTON	VA	none		132
JOHN ADAMS – VP	MA	Federalist		77
George Clinton	NY	Dem-Republican		50
Thomas Jefferson	VA	Dem-Republican		4
Aaron Burr	NY	Dem-Republican		1
1796				
JOHN ADAMS	MA	Federalist		71
THOMAS JEFFERSON – VP	VA	Dem-Republican		68[2]
Thomas Pinckney	SC	Federalist		59
Aaron Burr	NY	Dem-Republican		30
Samuel Adams	MA	Dem-Republican		15
Oliver Ellsworth	CT	Dem-Republican		11
George Clinton	NY	Dem-Republican		7
John Jay	NY	Federalist		5
James Iredell	NC	—		3
George Washington	VA	—		2
Samuel Johnston	NC	—		2
C. C. Pinckney	SC	Federalist		1
1800				
THOMAS JEFFERSON	VA	Dem-Republican		73[3]
AARON BURR – VP	NY	Dem-Republican		73
John Adams	MA	Federalist		65
C. C. Pinckney	SC	Federalist		64
John Jay	NY	Federalist		1

Candidate	State	Party	Popular Vote	Electoral
1804				
THOMAS JEFFERSON and	VA	Dem-Republican		162
GEORGE CLINTON – VP	NY	Dem-Republican		162
C. C. Pinckney and	SC	Federalist		14
Rufus King – VP	NY	Federalist		14
1808				
JAMES MADISON and	VA	Dem-Republican		122
GEORGE CLINTON – VP	NY	Dem-Republican		113
C. C. Pinckney and	SC	Federalist		47
Rufus King – VP	NY	Federalist		47
George Clinton	NY	Dem-Republican	for Pres.	6[4]
John Langdon for VP	NH	Dem-Republican		9
James Madison for VP	VA	Dem-Republican		3
James Monroe for VP	VA	Dem-Republican		3
1812				
JAMES MADISON and	VA	Dem-Republican		128
ELBRIDGE GERRY – VP	MA	Dem-Republican		131
DeWitt Clinton and	NY	Federalist		89
John Ingersoll – VP	PA	Federalist		86
Three electors did not vote				
1816				
JAMES MONROE and	VA	Dem-Republican		183
DANIEL TOMPKINS – VP	NY	Dem-Republican		183
Rufus King and	NY	Federalist		34
John E. Howard – VP	MD	Federalist		22
James Ross for VP	PA	Federalist		5
John Marshall for VP	VA	Federalist		4
Robert Harper for Pres.	MD	Federalist		3
1820				
JAMES MONROE and	VA	Dem-Republican		231
DANIEL D. TOMPKINS – VP	NY	Dem-Republican		218
John Quincy Adams	MA	Dem-Republican		1
Richard Stockton for VP	NJ	Dem-Republican		8
Daniel Rodney for VP	DE	Dem-Republican		1
Richard Rush for VP	PA	Dem-Republican		1
1824				
Andrew Jackson	TE	Dem-Republican	152,901	99[5]
JOHN QUINCY ADAMS	MA	Dem-Republican	114,023	84
William H. Crawford	GA	Dem-Republican	46,979	41
Henry Clay	KY	Dem-Republican	47,217	37
JOHN C. CALHOUN – VP	SC	Dem-Republican		182
Nathan Sanford for VP	NY	Dem-Republican		30
Nathaniel Macon for VP	NC	Dem-Republican		24
Andrew Jackson for VP	TE	Dem-Republican		13
Martin Van Buren for VP	NY	Dem-Republican		9
Henry Clay for VP	KY	Dem-Republican		2

Candidate	State	Party	Popular Vote	Electoral
		1828		
ANDREW JACKSON and	TE	Democrat	647,276	178
JOHN C. CALHOUN – VP	SC	Democrat		171
John Quincy Adams and	MA	Nat. Republican	508,074	83
Richard Rush – VP	PA	Nat. Republican		83
William Smith for VP	SC	Democrat		7
		1832		
ANDREW JACKSON and	TE	Democrat	687,502	219
MARTIN VAN BUREN – VP	NY	Democrat		189
Henry Clay and	KY	Nat. Republican	530,189	49
John Sergeant – VP	PA	Nat. Republican		49
John Floyd and	VA	Ind. Democrat		11
Henry Lee – VP	MA	Ind. Democrat		11
William Wirt and	MD	Anti-Masonic		7
Amos Ellmaker – VP	PA	Anti-Masonic		7
William Wilkins for VP	PA	Democrat		30
Two electors did not vote				
		1836		
MARTIN VAN BUREN and	NY	Democrat	763,978	170
RICHARD M. JOHNSON – VP	KY	Democrat		147[6]
William Henry Harrison	OH	Whig	549,508	73[7]
Hugh L. White	TE	Whig	145,352	26
Daniel Webster	MA	Whig	41,287	14
Willie P. Magnum	NC	Whig		11
Frances Granger for VP	NY	Anti-Masonic		77
John Tyler for VP	VA	Whig		47
William Smith for VP	AL	Whig		23
		1840		
WILLIAM HENRY HARRISON	OH	Whig	1,275,016	234
and JOHN TYLER – VP	VA	Whig		234
Martin Van Buren and	NY	Democrat	1,129,102	60
Richard Johnson – VP	KY	Democrat		48
Littleton Tazewell – VP	VA	Democrat		11
James K. Polk – VP	TE	Democrat		1
James G. Birney	NY	Liberty	7,069	
		1844		
JAMES KNOX POLK and	TE	Democrat	1,337,243	179
GEORGE M. DALLAS – VP	PA	Democrat		179
Henry Clay and	KY	Whig	1,299,062	105
Theodore Frelinghuysen – VP	NJ	Whig		105
James G. Birney	NY	Liberty	62,300	
		1848		
ZACHARY TAYLOR and	LA	Whig	1,360,099	163
MILLARD FILLMORE – VP	NY	Whig		163

Candidate	State	Party	Popular Vote	Electoral
		1848 *(continued)*		
Lewis Cass and	MI	Democrat	1,220,544	127
William O. Butler – VP	KY	Democrat		127
Martin Van Buren and	NY	Free Soil	291,283	
Charles F. Adams – VP	MA	Free Soil		
		1852		
FRANKLIN PIERCE and	NH	Democrat	1,601,274	254
WILLIAM R. KING – VP	AL	Democrat		254
Winfield Scott and	NJ	Whig	1,386,580	42
William A. Graham – VP	NC	Whig		42
John P. Hale and	NH	Free Soil	156,667	
George W. Julian – VP	IN	Free Soil		
		1856		
JAMES BUCHANAN and	PA	Democrat	1,838,169	174
JOHN BRECKINRIDGE – VP	KY	Democrat		174
John C. Fremont and	CA	Republican	1,341,264	114
William L. Dayton – VP	NJ	Republican		114
Millard Fillmore and	NY	Native Amer.	874,534	8[8]
Andrew J. Donelson – VP	TE	Native Amer.		8
		1860		
ABRAHAM LINCOLN and	IL	Republican	1,866,452	180
HANNIBAL HAMLIN – VP	ME	Republican		180
Stephen A. Douglas and	IL	Democrat	1,376,957	12
Herschel Johnson – VP	GA	Democrat		12
John C. Breckinridge	KY	South. Demo.	849,781	72
and Joseph Lane – VP	OR	South. Demo.		72
John Bell and	TE	Constit. Union	588,879	39
Edward Everett – VP	MA	Constit. Union		39
		1864		
ABRAHAM LINCOLN and	IL	Republican	2,330,552	234[9]
ANDREW JOHNSON – VP	TE	Nation. Union		234
George McClellan and	NY	Democrat	1,835,985	21
George Pendleton – VP	OH	Democrat		21
One elector died without voting				
		1868		
ULYSSES S. GRANT and	IL	Republican	3,012,833	294
SCHUYLER COLFAX – VP	IN	Republican		294
Horatio Seymour and	NY	Democrat	2,703,249	80
Francis Blair, Jr. – VP	MO	Democrat		80
		1872		
ULYSSES S. GRANT and	IL	Republican	3,597,132	352
HENRY WILSON – VP	MA	Republican		352
Horace Greeley and	NY	Liberal Rep.	2,834,125	0[10]
B. Gratz Brown – VP	MO	Liberal Rep.	for VP	27
Thomas A. Hendricks	IN	Democrat	for Pres.	42

Candidate	State	Party	Popular Vote	Electoral
		1872 *(continued)*		
B. Gratz Brown	MO	Lib. Rep-Dem.	for Pres.	18
Charles Jenkins	GA	Lib. Rep-Dem.	for Pres.	2
David Davis	IL	Lib. Rep-Dem.	for Pres.	1
George W. Julian	IN	Lib. Rep-Dem.	for VP	5
Alfred H. Colquitt	GA	Lib. Rep-Dem.	for VP	3
John M. Palmer III	IL	Lib. Rep-Dem.	for VP	3
Thomas Bramlette	KY	Lib. Rep-Dem.	for VP	3
Nathaniel J. Banks	MA	Lib. Rep-Dem.	for VP	1
William S. Groesbeck	OH	Lib. Rep-Dem.	for VP	1
Willis B. Machen	KY	Lib. Rep-Dem.	for VP	1
Charles O'Conor	NY	Old Line Dem.	29,489	
		1876		
RUTHERFORD B. HAYES and	OH	Republican	4,036,298	185[11]
WILLIAM WHEELER – VP	NY	Republican		185
Samuel J. Tilden and	NY	Democrat	4,300,590	184
Thomas A. Hendricks – VP	IN	Democrat		184
Peter Cooper	NY	Greenback	81,737	
Green Clay Smith	KY	Prohibition	9,522	
James B. Walker	IL	American	2,636	
		1880		
JAMES A. GARFIELD and	OH	Republican	4,454,416	214
CHESTER ALAN				
ARTHUR – VP	NY	Republican		214
Winfield Scott Hancock	PA	Democrat	4,444,952	155
and William English – VP	IN	Democrat		155
James B. Weaver and	IO	Greenback-Lab.	308,578	
Benjamin Chambers – VP	TX	Greenback-Lab.		
Neal Dow	ME	Prohibition	10,305	
		1884		
GROVER CLEVELAND and	NY	Democrat	4,914,986	401
THOMAS A. HENDRICKS – VP	IN	Democrat		401
James G. Blaine and	ME	Republican	4,854,981	182
John A. Logan – VP	IL	Republican		182
Benjamin F. Butler and	MA	Greenback-Lab.	175,365	
and Absolom West – VP	MS	Greenback-Lab.		
John P. St. John and	KS	Prohibition	150,369	
William Daniel – VP	MD	Prohibition		
		1888		
BENJAMIN HARRISON and	IN	Republican	5,439,853	233
LEVI P. MORTON – VP	NY	Republican		233
Grover Cleveland and	NY	Democrat	5,540,329	168
Allen Thurman – VP	OH	Democrat		168
Clinton B. Fisk and	NJ	Prohibition	249,506	
John A. Brooks – VP	MO	Prohibition		
Alson J. Streeter and	IL	Union Labor	146,934	

Candidate	State	Party	Popular Vote	Electoral
		1888 *(continued)*		
Charles Cunningham – VP	AR	Union Labor		
Robert H. Cowdrey	OH	United Labor	2,818	
		1892		
GROVER CLEVELAND and	NY	Democrat	5,556,918	277
ADLAI E. STEVENSON – VP	IL	Democrat		277
Benjamin Harrison and	OH	Republican	5,176,108	145
Whitelaw Reid – VP	NY	Republican		145
James B. Weaver and	IA	People's	1,041,028	22
James Field – VP	VA	People's		22
John Bidwell and	CA	Prohibition	264,133	
James B. Cranfill – VP	TX	Prohibition		
Simon Wing	MA	Socialist Labor	21,164	
		1896		
WILLIAM McKINLEY and	OH	Republican	7,111,607	271
GARRET A. HOBART – VP	NJ	Republican		271
William Jennings Bryan	NE	Dem-People's	6,731,635	176
Arthur Sewall – VP	ME	Democrat	for VP	149[12]
Thomas E. Watson – VP	GA	People's	for VP	27
John McC. Palmer and	IL	Nat. Dem.	134,645	
Simon B. Buckner – VP	KY	Nat. Dem.		
Joshua Levering and	MD	Prohibition	131,312	
Hale Johnson – VP	IL	Prohibition		
Charles Matchett	NY	Socialist Labor	36,373	
Charles E. Bentley	NE	Nat. Free Silver	13,968	
		1900		
WILLIAM McKINLEY and	OH	Republican	7,319,525	292
THEODORE ROOSEVELT				
– VP	NY	Republican		292
William Jennings Bryan	NE	Democrat	6,358,737	155
and Adlai Stevenson – VP	IL	Democrat		155
John C. Woolley and	IL	Prohibition	209,166	
Henry Metcalf – VP	RI	Prohibition		
Eugene V. Debs and	IN	Social Democrat.	94,864	
Job Harriman – VP	CA	Social Democrat.		
Wharton Barker	PA	People's	50,599	
Joseph Malloney	MA	Socialist Labor	33,322	
Seth Ellis	OH	Union Reform	5,598	
		1904		
THEODORE ROOSEVELT and	NY	Republican	7,628,785	336
CHARLES W. FAIRBANKS – VP	IN	Republican		336
Alton B. Parker and	NY	Democrat	5,084,338	140
Henry G. Davis – VP	WV	Democrat		140

Candidate	State	Party	Popular Vote	Electoral
		1904 *(continued)*		
Eugene V. Debs and	IN	Socialist	402,893	
Benjamin Hanford – VP	NY	Socialist		
Silas Comfort Swallow and	PA	Prohibition	258,750	
George Carroll – VP	TX	Prohibition		
Thomas E. Watson and	GA	People's	114,138	
Thomas H. Tibbles – VP	NE	People's		
Charles H. Corregan	NY	Socialist Labor	33,490	
		1908		
WILLIAM HOWARD TAFT and	OH	Republican	7,679,114	321
JAMES S. SHERMAN – VP	NY	Republican		321
William Jennings Bryan	NE	Democrat	6,410,665	162
and John W. Kern – VP	IN	Democrat		162
Eugene V. Debs and	IN	Socialist	420,890	
Benjamin Hanford – VP	NY	Socialist		
Eugene W. Chafin and	IL	Prohibition	253,840	
Aaron S. Watkins – VP	OH	Prohibition		
Thomas L. Hisgen	MA	Independence	83,651	
Thomas E. Watson	GA	People's	29,146	
August Gilhaus	NY	Socialist Labor	14,021	
		1912		
WOODROW WILSON and	NJ	Democrat	6,283,019	435
THOMAS R. MARSHALL – VP	IN	Democrat		435
Theodore Roosevelt and	NY	Progressive	4,119,507	88
Hiram Johnson – VP	CA	Progressive		88
William Howard Taft and	OH	Republican	3,484,956	8
James S. Sherman – VP	NY	Republican		0[13]
Nicholas M. Butler	NY	Republican	for VP	8
Eugene V. Debs and	IN	Socialist	962,573	
Emil Seidel – VP	WI	Socialist		
Eugene W. Chafin and	IL	Prohibition	207,928	
Aaron S. Watkins – VP	OH	Prohibition		
Arthur Reimer	MA	Socialist Labor	29,259	
		1916		
WOODROW WILSON and	NJ	Democrat	9,129,606	277
THOMAS R. MARSHALL – VP	IN	Democrat		277
Charles Evans Hughes and	NY	Republican	8,532,221	254
Charles Fairbanks – VP	IN	Republican		254
		1916		
Allen L. Benson and	NY	Socialist	585,113	
George Kirkpatrick – VP	NJ	Socialist		
James F. Hanly and	IN	Prohibition	220,606	
Ira D. Landrith – VP	TE	Prohibition		

Candidate	State	Party	Popular Vote	Electoral
		1916 *(continued)*		
Arthur Reimer	MA	Socialist Labor	13,403	
Allen L. Benson and	NY	Socialist	585,113	
George Kirkpatrick – VP	NJ	Socialist		
James F. Hanly and	IN	Prohibition	220,606	
Ira D. Landrith – VP	TE	Prohibition		
Arthur Reimer	MA	Socialist Labor	13,403	
		1920		
WARREN G. HARDING and	OH	Republican	16,153,115[14]	404
CALVIN COOLIDGE – VP	MA	Republican		404
James M. Cox and	OH	Democrat	9,133,092	127
Franklin Roosevelt – VP	NY	Democrat		127
Eugene V. Debs and	IN	Socialist	915,490	
Seymour Stedman – VP	IL	Socialist		
Parley Christensen and	UT	Farmer Labor	265,229	
Maxmillian Hayes – VP	OH	Farmer Labor		
Aaron S. Watkins and	OH	Prohibition	189,339	
David L. Colvin – VP	NY	Prohibition		
William W. Cox	MO	Socialist Labor	30,594	
		1924		
CALVIN COOLIDGE and	MA	Republican	15,725,616	382
CHARLES G. DAWES – VP	IL	Republican		382
John W. Davis and	WV	Democrat	8,386,704	136
Charles W. Bryan – VP	NE	Democrat		136
Robert M. LaFollette	WI	Progressive	4,832,532	13
and Burton Wheeler – VP	MT	Progressive		
Herman P. Faris and	MO	Prohibition	57,551	
Marie C. Brehm – VP	CA	Prohibition		
Frank T. Johns	OR	Socialist Labor	38,958	
William Z. Foster	IL	Worker's (Communist)	33,360	
Gilbert O. Nations	DC	American	24,340	
William J. Wallace	NJ	Single Tax	2,778	
		1928		
HERBERT CLARK HOOVER	CA	Republican	21,437,277	444
and CHARLES CURTIS – VP	KS	Republican		444
Alfred E. Smith and	NY	Democrat	15,007,698	87
Joseph Robinson – VP	AR	Democrat		87
Norman Thomas and	NY	Socialist	265,583	
James H. Maurer – VP	PA	Socialist		
William Z. Foster	IL	Worker's (Communist)	46,896	
Verne L. Reynolds	MD	Socialist Labor	21,586	
William F. Varney	NY	Prohibition	20,101	
Frank E. Webb	CA	Farmer Labor	6,810	

Candidate	State	Party	Popular Vote	Electoral
		1932		
FRANKLIN D. ROOSEVELT	NY	Democrat	22,829,501	472
and JOHN NANCE GARNER				
– VP	TX	Democrat		472
Herbert C. Hoover and	CA	Republican	15,760,684	59
Charles Curtis – VP	KS	Republican		59
Norman Thomas and	NY	Socialist	884,649	
James H. Maurer – VP	PA	Socialist		
William Z. Foster and	IL	Communist	103,253	
James W. Ford – VP	AL	Communist		
William D. Upshaw and	GA	Prohibition	81,872	
Frank S. Regan – VP	IL	Prohibition		
William H. Harvey and	AR	Liberty	53,247	
Frank B. Hemenway – VP	WA	Liberty		
Verne L. Reynolds	NY	Socialist Labor	34,038	
Jacob S. Coxey	OH	Farmer Labor	7,431	
		1936		
FRANKLIN D. ROOSEVELT	NY	Democrat	27,757,333	523
and JOHN NANCE GARNER				
– VP	TX	Democrat		523
Alfred M. Landon and	KS	Republican	16,684,231	8
Frank Knox – VP	IL	Republican		8
William Lemke and	ND	Union[15]	892,267	
Thomas C. O'Brien – VP	MA	Union		
Norman Thomas and	NY	Socialist	187,833	
George Nelson – VP	WI	Socialist		
Earl Browder and	KS	Communist	80,171	
James W. Ford – VP	NY	Communist		
D. Leigh Colvin	NY	Prohibition	37,677	
John W. Aiken	MA	Socialist Labor	12,788	
		1940		
FRANKLIN D. ROOSEVELT	NY	Democrat	27,313,041	449
and HENRY A. WALLACE				
– VP	IA	Democrat		449
Wendell L. Willkie and	IN	Republican	22,348,480	82
Charles L. McNary – VP	OR	Republican		82
Norman Thomas and	NY	Socialist	116,410	
Maynard C. Krueger – VP	Il	Socialist		
Roger W. Babson	MA	Prohibition	58,708	
Earl Browder	KS	Communist	46,259	
John W. Aiken	MA	Socialist Labor	14,883	
		1944		
FRANKLIN D. ROOSEVELT	NY	Democrat	25,612,610	531
and HARRY S. TRUMAN – VP	MO	Democrat		531
Thomas E. Dewey and	NY	Republican	22,017,617	99
John W. Bricker – VP	OH	Republican		99

Candidate	State	Party	Popular Vote	Electoral
		1944 *(continued)*		
Norman Thomas	NY	Socialist	79,003	
Claude A. Watson	CA	Prohibition	74,779	
Edward A. Teichert	PA	Socialist Labor	45,336	
"Texas Regulars" Ticket			135,444	
		1948		
HARRY S. TRUMAN and	MO	Democrat	24,179,345	303
ALBEN W. BARKLEY – VP	KY	Democrat		304
Thomas E. Dewey and	NY	Republican	21,991,291	189
Earl Warren – VP	CA	Republican		109
J. Strom Thurmond and	SC	States Rights	1,176,125	40[16]
Fielding L. Wright – VP	MS	States Rights		39
Henry A. Wallace and	IA	Progressive	1,157,326	
Glen Taylor – VP	ID	Progressive		
Norman Thomas and	NY	Socialist	139,572	
Tucker P. Smith – VP	MI	Socialist		
Claude A. Watson and	CA	Prohibition	103,900	
Dale H. Learn – VP	PA	Prohibition		
Edward A. Teichert	PA	Socialist Labor	29,272	
Farrell Dobbs	NY	Socialist Workers	13,614	
		1952		
DWIGHT D. EISENHOWER	NY	Republican	33,936,234	442
and RICHARD M. NIXON – VP	CA	Republican		442
Adlai E. Stevenson and	IL	Democrat	27,314,992	89
John Sparkman – VP	AL	Democrat		89
Vincent Hallinan and	CA	Progressive	140,023	
Charlotta A. Bass – VP	NY	Progressive		
Stuart Hamblen	OK	Prohibition	72,969	
Eric Hass	NY	Socialist Labor	30,376	
Darlington Hoopes	PA	Socialist	20,203	
Farrell Dobbs	NY	Socialist Workers	10,300	
Tickets supporting General				
Douglas MacArthur			17,205	
		1956		
DWIGHT D. EISENHOWER	NY	Republican	35,590,472	457
and RICHARD M. NIXON – VP	CA	Republican		457
Adlai E. Stevenson and	IL	Democrat	26,031,322	73
Estes Kefauver – VP	TE	Democrat		73
T. Coleman Andrews and	VA	States Rights	167,826	
Thomas H. Werdel – VP	CA	States Rights		
Harry F. Byrd and	VA	States Rts. of Ky.	134,128	
William E. Jenner – VP	IN	States Rts. of Ky.		
Eric Hass	NY	Socialist Labor	44,450	
Enoch Arden Holtwich	IL	Prohibition	41,937	

Candidate	State	Party	Popular Vote	Electoral
		1956 *(continued)*		
William E. Jenner	IN	Texas Constitution	30,999	
Farrell Dobbs	NY	Socialist Workers	5,707	
Walter B. Jones and	NC	Democrat[17]		1
Herman Talmadge – VP	GA	Democrat		1
		1960		
JOHN F. KENNEDY and	MA	Democrat	34,227,096	303
LYNDON B. JOHNSON – VP	TX	Democrat		318
Richard M. Nixon and	CA	Republican	34,108,546	219
Henry Cabot Lodge – VP	MA	Republican		220
Orval Faubus and	AR	Nat'l States Rts.	214,195	
John Crommelin – VP	AL	Nat'l States Rts.		
Independent Electors Slate in Louisiana			169,572	
Unpledged Democratic Electors Slate in Mississippi			116,248	
Harry F. Byrd[18]	VA	Independent Demo.	for Pres.	16
Eric Hass	NY	Socialist Labor	46,472	
Rutherford Decker	MO	Prohibition	45,919	
Farrell Dobbs	NY	Socialist Workers	39,541	
Charles Sullivan		Constitution	18,162	
		1964		
LYNDON B. JOHNSON and	TX	Democrat	43,167,895	486
HUBERT H. HUMPHREY – VP	MN	Democrat		486
Barry Goldwater and	AZ	Republican	27,146,969	52
William Miller – VP	NY	Republican		52
Eric Hass	NY	Socialist Labor	42,642	
E. Harold Munn	MI	Prohibition	23,267	
Clifton DeBerry	NY	Socialist Workers	22,249	
John Kasper	TE	Nat'l States Rts.	6,957	
Unpledged Democratic ticket in Alabama				210,732
		1968		
RICHARD M. NIXON and	NY	Republican	31,785,480	301
SPIRO T. AGNEW – VP	MD	Republican		301
Hubert H. Humphrey and	MN	Democrat	31,275,165	191
Edmund S. Muskie – VP	ME	Democrat		191
George C. Wallace and	AL	American Ind.	9,906,473	46
Curtis LeMay – VP	CA	American Ind.		46
Dick Gregory		Peace & Freedom	47,517	
Fred Halstead		Socialist Workers	41,390	
Eldridge Cleaver	CA	Peace & Freedom	8,736	
Eugene J. McCarthy	MN	Democrat (write-in)	25,552	
E. Harold Munn	MI	Prohibition	14,915	

Candidate	State	Party	Popular Vote	Electoral
		1972		
RICHARD M. NIXON and	NY	Republican	47,170,179	519
SPIRO T. AGNEW – VP	MD	Republican		520
George S. McGovern and	SD	Democrat	29,171,791	17
R. Sargent Shriver – VP	MD	Democrat		17
John G. Schmitz	CA	American Ind.	1,090,673	
Benjamin Spock		People's	78,751	
Louis Fisher		Socialist Labor	53,811	
Linda Jenness		Socialist Workers	37,423	
Gus Hall		Communist	25,343	
E. Harold Munn		Prohibition	12,818	
Evelyn Reed		Socialist Workers	5,575	
John Hospers		Libertarian	3,671	1[19]
		1976		
JIMMY CARTER and	GA	Democrat	40,830,763	297
WALTER MONDALE – VP	MN	Democrat		297
Gerald R. Ford and	MI	Repubican	39,147,793	240
Robert Dole – VP	KS	Republican		241
Eugene J. McCarthy	MN	Independent	756,691	
Roger MacBride	VA	Libertarian	173,010	
Lester Maddox	GA	Amer. Independent	170,531	
Thomas J. Anderson		American	160,773	
Peter Camejo		Socialist Workers	91,314	
Gus Hall		Communist	58,992	
Margaret Wright		People's	49,024	
Lyndon H. LaRouche		U.S. Labor	40,043	
Benjamin Buhar		Prohibition	15,934	
Jules Levin		Socialist Labor	9,616	
Frank P. Zeidler		Socialist	6,036	
Ronald Reagan		Republican		1[20]
		1980		
RONALD REAGAN and	CA	Republican	43,901,812	489
GEORGE BUSH – VP	TX	Republican		489
Jimmy Carter and	GA	Democrat	35,483,820	49
Walter Mondale – VP	MN	Democrat		49
John B. Anderson and	IL	Independent	5,719,722	
Patrick J. Lucey – VP	WI	Independent		
Edward E. Clark	CA	Libertarian	921,188	
Barry Commoner		Citizens	234,279	
Gus Hall		Communist	45,023	
John R. Rarick		Amer. Independent	41,268	
Clifton DeBerry		Socialist Workers	38,737	
Ellen McCormack		Right to Life	32,737	
Maureen Smith		Peace & Freedom	18,116	
Dierdre Griswold		Worker's World	13,300	
Benjamin C. Buber		Statesman	7,212	
David McReynolds		Socialist	6,895	
Percy L. Greaves		American	6,647	

Candidate	State	Party	Popular Vote	Electoral
		1980 (*continued*)		
Andrew Pulley		Socialist Workers	6,271	
Richard Congress		Socialist Workers	4,029	
		1984		
RONALD REAGAN and	CA	Republican	54,450,603	525
GEORGE BUSH – VP	TX	Republican		525
Walter F. Mondale and	MN	Democrat	37,573,671	13
Geraldine Ferraro – VP	NY	Democrat		13
David Bergland	CA	Libertarian	227,949	
Lyndon H. LaRouche Jr.		Independent	78,807	
Sonia Johnson		Citizens	72,200	
Bob Richards		Populist	66,336	
Dennis L. Serrette		Alliance	46,868	
Gus Hall		Communist	36,386	
Mel Mason		Socialist Workers	24,706	
Delmar Dennis		American	13,161	
Edward Winn		Workers League	10,801	
Earl F. Dodge		Prohibition	4,242	
		1988		
GEORGE BUSH and	TX	Republican	48,886,097	426
J. DANFORTH QUAYLE – VP	IN	Republican		426
Michael S. Dukakis and	MA	Democrat	41,809,074	112
Lloyd Bentsen – VP	TX	Democrat		113
Lloyd Bentsen	TX	Democrat	for Pres.	1[21]
Ron Paul	TX	Libertarian	432,179	
Lenora B. Fulani	NY	New Alliance	217,219	
David E. Duke	LA	Populist	47,047	
Eugene J. McCarthy	MN	Consumer	30,905	
James C. Griffin		Amer. Independent	47,818	
Lyndon H. LaRouche Jr		Independent	25,562	
William A. Marra		Right to Life	20,504	
Edward Winn		Workers League	18,693	
James Warren		Socialist Workers	15,604	
Herbert Lewin		Peace & Freedom	10,370	
Earl F. Dodge		Prohibition	8,002	
		1992		
BILL CLINTON and	AR	Democrat	44,908,254	370
ALBERT GORE, JR. – VP	TE	Democrat		370
George Bush and	TX	Republican	39,102,343	168
J. Danforth Quayle – VP	IN	Republican		168
Ross Perot and	TX	Independent	19,741,065	
James Stockdale – VP	CA	Independent		
Andre Marrou		Libertarian	249,883	
Lenora B. Fulani		New Alliance	63,601	

There were numerous self-starter parties and independent candidates.

Candidate	State	Party	Popular Vote	Electoral
		1996		
BILL CLINTON and	AR	Democrat	47,402,357	379
ALBERT GORE, JR- VP	TN	Democrat		
Robert Dole and	KS	Republican	39,198,755	159
Jack Kemp-VP	NY	Republican		
Ross H. Perot and	TX	Reform	8,085,402	
Patrick Choate		Reform		
Ralph Nader	NY	Green	684,902	
Harry Browne		Libertarian	485,798	
Howard Phillips		U.S. Taxpayers	184,658	
John Hagelin		Natural Law	113,668	
Monica Moorehead		Workers World	29,083	
Marsha Feinland		Peace & Freedom	25,332	
Charles Collins		Independent	8,941	
James Harris		Socialist Workers	8,476	
others			49,851	
		2000*		
GEORGE W. BUSH and	TX	Republican	50,456,169	271
RICHARD CHENEY - VP	WY	Republican		271
Albert Gore, Jr. and	TN	Democrat	50,996,116	266
Joseph Lieberman	CT	Democrat		266
Ralph Nader	NY	Green	2,756,083	

(*Note: Al Gore and Joseph Lieberman defeated George W. Bush and Richard Cheney in the popular vote by approximately 539,947 votes, while George W. Bush and Richard Cheney won the Electoral College vote by one more than the minimum required. One Gore Elector abstained. These popular vote figures are from Associated Press. The results of the 2000 election may always be in question due to voting and counting irregularities in Florida, as well as U.S. Supreme Court decisions.)

1 Washington received a unanimous vote. Until 1804 each elector cast two ballots without indicating which was for President and which for Vice President. The person receiving second highest number of electoral votes was elected Vice President.

2 Pinckney was supposed to be John Adams' running mate, but due to maneuvering to place Pickering ahead of Adams, in response some of the pro-Adams Federalist electors "cut" a few votes to keep Pinckney from running ahead of Adams, thus giving Jefferson the second place by accident.

3 The Democratic Republicans voted solidly for Jefferson and his running mate, Aaron Burr, causing the tie, which put the vote into the House. Contrary to myth Burr was loyal to Jefferson and did nothing to get first place. The Federalists finally gave up the contest and some abstained to give Jefferson the victory in the House.

4 George Clinton made an effort to run for President although he was Madison's running mate, but only got six electoral votes.

5 Since no candidate had a majority of electoral votes the election was sent to

the House. Only the top three could be voted upon, and fourth place contestant Henry Clay threw his support to John Quincy Adams, who thus defeated Jackson. Adams later appointed Clay Secretary of State.

6   Richard M. Johnson failed by one vote of getting a majority of electors (since some Democrats did not approve of him) so the vote went to the Senate which elected Johnson.

7   The Whigs were not well-organized nationally and different candidates were nominated by state meetings.

8   Fillmore was also endorsed by the Whig convention in 1856 when that party was on its last legs.

9   In 1864 during the Civil War the Republicans ran as the National Union party, with Democrat Andrew Johnson running for Vice President since he was a strong pro-union Democrat.

10 The Liberal Republican candidates were endorsed by the Democratic convention. Horace Greeley died after the election, but before the electoral votes were counted. Many electors agreed to vote for popular Democrat Thomas A. Hendricks and others decided to vote for vice presidential candidate B. Gratz "Boozey" Brown. Those who voted for Brown for President had to cast their ballots for someone else for Vice President. It was all academic since Grant had won.

11 The Republicans challenged the election results in Louisiana, Florida, and South Carolina and one elector in Oregon in which it appeared that the Democratic ticket of Tilden and Hendricks had won. The Republicans submitted their own count in each case. The dispute was eventually sent to an electoral commission created by special legislation, made up of eight Republicans and seven Democrats. In each case

the commission voted eight to seven to accept the Republican count and reject the original Democratic count. This made Hayes President and Wheeler Vice President each by one electoral vote. It is not without reason that this is referred to as "The Stolen Election". The vote counts here are those accepted by the commission.

12 William Jennings Bryan was nominated by the Democrats with Sewall and then by the People's (Populist) party with Watson as his running mate.

13 Vice President Sherman died after the 1912 election, but before the electoral college voted. It was decided that Columbia University President Nicholas Murray Butler would receive his eight electoral votes. Murray agreed if it was sure he could not be elected.

14 The substantial increase in votes is due to giving the vote to women for the first time.

15 The Union Party was officially the National Union for Social Justice. It was conservative and anti-New Deal and had nothing to do with labor unions.

16 States' Rights (Dixiecrat) presidential candidate Strom Thurmond received the vote of one Tennessee Democratic elector who had been elected on a Truman slate.

17 One Democratic elector cast his ballot for Jones and Talmadge.

18 Byrd received the votes of independent (read states rights conservative) Democrats as well as one vote pledged to Nixon.

19 One Nixon-pledged elector cast his vote for John Hospers

20 One Ford-pledged elector cast his vote for Ronald Reagan.

21 Bentsen received an electoral vote for President by a West Virginia elector.

PRESIDENTIAL BIOGRAPHIES

GEORGE WASHINGTON (April 30, 1789–March 4, 1797, no party)

"Father of His Country," he was a Virginia planter, surveyor, and soldier. While a young man and still a British subject he was a lieutenant colonel in the French and Indian War, who was forced to surrender a frontier fort in 1754, after the French overwhelmed the Virginia volunteers and killed his commander. He was elected a delegate to the first Continental Congress in 1774, and after fighting broke out between patriot "Minute Men" and British troops in Massachusetts, he was named commander in the chief of the newly formed Continental Army in June 1775. He was a signer of the Declaration of Independence on July 4, 1776. The American army under Washington eventually won the Revolutionary War after many setbacks, trapping the bulk of the British army at Yorktown in October 1781. He retired to his inherited estate, Mount Vernon, but in 1787 was chosen as president of the Constitutional Convention. He was elected the first president of the United States with the unanimous vote of the Electoral College, and inaugurated April 30, 1789, at New York City, the temporary capital. Reelected unanimously in 1792, he established the tradition of a two-term maximum. He organized the first government when no parties existed, appointing Thomas Jefferson as secretary of state and Alexander Hamilton as secretary of the treasury, although those two differed both personally and philosophically. Washington managed to govern despite growing factionalism, which he deplored. He was married to widow Martha Custis and they had no children.

Born February 22, 1732, died December 14, 1799.

JOHN ADAMS (March 4, 1797–March 4, 1801, Federalist)

A Massachusetts patriot lawyer, he was a delegate to the Continental Congresses, urged naming George Washington to head the army, and Thomas Jefferson to draft the Declaration of Independence, of which Adams was a signatory. During the American Revolution, he was first chairman of the board of war and ordnance, and then minister to France. Under the Articles of Confederation, he was the first American minister to Great Britain. Adams was elected vice president to serve with Washington by receiving the second most votes. Elected in 1796 as the only Federalist president, he had difficulties with radical France, was hurt by the unpopularity of the repressive Alien and Sedition Acts, and lost the 1800 election to Thomas Jefferson. He and his wife, forceful early feminist Abigail Adams, had three sons and two daughters. Adams died on July 4, 1826, the same day as Jefferson. His last words were: "Jefferson survives."

Born October 30, 1735, died July 4, 1826.

THOMAS JEFFERSON (March 4, 1801– March 4, 1809, Democratic-Republican)

Virginia lawyer and landowner, he was a delegate to the Second Continental Congress, drafted the Declaration of Independence, and served as governor of Virginia (1779–81), minister to France under the Articles of Confederation, and first secretary of state. A multitalented man, he designed his home, Monticello, imported tomatoes and rice, wrote several historic treatises, and was president of the American Philosophical Society (1797). He founded the Democratic-Republican Party and became vice president as runner-up to Adams in the 1796 election. Tied with his running mate, Aaron Burr, under the original system of two votes per elector, he was elected, president in 1801 by the House after 36 ballots when his enemy Alexander Hamilton swung over to him. As president he made the Louisiana Purchase, doubling U.S. territory, sent the navy to defeat Barbary pirates, and settled problems with France. He was readily reelected in 1804. After his presidential terms he founded the University of Virginia. He and his wife, heiress Martha Wayles Skelton, had one son (who died young) and five daughters before her death in 1782. Later he had six children by his mulatto mistress, Sally Hemings, who was his wife's half-sister. He died on July 4, 1826, a few hours before John Adams.

Born April 13, 1743, died July 4, 1826.

JAMES MADISON (March 4, 1809–March 4, 1817, Democratic-Republican)

"Father of the Constitution" and a lawyer from Virginia, Madison outlined the Constitution ("the Virginia Plan"), and wrote some of the scholarly and popular Federalist Papers in support of the Constitution along with Alexander Hamilton and John Jay. He helped Jefferson found the Democratic-Republican Party, became a House member, and then secretary of state. He led the nation through the War of 1812, despite the burning and sacking of Washington. In 1786 he married the flamboyant charmer, Dolley Todd, and they had no children.

Born March 16, 1751, died June 28, 1736.

JAMES MONROE (March 4, 1817–March 4, 1825, Democratic-Republican)

The last of the "Virginia Dynasty," Monroe fought in the American Revolution, and became a lawyer and protégé of Jefferson. He served as congressman, senator, minister to France, governor of Virginia and as Madison's secretary of state. Elected in 1816, Monroe was reelected in 1820 with all but one vote in a brief "Era of Good Feelings." He promulgated the "Monroe Doctrine," which declared the Western Hemisphere off-limits to European interference, acquired Florida, and settled Canadian border disputes. Monroe married Elizabeth Kortright, and they had two daughters who survived infancy.

Born April 28, 1758, died July 4, 1831.

JOHN QUINCY ADAMS (March 4, 1825–March 4, 1829, National Republican)

Son of John Adams, he was a lawyer, diplomat, senator from Massachusetts, and Monroe's secretary of state. Originally a Federalist, Adams became a Democratic-Republican, and was one of four candidates for president in 1824. Designated a National Republican, he ran second in electoral votes to Andrew Jackson, but was elected by the House, after fourth-place candidate Henry Clay urged his supporters to vote for Adams. His administration was hampered by lack of a mandate and his support of high tariffs ("The Tariff of Abominations"), and he lost to Jackson in 1828. Elected to the House in 1833, he served until his death in 1848. He and his wife, British-born Louisa Johnson, had three sons and one daughter.

Born July 11, 1767, died February 23, 1848.

ANDREW JACKSON (March 4, 1829–March 4, 1837, Democrat)

Nick-named "Old Hickory" for his toughness, he was a lawyer, judge, congressman, and militia general. Born in South Carolina, he was a teenage courier for the Continental Army, moved to Tennessee, and became its first member of the House. Jackson served as a senator (1797–98). As a militia general he decisively defeated the British in the Battle of New Orleans in January 1815, fought Indians, was appointed military governor of Florida, and returned to the Senate in 1823. After losing for president in 1824, Jackson de-

feated incumbent John Quincy Adams in 1828. He made Democratic-Republicans officially the Democratic Party, defeated rechartering of the national bank, which he felt was subservient to financial interests, crushed "nullification" of federal tariff laws by state legislatures, set up the first major national convention in 1831, recognized the Republic of Texas, which had declared independence from Mexico, and led the populist Jacksonian era, in which the vote was extended to all white males. His wife, Rachel Robards, died between his election and inauguration. They had no children, but they legally adopted one and informally adopted another.

Born March 15, 1767, died June 8, 1845.

MARTIN VAN BUREN (March 4, 1837–March 4, 1841, Democrat)

A lawyer from New York, Van Buren was a close adviser and the hand-picked successor of Andrew Jackson. State attorney general, two-term senator and once governor of New York, called "Little Magician" for his political talents, Van Buren became Jackson's secretary of state and then vice president (1833). As president he set up an independent treasury system, but his popularity fell due to the 1837 depression. Defeated in 1840, he lost the Democratic nomination in 1844 and ran third as a Free Soiler candidate for president (1848). His wife, Hannah Hoes, died in 1819 after having four sons long before Van Buren became president.

Born December 5, 1782, died July 24, 1862.

WILLIAM HENRY HARRISON (March 4, 1841–April 4, 1841, Whig)

Son of a prominent Virginia family, and a professional soldier, he was appointed governor of Indiana Territory, fought Indians, and in the War of 1812 he defeated the Indians in the Battle of Tippicanoe in 1811 and the British Battle of the Thames on Canadian soil in 1813. He moved to Cincinnati, Ohio, where he was elected to the House and then the Senate. John Quincy Adams appointed him minister to Colombia, after which Harrison retired to his farm. He won 73 electoral votes as a Whig presidential candidate in 1836, and then defeated incumbent president Van Buren in 1840. Harrison caught pneumonia at his inauguration and died one month later. He and his wife, Anna Symmes, had six sons and four daughters. His grandson, Benjamin Harrison, became president.

Born February 9, 1773, died April 4, 1841.

JOHN TYLER (April 6, 1841– March 4, 1845, Whig)

A Virginia lawyer, Tyler served as representative, senator and governor. Always independent, he left the Democrats and became a Whig in 1836 in protest to Jacksonian policies. Elected vice president ("Tippicanoe and Tyler Too") in 1840, when President Harrison died after a month in office, Tyler insisted he was president and not "acting president." Never enjoying a clear mandate and facing conflicts with Whig congressional leadership, Tyler's major achievement was annexation of Texas in 1845 near the end of his term. His first wife, Letitia Christian, died while he was president in 1842, after having three sons and five daughters. Tyler then married young Julia Gardiner, and fathered five more sons and two daughters.

Born March 29, 1790, died January 18, 1862.

JAMES KNOX POLK (March 4, 1845–March 4, 1849, Democrat)

"Young Hickory" was a protégé of Andrew Jackson, who had moved from North Carolina to Tennessee, practiced law, served several terms in the House, became Speaker of the House (1835–39), and then was elected governor of Tennessee. Defeated for reelection, he wanted to run for vice president at the 1844 Democratic convention as an advocate of Texas annexation. When Van Buren declared against annexation, Polk became a "dark horse" presidential candidate, won the nomination, and defeated Whig Henry Clay. He took the nation into the Mexican War in 1846, capturing the southwest and California, split Oregon territory with British Canada at the 49th parallel, and successfully pushed for lower tariffs. Pledged to a single term, Polk did not seek reelection. Married to strong-willed Sarah Childress, Polk had no children.

Born November 2, 1795, died July 9, 1850.

ZACHARY TAYLOR (March 4, 1849–July 9, 1850, Whig)

"Old Rough and Ready," was a professional soldier, serving as an officer in the War of 1812 and Indian wars.

Born in Virginia and raised in Kentucky, he settled on a plantation in Louisiana. Called up as a general in the Mexican War, he won several battles, including the crucial fight at Buena Vista, although badly outnumbered, and became a national hero. Chosen by the Whigs for his popularity, Taylor (who had never voted) won the presidency in 1848 since the Free Soilers had split the Democrats. Much of his brief administration dealt with the problem of whether new states like California would be slave or free. Taylor died of apoplexy on July 9, 1850. He and his wife, Margaret Smith, had one son and five daughters.

Born November 24, 1784, died July 9, 1850.

MILLARD FILLMORE (July 9, 1850–March 4, 1853, Whig)

A self-taught New York lawyer and second-line Whig politician, Fillmore served three terms in the House. After losing a race for governor, Fillmore was elected state comptroller in 1847. He was nominated and elected vice president in 1848 as a protégé of New York Whig leader Thurlow Weed. When President Zachary Taylor died, Fillmore became president. As president he signed the Fugitive Slave Law, backed the Compromise of 1850, and saw entry of California into the union as a free state. Not renominated, he ran unsuccessfully for president as a Know Nothing in 1856. He and his wife, Abigail Flowers, a teacher who helped educate him, had one son and one daughter. Abigail died in 1853, and in 1858 Fillmore married widow Caroline McIntosh.

Born January 7, 1800, died March 8, 1874.

FRANKLIN PIERCE (March 4, 1853– March 4, 1857, Democrat)

Compromise "dark horse" nominee for president on a 49th convention ballot, Pierce, a lawyer, had served two terms in the House (1833–37) and five years in the Senate, resigning in 1842. A brigadier general in the Mexican War, he was in private life when nominated, after having promised his reclusive wife he would not return to politics. Pressured into signing the Kansas-Nebraska Act, which left slavery to squatters' votes in new states, he failed to be renominated. The death of one of his sons in a train wreck just before inauguration greatly depressed Pierce and his wife, Jane Appleton. Pierce reportedly drank heavily in the White House. He had three sons, only one of whom reached adulthood.

Born November 23, 1804, died November 8, 1869.

JAMES BUCHANAN (March 4, 1857– March 4, 1861, Democrat)

Pennsylvania politician and perpetual presidential aspirant, Buchanan was a lawyer, fought in the War of 1812, served five terms in the House, and as minister to Russia (1832–34), senator (1834–45), Polk's secretary of state, and Pierce's minister to Great Britain. Elected president in 1856, he sat fearful and inactive as the nation drifted toward civil war over slavery and states' rights. Although opposed to the right of any state to secede, Buchanan failed to take any action or consider force to halt the rebellion. The only bachelor President (when he was young his fiancée had committed suicide), his presidential hostess was his pretty but imperious niece, Harriet Lane.

Born April 23, 1791, died June 1, 1868.

ABRAHAM LINCOLN (March 4, 1861– April 15, 1865, Republican)

Lincoln was a frontier lawyer (born in Kentucky, but settled in Illinois), with frustrated political ambitions. He served five terms in the Illinois legislature (1834–42 and again in 1854) and one term in the House (1847– 49) as a Whig. Lincoln became the chief organizer of the new Republican Party in Illinois. By running as a Republican against Democratic senator Stephen Douglas in 1858, he gained national prominence through a series of seven debates in which he took a moderate anti-slavery stance, although he lost the Senate race 54–46 in the state legislature. At the 1860 Republican convention, fortuitously held in Chicago where the galleries were packed for him, Lincoln won the nomination over favorites like William Seward when his managers promised cabinet appointments for state delegations. He won election partly due to a three-way split among the opposition—Democrats, Southern Democrats, and Constitutional Union parties. Before he was sworn in, southern states had begun to secede from the union, to form the Confederate States of America. President Lincoln determined that the prime issue was preservation of the union and built up a Union army (but had trouble finding able, forceful generals). Lincoln stood steadfast in the face of military defeats, issued the Emancipation Proclamation, which freed slaves in war zones, and finally put generals Ulysses S. Grant and William Sherman into position to defeat the Confederacy. After his reelection in 1864, Lincoln called for "charity for all" for the returning states. Just after the end of the war, on April 14, 1865, while watching a play at Ford's Theater, Lincoln was shot by actor John Wilkes Booth and died the next morning. He was married to the volatile, unstable Mary Todd, and they had three sons, one of whom died while Lincoln was president.

Born February 12, 1809, died April 15, 1865.

ANDREW JOHNSON (April 15, 1865–March 4, 1869, Democrat elected vice president as Republican)

A tailor, Johnson was born in North Carolina and trekked to Tennessee where he set up shop and entered local politics. He served five terms in the House (1843–1853), as governor of Tennessee (1853–1857), and as senator, starting in 1857. As the only southern Democratic senator to stand by the Union, he did so with a dramatic Senate speech. In 1862 President Lincoln appointed him military governor of Tennessee, which had seceded. Nominated by the Republicans (with the behind-the-scenes support of Lincoln), he was elected vice president on the National Union ticket (basically Republican) in 1864. After Lincoln's assassination in April 1865, Johnson became president. Trying to follow Lincoln's policy of moderation in treatment of the defeated South, he granted amnesty to Confederate officers, got into trouble with "radical Republicans," and survived a politically motivated impeachment in 1868 by one vote. His wife, Eliza McCardle, taught Johnson to read and write and had three sons and two daughters. In 1875 he again won election to the Senate, the first ex-president to do so.

Born December 29, 1808, died July 31, 1875.

ULYSSES S. GRANT (March 4, 1869– March 4, 1877, Republican)

A graduate of West Point in 1843, he fought in the Mexican War and served in various military posts until 1854, when he resigned after being criticized for his heavy drinking. A store clerk when the Civil War broke out, Grant became a colonel of volunteers, rose to brigadier general, and won numerous key battles. Appointed general in chief of armies in March, 1864, Grant ground out Union victories and accepted Robert E. Lee's surrender on April 3, 1865. The unanimous nominee of Republicans (1868), he won easily. Despite western expansion and prosperity, his administration was dogged by insider corruption, which he failed to control. He won reelection over Horace Greeley, who ran on a Liberal Republican-Democratic coalition. Grant failed in an attempt to get a third nomination in 1880. He and his wife, Julia Dent (the first to be called "First Lady"), had three sons and a daughter.

Born April 27, 1822, died July 23, 1885.

RUTHERFORD B. HAYES (March 4, 1877–March 4, 1881, Republican)

Governor of Ohio, former congressman, volunteer general in the Civil War, and lawyer, Hayes was a "favorite son" candidate who became the compromise choice at the 1876 Republican National Convention. When Hayes lost the popular vote by over 215,000 across the country, Republicans challenged apparent Democratic victories in three states. Eventually the dispute was resolved by an electoral commission, made up of eight Republicans and seven Democrats, who voted 8–7 to give the electoral votes in those contested states to the Republicans, thereby electing Hayes by one electoral vote over Samuel J. Tilden. President Hayes withdrew federal troops from the South, ending reconstruction, and made tentative steps toward civil service reform. His wife Lucy Webb (known as "Lemonade Lucy" for her refusal to serve any alcohol in the White House) bore seven sons and one daughter.

Born October 4, 1822, died January 17, 1893.

JAMES A. GARFIELD (March 4, 1881– September 19, 1881, Republican)

When the forces of James G. Blaine, Ulysses S. Grant, and Senator John Sherman deadlocked at the 1880 Republican convention, the delegates turned to reluctant James A. Garfield, senator-elect from Ohio. President of Hiram College, he had volunteered for the Union army and rose to major general, and then was elected to the House nine times, starting in 1863. After four months in office, on July 2, 1881, as he walked through a Washington, D.C., railroad station, Garfield was shot by Charles Guiteau, a mentally unstable disappointed government officeseeker. Garfield lingered for two-and-half months until he died on September 19, 1881. He and his wife, Lucretia Rudolph, had four sons and a daughter.

Born November 19, 1831, died September 19, 1881.

CHESTER ALAN ARTHUR (September 19, 1881–March 4, 1885, Republican)

A smart, socially sophisticated lawyer with a reputation as the gentleman "hack" for the New York Republican machine, Arthur had done well as New York's quartermaster general during the Civil War. Arthur was offered the nomination for vice president by Garfield to please "stalwarts" (losing Grant supporters), although he had held no elective office and had been sacked as collector of customs in 1871 by Hayes. When Garfield died by assassination, Arthur surprised many by fighting for the Civil Service Reform bill (1883). He also set up a tariff commission, vetoed "pork barrel" legislation, and refused to make appointments of incompetents pushed by political bosses. He was not renominated and it later became known that by the end of his term he was terminally ill with Bright's Disease. His handsome wife, Ellen Herndon, died the year before he became vice president. They had two sons (one died in infancy) and a daughter.

Born October 5, 1829 (usually stated as October 5, 1830, but a family Bible entry shows that Arthur was actually born in 1829), died November 18, 1886.

GROVER CLEVELAND (March 4, 1885–March 4, 1889 and March 4, 1893–March 4, 1897, Democrat)

Elected reform governor of New York in 1882, Cleveland had been a lawyer, sheriff, and mayor of Buffalo. Nominated for president in 1884 over opposition of the Tammany Hall machine, Cleveland defeated James G. Blaine, thanks to a publicized claim of a Blaine supporter that the Democrats were the party of "Rum, Romanism and Rebellion." The accusation delivered the New York Catholic vote to Cleveland despite a double cross by the Tammany leadership, who refused to campaign for him, and charges that Cleveland had fathered an illegitimate son. In his first term, Cleveland vetoed numerous veterans' claims and spending bills, got through the Interstate Commerce Commission Act, and made appointments on merit. In 1888, although leading in popular votes, Cleveland lost the Electoral College vote to Benjamin Harrison. Four years later he again received the nomination and defeated Harrison. Cleveland's second term was clouded by a sharp recession, labor unrest, and the growing fight for silver as well as gold backing for the currency, in which Cleveland was solidly pro-gold. A bachelor when elected, he married his ward, Frances Folsom, at the White House (1886), when he was 49 and she was only 22. They had two sons and three daughters, including Ruth in 1891 for whom the "Baby Ruth" candy bar was named.

Born March 18, 1837, died June 24, 1908.

BENJAMIN HARRISON (March 4, 1889–March 4, 1893, Republican)

When numerous candidates cancelled each other out, the 1888 Republican National Convention turned to Benjamin Harrison, a former one-term senator, as a compromise because he had no enemies. He was President William Henry Harrison's grandson, and the party expected to lose anyway. Although behind 100,000 in the popular vote, he won 233 to 168 in electoral votes over incumbent Grover Cleveland. The only notable achievements of his administration were the Sherman Anti-Trust Act and the Sherman Silver Purchase Act, which were developed by Congress. He lost reelection to Cleveland in 1892, two weeks after the death of his wife, Caroline Scott, who had given him a son and a daughter. In 1896 he married Mary Dimmick, and they had a daughter.

Born August 20, 1833, died March 13, 1901.

WILLIAM McKINLEY (March 4, 1897–September 14, 1901, Republican)

A six-term House member known for the highly protective McKinley Tariff of 1890, who followed President Benjamin Harrison as governor of Ohio, McKinley was nominated and elected in 1896 as a pro-gold candidate over silverite William Jennings Bryan. His wealthy campaign manager, Mark Hanna, devised a "front porch" campaign in which McKinley stayed at home and met with delegations from around the country delivered by friendly railroads. A lawyer, he was the last president who fought in the Civil War. Disputes with Spain over Spanish oppressive actions in Cuba, and the blowing up of the U.S. battleship *Maine* in Havana harbor (probably an accident) led to the brief Spanish-American War in 1898. The Philippines, Guam, and Puerto Rico

thus became American possessions. Easily reelected in 1900, he was shot by a crazed anarchist while shaking hands at the Pan-American Exposition in Buffalo, New York, on September 6, 1901, and died on September 14, largely due to medical incompetence. He and his wife, Ida Saxton, had no children.

Born January 29, 1843, died September 14, 1901.

THEODORE ROOSEVELT (September 14, 1901–March 4, 1909, Republican)

A New York writer and politician, Teddy was only 42, when as vice president, he succeeded the assassinated William Mckinley. He had served in the legislature, as a federal civil service commissioner under Hayes, flamboyant reform police commissioner in New York City, and assistant secretary of the navy, before being named a colonel and second-in-command of a volunteer unit called the "Rough Riders," which helped win the battle of San Juan Hill in the Spanish-American War. His heroics led to his election as governor of New York in 1899, in which position he refused to follow boss Tom Platt's suggestions on appointments. In order to get Roosevelt out of New York, Platt pushed him for the vice presidential nomination, as did many of Teddy's friends. Five months after the 1901 inauguration, President McKinley was assassinated and Roosevelt became president. Roosevelt was an extremely energetic anti-trust, pro-conservation, favorable-to-expansion president, who easily won election in 1904 on the pledge of a "Square Deal." He attempted a political comeback in

1912 as the Progressive (Bull Moose) candidate for president, but lost. His first wife, Alice Lee, died two days after giving birth to daughter Alice in 1884. Two years later Teddy married Edith Carow, his childhood sweetheart, and they had four sons and a daughter.

Born October 27, 1858, died January 6, 1919.

WILLIAM HOWARD TAFT (March 4, 1909–March 4, 1913, Republican)

Son of a cabinet member, Taft was an Ohio lawyer, judge, U.S. solicitor general under Hayes, appointed civil governor of the Philippines and later Cuba, and Teddy Roosevelt's secretary of war, 1904–08. As Roosevelt's hand-picked successor, he was nominated for president in 1908 and defeated Democrat William Jennings Bryan. He continued anti-trust policies and set up the Department of Labor, but lacked Roosevelt's dynamism and dedication to conservation. After Taft won the 1912 Republican nomination, Teddy ran as the Progressive third-party candidate, splitting the vote so Taft ran third behind Woodrow Wilson and Roosevelt. In 1921 President Har-ding appointed him Chief Justice of the Supreme Court. He and his wife, Helen Herron, had two sons (one was Senator Robert Taft) and a daughter.

Born September 15, 1857, died March 8, 1930.

WOODROW WILSON (March 4, 1913–March 4, 1921, Democrat)

Virginia-born lawyer, constitutional scholar, college professor, and president of Princeton University (1902–10), he was elected governor of New Jersey in 1910 as a reformer and Democratic progressive. It took 46 ballots for him to get the two-thirds necessary for the nomination for president in 1912. Aided by the Republican split, he won, and his "New Freedom" administration created the Federal Reserve System, passed constitutional amendments which legalized the income tax and provided for direct election of senators, lowered tariffs, and pushed progressive conservation and consumer protection measures. Faced with growing German belligerence in the European War, Wilson ran for reelection in 1916 under the slogan "he kept us out of war." He won reelection in 1916 over Charles Evans Hughes by the margin of a razor-thin victory in California. When German submarines sank several American merchant ships supplying the Allies, Wilson asked Congress for a declaration of war in April 1917. The U.S. troops provided the impetus for an Allied victory in 1918. Wilson issued his "Fourteen Points" for postwar international peace, including formation of the League of Nations. While a hero abroad, Wilson ran into opposition to the League at home. On a speaking tour for the League, Wilson had a stroke, followed by another one, nearly died, and never fully recovered during his last 18 months in office, in which he was kept away from public view by his wife and doctors. Wilson's first wife bore three daughters, and died during his first term in 1914. In 1915 he married a widow, Edith Galt, who directed White House policies in his name during his illness, although she had no experience in government.

Born December 28, 1856, died February 3, 1924.

WARREN G. HARDING (March 4, 1921–August 2, 1923, Republican)

When all the leading contestants were deadlocked at the 1920 Republican convention in Chicago, Harding emerged from a "smoke-filled room" as the "dark horse" presidential choice of the party's political bosses. A small-town newspaper publisher from Ohio just completing his one term as senator, he was the product of a political machine that became known as the "Ohio gang." Campaigning against the League of Nations and for "normalcy," Harding won the presidency. His administration became the scene of corruption, pay-offs for leases of U.S. oil rights, and many scandals involving cabinet members and other appointees. Harding died suddenly after a year and half in office. He was married to divorcée Florence De Wolfe. They had no children, but Harding apparently had an illegitimate daughter by one of his mistresses.

Born November 2, 1865, died August 2, 1923.

CALVIN COOLIDGE (August 2, 1923–March 4, 1929, Republican)

"Silent Cal," the laconic first term governor of Massachusetts, had been nominated for vice president in 1920 by a spontaneous draft of delegates annoyed by the bosses' dictation of Warren Harding for president. He was born in Vermont, moved to Massachusetts, became a lawyer, served in the legislature, was elected lieutenant governor in 1915, and became governor in 1919. Coolidge gained national prominence with a tough declaration against the right of public employees to strike just when the Boston Police Strike had been quashed. Conservative, unimaginative, and tightfisted, Coolidge benefited from great prosperity. Easily reelected in 1924 as the clean successor to Harding's scandals, he was helped by the split of the opposition. When Coolidge declared he did not "choose to run" in 1928, the GOP looked to Herbert Hoover. He and his particularly charming wife, Grace Goodhue, had two sons.

Born July 4, 1872, died January 6, 1933.

HERBERT C. HOOVER (March 4, 1929–March 4, 1933, Republican)

"The Great Engineer," Hoover was an international mining engineer with reputations for both making money and public service. He directed private relief efforts during World War I, then served as Wilson's U.S. food administrator (1917), as director of relief and reconstruction (1918), and then as secretary of commerce under Harding and Coolidge. In 1928 he was easily nominated for president and elected on a theme of American "rugged individualism", with an expectation of a well-organized administration. Within the year the stock market crashed (October 1929), the Great Depression began, and millions of Americans lost their jobs or farms. Hoover's conventional responses proved inadequate, and his hopeful statements ("we have turned the corner") were sneered at. Renominated, he lost badly to Franklin D. Roosevelt. Born in Iowa and orphaned young, he was raised by relatives in Oregon and then moved to

California to attend Stanford University, where he met his wife, Lou Henry, also a trained engineer. They had two sons. Democratic president Harry Truman later appointed Republican Hoover to head a commission on efficiency in government, known as the "Hoover Commission."

Born August 10, 1874, died October 20, 1964.

FRANKLIN DELANO ROOSEVELT (March 4, 1933–April 12, 1945, Democrat)

Roosevelt was an upstate New York patrician and fifth cousin of Teddy Roosevelt. He became a lawyer, state senator, assistant secretary of the navy during World War I, and Democratic nominee for vice president in 1920. His political career was sidetracked when he contracted polio in 1921, and despite years of rehabilitation, never could walk or even stand without braces and crutches. Nevertheless he returned to politics to be elected governor of New York in 1928 and reelected in 1930. At the 1932 Democratic National Convention he squeaked through to get the two-thirds needed on the third ballot when House Speaker John Nance Garner threw his votes to FDR. Roosevelt came to the presidency in the heart of the Great Depression, with a program of relief, recovery, and reform that became the "New Deal." He embarked on a Hundred Days of administrative/legislative action that renewed confidence and brought some relief to the unemployed, desperate farmers, troubled banks, and businesses. Soon came stock market controls, labor relations legislation, and, eventually, social security.

Sweeping to reelection in 1936, his New Deal recovery stumbled a bit, but employment continued to grow. Roosevelt cautiously moved to aid the Allies against Nazi Germany and began rearmament. He became the first president to be elected to a third term (1940). After the Japanese bombed Pearl Harbor on December 7, 1941, Roosevelt directed a vigorous war effort and became the leading figure in the world, forging an alliance among Great Britain, the Soviet Union and China. As victory approached he urged the formation of the United Nations for international cooperation, and he was reelected again in 1944. He died from a stroke on April 12, 1945, less than a month before the German surrender and the founding meeting of the United Nations. Married to Teddy Roosevelt's niece, Eleanor Roosevelt, they had five sons (one dying in infancy) and a daughter. Originally shy, Mrs. Roosevelt became a potent force herself, writing a newspaper column, traveling widely, pushing issues such as civil rights, and, after FDR's death, serving as a UN delegate.

Born January 30, 1882, died April 12, 1945.

HARRY S. TRUMAN (April 12, 1945–January 20, 1953, Democrat)

Truman was a Missouri farmer, who did not attend college, became an artillery captain at the front in World War I, failed in a haberdashery shop, was elected county judge (supervisor/commissioner) in 1922, lost in 1924, and returned from 1926 to 1933, when he became state reemployment director. Elected U.S. senator in 1934 and reelected in 1940, Truman became nationally famous as chairman of a committee investigating war production waste. He was drafted for nomination as vice president at the 1944 Democratic convention, defeating incumbent Henry A. Wallace, too liberal and nonpolitical for many Democratic leaders. On Franklin D. Roosevelt's death Truman became president less than a month before the German surrender in World War II, the United Nations founding conference, and the final testing of the atom bomb. Truman approved the dropping of two atom bombs in August 1945, which forced Japan's surrender, proposed the Marshall Plan for rehabilitation of Europe, responded to increased aggressiveness by the Soviet Union with the "Truman Doctrine" to provide military aid to threatened nations, established the North Atlantic Treaty Organization, created the Department of Defense and the CIA, supported the founding of the nation of Israel as a Jewish homeland, desegregated the armed services, and benefited from postwar prosperity. With a vigorous "whistle stop" campaign for what he called a "Fair Deal" he overcame bad public opinion polls and third parties on the left and right (Progressive and Dixiecrats) to upset Thomas E. Dewey in the 1948 election. In his second term he sent American troops into South Korea as a UN "police force" to halt a North Korean invasion, but the Korean War became unpopular as it dragged on. His wife was Elizabeth (Bess) Wallace, and they had a daughter, Margaret (Daniels).

Born May 8, 1884, died December 26, 1972.

DWIGHT D. EISENHOWER (January 20, 1953–January 20, 1961, Republican)

A professional soldier born in Texas and raised in Kansas, Eisenhower graduated from West Point, became aide to the secretary of war (1929–32) and then to Chief of Staff Douglas MacArthur. In 1942 he was appointed commander of the European Theater of Operations, led the invasion of North Africa, became a full general, and then supreme commander of all Allied forces, directing the invasion of occupied France in 1944 and Germany in 1945. He served as president of Columbia University, wrote *Crusade in Europe*, and in 1951 became commander of NATO forces. In early 1952 Eisenhower said he would accept the Republican nomination for president if offered, and defeated Senator Robert A. Taft at the national convention. Running as a nonpolitician, "Ike" defeated Illinois governor Adlai Stevenson in 1952 and again in 1956. He negotiated a cease-fire in Korea and led a moderate administration amidst general prosperity. He continued foreign aid, supported a policy of "brinkmanship" (apparent willingness to use military force without actually doing so), and, except for a brief military presence in Lebanon, stayed out of armed conflicts. He sent the National Guard to integrate schools, and gave Vice President Richard Nixon the nasty political chores. While in office, Eisenhower suffered a heart attack, an intestinal blockage, and a stroke, but he recovered. Toward the close of his tenure, there were two international embarrassments: the Soviets placed a satellite (*Sputnik*) in orbit and then captured an American spy plane and pilot. In a parting speech he warned against the power of the "military-industrial complex." He was married to Marie ("Mamie") Doud and they had one surviving son.

Born October 14, 1890, died March 28, 1969.

JOHN F. KENNEDY (January 20, 1961–November 22, 1963, Democrat)

The first Roman Catholic president was born in Massachusetts, the son of millionaire Joseph Kennedy, who had been ambassador to Great Britain. Kennedy graduated from Harvard, joined the navy, and rescued his crew after his torpedo boat was sunk by the Japanese. He was elected to the House in 1946 and served through 1952, when he won a seat in the Senate. Bothered by back injuries and Addison's disease (a shortage of adrenal steroids), he wrote Pulitzer Prize–winning *Profiles in Courage* (1957) during a hospitalization. Nominated for president in 1960, calling for reaching out to a "New Frontier," he defeated Vice President Richard Nixon in a close race, in part due to Kennedy's effectiveness in television debates, response to anti-Catholic attacks, and his "charisma." He stumbled initially with the "Bay of Pigs," a CIA–planned attempted invasion of Cuba, but started the Peace Corps and the Alliance for Progress, gave government backing to school integration, advocated voting rights for blacks in segregated southern states, and launched a program to put a man on the moon within a decade. In 1962 he forced the Soviet Union to honor a blockade against shipment of arms to Cuba and to dismantle Cuban missile

sites. On November 22, 1963, he was assassinated by sniper Lee Harvey Oswald while riding in a motorcade in Dallas, Texas. His wife was Jacqueline Bouvier, and they had a daughter and son, plus an infant boy who died soon after birth.

Born May 29, 1917, died November 22, 1963.

LYNDON B. JOHNSON (November 22, 1963–January 20, 1969, Democrat)

A powerful majority leader of the Senate from rural Texas, in 1960 Johnson accepted the vice presidential place on the ticket with Kennedy, after running second to JFK for the presidential nomination. He had been a high school teacher, congressional aide, state director of the National Youth Administration, and was elected to Congress in 1937, serving six terms. He lost for the U.S. Senate in 1941, but won in 1948, after a contested primary vote count. Mastering negotiation and manipulation skills, he became minority leader (1953) and majority leader (1955) of the Senate. Upon Kennedy's death, Johnson became president, quickly got Kennedy's voting rights act through Congress, and then announced his own "Great Society," a package of anti-poverty programs, plus "Head Start" schooling for disadvantaged pre-schoolers, job training, and other innovations, which were soon passed. After handily defeating (1964) Republican senator Barry Goldwater, who was portrayed as a dangerous warmonger, Johnson rapidly increased American military presence on behalf of South Vietnam against communist North Vietnam. By 1966 the United States was involved in a full-scale, undeclared war at great cost in American funds and lives, draining financial support from the "Great Society." Public opposition to the war grew, and when Johnson lost the New Hampshire primary (and faced defeat in Wisconsin) to anti-war senator Eugene McCarthy, and Senator Robert Kennedy entered the race, he announced he would not seek reelection. He and his wife, Claudia ("Lady Bird") Johnson, an active conservationist, had two daughters.

Born August 27, 1908, died January 22, 1973.

RICHARD M. NIXON (January 20, 1969–August 9, 1974, Republican)

A California lawyer and navy veteran, Nixon was elected to the House in 1946 and the Senate in 1950. Chosen as a youthful running mate for Eisenhower, Nixon was almost dropped from the ticket when a secret political fund was exposed, but he explained the matter on television in what became known as the "Checkers speech," dramatically stating he would not give up a supporter's gift of a dog, Checkers. As vice president he managed crises caused by Eisenhower's illnesses, made diplomatic trips, and became the administration's "hatchet man" attacking Democratic candidates for Congress. In 1960 he lost the presidential election to Kennedy by an eyelash, and in 1962 was defeated for governor of California by Edmund G. "Pat" Brown. Then he practiced law in New York and made a comeback, winning the 1968 nomination and election over Hubert Humphrey. In his first term he opened diplomatic relations with China, trav-

eled to the Soviet Union, pursued a conservative domestic agenda while the economy did well, and after considerable delays arranged U.S. withdrawal from Vietnam. Winning in 1972 by a landslide, Nixon was soon in trouble. Vice President Spiro Agnew was forced to resign after pleading guilty to tax evasion based on bribe taking (October 1973). Worse was the Watergate scandal, in which Nixon attempted to cover-up his knowledge of a break-in and telephone bugging of Democratic offices in the Watergate complex. Tapes of conversations in the Oval Office revealed that Nixon and his top aides had known of the burglary, blocked the investigation, and lied about it. Facing impeachment, Nixon resigned on August 9, 1964, to be succeeded by Gerald Ford, who had been appointed vice president under the 25th Amendment. Although several of his staff and campaign leaders were sent to prison, Nixon was given a blanket pardon by Ford. Married to Thelma ("Pat") Ryan, Nixon had two daughters.

Born January 9, 1913, died April 22, 1994.

GERALD R. FORD (August 9, 1974–January 20, 1977, Republican)

A star Michigan University football center, Ford (born Leslie King Jr., but adopted by his stepfather, Gerald Rudolph Ford Sr.) played in the East-West Shrine and the College All-Star games, and then earned his law degree at Yale while working as an assistant coach. After practicing law, he served as an officer in the navy in the South Pacific during World War II. Elected to the House in 1948, he served for 25 years, eventually becoming Republican leader in 1965. Upon Spiro Agnew's resignation, President Nixon nominated Ford for vice president on October 13, 1973, and Ford was confirmed by Congress. After President Nixon resigned on August 9, 1974, Ford was sworn in president. A month later he pardoned Nixon, thus blocking any criminal charges against the former president. He worked against inflation, negotiated a further arms reduction with the Soviets, visited China, and vetoed numerous spending bills. He lost election to Jimmy Carter in 1976 in a close race. He and his wife, Elizabeth Bloomer (best known for founding the Betty Ford Clinic for treatment of drug and alcohol addiction), had three sons and a daughter.

Born July 14, 1913.

JIMMY CARTER (January 20, 1977–January 20, 1981, Democrat)

Carter (full name James Earl Carter Jr.) was a graduate of the Naval Academy, served in the nuclear submarine program, and in 1953 resigned to take over the family's peanut-raising business. He served on a local school board, then in the state senate, lost for governor of Georgia in 1966, and finally won the governorship in 1970, as a progressive on racial issues. With a two-year campaign effort he won the Democratic nomination in 1976, and defeated incumbent Gerald Ford. He laid out a liberal domestic agenda, championed international human rights, and brought about a peace pact between Israel and Egypt (Camp David Accords). However, his administration was plagued by mounting inflation and the inability to free 52 hostages taken by the government of Iran. He lost

reelection to Republican Ronald Reagan in 1980, only to see the hostages freed on inauguration day. He and his wife, Rosalynn Smith (who was influential on policies), had three sons and a daughter. Known for being an acknowledged "born-again" Christian, but politically liberal, as an ex-president Carter gained worldwide respect for his personal work on developing self-help housing for low-income families, and for monitoring elections (sometimes in conjunction with ex-president Ford) in newly democratic nations, negotiating the removal of Haitian dictator Gen. Raoul Cédras, and a voice for human rights.

Born October 1, 1924.

RONALD REAGAN (January 20, 1981–January 20, 1989, Republican)

A long-time movie actor and television host, Reagan, once a liberal Democrat, became an active Republican in the early 1960s. He was born in Illinois, lived in Iowa where he was a sports announcer, and moved to California when he began his movie career. He gained popularity with Republican leaders and financial backers, in part due to an effective television commercial for 1964 candidate Barry Goldwater. Reagan was elected governor of California in 1966. Elected again in 1970, Reagan made forays for the presidency in 1968 and 1976, before winning the nomination in 1980. An accomplished speaker, dubbed "The Great Communicator," he defeated President Carter and routed former vice president Walter Mondale to win reelection in 1984. Shortly after his first inauguration he nearly died after being shot in an assassination attempt by an insane young man, but he made a strong recovery. Reagan got through Congress major increases in military spending while obtaining tax cuts, which brought higher incomes into lower tax brackets (1986). He took the American military into Lebanon and Grenada without declarations of war and supplied aid to anti-communist governments. Despite his having labeled the Soviet Union as the "evil empire," Reagan developed a rapport with President Mikhail Gorbachev, signed an arms reduction pact, and gave the Soviets assistance as their economy collapsed—taking credit for the failure of international communism. Called the "teflon president" because bad news would not stick to him, toward the end of his administration, it was revealed that there had been secret sales of arms to Iran in exchange for freeing hostages and the illegal diversion of the funds to the contras, guerrillas fighting against the leftist government of Nicaragua. His deregulation of the savings and loan industry resulted in frauds and losses to depositors in the tens of billions of dollars. Increased military spending and lower taxes had quadrupled the deficit, but by the time all that became obvious, Reagan had left office. The oldest and only divorced president, Reagan had been married to movie star Jane Wyman, with whom he had a son and a daughter, and, in 1952, he married Anne ("Nancy") Davis, with whom he had another son and daughter.

Born February 6, 1911.

GEORGE H. W. BUSH (January 20, 1989–January 20, 1993, Republican)

Son of Connecticut senator Prescott Bush, President Bush (full name George Herbert Walker Bush), was born in Massachusetts, became a navy flier by lying about his age, was shot down in the South Pacific, and graduated from Yale where he captained the baseball team. Bush then moved to Texas where he started an oil business in 1951. After losing a race for the Senate in 1964, he was elected in 1966 to the House for the first of two terms and then lost for the Senate in 1970. Presidents Nixon and Ford appointed him to several positions: ambassador to the UN (1971–73), Republican national chairman (1973–74), chief liaison officer to China (1974–76), and director of the CIA (1976–77). Losing the presidential nomination to Reagan, he became the vice presidential candidate. Nominated in 1988 for president, he defeated Massachusetts governor Michael Dukakis, after trailing in the early polls. He faced the inherited savings and loan debacle, calls to reduce military spending as the Soviet threat dissolved, and rumors of his own involvement in the Iran-Contra secret arms sales for profit diversion scandal. However, when Iraq's Saddam Hussein invaded oil-rich Kuwait, Bush won a resolution from the UN and congressional authority (by a narrow margin) for use of the U.S. military to oust the Iraqis. Heavy bombing, followed by a successful lightning ground war with low American casualties that chased Hussein out of Kuwait, gave him very high ratings in popularity polls. He seemed unbeatable for 1992, but an increasingly shaky economy, his persistent late-life anti-abortion stand, failure to attack the deficit, feeble support for ex-communist states, lack of empathy with the people, and the candidacy of independent millionaire Ross Perot, caused his lead to melt away. He lost to Governor Bill Clinton in 1992 in a three-way contest. He and his wife, Barbara Pierce, had four sons (one of whom died young), including President George W. Bush and Governor Jeb Bush of Florida, and two daughters.

Born June 12, 1924.

BILL CLINTON (January 20, 1993–January 20, 2001, Democrat)

The youthful governor of Arkansas was born after his father's death in an automobile accident and was named William Jefferson Blythe Jr. He took his stepfather's last name of Clinton when he was 16. Although of humble beginnings he graduated from Georgetown University, was a Rhodes Scholar at Oxford, and earned his law degree at Yale. He briefly taught law at the University of Arkansas, and was elected state attorney general in 1976. In 1978 he was elected governor, lost two years later, and came back for four more terms. Despite charges of avoidance of the draft during the Vietnam War (which he had opposed) and claims of marital infidelity, Clinton swept to the Democratic nomination. As a centrist "new Democrat," progressive but pragmatic, he defeated incumbent president George H. W. Bush and Independent industrialist Ross Perot, although Clinton did not win a majority of the popular vote. After an uncertain first two years in which a universal health plan (developed under the direction of Clinton's wife, Hillary Rodham Clinton) was defeated and the Republicans captured control of both houses of Congress, his program of economic stimulation led to a boom in the national economy, high employment,

minimal inflation, and large tax revenue surpluses that made reduction of the national debt possible. With the passage of NAFTA (North America Trade Agreement), relaxed trade relations with China (despite opposition of organized labor), compromised environmental controls, some handgun control, family medical leave, substantial reductions of the federal payroll, and large reductions in crime, Clinton easily won reelection in 1996 over Senator Robert Dole. Clinton's envoys helped achieve a truce in Northern Ireland, brought Israeli and Palestinian leaders to a White House agreement, and by a controversial use of air power forced the Yugoslav government to halt "ethnic cleansing" in the province of Kosovo, without loss of a single American life. His second term was clouded by the persistent investigation by independent counsel Kenneth Starr into allegations that President and Mrs. Clinton had profited from a questionable real estate transaction while he was governor of Arkansas. The charges were eventually found to be groundless. However, Starr used his powers to investigate Clinton's testimony in a civil lawsuit by an Arkansas state female employee, who claimed Clinton had made an indecent proposition to her while he was governor. Starr contended that Clinton had lied under oath about a sexual liaison with a young female White House intern, which he later denied in a press conference televised around the world. This led to impeachment charges brought in the House by the Republican leadership, contending that Clinton had committed a felony by committing perjury and obstructing justice. At a dramatic trial in the Senate the president was readily acquitted. During all these travails, public opinion polls showed the approval rating of Clinton's job performance by an historic margin well above 60 percent. In the final year of his presidency, the Clintons bought a house in Chappaqua, New York, established residency there, and Hillary Rodham Clinton ran for and was elected U.S. senator from that state over Republican representative Rick Lazio after New York City mayor Rudolph Giuliani dropped out of the race due to health problems. The Clintons have a daughter, Chelsea, who was a student at Stanford University during his second term.

Born August 19, 1946.

GEORGE W. BUSH (January 20, 2001– , Republican)

Eldest son of President George Herbert Walker Bush, he was elected in 2000 after serving six years as governor of Texas. In the election Bush ran more than 500,000 popular votes behind Democrat vice president Al Gore Jr., and the election result in the electoral college was not determined until a 36-day dispute over the results in Florida, where brother Jeb Bush was governor. In the most contentious result since 1876, the U.S. Supreme Court ruled in a 5–4 vote that attempts to recount ballots (many from antiquated voting machines) violated the equal rights provision of the 14th Amendment on the basis that different counties used different standards of judging contested ballots and there was no time to recount the entire state, thus giving Bush Florida by less than 500 votes and the election by one electoral vote over the minimum required. Governor Bush, nicknamed "Dubya" or "W", was the first son of

a president elected to the top office since John Quincy Adams in 1824 and the first popular vote loser to win the electoral vote since 1888. Born in Connecticut in 1946, he grew up in Texas where his father was in the oil exploration business. He attended Philips Andover Academy, graduated from Yale, joined the Texas National Guard, learned to fly a fighter jet, but was not called up during the Vietnam War. After various jobs, he went to Harvard Business School between 1972 and 1975, earning an M.B.A. Back in Texas he started an oil and gas company, married Laura Welch, ran a losing race for Congress, merged his company that was losing money, and the new operation was sold during a down period in the oil business, although Bush eventually made a profit on his stock. Bush readily admits that during his college years he was a fraternity activist who drank too much. In 1986 Bush stopped drinking the day after his 49th birthday, and joined his wife's Methodist Church. In 1988 he worked on his father's successful presidential campaign and then returned to Texas where he put together a group of investors who bought the Texas Rangers baseball franchise, of which he became managing partner, eventually selling his minority share for a profit of more than $14 million. In 1994 he was elected governor in an upset of incumbent Ann Richards (nationally famous for her keynote speech in which she quipped that father George Bush "was born with a silver foot in his mouth"). Four years later Bush breezed to reelection over nominal Democratic opposition. With cooperation of the legislative Democrats, during Bush's first term property taxes were lowered, test scores were pushed in schools and limits on tort lawsuit recoveries were imposed. During Bush's governorship, more people were executed in one year than in any other state under any governor. Bush also signed legislation into law to allow carrying concealed weapons. Bush announced his candidacy for president as a "compassionate conservative" with backing from many of his father's friends and colleagues, and an experienced political team he had developed in Texas. In the primaries, he overcame tenacious opponent, Senator John McCain, a war hero and champion of election law reform. In the final campaign he countered his relative inexperience by recruiting experts and veterans of his father's administration as advisers, emphasized his good nature, and concentrated on messages capsulized in slogans like "a uniter and not a divider" and "returning dignity to the White House." He was also able to take advantage of candidate Gore's surprisingly uncertain performances in a series of three televised debates. Despite the strong economy, which was expected to benefit Gore as a part of a successful administration, the race turned out to be the closest in popular vote since 1960 and the tightest in the electoral vote since 1876. The Bushes have twin daughters.

Born July 6, 1946.

VICE PRESIDENTIAL BIOGRAPHIES

JOHN ADAMS (1789–1797), Federalist.

Adams was a lawyer from Massachusetts and early patriot who protested against British policies and signed the Declaration of Independence. He served as chair of a committee on munitions and then commissioner to France during the American Revolution, wrote the constitution of Massachusetts, and was appointed the first minister to Great Britain. In the first election in 1789, he was elected vice president as a northerner to balance Virginian George Washington, receiving 34 votes of the 69 electors. Adams arrived at the temporary capital, New York, 10 days before Washington did, and between April 20, 1789, and April 30, 1789, when Washington took the oath of office, the United States had a vice president, but no president. As V.P. Adams was often bored, and spent an inordinate amount of time on matters of protocol. In 1796 as the candidate of the emerging Federalist Party Adams was reelected V.P. In February 1801, Adams was elected president by the Electoral College by a margin of three votes over Thomas Jefferson. See Presidents for more information on Adams.

Born October 30, 1735, died July 4, 1826, age 90.

THOMAS JEFFERSON (1797–1801), Democratic-Republican.

Lawyer, author of the Declaration of Independence, governor of Virginia, minister to France, and the first secretary of state, Jefferson was nominated for president by a caucus of Democratic-Republican congressmen. The new Constitution provided that each elector cast two ballots without identifying the office, the person getting the second highest total would be vice president. A split among the Federalists put Jefferson in second place, and therefore elected him V.P. He wrote a manual of rules that remains as the basis for conduct of business in the Senate. Back at his home, Monticello, he fathered the sixth of his children by his slave-mistress Sally Hemings. See Presidents for more information on Jefferson.

Born April 13, 1743, died July 4, 1826, age 83.

AARON BURR (1801–1805), Democratic-Republican.

Grandson of Jonathan Edwards, the famed preacher, New York lawyer, Revolutionary War hero at 24, Burr was known for his ambition and political organizing skills. Elected state assemblyman, attorney general, and U.S. senator, he was the unsuccessful vice presidential nominee of the Democratic-Republicans in 1796. As running mates in 1800 Jefferson and Burr tied with 73 electoral votes (one elector was supposed to vote for a noncandidate so Burr would run second), creating a constitutional crisis. The tied election was sent to the

House of Representatives, and for 36 ballots Jefferson could not get a majority of states. Finally the Federalists gave in and one member abstained, electing Jefferson. Burr established a reputation as an able and fair presiding officer of the Senate. Alexander Hamilton attacked Burr's honesty that led to a duel in which Burr shot and killed Hamilton, effectively ending his own political career. Later Burr was involved in a scheme to create a new nation out of western lands, leading to a charge of treason of which he was acquitted.

Born February 6, 1756, died September 14, 1836, age 80.

GEORGE CLINTON (March 4, 1805–April 12, 1812), Democratic-Republican.

Clinton was a lawyer and first American governor of New York, who served seven terms. During the revolution, he led militia forces in a series of defensive actions against the British. Originally opposed to a new constitution he eventually agreed to support it in the name of national unity. In 1792 he was a losing candidate for vice president, while supporting Washington who was unopposed. To provide a north-south balance, he was Jefferson's running mate in 1804 under the 12th Amendment, which separately identified the votes for president and vice president. Running with James Madison in 1808, he was reelected. Clinton was aging, often did not attend sessions of the Senate, and died in office.

Born July 26, 1839, died April 20, 1812, age 73.

ELBRIDGE GERRY (March 4, 1813–November 23, 1814), Democratic-Republican.

A Massachusetts merchant, he was a signer of the Declaration of Independence, member of Congress, negotiator with France, and governor. As a delegate to the Constitutional Convention Gerry refused to sign the new Constitution, due to several objections including the creation of the vice presidency. As governor Gerry signed a bill creating a sprawling House district favorable to the Democratic-Republicans, which a cartoonist likened to a salamander. So the process of drawing districts in strange configurations for political advantage became known as "gerrymandering." He was elected as Madison's vice president in his race for reelection in 1812. Gerry died less than two years into his term.

Born July 17, 1744, died November 13, 1814, age 70.

DANIEL D. TOMPKINS (1817–1825), Democratic-Republican.

Handsome, personable, and a skilled politician, Tompkins was a lawyer, a congressman, and state court justice before being elected governor of New York when just 32. He was Governor for 10 years (1807–17) and during the War of 1812 led the resistance to British invasions of his state. Only 42 years old when nominated by the Democratic-Republican caucus as the vice presidential running mate of Virginian James Monroe, he was easily elected in 1816 and reelected in 1820. While he was vice president, he became embroiled with the New York legislature over his claims for personal funds he had spent for state defense during the war. Tompkins began drinking heavily and by the end of his second term, he was a hopeless alcoholic. He died of alcoholism only three months after leaving office.

Born June 21, 1774, died June 11, 1825, age 50.

JOHN C. CALHOUN
(1825–December 28, 1832), Democratic-Republican (first term), Democrat (second term).

South Carolinian Calhoun was the champion of southern interests and states' rights for 40 years. A Yale-educated lawyer, he had been a state legislator, member of the House of Representatives (1811–17), and a leading "War Hawk" favoring war with Great Britain, before President Monroe appointed him secretary of war in 1817. He became a candidate for vice president when the Pennsylvania caucus of Democratic-Republicans endorsed him for that position. The idea spread to other states. While none of the four presidential candidates could get a majority of the Electoral College, Calhoun was easily elected vice president and served with President John Quincy Adams. When Jackson defeated Adams in 1828, Calhoun was Jackson's running mate. Calhoun and Jackson had a falling out when the vice president claimed that states could "nullify" federal laws, and because he snubbed the wife of the secretary of war. Calhoun resigned the vice presidency in the final year of his term to accept election to the U.S. Senate.

Born March 18, 1782, died March 31, 1850, age 68.

MARTIN VAN BUREN
(1833–1837), Democrat.

Nicknamed "the Little Magician" for his skills in leading the Democratic-Republicans (later Democrats) of New York, the young lawyer was a state senator, state attorney general, U.S. senator (1821–28), and briefly governor of New York, until appointed secretary of state by President Jackson. He was soon Jackson's closest political adviser. Jackson insisted that Van Buren be his vice presidential teammate in 1832. To guarantee this, Jackson called the first Democratic Party national convention in Baltimore, where the delegates nominated Van Buren. As vice president he led the Jackson Democrats in the Senate, but avoided entering into debates. In 1835 he was nominated for president and in 1836 was elected. See Presidents for more information on Van Buren.

Born December 5, 1782, died July 14, 1862, age 79.

RICHARD MENTOR JOHNSON
(1837–1841), Democrat.

A Kentucky lawyer, Johnson had served two terms in the House, 10 years as a senator, and another four terms as a representative until nominated by the Democrats to run with Van Buren in 1836. Johnson gained fame in the War of 1812. In the battle of the Thames during an invasion of Canada, Johnson led a charge that turned the tide of battle. He claimed to have killed Shawnee chief Tecumseh, who was actually shot by a fusillade from the American troops. Although Van Buren gained a clear majority of electors, several Democrats voted for an Anti-Masonic candidate for vice president, leaving Johnson one vote short (with only 73) of a clear majority, and the election was sent to the Senate, which promptly elected Johnson. While vice president bachelor Johnson lived openly with his part-black mistress (whom he was prohibited by law from marrying) and introduced his two quadroon daughters to Washington society. At the 1840 Democratic National Convention, there was considerable opposition to Johnson, so the delegates picked Van Buren for reelection, but they did not endorse Johnson for V.P., but he ran anyway, and lost along with Van Buren.

Born October 17, 1780, died November 19, 1850, age 70.

JOHN TYLER (March 4, 1841–April 4, 1841), Whig.

A former representative, governor, and senator from Virginia, Tyler was the unsuccessful vice presidential nominee of the "States' Rights" Whigs in 1836 after he was a lonely vote against giving President Jackson the power to use troops to enforce tariffs in southern states. On December 4, 1839, the Whig National Convention nominated Tyler as William Henry Harrison's running mate for 1840 because he was a well-known former Democrat and a supporter of Henry Clay at the convention. Under the slogan "Tippicanoe and Tyler Too" they won easily. Tyler was only vice president for one month, when he was notified that President Harrison had died from pneumonia caught in the rain at the inaugural. During his horseback ride from his home in Virginia, Tyler determined that he would be sworn in as president, and not as "acting president" which some cabinet members would have liked since it would diminish Tyler's political strength. On April 6, 1840, he took the presidential oath in Washington as president, an important precedent. See Presidents for more information on Tyler.

Born March 29, 1790, died January 18, 1862, age 71.

GEORGE MIFFLIN DALLAS (March 4, 1845–March 4, 1849), Democrat.

From a prominent Pennsylvania family, Dallas was mayor of Philadelphia, U.S. attorney, two years as U.S. senator (1831–33), then attorney general of Pennsylvania and minister to Russia. He was nominated for V.P. at the chaotic Democratic national convention in 1844. The favorite for the Democratic presidential nomination was ex-president Van Buren, with former Tennessee governor James Knox Polk the probable vice presidential nominee. Then three weeks before the convention Van Buren announced he was opposed to annexing the Republic of Texas. When pro-annexation delegates kept Van Buren from getting the two-thirds vote he needed, pro-Texas Polk was put forward on the eighth ballot and on the ninth was nominated, leaving the vice presidential slot open. The delegates nominated Senator Silas Wright Jr. of New York. However, the convention results in Baltimore were sent to Washington, D.C., by the newly invented telegraph. Senator Wright declined the nomination by return wire. Dallas's brother-in-law, Senator Robert Walker of Mississippi, began a winning floor campaign for the nomination of Dallas, a vocal advocate of Texas annexation. As vice president, Dallas courageously broke a Senate tie in favor of a low tariff bill opposed by industries in his home state. He also urged Polk to reach a settlement with Britain over the division of Oregon Territory. Dallas, Texas, is named for him.

Born July 10, 1792, died December 31, 1864, age 72.

MILLARD FILLMORE (March 4, 1849–July 9, 1850), Whig.

Fillmore was nominated for vice president at the 1848 Whig national convention as a political favorite of New York State party boss Thurlow Weed, and as a balance to nonpolitical presidential nominee, General Zachary Taylor. A largely self-taught attorney, Fillmore had served four terms in Congress, lost a race for governor, and the year before the convention had been elected state comptroller. He served as vice president for less than a year and a half when Taylor suddenly died. See Presidents for more information on Fillmore.

Born January 7, 1800, died March 8, 1874, age 74.

WILLIAM RUFUS DEVANE KING (March 4, 1853–April 18, 1853), Democrat.

After an exhausting multiballot nomination went to compromise darkhorse Franklin Pierce, the Democratic delegates at their June 1852 convention quickly nominated long-time Senate leader King for vice president. A graduate of the University of North Carolina, he became a lawyer at 20, a state legislator at 21, and was elected to Congress when only 25. After two terms he moved to Alabama, and was elected one of that state's first senators. In the 1820s he founded the town of Selma. He was a Jacksonian leader in the Senate, 10 years as President Pro Tem, until he was appointed minister to France (1844–1846), and was appointed to a vacant seat in the Senate for four more years, serving again as President Pro Tem. What the delegates did not know was that Senator King was severely ill with tuberculosis. The Pierce-King ticket swept to a landslide victory. In December, King went to Cuba in a futile attempt to restore his health. Congress passed a bill to allow him to take the oath of office in Cuba, so he was sworn in at Havana, so weak he had to be held erect by aides. Desiring to return to the United States, Vice President King was shipped home to his plantation, King's Bend. He died a day after his arrival, having served only a month and a half.

Born April 7, 1786, died April 18, 1853, age 67.

JOHN CABELL BRECKINRIDGE (March 4, 1857–March 4, 1861), Democrat.

At 35 the youngest vice president, Breckinridge was nominated from the floor by a Democratic delegate at the 1856 Democratic convention, and despite his vocal protests he was quickly chosen to run with James Buchanan. John was the grandson of John Breckinridge, representative, senator, and attorney general appointed by Jefferson. Tall, handsome, and a well-known orator, John C. Breckinridge was an officer in the Mexican War, served in the Kentucky state legislature and won two terms in Congress (1851–55) before declining to run again because he needed to rebuild his law practice. As vice president he was only consulted by President Buchanan once (on whether to hold a national day of prayer), despite his potential influence on border states on the issue of secession. In 1860, he was nominated for president by the southern Democrats when the national convention split into two factions. In the four-way race in 1860 won by Abraham Lincoln, Breckinridge finished third in popular vote, but second in electoral votes. In late 1860 he was elected a U.S. senator to begin service when his V.P. term ended in March 1861. The last southern senator to leave the Senate for the Confederacy, Breckinridge did not officially resign, and was therefore expelled by resolution on December 4, 1861. He became a brigadier general and later secretary of war for the Confederacy. Breckinridge fled to Europe, returned to Kentucky in 1868, and helped found a railroad.

Born January 21, 1821, died May 17, 1875, age 54.

HANNIBAL HAMLIN (March 4, 1861–March 4, 1865), Republican.

When the second Republican national convention (1860) surprisingly chose Abraham Lincoln of Illinois as its standard bearer, the delegates geographically balanced the ticket with Maine senator Hannibal Hamlin, a lawyer and former Democrat who had split with his old party over the issue of slavery. He and Lincoln, who had never met before the campaign, won easily over divided opposition, but the southern secession began even before they were inaugurated. Hamlin urged Lincoln to issue the Emancipation Proclamation and to authorize black recruits in the Union army. Hamlin was not renominated, but in 1866 was again elected to the Senate, serving for two more terms, followed by an ambassadorship to Spain.

Born August 27, 1809, died July 4, 1891, age 81.

ANDREW JOHNSON (March 4, 1865–April 15, 1865), Democrat elected on National Union (Republican) ticket.

Tough Tennesee Democrat Johnson started life as an illiterate tailor, who built up a business, learned to read from his wife and children, and entered local politics. He was elected a representative (1843–53), governor (1853–57), and senator in 1857. When the Civil War began, he was the only southern senator to stick with the Union, which he announced with a dramatic speech on the Senate floor. Appointed military governor of Tennessee by President Lincoln in 1862, he administered those sections of war-ravaged Tennessee occupied by Union forces and managed to keep the state from the Confederacy. To form a unity ticket with the best chance of winning in 1864, Lincoln worked quietly to get Johnson the V.P. nomination on the Republican "National Union" slate, without insulting loyal Hamlin. With the Union armies doing well, Lincoln and Johnson won easily. At the inaugural, Johnson was suffering from influenza, took several strong drinks of brandy, and made a rambling speech to the Senate, causing rumors that he was a drunkard. On the night of April 14, 1865 (just 40 days into the term), President Lincoln was shot while watching a play at Ford's Theater. One plotter stabbed but did not kill Secretary of State William Seward at his home. The assassin assigned to Johnson lost his nerve and got drunk. Notified of the shooting of Lincoln, Johnson walked to the house where Lincoln lay, and consoled Mrs. Lincoln. The next morning Lincoln died and Johnson was sworn in as president. See Presidents for more information on Johnson.

Born December 29, 1808, died July 31, 1875, age 66.

SCHUYLER COLFAX (March 4, 1869–March 4, 1873), Republican.

An Indiana newspaper publisher and former Whig, Colfax was a founder of the Republican Party in 1854 and was elected to seven terms in the House beginning that year. Elected Speaker of the House in 1862, he was nominated by the Republican National Convention in Chicago in 1868 for vice president with General Ulysses S. Grant for president. They easily swamped the Democrats. During the first Grant term the Credit Mobilier scandal came to light in which congressmen had been given stock in return for favorable votes on railroad subsidies and other benefits for railways. One of those who had received stock was Colfax. Tarnished by charges of bribe-taking, Colfax was unable to overcome the opposition of Grant to his renomination. Never officially charged with corruption, Colfax became a lecturer.

Born March 23, 1823, died January 13, 1885, age 61.

HENRY WILSON (March 4, 1873–November 22, 1875), Republican.

To replace Colfax for Grant's 1872 reelection bid, the Republican convention nominated Massachusetts senator Henry Wilson. Wilson, born Jeremiah Jones Colbaith, had officially changed his name when he turned 21. He was an apprentice cobbler, who soon owned his own shoe company. Elected to the state legislature as a Whig, he later published an anti-slavery Free Soil newspaper and wrote history books. He was elected to the U.S. Senate in 1854 by a coalition of Native Americans (Know Nothings), Free Soilers, and anti-slavery Democrats, but within a year joined the newly formed Republican party. During the Civil War he was chairman of the Senate Committee on military affairs. Fortunately for Wilson, although he had received some railroad stock, he had returned it. During his third year in office he died of a heart attack in the Capitol, and was the only incumbent vice president to lie in state in the Capitol rotunda.

Born February 16, 1812, died November 22, 1875, age 63.

WILLIAM A. WHEELER (March 4, 1877–March 4, 1881), Republican.

The 1876 Republican presidential nominee, Ohio governor Rutherford B. Hayes, was untainted by the scandals of the Grant administration. For vice president the party leadership wanted an honest man from vote-rich New York, and William A. Wheeler was a straight arrow from that state. A lawyer and former district attorney he had served five nonconsecutive and inconspicuous terms in the House of Representatives. When his name was first mentioned to Governor Hayes, he asked, "Who's Wheeler?" They were elected in the so-called stolen election of 1876 when the Democratic ticket had the popular majority, but the Republicans challenged the vote count in three southern states and Oregon, and a commission voted 8 to 7 to accept the Republican count, giving Hayes and Wheeler the election by 185 to 184 electoral votes, announced two days before inauguration day. As vice president Wheeler became a close friend of President Hayes and his wife Lucy, and was a frequent guest at the White House.

Born June 30, 1819, died June 4, 1887, age 67.

CHESTER ALAN ARTHUR (March 4, 1881–September 20, 1881), Republican.

A bright (Phi Beta Kappa) New York lawyer, he first gained attention by successfully suing to desegregate New York City's streetcars. Arthur was the state's quartermaster general during the Civil War. A debonair operative for the Republican state machine, he was rewarded by President Grant with appointment to the lucrative job of collector of the port of New York, responsible for handing out jobs to the party faithful. President Hayes removed Arthur as a symbol of the "spoils" system. At the 1880 national convention, Grant's attempt to run again was blocked and after 36 ballots Congressman James A. Garfield was nominated. Garfield wanted to mend fences by picking one of Grant's backers (known as "Stalwarts"). Angry

New York state boss Roscoe Conkling vetoed the idea, but when Arthur, who had never held elective office, was approached about taking the second place, he readily accepted. After only four months in office, President Garfield was shot by a demented office seeker, lingered for two months, and died on September 19, 1881, making Arthur president. He surprised his critics by becoming a champion of civil service reform, vetoing pork barrel bills, and running an efficient and honest administration. See Presidents for more information on Arthur.

Born October 5, 1829 (he officially gave his birth as 1830, but an entry in the family Bible found in 1972 showed he was born in 1829, possibly switching years with his brother who died young) at either Fairfield, Vermont, or across the border in Canada, died November 18, 1886, age 56.

THOMAS A. HENDRICKS (March 4, 1885–November 25, 1885), Democrat.

A veteran politician from Indiana, lawyer Hendricks had been a state legislator, representative, senator, and governor of the state. In 1876 he had been Samuel J. Tilden's running mate in the so-called stolen election taken by Hayes. Hendricks was a "favorite son" hopeful for president at the 1884 convention, but was nominated for vice president to run with New York reform governor Grover Cleveland, as a balance, constituting a western pro-silver old pol to the eastern hard money political newcomer. Hendricks died suddenly on a visit to Indiana after only seven months in office.

Born September 7, 1819, died November 25, 1885, age 66.

LEVI P. MORTON (March 4, 1889–March 4, 1893), Republican.

An industrialist turned banker as a co-venturer with the J. P. Morgan interests, multimillionaire Morton had twice been elected to the House, served as ambassador to France, and in 1880 on the advice of New York boss, Roscoe Conkling, rejected an offer of the vice presidential nomination with Garfield. Chosen as running mate with Benjamin Harrison by the Republicans who believed they had little chance, the ticket upset Cleveland. Criticized for not cutting off dilatory tactics of senators, he was not renominated. In 1895 Morton was elected governor of New York.

Born May 16, 1824, died May 16, 1920, age 96.

ADLAI E. STEVENSON (March 4, 1893–March 4, 1897), Democrat.

An Illinois lawyer and political leader, Stevenson served two terms in the House before he was appointed assistant postmaster general in the first Cleveland administration. There he gained the nickname "Adlai the Ax" for replacing Republican postal workers with Democrats. He was selected for nomination in 1892 to represent party interests with independent-minded Cleveland. Stevenson was nominated again for V.P. in 1900 in a losing effort. He was grandfather of Adlai Stevenson, 1952 and 1956 Democratic presidential nominee.

Born October 25, 1835, died June 14, 1914, age 78.

GARRET A. HOBART (March 4, 1897–November 21, 1899), Republican.

Lawyer-banker Hobart's only government experience was 10 years in the New Jersey legislature. In 1896 his nomination for vice president was dictated by nominee William McKinley's campaign manager, Mark Hanna. Hanna liked Hobart because he was a Hanna ally on the Republican National Committee, a G.O.P. fundraiser, and more of a "hard money" man than McKinley. He died two and a half years into his term.

Born June 3, 1844, died November 21, 1899, age 55.

THEODORE ROOSEVELT (March 4, 1901–September 14, 1901), Republican.

After gaining notoriety as a young New York legislator, "Teddy" served on the federal Civil Service Commission for six years, and for two years was New York City police commissioner, routing out corruption. An early supporter of McKinley he was rewarded appointment as assistant secretary of the navy. An ardent outdoorsman, a goal he used to overcome childhood asthma, he recruited a volunteer unit for the Spanish-American War, called the "Rough Riders," and was hailed as a hero in the capture of Cuba. He was swept into the governorship in 1899. However, he annoyed Senator Thomas Platt by refusing to appoint Platt's favorites. He was pushed for the vice presidential nomination by friends and by Boss Platt, who wanted him out of New York. Mark Hanna was opposed, yelling: "Don't any of you realize that there is only one life between that madman and the Presidency?" Five months after inauguration, McKinley was shot by an anarchist while shaking hands at an exhibition, and died a few days later. Roosevelt was the first V.P. elevated to the presidency who won reelection. See Presidents for more information on Roosevelt.

Born October 27, 1858, died January 6, 1919, age 60.

CHARLES W. FAIRBANKS (March 4, 1905–March 4, 1909), Republican.

An Indiana lawyer, serving his second term in the Senate, Fairbanks was the choice of Republican leaders to provide a conservative balance to progressive, trust-busting Roosevelt, with whom he was never close. Fairbanks refused nomination with William Howard Taft in 1908, but did run for V.P. in the losing race of Charles Evans Hughes in 1916. The city of Fairbanks in Alaska is named for him.

Born May 11, 1852, died June 4, 1918, age 66.

JAMES SCHOOLCRAFT SHERMAN (March 4, 1909– October 30, 1912), Republican.

The 1908 Republican convention settled on veteran New York congressman "Sunny Jim" Sherman, known for his natty clothes, parliamentary skills, and good nature. He was renominated in 1912 in the tumultous convention when Roosevelt and the progressives walked out, but his health was precarious. Sherman died after the election that he and Taft had lost, his eight electoral votes being cast for university president Nicholas Murray Butler.

Born October 24, 1855, died October 30, 1912, age 57.

THOMAS R. MARSHALL (March 4, 1913–March 4, 1921), Democrat.

A small-town Indiana lawyer, Marshall was in his second term as governor with a reputation for impeccable honesty and as a liberal ("with the brakes on" he said). In the 1912 Democratic convention 45-ballot marathon for the presidential nomination finally won by Governor Woodrow Wilson, Indiana had switched Marshall's favorite son votes to Wilson. Wilson's manager recommended Marshall, and he was easily nominated. The funniest vice president, he was well known for interrupting a boring speaker with "what this country needs is a good five-cent cigar," and describing the vice presidency as a "catatonic state" in which he knew what was happening but could do nothing about it. Reelected with Wilson in 1916, he was the first V.P. since Daniel Tompkins (1817–25) to serve two complete terms. Wilson suffered a serious stroke with 18 months left in his second term, but Mrs. Wilson managed to keep Marshall from seeing the president. Despite urging by some government officials, Marshall refused to take any step which might be interpreted as usurping presidential powers.

Born March 14, 1854, died June 1, 1925, age 71.

CALVIN COOLIDGE (March 4, 1921–August 2, 1923), Republican.

Vermont-born Coolidge was a lawyer who rose from city councilman and mayor of Northhampton, Massachusetts, to the State Senate, two years as lieutenant governor, and two years as governor. He gained national fame by declaring during a Boston police strike: "There is no right to strike against the public safety, by anybody, anywhere, any time." After the party power brokers emerged from the "smoke-filled room" at the 1920 G.O.P. convention to back Senator Warren Harding for president, the delegates refused to accept dictation of a running mate. When a delegate nominated Coolidge from the floor, it triggered sustained applause, and a landslide first ballot win for him. After serving less than a year and a half, Harding died amid clouds of scandal. "Silent Cal" provided stability and rectitude without saying much. See Presidents for more information on Coolidge.

Born July 4, 1872, died January 5, 1933, age 60.

CHARLES G. DAWES (March 4, 1925–March 4, 1929), Republican.

Dawes was a lawyer, utility executive, founder of a major Chicago bank, brigadier general in charge of military purchases in Europe during World War I, first director of the Bureau of the Budget (under Harding), and winner of the Nobel Peace Prize for restructuring war reparation payments. When the delegates to the 1924 convention nominated former

Illinois governor Frank Lowden as Coolidge's running mate, Lowden declined. The leadership proposed Dawes, who was nominated in one ballot. He got off on the wrong foot with the Senate, lecturing them on their inefficiency and habits of delay. Then he overslept and failed to break a tie on Coolidge's nomination for attorney general, causing his defeat. He did not contend for the presidential nomination in 1928, but he was appointed to the Reconstruction Finance Corporation board by Democrat Franklin D. Roosevelt.

Born August 27, 1865, died April 23, 1951, age 85.

CHARLES CURTIS (March 4, 1929–March 4, 1933), Republican.

As Herbert Hoover's running mate the Republican leadership in 1928 chose Senate majority leader, 68-year-old Charles Curtis. A one-quarter Kaw Indian, he had lived on a reservation as a child, became a teenage jockey, and a lawyer at 21. First elected to the House when less than 30, he served eight terms before moving up to the Senate. Although popular with his colleagues he was never close to Hoover. They were both renominated in 1932 and lost to Franklin D. Roosevelt.

Born January 25, 1860, died February 8, 1936, age 76.

JOHN NANCE GARNER (March 4, 1933–January 20, 1941), Democrat.

Born in a Texas log cabin, Garner was a lawyer at 21, a judge, a state legislator, and in 1902 was elected to the

House of Representatives where he served 30 years, finally becoming Speaker in 1931. At the 1932 Democratic convention in Chicago, New York governor Franklin D. Roosevelt had a majority of delegates, but could not reach the required two-thirds. He was blocked by 1928 candidate Al Smith and Garner, who had upset Roosevelt in the California primary, with the backing of the Hearst newspapers in that state. After three ballots, at the urging of William Randolph Hearst, Garner released his California and Texas delegates to FDR, giving him the nomination. Garner took the proffered V.P. nomination although doubtful of giving up the Speaker's power. He was publicly loyal to Roosevelt, but did not like some New Deal innovations and stopped attending cabinet meetings. Nevertheless, FDR wanted the same team in 1936. Garner opposed a third term for the president in 1940. Garner's well-known evaluation of the vice presidency was "It ain't worth a pitcher of warm spit." He died just shy of 99 years old, the longest living vice president. John F. Kennedy stopped to congratulate Garner on his 95th birthday a few hours before JFK was assassinated.

Born November 22, 1868, died November 7, 1967, age 98.

HENRY A. WALLACE (January 20, 1941–January 20, 1945), Democrat.

Appointed secretary of agriculture by Roosevelt in 1933, Wallace was an agricultural economist, developer of hybrid corn, and pro-Roosevelt editorial writer for *Wallaces' Farmer and Iowa Homestead*. Originally a Republican (his grandfather was secretary of agriculture appointed by Harding), he became a fervent supporter of FDR and the New Deal. When Democratic Party leaders begged Roosevelt to run again in 1940, he demanded that they name Wallace as his running mate to assure strong support for his programs. Despite complaints that Wallace was too liberal and a drag on the ticket, he was nominated. Roosevelt gave Wallace more responsibility than any previous V.P., including head of the Economic Defense Board. However, he got into a public squabble with the secretary of commerce, which embarrassed the administration, and there was considerable opposition to his being renominated in 1944. At a raucous session, in which Wallace almost stampeded the convention with a vigorous seconding speech for FDR, the anti-Wallace forces successfully coalesced around Senator Harry Truman. He loyally campaigned for the Roosevelt-Truman ticket and was rewarded with appointment as secretary of commerce. Wallace later split with Truman, ran in 1948 as a protest candidate under a new Progressive Party banner, eventually rejoined the Republican Party, returned to plant genetics, and died of Lou Gehrig's disease.

Born October 7, 1888, died November 18, 1965, age 77.

HARRY S. TRUMAN (January 20, 1945–April 12, 1945), Democrat.

Missourian Truman entered politics after returning from World War I where as captain he whipped into shape a notoriously undisciplined volunteer outfit. Failing in the haberdashery business, he was elected county judge (commissioner) with the support of the Kansas City Pendergast machine, and also worked for the state automobile association. In 1934 the Pendergasts picked Truman to run for the U.S. Senate, since they needed a "clean" candidate. Reelected in 1940, he gained national fame as chair of the Special Committee to Investigate the National Defense Program. A tough investigator, he saved the nation billions of dollars by exposing inflated costs, corruption, and inefficiency. As the 1944 Democratic convention convened President Roosevelt stated that, although incumbent Wallace was his personal choice, Truman was acceptable to him, a broad hint that propelled Truman to the nomination. As vice president, Truman had little contact with the president, and had not been told of the development of the atomic bomb. Less than three months in office, Truman was suddenly thrust into the presidency when FDR died of a cerebral hemorrhage. See Presidents for more information on Truman.

Born May 8, 1884, died December 26, 1972, age 88.

ALBEN W. BARKLEY (January 20, 1949–January 20, 1953), Democrat.

A Paducah, Kentucky, attorney, he served seven terms in the House of Representatives before election to the Senate in 1926. Barkley was Senate majority leader 1937–47, and minority leader 1947–49. Barkley invigorated the dispirited delegates to the 1948 Democratic national convention with a tub-thumping keynote speech. When Truman was renominated he asked a committee of party leaders to make a recommendation and they

chose 70-year-old Barkley. The Truman-Barkley team campaigned hard and upset the favored Thomas E. Dewey and Earl Warren slate. While vice president, widower Barkley remarried. He added a word to the language, calling himself "Veep." After his term he was again elected to the Senate, but he died a year later.

Born November 24, 1877, died April 30, 1956, age 78.

RICHARD M. NIXON (January 20, 1953–January 20, 1961), Republican.

Nixon was a lawyer from southern California and a navy veteran when elected to the House in 1946, claiming that the incumbent was supported by communists. He received national attention as a member of the House Un-American Activities Committee (HUAC) by pursuing former diplomat Alger Hiss for allegedly lying about his connections with communists. In 1950 he was elected to the Senate. Promoted by Thomas E. Dewey, Nixon was chosen by nominee Dwight D. Eisenhower, as a youthful balance to the ticket. When it was reported that he had a secret fund for political and personal use, Nixon saved himself with a television speech in which he denied doing anything improper, best remembered for an emotional statement that he would not return the dog "Checkers" given to his family by a supporter. As V.P. he was a tough campaigner for Republican candidates (leaving Eisenhower to stay above the fray), but he faced two crises when Eisenhower first suffered a heart attack and later a stroke. Nixon saw to it that public confidence was maintained while careful not to take over any presidential powers. Eisenhower and Nixon were renominated and reelected in 1956. In 1960 Nixon was the first sitting vice president since John C. Breckinridge in 1860 to run for president. He lost a close race to John F. Kennedy, failed in a campaign for governor of California in 1962, but returned for a second nomination and election as president in 1968. See Presidents for more information on Nixon.

Born January 9, 1913, died April 22, 1994, age 81.

LYNDON B. JOHNSON (January 20, 1961–November 22, 1963), Democrat.

Johnson had been a school teacher, congressional aide, Texas state director of the National Youth Administration, and six-term representative in the House, when elected to the Senate in 1948. He became Democratic minority leader while still in his first term, and Senate majority leader in 1955. The chief rival to John F. Kennedy at the 1960 Democratic convention, Johnson accepted JFK's offer of support for the second place on the ticket. In the campaign LBJ helped deliver several southern states, probably the one time that the V.P. candidate made the difference in the result. During a trip to mediate a schism in the Texas Democratic Party, as the Kennedy motorcade entered Dallas the president was shot in the head by sniper Lee Harvey Oswald. When Kennedy was pronounced dead, Johnson summoned a federal judge to the presidential plane, where the judge administered the presidential oath with Kennedy's widow, Jacqueline (still splattered with her hus-

band's blood), standing by. Johnson used the national sympathy for the slain president to push through the Civil Rights Act of 1964 and other New Frontier legislation. See Presidents for more information on Johnson.

Born August 27, 1908, died January 22, 1973, age 64.

HUBERT H. HUMPHREY (January 20, 1965–January 20, 1969), Democrat.

As a young political science professor Humphrey had helped weld together a coalition between Minnesota's Farmer-Labor Party and the Democrats, and he was elected mayor of Minneapolis in 1945. He gained national prominence as the leader of the fight for a civil rights plank in the 1948 Democratic platform, and later that year was elected to the Senate. He entered the 1960 presidential primaries, but dropped out after losing to Kennedy in West Virginia. At the 1964 convention, President Johnson insisted on keeping his choice for running mate a secret until he could make a dramatic announcement from the podium. After previously hinting at others he named Senator Humphrey. As vice president, despite personal doubts, he loyally supported Johnson's policy of escalating military involvement in Vietnam. In March 1968, faced with mounting primary opposition from senators Eugene McCarthy and Robert Kennedy, Johnson announced he would not seek renomination. Humphrey became a candidate for president without entering primaries. At the tumultuous and violent 1968 convention, Humphrey won the nomination over the combined forces of McCarthy and Senator George McGovern, who had entered the race after the assassination of Robert Kennedy. In the fall he lost by a narrow margin, but was again elected to the Senate in 1972.

Born May 27, 1911, died January 13, 1978, age 67.

SPIRO T. AGNEW (January 20, 1969–October 10, 1973), Republican.

When Richard Nixon won the nomination at the 1968 Republican convention he appointed a committee to recommend a running mate, but in reality he had privately settled on the governor of Maryland, Spiro T. Agnew. A lawyer and Bronze Star winner in World War II, Agnew had been a zoning commissioner and elected administrator of Baltimore County. He achieved a reputation as a moderate with broad voter appeal by winning the governorship in 1966 over a right-wing Democrat. Agnew became the point man for the Nixon campaign and administration famed for his attacks on liberals, Democrats, and the media, which he called "the nattering nabobs of negativism." Along with Nixon he was swept back into office in the landslide of 1972. In the summer of 1973 the U.S. attorney in Baltimore stumbled upon evidence of a pattern of bribes to Agnew from contractors with the state of Maryland, including payments actually handed to him in the vice president's office. Agnew claimed it was a pack of lies, but faced with the proof and potential charges of fraud, corruption, and tax evasion, he agreed to resign and plead no contest to one charge of tax evasion, in return for no jail time. On October 10, 1973, this arrangement was stipulated at a quick hearing, and Agnew was gone.

Born November 9, 1918, died September 21, 1996, age 77.

GERALD R. FORD (December 6, 1973–August 9, 1974), Republican.

Ford (born Leslie King Jr., but given his stepfather's name), a Michigan University football star, worked his way through Yale Law School as an assistant coach. Returning from World War II navy service, he was elected to the House in 1948. Working his way up, he was chosen minority leader in 1965. With Agnew's resignation, under the 25th Amendment, Nixon submitted Ford's name to Congress as the proposed vice president. Chosen because he was personally popular with many Democrats in Congress as well as Republicans, Ford was confirmed as vice president by Congress on December 6, 1973. Senate hearings revealed Nixon's involvement in the Watergate scandal, and in the summer of 1994 the Judiciary Committee of the House passed Articles of Impeachment. Informed by a group of Republican senators that he would be convicted in the Senate, Nixon agreed to resign. Ford was informed that Nixon would announce his resignation on August 8, 1974, effective noon the next day. Chief Justice Warren Burger flew back from a trip to Europe to administer the oath to Ford in the Oval Office. See Presidents for more information on Ford.

Born July 14, 1913.

NELSON A. ROCKEFELLER (December 19, 1974–January 20, 1977), Republican.

To fill the new vacancy in the office of vice president, Ford chose former New York governor Nelson Rockefeller, a leader of the moderate wing of the Republican Party, who could get Democratic votes in Congress. A scion of the legendary billionaires, he had been the State Department's director of Latin American affairs (1940–44), assistant secretary of state for Latin America, held several advisory posts under Eisenhower, and was under secretary of health, education and welfare. In 1958 he was elected governor and served until 1973. In 1964, 1968, and 1972 he made unsuccessful tries for the G.O.P. presidential nomination. Congressional hearings on Rockefeller dragged on for four months, with most negative comments coming from conservatives. He was approved and sworn in on December 19, 1974. Despite attempts to show his conservative side, throughout his first year in office, he was dogged by complaints from the right wing of his party. Finally he announced he would not seek renomination.

Born July 8, 1908, died January 26, 1979, age 71.

WALTER MONDALE (January 20, 1977–January 20, 1981), Democrat.

A protégé of Senator Hubert Humphrey, Mondale (nicknamed "Fritz") was appointed attorney general of Minnesota only four years out of law school. He was appointed to the U.S. Senate to replace his mentor when Humphrey was elected vice president in 1964. Mondale was reelected senator twice before being selected by Jimmy Carter to be his running mate, after Carter personally interviewed several possible candidates. He worked closely with the president, and was the first vice president to have an office in the White House. He joined Carter in defeat in 1980. He won the Democratic nomination for president in 1984, and running with Congresswoman Geraldine Ferraro as the first woman vice presidential candidate he lost. Years later he was named ambassador to Japan by President Clinton.

Born January 5, 1928.

GEORGE H. W. BUSH (January 20, 1981–January 20, 1989), Republican.

Son of Connecticut senator Prescott Bush (1952–63), Bush enlisted as a navy flyer at age 18, and survived being shot down over the Pacific. After graduation from Yale he moved to Texas where he organized oil companies. Elected to two terms in the House, twice he lost races for the Senate. President Nixon appointed Bush ambassador to the United Nations (1971–73). He was chairman of the Republican National Committee (1973–74), chief liaison officer to the People's Republic of China (1974–76), and director of the Central Intelligence Agency, appointed by President Ford. The runner-up to Ronald Reagan for the Republican presidential nomination in 1980, Reagan selected Bush as his running mate. Only two months after inauguration, Reagan was badly wounded in an assassination attempt, which required Bush to act as liaison to the president during his recuperation and keep the White House staff running smoothly.

Both were reelected in 1984. As vice president he sat with the cabinet and often represented the United States at overseas events, including many state funerals. Easily nominated for president in 1988, he became the first sitting vice president to be elected president since Martin Van Buren in 1836. See Presidents for more information on Bush.

Born June 12, 1924.

J. DANFORTH QUAYLE (January 20, 1989–January 20, 1993), Republican.

Member of a prominent publishing family with newspapers in Indiana and Arizona, Dan Quayle practiced law briefly before being elected to the first of two terms in the House of Representatives at age 29. Four years later he upset Senator Birch Bayh in winning election to the U.S. Senate and was reelected in 1986. Young, handsome, and athletic, but nationally unknown, Quayle was George H. W. Bush's surprise personal choice for the vice presidential nomination in 1988. During the campaign he became known for slips of the tongue and when he compared himself to John F. Kennedy during a debate, Democratic Veep candidate Lloyd Bentsen skewered him with: "I knew President Kennedy, and you're no Jack Kennedy." As vice president he became a conservative spokesman for "family values," and criticized fictional television character Murphy Brown for having a baby out of wedlock, as a symbol of entertainment business immorality. Bush kept Quayle on the ticket for the reelection campaign in 1992, and they both lost.

Born February 4, 1947.

ALBERT GORE JR. (January 20, 1993–January 20, 2001), Democrat.

Son of three-term Tennessee senator Albert Gore, after graduation from Harvard, he volunteered for the army (1969–71) and served in Vietnam. He was a reporter for the *Nashville Tenneseean* (1971–76) while attending Vanderbilt University's school of religion for one year and then its law school. In 1976 Gore was elected to the first of four terms in the House of Representatives, and to the Senate in 1984. He made an abortive try for the Democratic nomination for president in 1988. Democratic nominee Bill Clinton picked Gore as his running mate although the selection violated the conventional wisdom about balancing a ticket: They were approximately the same age, came from neighboring states, and were of similar political philosophies. Once elected Clinton and Gore were a team (although the president was the controlling member), with Gore leading in numerous areas, including a task force on "Re-inventing Government," dealing with the emerging Internet, and such environmental issues as global warming. As the Democratic nominee for President in 2000 Gore won the popular vote, but lost the election to George W. Bush in the Electoral College.

Born March 31, 1948.

RICHARD BRUCE CHENEY (2001–), Republican.

Richard Cheney was born January 30, 1941, in Nebraska and raised in Wyoming. After earning a B.A. and M.A. in political science at the University of Wyoming, he served on the staff of two government agencies before becoming a staff assistant in the White House under President Richard M. Nixon. When Gerald Ford became President in 1974, Cheney was selected to be Deputy Assistant to the President's Chief of Staff. In 1975 he moved up to Ford's Chief of Staff. In 1978 Cheney was elected to the U.S. House of Representatives from Wyoming and served for 10 years, eventually rising to House minority whip. Appointed Secretary of Defense by President George H. W. Bush in 1989, he presided over the Gulf War against Iraq. At the end of the Bush administration, Cheney became Chairman of the Board and CEO of Halliburton Company, a Texas oil and energy corporation. In 2000 candidate George W. Bush chose Cheney to head a search committee to select a vice presidential candidate. Just days prior to the Republican National Convention, Cheney suddenly moved his residence from Texas back to his ranch in Wyoming and registered to vote there. Bush then named Cheney as his running mate, having solved the constitutional prohibition against both candidates coming from the same state. Although not noted for campaigning, Cheney distinguished himself in a congenial debate with Democratic vice presidential rival, Senator Joseph Lieberman, and helped assuage critics of his very conservative Congressional record. After election, Cheney played the major role in organization of the Bush-Cheney administration and selection of the Cabinet. In March, 2000 Cheney had his second heart surgery in five months, having suffered four heart attacks by the age of 60. He is married to his high school sweetheart, Lynne, who has a long record of political activity, including as Chair of the National Endowment for the Humanities under President Ronald Reagan. They have two grown daughters.

AMERICAN PRESIDENTS
AND THEIR VICE PRESIDENTS

	Term	Party	Born	Died
GEORGE WASHINGTON	1789–1797	None	2/22/32	12/14/99
John Adams	1789–1797	None	10/30/35	7/4/26
JOHN ADAMS	1797–1801	Federalist	10/30/35	7/4/26
Thomas Jefferson	1797–1801	Dem-Rep.	4/13/43	7/4/26
THOMAS JEFFERSON	1801–1809	Dem-Rep.	4/13/43	7/4/26
Aaron Burr	1801–1805	Dem-Rep.	2/6/56	9/14/36
George Clinton	1805–1809	Dem-Rep.	7/26/39	4/20/12
JAMES MADISON	1809–1817	Dem-Rep.	3/16/51	6/28/36
George Clinton	1809–1812[1]	Dem-Rep.	7/26/39	4/20/ 12
Elbridge Gerry	1812–1814[2]	Dem-Rep.	7/17/44	11/23/14
JAMES MONROE	1817–1825	Dem-Rep.	4/28/58	7/4/31
Daniel D. Tompkins	1817–1825	Dem-Rep.	6/21/74	6/11/25
JOHN QUINCY ADAMS	1825–1829	Nat. Rep.	7/11/67	2/23/48
John C. Calhoun	1825–1829	Dem-Rep.	3/18/82	3/31/50
ANDREW JACKSON	1829–1837	Democrat	3/15/67	6/8/45
John C. Calhoun	1829–1832[3]	Democrat	3/18/82	3/31/ 50
MARTIN VAN BUREN	1837–1841	Democrat	12/5/82	7/24/62
Richard M. Johnson	1837–1841	Democrat	10/17/80	11/19/50
WILLIAM HENRY HARRISON	1841[4]	Whig	2/9/73	4/4/41
John Tyler	1841	Whig	3/29/90	1/18/62
JOHN TYLER	1841–1845	Whig	3/29/90	1/18/62
No vice president				
JAMES KNOX POLK	1845–1849	Democrat	11/2/95	7/9/50
George M. Dallas	1845–1849	Democrat	7/10/92	12/31/64
ZACHARY TAYLOR	1849–1850[5]	Whig	11/24/84	7/9/50
Millard Fillmore	1849–1850	Whig	1/7/00	3/8/74
MILLARD FILLMORE	1850–1853	Whig	1/7/00	3/8/74
No vice president				
FRANKLIN PIERCE	1853–1857	Democrat	11/23/04	10/8/69
Wiliam R. King	1853[6]	Democrat	4/7/86	4/18/53

	Term	Party	Born	Died
JAMES BUCHANAN	1857–1861	Democrat	4/23/91	6/1/68
John C. Breckinridge	1857–1861	Democrat	1/21/2	15/17/75
ABRAHAM LINCOLN[7]	1861–1865	Republican	2/12/09	4/15/65
Hannibal Hamlin	1861–1865	Republican	8/27/09	7/4/91
Andrew Johnson[8]	1865	Republican	12/29/08	7/31/75
ANDREW JOHNSON	1865–1869	Republican	12/29/08	7/31/75
No vice president				
ULYSSES S. GRANT	1869–1877	Republican	4/27/22	7/23/85
Schuyler Colfax	1869–1873	Republican	3/23/23	1/13/85
Henry Wilson[9]	1873–1875	Republican	2/16/12	11/12/75
RUTHERFORD B. HAYES	1877–1881	Republican	10/4/22	1/17/93
William Wheeler	1877–1881	Republican	6/30/19	6/4/87
JAMES A. GARFIELD[10]	1881	Republican	11/19/31	9/19/81
Chester Alan Arthur	1881	Republican	10/5/29[11]	11/18/86
CHESTER ALAN ARTHUR	1881–1885	Repubican	10/5/29	11/18/86
No vice president				
GROVER CLEVELAND	1885–1889	Democrat	3/18/37	6/24/08
Thomas A. Hendricks	1885[12]	Democrat	9/7/19	11/25/85
BENJAMIN HARRISON	1889–1893	Republican	8/20/33	3/13/01
Levi P. Morton	1889–1893	Republican	5/16/24	5/16/20
GROVER CLEVELAND	1893–1897	Democrat	3/18/37	6/24/08
Adlai E. Stevenson	1893–1897	Democrat	10/25/35	6/14/14
WILLIAM McKINLEY	1897–1901	Republican	1/29/43	9/14/01
Garret A. Hobart	1897–1899[13]	Republican	6/3/44	11/21/99
Theodore Roosevelt[14]	1901	Republican	10/27/58	1/6/19
THEODORE ROOSEVELT	1901–1909	Republican	10/27/58	1/6/19
Charles W. Fairbanks	1905–1909	Republican	5/11/52	6/4/18
WILLIAM HOWARD TAFT	1909–1913	Republican	9/15/57	3/8/30
James S. Sherman	1909–1912[15]	Republican	10/24/55	10/30/12
WOODROW WILSON	1913–1921	Democrat	12/28/56	2/3/24
Thomas R. Marshall	1913–1921	Democrat	3/14/54	6/1/25
WARREN G. HARDING	1921–1923[16]	Republican	11/2/65	8/2/2 3
Calvin Coolidge	1921–1923	Republican	7/4/72	1/5/33
CALVIN COOLIDGE	1923–1929	Republican	7/4/72	1/5/33
Charles G. Dawes	1925–1929	Republican	8/27/65	4/23/51
HERBERT C. HOOVER	1929–1933	Republican	8/10/74	10/20/64
Charles Curtis	1929–1933	Republican	1/25/60	2/8/36

	Term	Party	Born	Died
FRANKLIN D. ROOSEVELT	1933–1945	Democrat	1/30/82	4/12/45
John Nance Garner	1933–1945	Democrat	11/22/68	7/7/67
Henry A. Wallace	1941–1945	Democrat	19/7/88	11/18/65
Harry S. Truman	1945[17]	Democrat	5/8/84	12/26/72
HARRY S. TRUMAN	1945–1953	Democrat	5/8/84	12/26/72
Alben W. Barkley	1949–1953	Democrat	11/24/77	4/30/56
DWIGHT D. EISENHOWER	1953–1961	Republican	10/14/90	3/28/6 9
Richard M. Nixon	1953–1961	Republican	1/9/13	4/22/94
JOHN F. KENNEDY	1961–1963[18]	Democrat	5/29/17	11/2 2/63
Lyndon B. Johnson	1961–1963	Democrat	8/27/08	1/22/73
LYNDON B. JOHNSON	1963–1969	Democrat	8/27/08	1/22/73
Hubert H. Humphrey	1965–1969	Democrat	5/27/11	1/13/78
RICHARD M. NIXON	1969–1974	Republican	1/9/13	4/22/94
Spiro T. Agnew[19]	1969–1973	Republican	11/9/18	9/21 /96
Gerald R. Ford[20]	1973–1974	Republican	7/14/13	-
GERALD R. FORD[21]	1974–1977	Republican	7/14/13	1/26/79
Nelson A. Rockefeller[22]	1974–1977	Republican	7/8/08	
JIMMY CARTER[23]	1977–1981	Democrat	10/1/24	-
Walter Mondale	1977–1981	Democrat	1/5/28	-
RONALD REAGAN	1981–1989	Republican	2/6/11	-
George Bush	1981–1989	Republican	6/12/24	-
GEORGE BUSH	1989–1993	Republican	6/12/24	-
J. Danforth Quayle	1989–1993	Republican	2/4/47	-
BILL CLINTON[24]	1993–2001	Democrat	8/19/46	-
Albert Gore Jr.	1993–2001	Democrat	3/31/48	-
GEORGE W. BUSH	2001–	Republican	7/6/46	-
Dick Cheney	2001–	Republican	1/30/41	-

[1] George Clinton died in office on April 12, 1812.

[2] Elbridge Gerry died in office on November 23, 1814.

[3] John C. Calhoun resigned as vice president on December 28, 1832, to take a seat in the United States Senate.

[4] President William Henry Harrison caught pneumonia at his inauguration and died one month later on April 4, 1841, and was succeeded by John Tyler.

[5] President Zachary Taylor died of apoplexy on July 9, 1850, making Millard Fillmore his successor.

[6] At the time of his election as vice president, William King was deathly ill with tuberculosis; he was sworn in at Havana, Cuba, on March 24, 1853, and returned to Alabama and died the day after he arrived on April 18, 1853.

[7] President Abraham Lincoln was shot on April 14, 1865, and died on April 15, 1865, leaving Andrew Johnson as president.

[8] Vice President Andrew Johnson had been a Democrat, but supported the Union and ran on the National Union ticket in 1864.

9 Vice President Henry Wilson was born Jeremiah Jones Colbath, but officially changed his name to Henry Wilson when he turned 21. Wilson died in office on November 22, 1875.

10 President James A. Garfield was shot on July 2, 1881, and died on September 19, 1881, making Chester Alan Arthur president.

11 Most historical sources give Chester Alan Arthur's birth year as 1830, but Arthur lied about his age and was actually born in 1829 according to the best evidence.

12 Vice President Thomas A. Hendricks died in office on November 25, 1885.

13 Vice President Garret A. Hobart died in office on November 21, 1899.

14 President William McKinley was shot on September 6, 1901, and died on September 14, 1901, making Theodore Roosevelt president.

15 Vice President James S. Sherman died in office on October 30, 1912, while a candidate for reelection.

16 President Warren G. Harding died of a heart attack on August 2, 1923, making Calvin Coolidge president.

17 President Franklin D. Roosevelt died of a stroke on April 12, 1945, making Harry S. Truman president.

18 President John F. Kennedy was shot and killed on November 22, 1963, making Lyndon B. Johnson president.

19 Vice President Spiro T. Agnew resigned on October 10, 1973, as part of a plea bargain in which he pled guilty to income tax evasion on profits from bribetaking.

20 Gerald Ford, then minority leader of the House, was nominated for vice president by President Nixon and approved by Congress on December 6, 1973. Gerald Rudolph Jr. was born Leslie King Jr., but was given his stepfather's name when he was a child.

21 President Richard M. Nixon resigned on August 9, 1974, while facing impeachment proceedings stemming from the Watergate scandal coverup, making Gerald R. Ford president.

22 Nelson A. Rockefeller was nominated for vice president by President Ford on August 20, 1974, and approved by Congress on December 19, 1974.

23 Jimmy Carter's legal name was James Earl Carter Jr.

24 President Clinton was born William Jefferson Blyth. He was a posthumous child. He changed his last name to Clinton, which was his stepfather's name, when he was 16.

INDEX

6 - 2009